THE SABBATH ANTHOLOGY

THE JPS HOLIDAY ANTHOLOGIES

UNIVERSITY OF NEBRASKA PRESS

LINCOLN

THE
SABBATH
ANTHOLOGY

Edited by Abraham E. Millgram

THE JEWISH PUBLICATION SOCIETY

PHILADELPHIA

Acknowledgments for the use of previously
published material appear on pages xxix–xxxi, which
constitute an extension of the copyright page.

First Nebraska paperback printing: 2018

Library of Congress Control Number: 2018935578

To My Wife

איטא חיה

CONTENTS

BOOK I

THE SABBATH IN PRACTICE

vii

Poems

            The *Rebbi* Works Wonders
            How to Support a Son-in-Law
            A Small Jew with a Big Stomach
            Fulfilling a Commandment
            Wine for *Kiddush* and *Habdalah*
            The Superstition of Sabbath Observance
            A Successful Sermon

BOOK II

THE SABBATH IN LITERATURE, ART AND MUSIC

BOOK III

THE SABBATH IN HISTORY

LIST OF ILLUSTRATIONS

(Facing page 320)

A NOTE FROM THE PUBLISHER

The JPS Holiday Anthologies are unequaled compilations of Bible, Talmud, prayer, poetry, and folklore.

When I first began studying Judaism, and later as a young rabbi, these books were indispensable aids in learning and teaching about the holidays. They took a place of pride on my essential reference bookshelf, right next to *The JPS Tanakh* and *The JPS Torah Commentary*.

Even in our digital age they deserve a similar place on the bookshelf of the next generation of rabbis, cantors, educators, and readers seeking the meaning and origin of the Sabbath and Jewish festivals.

These classics deserve to be available *m'dor l'dor*, from one generation to the next, and we are pleased to make that commitment in this reprint series.

Rabbi Barry L. Schwartz
Director, The Jewish Publication Society

PREFACE

ONE of the most eloquent pleas ever made in America for the revitalization of the Sabbath was in a paper read by Rabbi Israel Harburg at the 1937 meeting of the Central Conference of American Rabbis. His plea, though deeply stirring, and his practical suggestions, though thoroughly convincing, are now all but forgotten. Among other things Rabbi Harburg called attention to the *Sefer ha-Shabbat* which was published in Tel Aviv, Palestine. "Even a casual glance at this work," he said, "will make one see clearly that the Sabbath was uppermost in the minds of our greatest prophets and lawgivers, of saints and psalmists, of poets and philosophers, of our men of letters as well as of our greatest Jewish artists." Rabbi Harburg then added "that the Conference would render a great service for the cause of the Sabbath by publishing a similar work in English." The present volume, though not as all-inclusive as its prototype, the *Sefer ha-Shabbat*, is meant to serve a similar purpose. Its aim is to reaffirm the historic truth that the Sabbath is "the cornerstone of Judaism."

In planning this volume the compiler constantly bore in mind the needs of the American Jewish community. It was his purpose not only to make American Jewry more aware of the central importance of the Sabbath as an institution in the pattern of Jewish life, but also to provide the observant American Jew with a practical guide and handbook for Sabbath observance. To meet this general purpose, Hebrew prayers and hymns were transliterated in accordance with the Ashkenazic instead of the Sefardic pronunciation which is otherwise followed in this book.

A cursory reading of the book will also reveal the conscious plan to present and emphasize the positive elements of Sabbath observance — the elements that have rendered the Sabbath a day of delight to numberless generations of observant Jews throughout the world.

The compilation of a volume of this nature can hardly be the work of one person. Among those who contributed to this labor of love, and to whom the compiler is deeply indebted, are his collaborators Mrs. Rachel Wischnitzer-Bernstein who contributed the chapter on "The Sabbath in Art," and Professor A. W. Binder who contributed the chapter on "The Sabbath in Music" as well as all the musical selections. These contributions need no appraisal here. They speak for themselves.

The compiler is equally indebted to a number of people who read the manuscript and through their helpful criticisms greatly improved the book. Among these are the members of the Publication Committee of The Jewish Publication Society of America, and particularly Rabbi Max D. Klein, chairman of the Committee on the Sabbath and Holiday Series. His painstaking examination of the manuscript and his sound critical advice proved of inestimable value.

Parts of the manuscript were also read by Dr. Louis Finkelstein, President of the Jewish Theological Seminary of America, whose opinions regarding the general approach to the subject were enlightening. Above all, the compiler feels privileged to acknowledge his boundless gratitude to Professor Louis Ginzberg who personally helped in the revision of parts of the second chapter. Only those who have had the good fortune of being Professor Ginzberg's students can fully appreciate the privilege of being indebted to him for clarifying and simplifying obscure and intricate problems of scholarship.

In preparing a manuscript there are many who assist greatly though they are hardly aware of the full value of their assistance. Among these, in the present instance, is Professor Joseph Reider, librarian of the Dropsie College Library, who rendered invaluable service in making available to the compiler innumerable books from the Dropsie College Library. Without that great library at his disposal the compiler could not possibly have undertaken this work. The compiler is equally indebted to Miss Anna Kleban, of the Library of the Jewish Theological Seminary of America. Miss Kleban spent many hours of arduous work selecting and preparing many of the photographic illustrations. Mrs. Rachel Wischnitzer-Bernstein joins the compiler in thanking Miss Kleban for her gracious and valuable help.

In the original manuscript there was a chapter entitled "The Sabbath in the School." This chapter was eliminated from the book because, in addressing itself to Jewish educators, it proved too technical for the general reader. Thanks are nevertheless due to Dr. Azriel Eisenberg, director of the Cleveland Bureau of Jewish Education, and to Mr. Jacob M. Snyder, who read that chapter and greatly helped in bringing it to its final form. The compiler also gratefully records his indebtedness to his friend Mr. Nathan Zuckerberg who helped prepare the bibliography, and to Miss Muriel Steinman who helped prepare the manuscript for publication.

The compiler is deeply indebted to Mr. Maurice Jacobs, the Society's genial Executive Vice President, who has from the start encouraged and in numerous ways assisted in the complicated tasks. Mr. Jacobs' enthusiastic interest in the proposed volume and his faith in the compiler's ability to see it through proved highly infectious. If the book fulfills

only a small part of Mr. Jacobs' expectations it will prove
in every way a valuable contribution to the growing list
of the Society's publications.

But the man who has worked hardest and correspond-
ingly assisted most is the Society's Editor, Dr. Solomon
Grayzel. He carefully scrutinized every section of the book,
made numerous helpful suggestions, and has thus left his
imprint on almost every page. A mere expression of gratitude is altogether inadequate. Being, in more than one
sense, a partner in the work, his recompense can be expressed
only in terms of the book's usefulness to the American Jewish
community. It is the compiler's earnest hope that the reward
will be in full measure.

ABRAHAM E. MILLGRAM

Minneapolis, Minn.
June, 1944.

ACKNOWLEDGMENTS

The editor herewith expresses his sincere appreciation to the following publishers and authors, who have kindly granted permission to use the material indicated:

Behrman's Jewish Book House, New York: "Elijah, a Friend of the Poor," from *Elijah, a Study in Folklore*, by Samuel M. Segal, 1935; "The Twin Stars," by Joel Blau, from *Anthology of Modern Jewish Poetry*, by Philip M. Raskin, 1927; "A Deed of Daring," from *Hath Not the Jew*, by A. M. Klein, 1940; "The Sabbath as an Instrument of Personal and Social Salvation" and "The Three-Fold Meaning of Sabbath Observance," from *The Meaning of God in Modern Jewish Religion*, by Mordecai M. Kaplan, 1937; "The Sabbath of the Poor," by Mendele Moker Sefarim, from *The Jewish Anthology*, by Edmond Fleg, trans. by Maurice Samuel, 1925.

Bloch Publishing Company, New York: "How Danny Helped for *Shabbos*," from *What Danny Did*, by Sadie R. Weilerstein, 1928; "Sabbath Blessing," "A Jewish Home," "The Sabbath Visit," "*Habdalah*," and "Summer Sabbath," from *Around the Year in Rhymes for the Jewish Child*, 1920; "The Joyous Observance of the Sabbath Is Preferable to Monastic Retirement and Asceticism" and "The Sabbath, a Means of Preserving Israel's Strength and Lustre," from *Kitab Al Khazari*, by Judah Halevi, trans. by Hartwig Hirschfeld; "Israel, Thou Art a Puzzle!," by Mendele Moker Sefarim, from *Echoes of the Jewish Soul*, by Jospeh Cooper Levine, 1931; "The Sabbath Day," by Judah Halevi, and "Abba Tachna," from *The Jewish Year*, by Alice Lucas, 1926; "The Sabbath," from *Echoes from the Temple*, by Edith Ella Davis, 1926; "The Sabbath in Merchaviah," from *The Emek*, by Jessie E. Sampter, 1927; and the prayers of *zemirot*, culled from *The Standard Prayer Book*.

Brentanos, New York: "A Summer Sabbath in a Lithuanian Village," from *A Lithuanian Village*, by Leon Kobrin, 1920.

Bruce, Humphries, Boston: "A Sabbath Chant," by S. Benzion, and "Welcome, Queen Sabbath," by Zalman Shneiur, from *Gems of Hebrew*

Verse, by Harry H. Fein, 1940.

Central Conference of American Rabbis, Cincinnati: "Reform Home Service for Sabbath Eve," from the *Union Prayer Book*.

Croscup and Sterling Company, New York: "Princess Sabbath," from *The Works of Heinrich Heine*, trans. by Charles Godfrey, 1906.

Dodd, Mead and Company, New York: "Sabbath Hymn," by Aaron Cohen, from *The Standard Book of Jewish Verse*, by Joseph Friedlander, 1917.

Doubleday, Page and Company, New York: "The Hebrew's Friday Night," by Israel Zangwill, from *Apples and Honey*, by Nina Salaman, 1922.

Drujanoff, Mrs. A., Tel Aviv: selections from *Sefer ha-Bediḥah veha-Ḥidud*, 1935.

E. P. Dutton Company, New York: "Two Reasons for the Observance of the Sabbath" and "A Day of Rest," from *The Guide for the Perplexed*, by Moses Maimonides, trans. by M. Friedlander, 1910.

Furrows, New York: "Shambat," by Hayim Greenberg, 1942.

Goldin, Judah I.: translation of "*M'nuchoh v'Simchoh*."

Hasefer Agency for Literature, London: "The Sabbath Among the Ḥasidim," from *Leaders of Hassidism*, by S. A. Horodezky, 1928.

Hebrew Publishing Company, New York: selections from the *Code of Jewish Law*, by Hyman E. Goldin, 1928.

The Jewish Child, New York: "Remember the Sabbath Day" (1912), "Stars and Candles" (1918), and "The *Shabbos-Kugel*" (1916), by Shulamith Ish-Kishor.

Jewish National Workers Alliance, New York: "A Story About a Coin," by S. J. Agnon, trans. by Jacob Katzman, and "The Sabbath in Palestine," by Jacob Fichman, trans. by Abraham Regelson, from *Oneg Shabbot*.

Jonathan Cape and Robert Ballou, New York: "Thrice He Laughed," from *The Golden Mountain*, by Meyer Levin, 1932.

J. M. Dent and Sons, London: "The Severe Penance," from *Jewish Mysticism and the Legends of Baalshem*, by Martin Buber, trans. by Lucy Cohen, 1931.

Labovich, Shirley: "*Sabbath Candles*" and "My Sabbath Call."

The Macmillan Company, New York: "The Most Important Institution of the Synagogue," from *Jewish Theology*, by K. Kohler, 1918; "Sabbath Among the Marranos," from *A History of the Inquisition of Spain*, by Henry Charles Lea, 1907.

Oneg Shabbot Society, Tel Aviv: "The Sabbath Is the Cornerstone of

Judaism," by Ḥayyim Naḥman Bialik, "The Sabbath Among the Karaites," by Ephraim Deinard, "The Sabbath Among the Falashas," by J. Faitlovitch, "The Sabbath Among the 'Bene Israel' of India," by Solomon Rinman, and "Sabbath Among the Marranos," by Nahum Slouschz, from *Sefer Ha-Shabbat*, 1936.

Oxford University Press, London: "The Sabbath Among the Samaritans," from *The Samaritans*, by Moses Gaster, 1925; "The Maccabees Decide to Defend Themselves on the Sabbath," from *The Apocrypha*, The Authorized Version.

The Reconstructionist, New York: "*Shabbat*," by E. Grindell, 1942.

The Rosenbach Company, Philadelphia: "Hymn of Welcome to the Sabbath," from *When Love Passed By and Other Poems*, by Solomon Solis-Cohen, 1929.

Sci-Art Publishers, Cambridge MA: "Outgoing Sabbath," from *The Golden Peacock*, by Joseph Leftwich, 1939.

Siegel, Mrs. Julius L., New York: "The Sabbath, a Product of *Halakah* and *Hagadah*," from *Law and Legend*, by Ḥayyim Naḥman Bialik, trans. by Julius L. Siegel, 1923.

The Sinai Press, Cincinnati: "Beyond the Sambatyon," from *The Unconquered*, by Joseph Gaer, 1932.

The Soncino Press, London: "The Dignity of Labor," from *The Pentateuch and Haftorahs*, by J. H. Hertz, 1938.

The Women's League of the United Synagogue of America, New York: "How K'tonton Took a Ride on a Chopping-Knife and Wished He Hadn't," from *The Adventures of K'tonton*, by Sadie R. Weilerstein, 1935.

Young Judaea, New York: "Sabbath Eve," from *Poems for Young Judaeans*, 1917; "Sabbath Thought," by Shulamith Ish-Kishor, from *Sabbath Program*, by Leo W. Schwarz, 1928.

The Young Judean, New York: "Ariel," by B. S. Levner, 1927; "The Princess Sabbath," by Jehudi, 1912; "The Sabbath Queen," by B. S. Levner, 1925.

Zobel, Moritz, Berlin: "The Sabbath Among the Karaites," from *Der Shabbat*, 1935.

BOOK ONE

THE SABBATH IN PRACTICE

CHAPTER I

THE TRADITIONAL SABBATH

יוֹתֵר מִשֶּׁיִשְׂרָאֵל שָׁמְרוּ אֶת הַשַּׁבָּת

שָׁמְרָה הַשַּׁבָּת אוֹתָם. (אחד העם)

More than Israel has kept the Sabbath,
it is the Sabbath that has kept Israel.
AHAD HA-'AM

"MORE than Israel has kept the Sabbath, it is the Sabbath that has kept Israel." Thus did the brilliant Hebrew essayist, Ahad Ha-'Am, epitomize the historical significance of the Sabbath for the Jewish people. Nor is Ahad Ha'Am alone in his exalted opinion of the role that the Sabbath has played in the history of the Jews. He reflects the universal regard for the Sabbath as it revealed itself in the life and literature of the Jew up to the nineteenth century.

Even in ancient times the Sabbath was singled out as the most important of all the festivals. The Sabbath alone was included in the Ten Commandments wherein the Hebrews were enjoined to "remember the sabbath day, to keep it holy."[1] The post-biblical rabbinic literature not only exhorts the Jews to observe the Sabbath, but also dwells on the blessings of the Sabbath both for the individual Jew and for Israel. On Friday night, we are told, the Jew is accompanied on his way home from synagogue by two angels, one good and one evil. When the Jew enters his home and finds the Sabbath lights kindled and the home radiant with the joyous Sabbath atmosphere, the good angel blesses the

1

home and says, "May this home always be an abode of happiness;" and the wicked angel grudgingly answers, "Amen." But if the Jew, on coming home, finds the Sabbath lights unlit and the house filled with gloom, the wicked angel curses the home and says, "May this home never know the joy of Sabbath." Then the good angel weeps and perforce answers, "Amen."

In rabbinic tradition the Sabbath is further associated with the personal salvation of man by being called a fore-taste of the bliss which is stored up for the righteous in the world to come. According to the rabbis, the joys of the Sab-bath transcend all earthly bliss. And so attractive was the bliss of the Hereafter, as reflected by the Sabbath "delight," that it undoubtedly encouraged many a Jew to strive for a better life in order to be deserving of that great reward. No wonder, therefore, that the Jew lavished so much love on the Sabbath. He personified it as a lovely Bride, a charm-ing Princess, a gracious Queen. On Friday the Jew received his Sabbath Bride with hymns of welcome both in the syna-gogue and in his home. On Friday afternoons the mystics of Safed actually marched to the outskirts of the city in order to receive their Queen, the Sabbath.

The Jew was amply rewarded for this love of the Sabbath. Not the least of his rewards was the miraculous transforma-tion which he experienced on that day. The Sabbath changed his very soul. It changed even the expression of his face. Sholem Asch, in his novel, *Salvation*, speaks of the two mothers a Jewish child used to have, a weekday mother and a Sabbath mother. The same may be said of every Jew. There was a weekday Jew and a Sabbath Jew. Hein-rich Heine observed this miraculous transformation. In one of his poems, "Princess Sabbath,"[2] he speaks of the Jew in terms of an Arabian legend in which a prince is magically transformed into a dog. Six days in every week the Jew was a hounded creature; but on the Sabbath he regained his princely state. But no sooner was the Sabbath gone than the prince once more returned to his lowly existence. The Jew explained this almost unbelievable, yet real, transformation by a strange hypothesis, namely, that he temporarily possessed a *Neshamah Yeterah*, an additional soul. This soul came to him every Friday evening and stayed with him till the end of the Sabbath.

Equally profound was the influence which the Sabbath exerted on the group life of the Jews. It is no exaggeration to state that the Sabbath was to a large degree responsible for the development of the synagogue. The rest which prevailed on the Sabbath day gave rise to the ancient practice of periodically visiting the prophet for edification and instruction. These weekly Sabbath gatherings were undoubtedly the seeds out of which the synagogue as an institution of prayer and instruction later developed.[3] The Sabbath, too, is in large measure to be credited with the elimination of illiteracy from among the Jews and with the development of their unusual love of learning. The first-century historian Josephus, in his apologetic treatise *Against Apion* (2.18), praises Moses who "caused the people to abandon all other employments and to assemble to hear the Law and to study it carefully every week — a thing all other legislators failed to do." Likewise, the Alexandrian Jewish philosopher Philo, in his essay *On the Sabbath*, says, "On the seventh day there are spread before the people in every city innumerable lessons in prudence, justice and all the other virtues .... and so the lives of all are improved." Indeed, it has always been the custom of Jews to assemble in the synagogues on the Sabbath for learning and for edification. Even in the Middle Ages which, in the history of Western Europe, are characterized by ignorance and superstition, the Jews hardly knew of illiteracy and produced numerous scholars under whose guidance learning flourished in all the Jewish communities. Without the Sabbath, when the humble poor and the proud rich met in the synagogue for prayer and instruction, learning and piety might have become the domain of the rabbis and scholars instead of the heritage of the entire people.

The Jew's high regard for the Sabbath was not based on tradition alone. It was founded on deep religious convictions and on sound moral principles. To begin with, it was a religious institution, "a sabbath unto the Lord," associated with the divine creative faculty. By observing the Sabbath the Jew paid tribute to the Creator and reaffirmed his faith in the creative powers of man. Since God created the world in six days and rested on the seventh, the Jew emulated this divine pattern. By working six days in the week he glorified the dignity of labor, and by resting on the seventh day he raised the dignity of human personality.

But to be creative, man must necessarily be free to exercise his God-given faculties. The observance of the Sabbath was therefore conceived of as a tribute to the ideal of freedom. The Sabbath not only commemorated the creation of the world, it also served as "a memorial of the deliverance from Egypt." And just as the deliverance from Egyptian bondage was a prerequisite to the hoped-for realization of the Hebrew national goal —"a kingdom of priests and a holy nation"— so the periodic freedom from the enslaving burdens and anxieties of daily life became a necessary prerequisite to the realization of a productive and creative life for each individual.

Finally, the Sabbath was a "sign" and a perpetual witness of the covenant between God and Israel. "It was in this respect even more significant than circumcision. The latter sign of the covenant was imposed on an infant . . . solely by virtue of his descent; whereas the keeping of the Sabbath in the face of persecution or the permanent and more insidious temptations of worldly interest was a standing evidence of the intelligent and self-determined fidelity of the man to the religion in which he was brought up ..."[4] History records many instances when Jews preferred to die a martyr's death rather than desecrate this "sign" of Israel's covenant with God.

If the Sabbath, as a religious institution, was really to strengthen, exalt, and purify the spiritual nature of the Jewish people, it had to be observed in a specific manner, as prescribed by the Bible and the Talmud. Accordingly, the Sabbath was instituted as a day of rest for all — for man and beast, for master and slave. But mere cessation from labor would have served the body alone. The Sabbath was therefore made into a day of holiness in order to edify, inspire and ennoble the life of the observant Jew.

The many restrictions which were instituted to insure complete rest were not burdensome, as common belief has it. The Jewish Sabbath, to quote Solomon Schechter, had none of "the bleak and dismal characteristics of a seventeenth-century Calvinist Sunday in Scotland, as described by continental writers." The Jewish Sabbath was "a day of *joyful* rest." The atmosphere both at home and in the synagogue was bright and cheerful. Many lights were kindled; the best food was prepared; the finest garments were worn. There was joy and gladness everywhere. By avoiding vulgar enjoyments, strenuous exercises and coarse diversions, the Sabbath was rendered "a day of mystic sweetness and spirituality." While physical exertions were prohibited, spiritual and intellectual occupations were encouraged and even prescribed by religious statute. Such occupations counterbalanced the prohibitions of Sabbath observance, which are usually singled out by critics as the sole characteristics of the day. By making the Sabbath a day of edification and contemplation as well as a day of rest, the Jews saved it from the danger of becoming a gloomy, austere and solemn day. Instead, the Sabbath assumed a sublime serenity and a holy peace which rendered it a day of delight. The Talmud does not exaggerate when it says: "The Holy One, blessed be He, said unto Moses, 'I have a precious gift in my treasure house, and Sabbath is its name. I wish to present it to Israel. Go and bring them the good tidings.' "[5] A valuable gift indeed was the Sabbath. It strengthened the Jew and enabled him to face the trials of a hostile world with dignity, courage, faith and hope. Poverty, insecurity, physical torment and constant humiliation could not destroy the optimism of the Jew. The sweet memory of the preceding Sabbath and the fervent anticipation of the coming Sabbath transcended all the realities of the six days of the week.

But modernity, which belatedly arrived among the Jews during the nineteenth century, has brought with it many powerful forces tending to uproot everything unique in Jewish life. These forces have all but destroyed the Jewish Sabbath in America. And, if it is true, as the Hebrew poet Hayyim Nahman Bialik claims, that "the Sabbath is the cornerstone of Judaism," then Jewish life in America is gravely endangered. Just as the traditional Sabbath enriched the life of the individual Jew and gave stability and permanence to Jewish group life, so the anemic Sabbath of today impoverishes the life of the individual Jew and endangers the survival of the American Jewish community. If in the past the Sabbath rest led to the development of the synagogue which, in turn, led to common worship and public instruction, in our day the elimination of the Sabbath inevitably leads to the weakening of the synagogue and to the general decline of Judaism in America. One of the outstanding religious leaders of American Jewry summed up this unfortunate situation in the following statement: "What, then, has weakened the Jewish sentiment that was so strong a feature in the maintenance of the synagogue in the past? Many elements, undoubtedly, have contributed to the undermining of that sentiment, but chief of all is the dwindling of Sabbath observance. Kept away from attendance at the synagogue on the traditional day of rest and common worship, the Jew finds little motive for being identified with the synagogue, and, when he finds himself out of touch with synagogue life, it cannot be long before he becomes entirely cold to Jewish traditions and ideals. Hence, among the principal measures for the upbuilding of the synagogue must be the restoration of the Sabbath, a measure which cannot be brought about except by the united efforts of all elements in the Jewish community."[6]

The task of restoring the Sabbath to its place of primacy in Jewish life is, to say the least, extremely difficult. But floods have been dammed by cooperative human effort, and powerful armies have been stopped by heroic counter-attacks. The Sabbath can be reinvigorated provided the American Jews realize that "the Sabbath is the vessel that contains the soul of Judaism,"[7] and that the survival or extinction of the Jewish people is tied up with the Sabbath.

CHAPTER II

THE SABBATH IN THE HOME

הַבַּיְתָה נָשׁוּבָה בְּלֵב מָלֵא גִילָה;

שָׁם עָרוּךְ הַשֻּׁלְחָן, הַנֵּרוֹת יָאִירוּ,

כָּל פִּנּוֹת הַבַּיִת יִזְרְחוּ יַזְהִירוּ. ‏(ח. נ. ביאליק)

We go slowly homewards, our hearts full of grace,
The table is spread there, the candles give light,
Every nook in the house is shining and bright.
H. N. BIALIK

THE JEWISH HOME ON THE SABBATH

WE associate the Sabbath primarily with the home. Even the Jew who has deliberately severed all ties with Jewish life frequently recalls with longing the "mystic sweetness and spirituality" that reigned in his home when the Sabbath lights were kindled by his mother and the *Kiddush* was recited by his father. Even the renegade cannot free himself from the sweet recollection of "the dim religious light" of the late Sabbath afternoons in winter, when his mother piously recited the prayer "O God of Abraham, Isaac and Jacob." These and other Sabbath observances not only hallowed the Sabbath but also sanctified the Jewish home, making it a *Miḳdash Me'aṭ*, a miniature sanctuary, in which the parents were the priests and the family table was the altar. Such Sabbath observances exerted a powerful influence on the family as an institution, and on its individual members. They strengthened those domestic virtues and graces which to this day distinguish

8

Jewish home life for its unusual stability and its beneficent influence on the children.

The Sabbath has always been associated with filial piety, as is indicated by the biblical command, "Ye shall fear every man his mother and his father, and ye shall keep My sabbaths: I am the Lord your God" (Lev. 19.3). That the reverence for father and mother is linked with the keeping of the Sabbath is evident from the Sabbath custom of bringing together the scattered members of the family. Sabbath observance thus helped to cement family ties which might otherwise have been loosened. The atmosphere of enchantment which the Sabbath Queen brought into the home strengthened family unity in sweet forgetfulness of weekday sorrows.

To understand the Jewish home as it was transformed by the Sabbath, and to appreciate the unique role of the Sabbath in the life of the Jew, let us look into a traditional Jewish home on a Sabbath day. As a rule, observance of the Sabbath in the Jewish home begins on Thursday when most of the shopping is done. But it is on Friday that the real commotion begins. Mother and daughters rise early and work incessantly till evening when the Sabbath is ushered in. There is much to be done for the Sabbath. Shopping must be completed, and nothing but the best is purchased in honor of Queen Sabbath. Much cooking and baking is necessary, not only to insure sufficient food for the Sabbath when no cooking is permissible, but to provide many delicacies and such special Sabbath foods as *Gefilte* (stuffed) or fried fish and *Kugel* (Sabbath pudding). In former days the housewife would even bake her own *Hallot* (Sabbath bread), a task which made it necessary for her to rise before daybreak. Then there is the house cleaning, which is especially thorough on Friday. How else is one to receive the most welcome of guests, Queen Sabbath?

Although these preparations are the special task of the womenfolk, it is not unusual for the men to assist in this holy work. The Talmud holds up for emulation several of the sages who personally assisted in the preparations for the Sabbath by performing certain specific tasks, such as splitting wood, kindling and fanning the fire, or salting the fish (Shab. 119a).

On Friday afternoon the house begins to look Sabbath-like. Everyone wears his best garments and puts away such mundane things as money, sewing kits, and cooking utensils. The table is covered with a white cloth and is set for the Sabbath meal. On it are placed two *Hallot*, covered with a specially embroidered cover; a bottle of wine and a goblet; the candlesticks with their candles; and, in some homes, Sabbath flowers. These preparations concluded, the family is ready to receive the Sabbath.

The housewife is singled out for the honor of receiving the Sabbath. It is a fitting choice, for the Sabbath is primarily a home festival, and the wife, according to the rabbis of the Talmud, is synonymous with the home (Shab. 118b). It is the wife, therefore, who ushers in the Sabbath by kindling the Sabbath lights. This act, which is preceded by the dropping of a coin into a charity box, is accompanied by a suitable prayer for God's blessing on the family. The housewife recites this prayer in silent reverence, her eyes shielded with the palms of her hands. The kindling of the Sabbath lights is one of the most impressive home ceremonies, symbolizing the essential characteristics of the Sabbath — light, joy, and good cheer.

Equally impressive is the blessing of the children by the father. No ceremony is recalled with more tenderness than this simple ceremony in which the father places his hands on the bowed head of each child and recites the blessing (for a boy), "May God make you like unto Ephraim and

Manasseh," and (for a girl) "May God make you like unto Sarah, Rebekah, Rachel and Leah." The blessing is followed by the priestly benediction and any other personal prayer that the father chooses to offer.

The woman's place of honor on the Sabbath and her exalted position in the Jewish home are again emphasized by the husband's recital of the last section of the book of Proverbs, wherein the housewife is praised in the most glowing terms. "A woman of valour who can find? For her price is far above rubies. The heart of her husband doth safely trust in her, and he hath no lack of gain. She doeth him good and not evil all the days of her life" (Prov. 31.10–12).

The Sabbath meal proper is begun with the sanctification of the Sabbath over a cup of wine, which, like the kindling of the Sabbath lights, symbolizes joy and cheer. The late Henry Berkowitz, in his book *Sabbath Sentiment*, speaks of the *Kiddush* in the following enthusiastic terms: "What a work of genius is that simple, homely and beautiful creation of the Jewish spirit — the *Kiddush!* It is the very essence of poetry wrought into an institution of family life. It has cultivated and nourished the idealism of generations. It has proven a factor of incalculable worth in linking loving hearts to home, to kindred, to Israel and to God."

After the master of the house has recited the *Kiddush* and everyone has tasted of the wine, he recites the blessing over the bread (*Ha-Moṣi'*), and gives a piece of the *Ḥallah* to each member of the family. The meal has now formally begun. The distinguishing characteristics of the Sabbath meal, however, are not the special Sabbath dishes but rather the Sabbath table-hymns known as *Zemirot*. These songs are unique in their peculiar blending of the holy and the secular, the serious and the playful. As the families of past generations sang these unique religious hymns, they forgot

their weekday burdens, worries and sorrows. Complete
mental and physical relaxation was their happy lot. Today
these medieval *Zemirot* are sometimes supplemented by
modern songs both in Hebrew and in the vernacular.

Another feature of the Sabbath, one no longer in vogue,
was the frequent presence of an *Ore-aḥ* (guest) at the Sabbath
table. This *Ore-aḥ*, usually a poor Jew, ofttimes a student,
would be invited and brought home from the synagogue as
the Sabbath guest. Since there were not enough guests for
all, the successful host felt signally honored, and treated the
Sabbath guest with singular reverence.

After chanting grace, the family either spends the evening
at home in weekly reunion or goes to the synagogue to par-
ticipate in a late Friday evening service.

The Sabbath day itself is not so crowded with observances.
In the morning the family attends the synagogue services.
At the conclusion of the services everyone greets his neighbor
with the customary Sabbath greeting, *Gut Shabbos* or
Shabbat Shalom (a peaceful Sabbath), to which he receives
the customary reply of *Gut Shabbos* or *Shabbat Shalom u-
Berakah* (a peaceful and blessed Sabbath).[1]

The family again gathers at the table for the Sabbath
meal. The father recites *Kiddush* and *Ha-Moṣi'*, and the
family leisurely partakes of the meal. They sing *Zemirot*
and conclude the meal with the chanting of grace.

The Sabbath afternoon is spent in various ways, depending
on the season of the year and the age of the individuals.
The older people usually rest. The younger ones prefer a
walk. All enjoy the custom of making social calls on Sabbath
afternoon. If a child is blessed with grandparents, he simply
must visit them on Saturday afternoons to eat some of the
cookies grandmother prepared for the Sabbath. In the
summer, when the afternoons are long, there is another duty,

that of reading a chapter of the *Pirke Abot* (The Ethics of the Fathers). Since this ethical treatise has only six chapters, the observant Jew reviews its contents several times a year.

The conclusion of the Sabbath is replete with mystic beauty. After the Sabbath afternoon service, the family eats the third Sabbath meal. This meal, called *Se'udah Shelishit,* or less correctly, *Shalosh Se'udot,* is in no way comparable to the other Sabbath meals. It is too near the end of the Sabbath to retain the genuine joy and relaxation of the other meals. The *Zemirot* are sung without enthusiasm. The weekday spirit is beginning to crowd out the Sabbath delight which has filled the home since the kindling of the Sabbath lights on the previous night.

But the Sabbath Queen is not allowed to depart without a fitting farewell. Since the Jew is loath to part with the Sabbath, he prolongs the day until it is so dark that at least three stars are visible to the naked eye. In this twilight hour the mother recites the well-known prayer which begins with the words, "O God of Abraham, Isaac and Jacob, guard Thy people Israel for Thy praise!"

After the stars appear, the Sabbath ends with the *Habdalah* ceremony. This ceremony contains several symbols which are associated with the parting of the Sabbath. The *Habdalah* prayer itself deals with the distinction that God has made between the holy and the profane, between light and darkness, between Israel and the nations. The ceremony contains a blessing for the light in remembrance of its creation on the first day of the week, and a blessing over spices, the smelling of which symbolically constitutes a spiritual feast for the *Neshamah Yeterah* (extra soul) which leaves the Jew at the conclusion of the Sabbath. After the *Habdalah* the family sings *Zemirot* in which the central theme is the longing for the appearance of the prophet Elijah, who will bring the good tidings of the coming of the Messiah.

The *Ḥasidim* take leave of the Sabbath Queen in a more realistic manner. In addition to the *Habdalah* and the *Zemirot*, they gather on Saturday night for a feast known as a *Melaveh Malkah*, a farewell feast in honor of Queen Sabbath.

With the conclusion of the *Habdalah* the Sabbath spirit is gone. Weekday duties and tasks are resumed, and the traditional Jewish home again looks in joyous anticipation towards the return of the Sabbath Queen.

The Sabbath, as described in the preceding paragraphs, once prevailed in every Jewish home. But now it is the exception rather than the rule. The decline of such total Sabbath observance is due to many causes which will be discussed elsewhere in this book. Here it is well to note that many men, employed on Saturday mornings, still observe Friday evenings in the prescribed manner and resume their Sabbath observance on Saturday afternoon. The family thus maintains a Sabbath atmosphere throughout the day, and the younger children experience that Sabbath delight which they will later prize as among their sweetest memories.

SABBATH CUSTOMS IN THE HOME[2]

1. *Why Is the Sabbath Table Always Covered with a White Cloth?*

In olden times tablecloths were used only on festive occasions and were usually white. The Sabbath thus became associated with the white tablecloth. This custom has been reinterpreted, and now it is generally explained that the white cloth symbolizes the manna, a double portion of which was gathered on Friday to last through the Sabbath. The color of the manna was white and "fine like a hoarfrost."

2. *Why Are Candles Kindled on the Sabbath?*

The custom originated, most likely, as a protest against the old Babylonian superstition which considered the "movable" Sabbath of the Babylonians as an unlucky and gloomy day on which people would use neither fire nor light.[3]

Another probable explanation is the fact that the last work performed before the Sabbath was the preparation of the light. In time this normal act became associated with the ushering in of the Sabbath and thus became a religious ceremony.

In later times the lights were interpreted as commemorating the ancient custom of weekly refilling and rekindling the Menorah in the Temple.

Today the importance of the candlelights lies in their being the symbol of the joyful delight that fills the Jewish home on the Sabbath.

3. *Why Are There Usually Two Sabbath Lights?*

In early talmudic times the average dwelling had three rooms: a kitchen, a living room, and a bedroom. Normally two candles were lighted, one for the kitchen and one for the living room. This normal act, once it became associated with the ushering in of the Sabbath, became an established religious rite.

A later explanation is that *two lights* are kindled in honor of the *two versions* of the Sabbath commandment. The first one (Ex. 20.8) begins with the words *"Remember* the sabbath day," and the other (Deut. 5.12) begins with the words *"Observe* the sabbath day."

4. *Why Does the Woman who Kindles the Sabbath Lights Shield her Eyes with the Palms of her Hands?*

All benedictions are recited *before* the performance of a rite. Since the benediction over the lights officially ushers in the Sabbath, the woman necessarily kindles the lights before the benediction but shields her eyes so as not to "see" the lights till after the benediction.

Another purpose of shielding the eyes is to aid devotion during the prayer.

5. Why Is "Kiddush" Recited over Wine at the Beginning of the Sabbath Meal?

In the early centuries of the Common Era, every festive meal began with a cup of wine. Since the cup of wine was the beginning of the Friday evening meal at the beginning of the Sabbath, it was logical to recite the prayer declaring the holiness of the Sabbath immediately before drinking that cup of wine. When the practice of starting a meal with a cup of wine was no longer in vogue, the cup of wine before the Sabbath meal was nonetheless retained as a religious rite.

In time a new reason was given for the use of wine to welcome the Sabbath. The Sabbath is the harbinger of joy, and it is therefore fitting to declare its sanctity over a cup of wine which is the symbol of joy.

6. Why Is the "Kiddush" Recited in the Synagogue During the Friday Evening Service?

This custom was introduced in Babylonia where the quarters for the transient poor were attached to the synagogue. It was found more economical to have the *Kiddush* recited in the synagogue than to provide each transient with a cup of wine. Eventually this practice spread to all Jewish communities.

7. Why Is the Sabbath Bread Called "Hallah"?

In biblical as well as in later Hebrew, *Hallah* means a round loaf or cake. In a more specific sense *Hallah* means the share of dough, one loaf, given to the priest. The Sabbath loaf retained the Hebrew name. But in the vernacular any *white* bread whether used on Sabbath or weekdays is called *Ḥallah*, because it gradually became identified with the white wheat bread made for the Sabbath as distinct from the rye bread usually made for weekdays.

8. *Why Do the German Jews Call Their Sabbath Bread "Berches"?*

During the early Middle Ages the German women used to bake twisted bread in honor of the goddess of vegetation, Berchta, and they called the loaves by the name of this goddess. The Jewish women of Germany baked twisted white loaves in honor of the Sabbath, and they often called these loaves by the German name. The word *Berches* or *Barches* is a corruption of the word *Berchta*.

There is also a popular explanation that the word *Berches* is a corruption of the Hebrew word *Birkat* from the verse (Prov. 10.22) *Birkat Adonai Hi Ta'ashir* (The blessing of the Lord, it maketh rich), a verse still found on knives used on Sabbaths for cutting *Ḥallah*.

9. *Why Do We Always Place Two "Ḥallot" on the Sabbath Table?*

In ancient times, the number of loaves served at a meal corresponded to the number of dishes. On weekdays only one dish was served and, therefore, only one loaf of bread was broken. On the Sabbath it was customary to serve two dishes. Therefore two *Ḥallot* were broken.

This practice, too, was later reinterpreted, and the reason popularly given for the two *Ḥallot* was that they commemorated the double portion of manna which the Hebrews gathered on Fridays during their sojourn in the desert (Ex. 16.22, 23).

10. *Why Are the "Ḥallot" Covered Before the Meal?*

In olden times the cup of wine ushered in the Sabbath. After that the table (tray) with the bread was brought in. Later, when it became customary to set the table before the *Kiddush*, the *Ḥallot* were covered to signify that the Sabbath meal was served after the *Kiddush*.

A later explanation is that the observant Jew is anxious to honor not only the Sabbath but each of its symbols. Since the recital of the *Kiddush* precedes the benediction over the *Ḥallot*, it might be inferred that the one ceremony is preferred to the other. By covering the *Ḥallot* the observant Jew does away with this seeming preference.

11. *Why Do We Eat Fish and "Kugel" on the Sabbath?*

Fish and *Kugel* (pudding) have been popular Sabbath dishes for many centuries and have become characteristic of the Sabbath meals.

The eating of fish — stuffed (*gefilte*) or otherwise — has been interpreted as a symbol of the blessing that the children of Israel would multiply like the stars in the heavens and the sand of the sea.

The word *Kugel* (pudding) is a corruption of the Hebrew word *Ke'ugal* (round-shaped) and is supposed to remind us of the manna which consisted of globules.

12. *Why Was It Customary to Eat "Cholent" or "Schalet" on the Sabbath?*

The words *Cholent* and *Schalet* come from the old French word *chald*, or the modern French word *chaud*, meaning warm. The Jews wanted to eat warm food on the Sabbath. They therefore put the food in the oven, which was sealed on Friday so as to retain its heat. The food which was thus kept warm was called in Germany *Schalet*, and in Eastern

Europe *Cholent.* In time the words *Schalet* and *Cholent* assumed specialized meanings. The German Jews used the word *Schalet* to designate the warm Sabbath pudding, while the Eastern Jews used the word *Cholent* to designate the warm Sabbath soup.

13. *Why Are Three Meals Prescribed for the Sabbath?*

In olden times people ate two meals daily — one at about 10 A. M. and the main meal in the evening. The first Sabbath meal on Friday evening was the regular evening meal of that day. The other two meals on the Sabbath day were the two regular meals of that day, except that in honor of the Sabbath the evening meal was taken *before* the night set in.

It has also been explained that we eat three Sabbath meals in honor of the three Patriarchs, Abraham, Isaac, and Jacob, who observed the Sabbath even before the giving of the Torah.

14. *Why Is a Special Prayer, Known as the "Habdalah," Recited over a Cup of Wine at the Conclusion of the Sabbath?*

Just as it used to be customary to begin the meal with a cup of wine, so was it customary to end the meal with a cup of wine. Since the third Sabbath meal was eaten shortly before dusk, it normally ended when the Sabbath was already over. The importance of the Sabbath and its holiness were then expressed over the cup of wine which brought that meal to a close.

Habdalah means separation. The service indicates that the holiness and joy of the Sabbath are terminated, and that the weekdays of toil and worry have begun. The *Habdalah* prayer reads, in part, "Blessed art Thou, O Lord, our God, King of the Universe, who makest a distinction between holy and profane, between light and darkness, between Israel and other peoples, between the seventh day and the six working days. Blessed art Thou, O Lord, who makest a distinction between the holy and the profane."

15. *Why Is a Lighted Candle Held at the "Habdalah" Service and Why Is a Blessing Recited over It?*

When the last Sabbath meal was over and the cup of wine was served, light was brought in, for night had already set in. The *Habdalah* which was then recited became associated with the light in the same manner as it became associated with the wine.

A more popular explanation associates this custom with the tradition that light was created at the beginning of the week. A benediction is therefore pronounced over the light to thank God for this blessing (Gen. Rab. 12.6).

16. *Why Do People Close and Open Their Hands and Gaze at Their Fingers after the Benediction over the Light?*

By looking at their hands people are making use of the light. Not to make use of it would render the benediction a *Berakah le-Vatalah* — a useless blessing.

17. *Why Is the "Habdalah" Candle Usually Made of Many Strands and Wicks?*

Light has many manifestations, hence the benediction over light uses the plural (lights). The *Habdalah* candle, by having several wicks, produces a compound light and thus corresponds to the plural form of the prayer. The Friday night candles, however, have only one wick each, sufficient to light the room for which they were originally meant (see No. 3, p. 15).

18. Why Are Spices Used at the "Habdalah" Service?

In ancient times, before meat-forks came into use, it was customary to cleanse the hands after a meal by passing them over spices on hot coals. On the Sabbath this custom was necessarily dispensed with. But after the third Sabbath meal which was eaten at dusk, the spices were brought in. Like the kindling of the light, they became a symbol of the conclusion of the Sabbath. The spices thus became associated with the *Habdalah* service.

A later, mystical reason given for the use of spices is that smell is the most non-material perception of the senses and consequently the most spiritual of sense satisfactions. Since the "special soul" (*Neshamah Yeterah*) leaves at the end of the Sabbath, the smelling of spices is a sort of spiritual feast to comfort the *Neshamah Yeterah* which grieves when the Sabbath ends.

19. Why Do the Religious Hymns of Saturday Night Deal Primarily with the Prophet Elijah?

According to tradition, the Prophet Elijah, messenger of the good tidings of the Messiah's coming, will not arrive on Friday when everyone is busy preparing for the Sabbath, nor on Saturday when Jews are at rest. Consequently he is expected immediately after the Sabbath. The hymns express the hope that the Prophet Elijah will appear during the coming week and bring the good tidings of redemption for Israel and humanity.

20. Why Do Some Jews Eat a Fourth Sabbath Meal on Saturday Night?

Many people preferred to have their main meal after the *Habdalah*, when they could have freshly cooked food. Since the rabbis could not prevent the people from having an additional fresh and warm meal after the outgoing of the Sabbath, they insisted that this meal too be considered in honor of Queen Sabbath. The meal was therefore named *Melaveh Malkah* — farewell feast for the departing Queen Sabbath.

The Saturday evening meal has also been called the feast of King David. The Talmud relates that in answer to King David's plea, "Lord make me to know mine end" (Ps. 39.5), David learned that his death would occur on a Sabbath. After each Sabbath, King David would celebrate because he was assured of life for at least one more week.

CHAPTER III

HOME SERVICE FOR THE SABBATH

וָאֹמַר אֶל בְּנֵיהֶם ...

בְּחֻקּוֹתַי לֵכוּ ...

וְאֶת שַׁבְּתוֹתַי קַדֵּשׁוּ (יחזקאל, י"ח-כ')

And I said unto their children ...
Walk in My statutes ...
And hallow My sabbaths (Ezek. 20.18–20).

I

TRADITIONAL HOME SERVICE FOR SABBATH EVE

1. KINDLING THE SABBATH LIGHTS

Before kindling the Sabbath lights, the following preparations are made. The table is set for the meal; two
Ḥallot (covered with a napkin or a specially embroidered
cover) and a cup of wine are placed at the head of the
table; the candlesticks with the candles are placed in the
center of the table; in accordance with ancient custom
money is dropped into a charity box. The mistress of the
house then kindles the lights, shields her eyes with the
palms of her hands, and silently recites the following
blessing and prayer:[1]

בָּרוּךְ אַתָּה יְיָ אֱלֹהֵינוּ מֶלֶךְ הָעוֹלָם. אֲשֶׁר קִדְּשָׁנוּ
בְּמִצְוֹתָיו וְצִוָּנוּ לְהַדְלִיק נֵר שֶׁל־שַׁבָּת:

Blessed art Thou, O Lord our God, King of the universe, who
hast sanctified us by Thy commandments, and commanded us
to kindle the Sabbath lights.

May the Sabbath-light which illumines our dwelling cause
peace and happiness to shine in our home. Bless us, O God, on
this holy Sabbath, and cause Thy divine glory to shine upon us.
Enlighten our darkness and guide us and all mankind, Thy
children, towards truth and eternal light. Amen.

2. BLESSING THE CHILDREN

After kindling the Sabbath lights, or immediately before the *Kiddush*, the father places his hands on the head of each child and recites the following blessing:

FOR SONS

יְשִׂמְךָ אֱלֹהִים כְּאֶפְרַיִם וְכִמְנַשֶּׁה:

יְבָרֶכְךָ יְיָ וְיִשְׁמְרֶךָ: יָאֵר יְיָ פָּנָיו אֵלֶיךָ וִיחֻנֶּךָּ:
יִשָּׂא יְיָ פָּנָיו אֵלֶיךָ וְיָשֵׂם לְךָ שָׁלוֹם:

May God make thee as Ephraim and Manasseh.

May the Lord bless thee and keep thee:
May the Lord cause His countenance to shine upon
thee, and be gracious unto thee:
May the Lord lift up His countenance towards
thee and give thee peace.

(A personal prayer may be added)

FOR DAUGHTERS

יְשִׂמֵךְ אֱלֹהִים כְּשָׂרָה רִבְקָה רָחֵל וְלֵאָה:

יְבָרֶכְךָ יְיָ וְיִשְׁמְרֶךָ: יָאֵר יְיָ פָּנָיו אֵלֶיךָ וִיחֻנֶּךָּ:
יִשָּׂא יְיָ פָּנָיו אֵלֶיךָ וְיָשֵׂם לְךָ שָׁלוֹם:

May God make thee as Sarah, Rebekah, Rachel,
and Leah.

May the Lord bless thee and keep thee:
May the Lord cause His countenance to shine upon
thee, and be gracious unto thee:
May the Lord lift up His countenance towards
thee and give thee peace.

(A personal prayer may be added)

3. HYMN OF WELCOME TO THE SABBATH
ANGELS OF PEACE

(Sung before the *Kiddush*)

שָׁלוֹם עֲלֵיכֶם

שָׁלוֹם עֲלֵיכֶם מַלְאֲכֵי הַשָּׁרֵת מַלְאֲכֵי עֶלְיוֹן
מִמֶּלֶךְ מַלְכֵי הַמְּלָכִים הַקָּדוֹשׁ בָּרוּךְ הוּא.

בּוֹאֲכֶם לְשָׁלוֹם מַלְאֲכֵי הַשָּׁלוֹם מַלְאֲכֵי עֶלְיוֹן
מִמֶּלֶךְ מַלְכֵי הַמְּלָכִים הַקָּדוֹשׁ בָּרוּךְ הוּא.

בָּרְכוּנִי לְשָׁלוֹם מַלְאֲכֵי הַשָּׁלוֹם מַלְאֲכֵי עֶלְיוֹן
מִמֶּלֶךְ מַלְכֵי הַמְּלָכִים הַקָּדוֹשׁ בָּרוּךְ הוּא:

צֵאתְכֶם לְשָׁלוֹם מַלְאֲכֵי הַשָּׁלוֹם מַלְאֲכֵי עֶלְיוֹן
מִמֶּלֶךְ מַלְכֵי הַמְּלָכִים הַקָּדוֹשׁ בָּרוּךְ הוּא.

3. HYMN OF WELCOME TO THE SABBATH
ANGELS OF PEACE

שָׁלוֹם עֲלֵיכֶם

I. GOLDFARB, arr. by A. W. B.

mf Andantino

1. Sho - lōm a - lĕ - chem mal a - chĕ ha - sho - rēs mal-
4. Tsēs - chem l' - sho - lōm mal a - chĕ ha - sho - lōm, mal-

a - chĕ el - yōn; mi - me - lech
a - chĕ el - yōn; mi - me - lech

mal - chĕ ham - lo - chīm, ha - ko - dōsh bo - ruch hu.
mal - chĕ ham - lo - chīm, ha - ko - dōsh bo - ruch hu.

FINE

2. Bŏ - a - chem l' - sho - lŏm mal - a - chē ha - sho - lŏm,
3. Bor chu - nĭ l' - sho - lŏm mal - a - chē ha - sho - lŏm,

mal - a - chē el - yŏn, mi - me - lech
mal - a - chē el - yŏn,

D. C. al Fine

mal - chē ham - lo - chĭm ha - ko - dŏsh bo - ruch hu. Bor' hu.

3. HYMN OF WELCOME TO THE SABBATH
ANGELS OF PEACE

(Sung before the *Kiddush*)

SHOLOM ALECHEM

(Peace Be Unto You)

Peace be unto you,
Ye ministering angels,
Ye angels from on high,
From the King
Who is King over kings
The holy One, blessed be He.

May your coming be in peace,
Ye angels of peace,
Ye angels from on high,
From the King
Who is King over kings
The holy One, blessed be He.

Bless us with peace,
Ye angels of peace,
Ye angels from on high,
From the King
Who is King over kings
The holy One, blessed be He.

May your going be in peace,
Ye angels of peace,
Ye angels from on high,
From the King
Who is King over kings
The holy One, blessed be He.

4. A TRIBUTE TO THE MISTRESS OF THE HOUSE

A WOMAN OF VALOR — אֵשֶׁת חַיִל

Andante

mf

E - shes cha - yil mī— yim - tso v'ro - chŏk mip - nī - nīm

mich - roh   Bo - tăch boh lĕv bal - a - loh——

v'sho - lol lŏ——— yech - sor——— yech - sor. G'mo-

las - hu tŏv v'- lŏ ro kŏl y'- mē cha - ye - ho. G'mo-

las - hu tŏv v'- lŏ ro kŏl y'- mē cha - ye - ho.

4. A TRIBUTE TO THE MISTRESS OF THE HOUSE

(Recited by the Husband before the *Kiddush*)

ESHES CHAYIL*

(A Woman of Valor)

A woman of valour who can find?
    For her price is far above rubies.
The heart of her husband doth safely trust in her,
    And he hath no lack of gain.
She doeth him good and not evil
    All the days of her life.
She giveth food to her household,
    And a portion to her maidens.
She stretcheth out her hand to the poor;
    Yea, she reacheth forth her hands to the needy.
Strength and dignity are her clothing;
    And she laugheth at the time to come.
She openeth her mouth with wisdom;
    And the law of kindness is on her tongue.
She looketh well to the ways of her household,
    And eateth not the bread of idleness.
Her children rise up, and call her blessed;
    Her husband also, and he praiseth her:
'Many daughters have done valiantly,
    But thou excellest them all.'
Grace is deceitful, and beauty is vain;
    But a woman that feareth the Lord, she shall be praised.
Give her of the fruit of her hands;
    And let her works praise her in the gates.

(Prov. 31.10–12, 15, 20, 25–31)

---

* Verses 13, 14, 16–19, and 21–24 were omitted in the translation because they are not relevant to modern life.

5. KIDDUSH FOR FRIDAY EVENING

After singing *Sholōm Alēchem* and reciting *Eshes Chayil*, the head of the household raises the cup of wine and recites the *Kiddush*. The wine is then passed to everyone at the table. If wine is not available, the *Kiddush* is recited over the *Ḥallah* and the benediction הַמּוֹצִיא לֶחֶם is substituted for the benediction בּוֹרֵא פְּרִי הַגָּפֶן מִן הָאָרֶץ.

וַיְהִי עֶרֶב וַיְהִי בֹקֶר:

יוֹם הַשִּׁשִּׁי: וַיְכֻלּוּ הַשָּׁמַיִם וְהָאָרֶץ וְכָל צְבָאָם: וַיְכַל אֱלֹהִים בַּיּוֹם הַשְּׁבִיעִי מְלַאכְתּוֹ אֲשֶׁר עָשָׂה וַיִּשְׁבֹּת בַּיּוֹם הַשְּׁבִיעִי מִכָּל־מְלַאכְתּוֹ אֲשֶׁר עָשָׂה: וַיְבָרֶךְ אֱלֹהִים אֶת־יוֹם הַשְּׁבִיעִי וַיְקַדֵּשׁ אֹתוֹ. כִּי בוֹ שָׁבַת מִכָּל־מְלַאכְתּוֹ אֲשֶׁר־בָּרָא אֱלֹהִים לַעֲשׂוֹת:

בָּרוּךְ אַתָּה יְיָ אֱלֹהֵינוּ מֶלֶךְ הָעוֹלָם בּוֹרֵא פְּרִי הַגָּפֶן:

בָּרוּךְ אַתָּה יְיָ אֱלֹהֵינוּ מֶלֶךְ הָעוֹלָם אֲשֶׁר קִדְּשָׁנוּ בְּמִצְוֹתָיו וְרָצָה בָנוּ וְשַׁבַּת קָדְשׁוֹ בְּאַהֲבָה וּבְרָצוֹן הִנְחִילָנוּ זִכָּרוֹן לְמַעֲשֵׂה בְרֵאשִׁית. כִּי הוּא יוֹם תְּחִלָּה לְמִקְרָאֵי קֹדֶשׁ זֵכֶר לִיצִיאַת מִצְרָיִם. כִּי־בָנוּ בָחַרְתָּ וְאוֹתָנוּ קִדַּשְׁתָּ מִכָּל־הָעַמִּים וְשַׁבַּת קָדְשֶׁךָ בְּאַהֲבָה וּבְרָצוֹן הִנְחַלְתָּנוּ. בָּרוּךְ אַתָּה יְיָ מְקַדֵּשׁ הַשַּׁבָּת:

5. KIDDUSH FOR FRIDAY EVENING[2]

Quasi recitative

After a version by L. LEWANDOWSKI

mf

Bo-ruch a-toh a-dō-noy e - lō - hē - nu me-lech ho-ō - lom

bō - rē pe - rī ha-go - fen Bo-ruch a-toh a-dō-noy

Ē - lō - hē - nu me-lech ho - ō - lom A -

sher ki - d'-sho-nu b'-mitz-vō-sov v'- ro - tsoh vo - nu v' - sha-

bas ko - d' - shō b' - a - ha - voh ur - ro - tsōn hin - chī

lo - nu zi - ko - rōn — l'-ma - a - sēh v' - rē - -

shīs. Kī hu yōm t'-chi - loh l'-mik-ro - ē kō-desh, zē - cher

liğ-tsï-as mitz-rǒ-yïm. Kï vo-no vo-char-to v'ŏ-
so-nu kï-dash-to mi-kol ho-a - mim   v'-
sha-bas kod-sh' cho b'-a-ha-voh uv-ro - tsōn
hin-chal-to - nu. Bo-ruch a-toh a-dō-noy
m - ka - dēsh ha-sha - bos.

5. KIDDUSH FOR FRIDAY EVENING

After singing *Sholōm Alēchem* and reciting *Eshes Chayil,*
the head of the household raises the cup of wine and
recites the *Kiddush.* The wine is then passed to everyone
at the table. If wine is not available, the *Kiddush* is
recited over the *Ḥallah* and the benediction הַמּוֹצִיא לֶחֶם
מִן הָאָרֶץ is substituted for the benediction בּוֹרֵא פְּרִי הַגָּפֶן.

And it was evening and it was morning — the sixth day.

And the heaven and the earth were finished and all their
host. And on the seventh day God had finished His work
which He had made; and He rested on the seventh day from
all His work which He had made. And God blessed the
seventh day, and He hallowed it, because He rested thereon
from all His work which God had created and made.

Blessed art Thou, O Lord our God, King of the universe,
Creator of the fruit of the vine.

Blessed art Thou, O Lord our God, King of the universe,
who hast sanctified us by Thy commandments and hast
granted us Thy favor and given us Thy holy Sabbath as an
inheritance. It is a memorial of the creation. It is a special
day, first of the days of holy assembly, a memorial of the
departure from Egypt. Thou hast chosen Israel and Thou
hast sanctified us among the peoples in that with love and
favor Thou hast given us Thy holy Sabbath as an inheritance. Blessed art Thou, O Lord, who sanctifiest the
Sabbath Day.

6. GRACE BEFORE THE MEAL

Blessing After Washing of Hands for the Meal

בָּרוּךְ אַתָּה יְיָ. אֱלֹהֵינוּ מֶלֶךְ הָעוֹלָם. אֲשֶׁר קִדְּשָׁנוּ בְּמִצְוֹתָיו. וְצִוָּנוּ עַל נְטִילַת יָדַיִם:

Blessed art Thou, O Lord our God, King of the universe, who hast sanctified us by Thy commandments, and hast commanded us concerning the washing of the hands.

Blessing Before Partaking of the *Hallah*

בָּרוּךְ אַתָּה יְיָ. אֱלֹהֵינוּ מֶלֶךְ הָעוֹלָם. הַמּוֹצִיא לֶחֶם מִן הָאָרֶץ:

Blessed art Thou, O Lord our God, King of the universe, who bringest forth bread from the earth.

---

7. ZEMIROT*

TABLE-HYMNS FOR FRIDAY EVENING

יָהּ רִבּוֹן

יָהּ רִבּוֹן עָלַם וְעָלְמַיָּא, אַנְתְּ הוּא מַלְכָּא מֶלֶךְ מַלְכַיָּא.

עוֹבַד גְּבוּרְתֵּךְ וְתִמְהַיָּא, שַׁפִּיר קֳדָמָךְ לְהַחֲוָיָה: ‏[ויה רבון]‏

שְׁבָחִין אֲסַדֵּר צַפְרָא וְרַמְשָׁא, לָךְ אֱלָהָא דִי בְרָא כָל־נַפְשָׁא.

עִירִין קַדִּישִׁין וּבְנֵי אֱנָשָׁא, חֵיוַת בָּרָא וְעוֹפֵי שְׁמַיָּא: ‏[ויה רבון]‏

רַבְרְבִין עוֹבְדָיךְ וְתַקִּיפִין, מָכֵךְ רָמַיָּא, זָקֵף כְּפִיפִין.

לוּ יְחֵא גְבַר שְׁנִין אַלְפִין, לָא יֵעוֹל גְּבוּרְתֵּךְ בְּחֻשְׁבְּנַיָּא: ‏[ויה רבון]‏

אֱלָהָא דִי לֵהּ יְקַר וּרְבוּתָא, פְּרֹק יָת־עָנָךְ מִפּוּם אַרְיָוָתָא.

וְאַפֵּק יָת עַמָּךְ מִגּוֹא גָלוּתָא, עַמָּךְ דִי בָחַרְתְּ מִכָּל־אֻמַּיָּא: ‏[ויה רבון]‏

לְמִקְדָּשָׁךְ תּוּב וּלְקֹדֶשׁ קֻדְשִׁין, אֲתַר דִּי בֵהּ יֶחֱדוּן רוּחִין וְנַפְשִׁין.

וִיזַמְּרוּן שִׁירִין וְרַחֲשִׁין, בִּירוּשְׁלֵם קַרְתָּא דִי־שֻׁפְרַיָּא: ‏[ויה רבון]‏

1

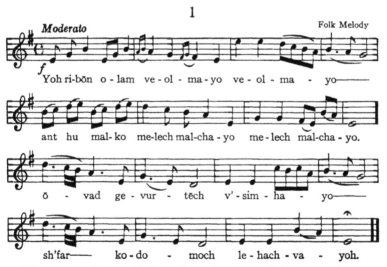

*One or more of these table-hymns is usually sung at the Friday evening meal.
Other suitable hymns may be chosen from the ‘Oneg Shabbat songs at the end of
this volume.

2

I. GOLDFARB

Moderato

Yoh ri - bŏn o - lam v' - ol - ma - yo

ant hu mal - ko—— me - lech mal' - cha - yoh,—— ŏ -

vad g' - vur - tĕch v' - sim - ha - yo.... shap -

pir — ko - do - moch l' - hach' - va - yoh——

REFRAIN

Yoh ri - bŏn o - lam v' - ol - ma - yo.........

ant.... hu.... mal - ko.... me-lech mal - cha.... yo.——

7. ZEMIROT

TABLE-HYMNS FOR FRIDAY EVENING

YOH RIBBON

ISRAEL NAJARA (1555–1628)

(Translated from the Hebrew by ISRAEL ABRAHAMS)

God of the world, eternity's sole Lord!
King over kings, be now Thy name adored!
Blessed are we to whom Thou dost accord
    This gladsome time Thy wondrous ways to scan!

Refrain

    God of the world, eternity's sole Lord!
    King over kings, be now Thy name adored!

Early and late to Thee our praises ring,
Giver of life to every living thing!
Beasts of the field, and birds that heavenward wing,
    Angelic hosts and all the sons of man!

Refrain

Though we on earth a thousand years should dwell,
Too brief the space Thy marvels forth to tell!
Pride Thou didst lower, all the weak who fell
    Thy hand raised up e'er since the world began!

Refrain

Thine is the power, Thine the glory be!
When lions rage, O deign Thy flock to free!
Thine exiled sons, O take once more to Thee,
    Choose them again as in Thine ancient plan!

Refrain

Turn to Thy city, Zion's sacred shrine!
On yon fair mount again let beauty shine!
There, happy throngs their voices shall combine,
    There, present joy all former ill shall ban!

Refrain

מְנוּחָה וְשִׂמְחָה

מְנוּחָה וְשִׂמְחָה, אוֹר לַיְּהוּדִים.
יוֹם שַׁבָּתוֹן יוֹם מַחֲמַדִּים.
שׁוֹמְרָיו וְזוֹכְרָיו הֵמָּה מְעִידִים.
כִּי לְשִׁשָּׁה כֹּל בְּרוּאִים וְעוֹמְדִים:

שְׁמֵי שָׁמַיִם אֶרֶץ וְיַמִּים.
כָּל צְבָא מָרוֹם גְּבוֹהִים וְרָמִים.
תַּנִּין וְאָדָם וְחַיַּת רְאֵמִים.
כִּי בְּיָהּ יְיָ צוּר עוֹלָמִים:

הוּא אֲשֶׁר דִּבֶּר לְעַם סְגֻלָּתוֹ.
שָׁמוֹר לְקַדְּשׁוֹ מִבּוֹאוֹ וְעַד צֵאתוֹ.
שַׁבַּת קֹדֶשׁ יוֹם חֶמְדָּתוֹ.
כִּי בוֹ שָׁבַת אֵל מִכָּל מְלַאכְתּוֹ:

בְּמִצְוַת שַׁבָּת אֵל יַחֲלִיצָךְ.
קוּם קְרָא אֵלָיו יָחִישׁ לְאַמְּצָךְ.
נִשְׁמַת כָּל חַי וְגַם נַעֲרִיצָךְ.
אֱכוֹל בְּשִׂמְחָה כִּי כְבָר רָצָךְ:

בְּמִשְׁנֶה לֶחֶם וְקִדּוּשָׁא רַבָּה.
בְּרוֹב מַטְעַמִּים וְרוּחַ נְדִיבָה.
יִזְכּוּ לְרַב טוּב הַמִּתְעַנְּגִים בָּהּ.
בְּבִיאַת גּוֹאֵל לְחַיֵּי הָעוֹלָם הַבָּא:

M'NUCHOH V'SIMCHOH — מְנוּחָה וְשִׂמְחָה

M'nu - choh v' - sim - choh ōr la - y' - hu - dīm,

yōm sha - bo - sōn yōm mach-ma-dīm shōm-rov v'-zōch-rov

hĕ - moh m' - ī - dīm, Kī l'-shi-shoh kōl b' - ru - īm v'- ōm dīm.

Sh'mĕ sho - ma - yīm e - retz v' - ya - mīm Kol ts'vo mo - rōm

g'vō - hīm v - ro - mīm ta - nīn v' - o - dom

v'cha - yas r' - ĕ - mīm kī b'yoh a - dō - noy. tsur ō - lo-mīm.

M'NUCHOH V'SIMCHOH

AUTHOR UNKNOWN

(Translated from the Hebrew by JUDAH I. GOLDIN)

Rest and rejoicing and light for the Jews!
    Sabbath day, Sabbath, O day of delights!
All them that keep it so proudly declare
    The world was created in six days and nights.

Heaven on heaven, the earth and the seas,
    Hosts of the skies all excelling in height,
Monster and mankind and beast of the field
    Proclaim God is Lord, for in Him is all might.

Thus did He speak to the people He chose:
    Hallow the Sabbath throughout its long run.
Holy is Sabbath, O day of His joy —
    For on it God rested, His labor was done.

God shall protect thee for dear Sabbath's sake.
    Rise now and call Him; to thee He will haste.
Sing all the prayers thy *siddur* prescribes;
    Now eat thou in gladness: thou art to His taste.

Double thy portion of bread, and sip wine;
    Pile on more dainties, in more ample sum!
May all those rejoicing inherit much good,
    And bring, O Redeemer, the world that's to come.

צוּר מִשֶּׁלּוֹ

צוּר מִשֶּׁלּוֹ אָכַלְנוּ, בָּרְכוּ אֱמוּנַי.
שָׂבַעְנוּ וְהוֹתַרְנוּ כִּדְבַר יְיָ: [צור]

הַזָּן אֶת עוֹלָמוֹ, רוֹעֵנוּ, אָבִינוּ.
אָכַלְנוּ אֶת לַחְמוֹ וְיֵינוֹ שָׁתִינוּ.
עַל כֵּן נוֹדֶה לִשְׁמוֹ וּנְהַלְלוֹ בְּפִינוּ.
אָמַרְנוּ וְעָנִינוּ, אֵין קָדוֹשׁ כַּיְיָ: [צור]

בְּשִׁיר וְקוֹל תּוֹדָה נְבָרֵךְ אֱלֹהֵינוּ.
עַל אֶרֶץ חֶמְדָּה, שֶׁהִנְחִיל לַאֲבוֹתֵינוּ.
מָזוֹן וְצֵידָה הִשְׂבִּיעַ לְנַפְשֵׁנוּ,
חַסְדּוֹ גָּבַר עָלֵינוּ וֶאֱמֶת יְיָ: [צור]

רַחֵם בְּחַסְדֶּךָ עַל עַמְּךָ צוּרֵנוּ.
עַל צִיּוֹן מִשְׁכַּן כְּבוֹדֶךָ, זְבוּל בֵּית תִּפְאַרְתֵּנוּ.
בֶּן־דָּוִד עַבְדֶּךָ יָבֹא וְיִגְאָלֵנוּ,
רוּחַ אַפֵּינוּ, מְשִׁיחַ יְיָ: [צור]

יִבָּנֶה הַמִּקְדָּשׁ, עִיר צִיּוֹן תְּמַלֵּא.
וְשָׁם נָשִׁיר שִׁיר חָדָשׁ, וּבִרְנָנָה נַעֲלֶה.
הָרַחֲמָן הַנִּקְדָּשׁ, יִתְבָּרַךְ וְיִתְעַלֶּה
עַל כּוֹס יַיִן מָלֵא, כְּבִרְכַּת יְיָ: [צור]

TSUR MISHELO – צוּר מִשֶּׁלּוֹ

Tsur—— mi-she-lō o-chal-nu bo-ra-chu e-mu-noy So-va-nu, so-va-nu, so-va-nu v'-hō-sar-nu kid-var a-dō-noy. Ha-zon—— es ō-lo-mō rō-ē-nu o-vī-nu o-chal-nu——es—— lach-mō v'-yē-nō sho-sī-nu.

Al—— kēn nō-de—lish-mō un ha-le-lō b'-fī-nu o-mar-nu v'o-nī———nu ēn ko-dōsh ka-dō-noy.

TSUR MISHELO

AUTHOR UNKNOWN

(Translated from the Hebrew by NINA SALAMAN)

Refrain

Rock from whose store we have eaten —
Bless Him, my faithful companions.
Eaten have we and left over —
  This was the word of the Lord.

Feeding His world like a shepherd —
Father whose bread we have eaten,
Father whose wine we have drunken.
Now to His name we are singing,
Praising Him loud with our voices,
Saying and singing for ever:
  Holy is none like the Lord. [*Refrain*]

Singing with sound of thanksgiving,
Bless we our God for the good land
Given of old to our fathers;
Bless we Him now who has given
Food for our hunger of spirit;
Strong over us is His mercy,
  Mighty the truth of the Lord. [*Refrain*]

Mercy, O Rock, for Thy people!
Pity the place of Thy glory,
Zion, the house of our beauty.
Soon shall he come to redeem us —
Offspring of David, Thy servant,
He that is breath of our spirit —
  Send Thine anointed, O Lord! [*Refrain*]

O that the Temple were builded,
Filled again Zion our city —
There a new song shall we sing Him,
Merciful, holy and blessed —
Bless we Him now and for ever,
Over the full brimming wine-cup,
  Blest as we are of the Lord. [*Refrain*]

שָׁלוֹם לָךְ יוֹם הַשְּׁבִיעִי

עַל־אַהֲבָתֶךָ אֶשְׁתֶּה גְבִיעִי,
שָׁלוֹם לָךְ שָׁלוֹם, יוֹם הַשְּׁבִיעִי!

שֵׁשֶׁת יְמֵי מַעֲשֶׂה לָךְ כַּעֲבָדִים,
אִם אֶעֱבֹד בָּהֶם, אֶשְׂבַּע נְדוּדִים.
כֻּלָּם בְּעֵינַי הֵם יָמִים אֲחָדִים.
מֵאַהֲבָתִי בָךְ, יוֹם שַׁעֲשׁוּעָי. [שלום]

אֵצֵא בְּיוֹם רִאשׁוֹן לַעֲשׂוֹת מְלָאכָה,
לַעֲרֹךְ לְיוֹם שַׁבָּת הַמַּעֲרָכָה,
כִּי הָאֱלֹהִים שָׁם שָׂם הַבְּרָכָה,
אַתָּה לְבַד חֶלְקִי מִכָּל יְגִיעִי. [שלום]

מָאוֹר לְיוֹם קָדְשִׁי מֵאוֹר קְדוֹשִׁי,
שֶׁמֶשׁ וְכוֹכָבִים קִנְאוּ לְשִׁמְשִׁי.
מַה־לִּי לְיוֹם שֵׁנִי אוֹ לַשְּׁלִישִׁי?
יַסְתִּיר מְאוֹרוֹתָיו יוֹם הָרְבִיעִי. [שלום]

אֶשְׁמַע מְבַשֵּׂר טוֹב מִיּוֹם חֲמִישִׁי,
כִּי מָחֳרָת יִהְיֶה נֹפֶשׁ לְנַפְשִׁי:
בֹּקֶר לַעֲבוֹדָתִי, עֶרֶב לְחָפְשִׁי,
קָרוֹא אֱלֵי שֻׁלְחַן מַלְכִּי וְרוֹעִי. [שלום]

SHOLOM LOCH YOM HA-SHEVI-I — שָׁלוֹם לְךָ יוֹם הַשְּׁבִיעִי

Andante

SOLOMON LAMPORT, arr. by A. W. B.

mf

1. She - shes ye - me ha-ma - a - seh—— loch ka-avo - dim,
2. E - tse b' - yom— ri - shon la-a - sos m' - lo - choh,

Im e-evod bo - hem es - ba n'— du— dim Ku-
La - a-roch l'yom sha - bos - ha - ma - a'ro— choh, Ki-

lom b' - e — nay hem yo - mim a - cho - dim, Me-
hu - e - lo — him shom—— som ha - b'ro—choh,' A-

a - ha-vo - si b' - cho— yom ma - r'go - i.
toh l' - vad chel - ki mi - kol y' - gi - i.

אֶמְצָא בְיוֹם שִׁשִּׁי נַפְשִׁי שְׂמֵחָה,
כִּי קָרְבָה אֵלַי עֵת הַמְּנוּחָה.
אִם נָע וָנָד אֵלֵךְ לִמְצֹא רְוָחָה,
עֶרֶב וְאֶשְׁכַּח כָּל נוֹדִי וְנוֹעִי. [שלום]

מַה־נָּעֲמָה לִי עֵת בֵּין הַשְּׁמָשׁוֹת
לִרְאוֹת פְּנֵי שַׁבָּת, פָּנִים חֲדָשׁוֹת,
בֹּאוּ בְתַפּוּחִים, הַרְבּוּ אֲשִׁישׁוֹת,
זֶה יוֹם מְנוּחִי, זֶה דּוֹדִי וְרֵעִי! [שלום]

אָשִׁיר לְךָ, שַׁבָּת, שִׁירֵי יְדִידוֹת,
כִּי יָאֲתָה לְךָ, כִּי אַתְּ יוֹם חֲמוּדוֹת,
יוֹם תַּעֲנוּגִים גַּם שָׁלֹשׁ סְעוּדוֹת
תַּעֲנוּג לְשֻׁלְחָנִי, תַּעֲנוּג יְצוּעִי.
שָׁלוֹם לְךָ שָׁלוֹם, יוֹם הַשְּׁבִיעִי!

SHOLOM LOCH YOM HA-SHEVI-I

Judah Halevi

(Translated from the Hebrew by Solomon Solis-Cohen)

I greet my love with wine and gladsome lay;
Welcome, thrice welcome, joyous Seventh Day!

Six slaves the weekdays are; I share
With them a round of toil and care,
Yet light the burdens seem, I bear
    For thy sweet sake, Sabbath, my love!

On First-day to the accustomed task
I go content, nor guerdon ask,
Save in thy smile, at length, to bask —
    Day blest of God, Sabbath, my love!

Is Second-day dull, Third-day unbright?
Hide sun and stars from Fourth-day's sight?
What need I care, who have thy light,
    Orb of my life, Sabbath, my love!

The Fifth-day, joyful tidings ring;
"The morrow shall thy freedom bring!"
At dawn a slave, at eve a king —
    God's table waits, Sabbath, my love!

On Sixth-day doth my cup o'erflow,
What blissful rest the night shall know,
When, in thine arms, my toil and woe
    Are all forgot, Sabbath, my love!

'Tis dusk. With sudden light distilled
From one sweet face, the world is filled;
The tumult of my heart is stilled —
    For thou art come, Sabbath, my love!

Bring fruits and wine, and sing a gladsome lay,
Chant: "Come in peace, O blissful Seventh Day!"

שַׁבָּת הַמַּלְכָּה

הַחַמָּה מֵרֹאשׁ הָאִילָנוֹת נִסְתַּלְּקָה –
בֹּאוּ וְנֵצֵא לִקְרַאת שַׁבָּת הַמַּלְכָּה,
הִנֵּה הִיא יוֹרֶדֶת, הַקְּדוֹשָׁה, הַבְּרוּכָה,
וְעִמָּהּ מַלְאָכִים צְבָא שָׁלוֹם וּמְנוּחָה,
בֹּאִי בֹאִי, הַמַּלְכָּה!
בֹּאִי בֹאִי, הַמַּלְכָּה! –
שָׁלוֹם עֲלֵיכֶם, מַלְאֲכֵי הַשָּׁלוֹם!

———

קִבַּלְנוּ פְּנֵי שַׁבָּת בִּרְנָנָה וּתְפִלָּה,
הַבַּיְתָה נָשׁוּבָה בְּלֵב מָלֵא גִילָה;
שָׁם עָרוּךְ הַשֻּׁלְחָן, הַנֵּרוֹת יָאִירוּ,
כָּל־פִּנּוֹת הַבַּיִת יִזְרָחוּ, יַזְהִירוּ.
שַׁבָּת שָׁלוֹם וּבְרָכָה,
שַׁבָּת שָׁלוֹם וּמְנוּחָה –
בּוֹאֲכֶם לְשָׁלוֹם, מַלְאֲכֵי הַשָּׁלוֹם!

———

שְׁבִי, זַכָּה, עִמָּנוּ וּבְזִיוֵךְ נָא אוֹרִי
לַיְלָה וָיוֹם – אַחֲרֵי־כֵן תַּעֲבֹרִי;
וַאֲנַחְנוּ נְכַבְּדֵךְ בְּבִגְדֵי חֲמֻדוֹת

בִּזְמִירוֹת וּתְפִלּוֹת וּבְשָׁלֹשׁ סְעוּדוֹת,

וּבִמְנוּחָה שְׁלֵמָה

וּבִמְנוּחָה נָעֵמָה

בָּרְכוּנִי לְשָׁלוֹם, מַלְאֲכֵי הַשָּׁלוֹם!

הַחַמָּה מֵרֹאשׁ הָאִילָנוֹת נִסְתַּלְּקָה —

בֹּאוּ וּנְלַוֶּה אֶת־שַׁבָּת הַמַּלְכָּה.

צֵאתֵךְ לְשָׁלוֹם, הַקְּדוֹשָׁה הַזַּכָּה!

דְּעִי, שֵׁשֶׁת יָמִים אֶל־שׁוּבֵךְ נְחַכֶּה,

כֵּן לַשַּׁבָּת הַבָּאָה,

כֵּן לַשַּׁבָּת הַבָּאָה!

צֵאתְכֶם לְשָׁלוֹם, מַלְאֲכֵי הַשָּׁלוֹם!

SHABBOS HA-MALKOH¹ — שַׁבָּת הַמַּלְכָּה

P. Minkowsky

Andantino

mf

Ha-cham-moh mē - rōsh ho - i - lo-nōs nis - tal-koh   Bŏ-
Ki - bal - nu p'nē shab-bos bir - no-noh u - s' fi-loh,   Ha -

uh - v' - nē - tsē lik-ras sha-bos ha - mal - koh. Hi - nēh
bay-so no - shu - vo b'- lēv mo-lēh v' - gil   loh. Shom

hi— yō - re - des hak - dŏ - shoh ha - b'ru - cho v' -
o-ruch ha - shul-chon ha - nē - rōs yo - i - ru. Kol

im - moh mal - o - chim ts'vo sho - lōm um - nu - choh.
pi - nōs ha - ba - yis yiz - ro - chu yaz - hī - ru.

f

Bŏ - i, bŏ - i, ha - mal - - koh, bŏ - i, bŏ - i ha -
Sha - bos sho - lōm u - m'vŏ - - roch, Sha - bas Sho - lōm u -

kal - - loh, Sho - lōm a - lē-chem mal - a-chē ha - sho-lōm.
m'vo - - roch, Bŏ - a-chem l' - sho-lōm mal - a-chē ha - sho-lōm.

SABBATH THE QUEEN

HAYYIM NAHMAN BIALIK
(Translated from the Hebrew by I. M. LASK)

The sun o'er the treetops is no longer seen;
Come, let us go forth to greet Sabbath the Queen!
Behold her descending, the holy and blest,
And with her the angels of peace and of rest.
> Welcome, O Queen, welcome!
> Enter thou, enter, O Bride!
Unto you be there peace, ye angels of peace.

The Sabbath is greeted with song and with praise,
We go slowly homewards, our hearts full of grace.
The table is spread there, the candles give light,
Every nook in the house is shining and bright.
> Sabbath is peace and rest.
> Sabbath is peaceful and blest.
Enter in peace, ye angels of peace.

O pure one, be with us and light with thy ray
The night and the day, then go on thy way,
And we do thee honor with garments most fine,
With songs and with psalms and with three feasts with wine.
> And by sweetest peace,
> And by perfect peace.
Bless us in peace, ye angels of peace!

The sun in the treetops is no longer seen,
Come forth; we will speed our Sabbath the Queen,
Go thou in peace, our holy and pure one!
Know that for six days we wait you, our sure one!
> Thus for the coming Sabbath,
> Thus for the coming Sabbath!
Pass forth in peace, ye angels of peace.

THE SABBATH BRIDE

ISAAC S. MOSES

O holy Sabbath-day draw near,
Thou art the source of bliss and cheer;
The first in God's creative thought,
The final aim of all He wrought,
Welcome, welcome, day of rest,
Day of joy the Lord hath bless'd.

Rejoice ye now with all your might:
The Sabbath, freedom brings us light;
Let songs of praise to God ascend,
And voices sweet in chorus blend.
Welcome, welcome, day of rest,
Day of joy the Lord hath bless'd.

Now come thou blessed Sabbath-Bride,
Our joy, our comfort and our pride;
All cares and sorrows bid thou cease,
And fill our waiting hearts with peace.
Welcome, welcome, day of rest,
Day of joy the Lord hath bless'd.

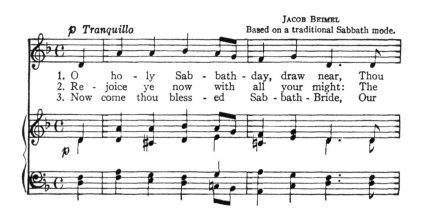

art the source of bliss and cheer; The first in God's cre-
Sab-bath free-dom brings you light; Let songs of praise to
joy, our com-fort and our pride; All cares and sor-rows

a-tive thought, The fi-nal aim of all He wrought, Wel-come,
God as-cend, And voic-es sweet in cho-rus blend. Wel-come,
bid thou cease, And fill our wait-ing hearts with peace. Wel-come,

wel-come, day of rest, Day of joy the Lord hath bless'd.
wel-come, day of rest, Day of joy the Lord hath bless'd.
wel-come, day of rest, Day of joy the Lord hath bless'd.

SABBATH BLESSING

Jessie E. Sampter

The Sabbath light is burning bright;
Our prettiest cloth is clean and white,
    With wine and bread for Friday night.

At set of sun our work is done;
The happy Sabbath has begun;
    Now bless us, Father, ev'ry one.

O Sabbath guest, dear Sabbath guest,
Come, share the blessing with the rest,
    For all our house tonight is blest.

SABBATH BLESSING

A. W. B.

mf Andante

1. The Sab-bath light is burn-ing bright; Our pret-tiest cloth is
2. At set of sun our work is done; The hap-py Sab-bath
3. O Sab-bath guest, dear Sab-bath guest, Come, share the bless-ing

clean and white, With wine and bread for Fri-day night.
has be-gun; Now bless us, Fa-ther, ev-'ry one.
with the rest, For all our house to-night is blest.

8. GRACE AFTER MEALS*

INTRODUCTORY PSALM

Psalm 126

שִׁיר הַמַּעֲלוֹת.

בְּשׁוּב יְיָ אֶת־שִׁיבַת צִיּוֹן הָיִינוּ כְּחֹלְמִים:

אָז יִמָּלֵא שְׂחֹק פִּינוּ וּלְשׁוֹנֵנוּ רִנָּה

אָז יֹאמְרוּ בַגּוֹיִם הִגְדִּיל יְיָ לַעֲשׂוֹת עִם־אֵלֶּה:

הִגְדִּיל יְיָ לַעֲשׂוֹת עִמָּנוּ הָיִינוּ שְׂמֵחִים:

שׁוּבָה יְיָ אֶת־שְׁבִיתֵנוּ כַּאֲפִיקִים בַּנֶּגֶב:

הַזֹּרְעִים בְּדִמְעָה בְּרִנָּה יִקְצֹרוּ:

הָלוֹךְ יֵלֵךְ וּבָכֹה נֹשֵׂא מֶשֶׁךְ־הַזָּרַע

בֹּא־יָבֹא בְרִנָּה נֹשֵׂא אֲלֻמֹּתָיו:

---

*The full Grace After Meals will be found in the music supplement, below, pp. 438–456.

8. GRACE AFTER MEALS

INTRODUCTORY PSALM

Psalm 126

A Song of Ascents.

When the Lord brought back those that returned to Zion,
We were like unto them that dream.
Then was our mouth filled with laughter,
And our tongue with singing;
Then said they among the nations:
'The Lord hath done great things with these.'
The Lord hath done great things with us;
We are rejoiced.

Turn our captivity, O Lord,
As the streams in the dry land.
They that sow in tears
Shall reap in joy.
Though he goeth on his way weeping that beareth the measure
of seed,
He shall come home with joy, bearing his sheaves.

8. GRACE AFTER MEALS

INTRODUCTORY PSALM

SHIR HAMA‘ALOS — שִׁיר הַמַּעֲלוֹת

oz— yōm - ru ba - gō - yīm hig - dil adō - noy
Ho-loch yē - lēch u - vo - chōh no - se me - shech

la - a - sōs im ē - leh hig - dīl adō - noy
ha - zo - ra— Bō— yo - vō

la - a - sōs im-o - nu Ho - - yī - nu s'mē - chim.
b'ri - - noh nō - sē a'lu - mō - sov.

RESPONSES

1. הָנֵן אֶת הַכֹּל

Bō-ruch a - toh a - dō - noy ha - zon— es ha - kōl.

2. בְּכָל יוֹם

B' chol yōm, uv - chol ēs uv'-chol sho— oh

3. כְּכָתוֹב

Ka - ko - suv v'— o - chal - to v' - so - vo - toh.

4. עַל הָאָרֶץ וְעַל הַמָּזוֹן

Bo - ruch a - toh a - do - noy al ho -
o - retz v'al ha - mo - - zon.

5. אֱלֹהֵינוּ אָבִימ

E - lo - he - nu o - vi - nu re - e - nu zu - ne - nu

par - n'se - nu v'- chal - ke - le - nu v'- har - vi - che - nu.

yōm vo - yōm hu hē - tīv hu mē -

tīv hu yē - tīv lo - nu.

8. וְנִמְצָא חֵן

V'-nim - tso chēn v' - sē - chel

tōv b' - ē - nē e lō - him v'o - dom.

9. מִגְדּוֹל יְשׁוּעוֹת

Moderato

f

Mig - dōl y' - shu - ōs mal - kō

v'ō - seh che - sed lim - shi — chō l' - do - vid ul -

zar - ŏ   ad   ŏ - lom.   O - seh sho - lŏm

bim - rŏ - mov   Hu   ya - aseh sho - lŏm   o -

le - nu v'al kol yis - ro - ēl v'im - ru   o   - men.

10. ה' עֹז

Broadly

A - do - noy   oz   l' - a - mo   yi - ten

a - do - noy ye - vo'——rech   es a - mo ba - sho - lom.

II

REFORM HOME SERVICE
FOR
SABBATH EVE

1. LIGHTING THE SABBATH CANDLES

Come, let us welcome the Sabbath. May its radiance illumine our hearts as we kindle these tapers.

Light is the symbol of the divine. The Lord is my light and my salvation.

Light is the symbol of the divine in man. The spirit of man is the light of the Lord.

Light is the symbol of the divine law. For the commandment is a lamp and the law is a light.

Light is the symbol of Israel's mission. I, the Lord, have set thee for a covenant of the people, for a light unto the nations.

Therefore, in the spirit of our ancient tradition that hallows and unites Israel in all lands and all ages, do we now kindle the Sabbath lights.

בָּרוּךְ אַתָּה יְיָ אֱלֹהֵינוּ מֶלֶךְ הָעוֹלָם אֲשֶׁר קִדְּשָׁנוּ בְּמִצְוֹתָיו
וְצִוָּנוּ לְהַדְלִיק נֵר שֶׁל־שַׁבָּת:

Blessed art Thou, O Lord our God, King of the universe, who hast sanctified us by Thy laws and commanded us to kindle the Sabbath light.

May the Lord bless us with Sabbath joy.

May the Lord bless us with Sabbath holiness.

May the Lord bless us with Sabbath peace.   *Amen.*

2. KIDDUSH

קִדּוּשׁ

The table is given a festive appearance. A wine-cup and a loaf of bread for the blessing are set before the head of the household. The ceremony of ushering in the Sabbath is begun by the kindling of the lights, during which a blessing by the wife is silently asked upon the home and the dear ones. The following may be used:

May our home be consecrated, O God, by Thy light. May it shine upon us all in blessing as the light of love and truth, the light of peace and goodwill.   *Amen.*

(When all are seated, the head of the household says:)

Come, let us welcome the Sabbath in joy and peace! Like a bride, radiant and joyous, comes the Sabbath. It brings blessings to our hearts; workday thoughts and cares are put aside. The brightness of the Sabbath light shines forth to tell that the divine spirit of love abides within our home. In that light all our blessings are enriched, all our griefs and trials are softened.

At this hour, God's messenger of peace comes and turns the hearts of the parents to the children, and the hearts of the children to the parents, strengthening the bonds of devotion to that pure and lofty ideal of the home found in Sacred Writ.

(The verses quoted above, p. 31, from Chapter 31 of the Book of Proverbs may be added.)

(The head of the household lifts the wine-cup and says:)

Let us praise God with this symbol of joy, and thank Him for the blessings of the past week, for life, health, and strength, for home, love and friendship, for the discipline of our trials and temptations, for the happiness that has come to us out of our labors. Thou hast ennobled us, O God, by the blessings of work, and in love and kindness Thou hast sanctified us by the blessings of rest through the commandment: Six days shalt thou labor and do all thy work, but the seventh day is the Sabbath hallowed unto the Lord, thy God.

Praised be Thou, O Lord our God, King of the universe, who hast created the fruit of the vine.

בָּרוּךְ אַתָּה יְיָ אֱלֹהֵינוּ מֶלֶךְ הָעוֹלָם בּוֹרֵא פְּרִי הַגָּפֶן:

(The wine-cup is passed round the table and each in turn drinks from it.

The head of the household then breaks the bread and, dipping a piece of it in salt, pronounces the blessing:)

Praised be Thou, O Lord our God, King of the universe, who causest the earth to yield food for all.

בָּרוּךְ אַתָּה יְיָ אֱלֹהֵינוּ מֶלֶךְ הָעוֹלָם הַמּוֹצִיא לֶחֶם
מִן הָאָרֶץ:

(Each one at the table likewise partakes of bread and salt.

Then the parent, with hands upon the head of each child in turn, silently pronounces such a blessing as the heart may prompt, or uses the following formula:)

May the God of our fathers bless you. May He who has guided us unto this day lead you to be an honor to our family. May He who has protected us from all evil make you a blessing to Israel and to all mankind. *Amen.*

---

3. GRACE AFTER MEALS

O Lord, Thou art our Shepherd, and we shall not want. Thou openest Thy hand and satisfiest the needs of every living being. We thank Thee for the gifts of Thy bounty which we have enjoyed at this table. As Thou hast provided for us hitherto, so mayest Thou sustain us throughout our lives. Thy kindness endureth forever, and we put our trust in Thee.

While we enjoy Thy gifts, may we never forget the needy, nor allow those who want, to be forsaken. May our table be an altar of lovingkindness, and our home a temple in which Thy spirit of goodness dwells.

בָּרוּךְ אַתָּה יְיָ הַזָּן אֶת־הַכֹּל:

We praise Thee, O Lord, who in kindness sustainest the world. *Amen.*

III

TRADITIONAL HOME SERVICE FOR THE SABBATH DAY

1. KIDDUSH FOR SABBATH MORNING

Before the Sabbath noon meal, the head of the household raises the cup of wine and recites the *Kiddush*. The wine is then passed to everyone at the table. In the absence of wine the *Kiddush* is recited over the *Ḥallah*.

וְשָׁמְרוּ בְנֵי־יִשְׂרָאֵל אֶת־הַשַּׁבָּת. לַעֲשׂוֹת אֶת־הַשַּׁבָּת לְדֹרֹתָם בְּרִית עוֹלָם בֵּינִי וּבֵין בְּנֵי יִשְׂרָאֵל אוֹת הִיא לְעוֹלָם. כִּי־שֵׁשֶׁת יָמִים עָשָׂה יְיָ אֶת־הַשָּׁמַיִם וְאֶת־הָאָרֶץ וּבַיּוֹם הַשְּׁבִיעִי שָׁבַת וַיִּנָּפַשׁ:

עַל־כֵּן בֵּרַךְ יְיָ אֶת־יוֹם הַשַּׁבָּת וַיְקַדְּשֵׁהוּ:

בָּרוּךְ אַתָּה יְיָ אֱלֹהֵינוּ מֶלֶךְ הָעוֹלָם. בּוֹרֵא פְּרִי הַגָּפֶן:

1. KIDDUSH FOR SABBATH MORNING

Before the Sabbath noon meal, the head of the household raises the cup of wine and recites the *Kiddush*. The wine is then passed to everyone at the table. In the absence of wine the *Kiddush* is recited over the *Ḥallah*.

And the children of Israel shall keep the Sabbath, to observe the Sabbath throughout their generations, for an everlasting covenant. It is a sign between Me and the children of Israel for ever, that in six days the Lord made the heavens and the earth, and on the seventh day He rested, and ceased from His work (Ex. 31.16–17).

Wherefore the Lord blessed the sabbath day and hallowed it.

Blessed art Thou, O Lord our God, King of the universe, who createst the fruit of the vine.

2. GRACE BEFORE THE MEAL

Blessing After Washing of Hands for the Meal

בָּרוּךְ אַתָּה יְיָ אֱלֹהֵינוּ מֶלֶךְ הָעוֹלָם אֲשֶׁר קִדְּשָׁנוּ בְּמִצְוֹתָיו
וְצִוָּנוּ עַל נְטִילַת יָדְיִם:

Blessed art Thou, O Lord our God, King of the universe, who hast sanctified us by Thy commandments, and hast commanded us concerning the washing of the hands.

Blessing Before Partaking of the *Hallah*

בָּרוּךְ אַתָּה יְיָ אֱלֹהֵינוּ מֶלֶךְ הָעוֹלָם. הַמּוֹצִיא לֶחֶם מִן הָאָרֶץ:

Blessed art Thou, O Lord our God, King of the universe, who bringest forth bread from the earth.

For Grace After Meals see pp. 438–456.

3. ZEMIROT*

Table-Hymns for the Sabbath Noon Meal

יוֹם זֶה לְיִשְׂרָאֵל

יוֹם זֶה לְיִשְׂרָאֵל, אוֹרָה וְשִׂמְחָה, שַׁבַּת מְנוּחָה.

צִוִּיתָ פִּקּוּדִים, בְּמַעֲמַד סִינַי,
שַׁבָּת וּמוֹעֲדִים, לִשְׁמוֹר בְּכָל־שָׁנַי,
לַעֲרוֹךְ לְפָנַי,
מַשְׂאֵת וַאֲרֻחָה, שַׁבַּת מְנוּחָה.

(יוֹם זֶה)

חֶמְדַּת הַלְּבָבוֹת, לְאֻמָּה שְׁבוּרָה,
לִנְפָשׁוֹת נִכְאָבוֹת, נְשָׁמָה יְתֵרָה,
לְנֶפֶשׁ מְצֵרָה,
יָסִיר אֲנָחָה, שַׁבַּת מְנוּחָה.

(יוֹם זֶה)

קִדַּשְׁתָּ בֵּרַכְתָּ אוֹתוֹ מִכָּל־יָמִים,
בְּשֵׁשֶׁת כִּלִּיתָ, מְלֶאכֶת עוֹלָמִים,
בּוֹ מָצְאוּ עֲגוּמִים,
הַשְׁקֵט וּבִטְחָה, שַׁבַּת מְנוּחָה.

(יוֹם זֶה)

לֶאֱסוֹר מְלָאכָה צִוִּיתָנוּ נוֹרָא,
אֶזְכֶּה הוֹד מְלוּכָה, אִם שַׁבָּת אֶשְׁמוֹרָה,
אַקְרִיב שַׁי לַמּוֹרָא,
מִנְחָה מֶרְקָחָה, שַׁבַּת מְנוּחָה.

(יוֹם זֶה)

---

*One or more of these table-hymns is usually sung at the Sabbath noon meal. Other suitable hymns may be chosen from the 'Oneg Shabbat songs below, pp. 457–470.

חַדֵּשׁ מִקְדָּשֵׁנוּ, זָכְרָה נֶחֱרֶבֶת,
טוּבְךָ מוֹשִׁיעֵנוּ, תְּנָה לַנֶּעֱצֶבֶת,
בְּשַׁבָּת יוֹשֶׁבֶת
בִּזְמִיר וּשְׁבָחָה, שַׁבַּת מְנוּחָה.

(יום זה)

3. ZEMIROT

Table-Hymns for the Sabbath Noon Meal

YOM ZEH L'YISROEL — יוֹם זֶה לְיִשְׂרָאֵל

ISAAC LURIA

(Translated from the Hebrew by NINA SALAMAN)

This day is for Israel light and rejoicing,
A Sabbath of rest.

Thou badest us, standing assembled at Sinai,
That all the years through we should keep Thy behest —
To set out a table full-laden, to honor
The Sabbath of rest.

This day is for Israel light and rejoicing,
A Sabbath of rest.

Treasure of heart for the broken people,
Gift of new soul for the souls distrest,
Soother of sighs for the prisoned spirit —
The Sabbath of rest.

This day is for Israel light and rejoicing,
A Sabbath of rest.

When the work of the worlds in their wonder was finished,
Thou madest this day to be holy and blest,
And those heavy-laden found safety and stillness,
A Sabbath of rest.

This day is for Israel light and rejoicing,
A Sabbath of rest.

If I keep Thy command I inherit a kingdom,
If I treasure the Sabbath I bring Thee the best —
The noblest of offerings, the sweetest of incense —
A Sabbath of rest.

This day is for Israel light and rejoicing,
A Sabbath of rest.

Restore us our shrine — O remember our ruin
　　And save now and comfort the sorely opprest
Now sitting at Sabbath, all singing and praising
　　The Sabbath of rest.

　　This day is for Israel light and rejoicing,
　　A Sabbath of rest.

יוֹם זֶה מְכֻבָּד

יוֹם זֶה מְכֻבָּד מִכָּל יָמִים,
כִּי בוֹ שָׁבַת צוּר עוֹלָמִים.

שֵׁשֶׁת יָמִים תַּעֲשֶׂה מְלַאכְתֶּךָ
וְיוֹם הַשְּׁבִיעִי לֵאלֹהֶיךָ,
שַׁבָּת לֹא תַעֲשֶׂה בוֹ מְלָאכָה,
כִּי כֹל עָשָׂה שֵׁשֶׁת יָמִים
יום זה . . .

רִאשׁוֹן הוּא לְמִקְרָאֵי קֹדֶשׁ,
יוֹם שַׁבָּתוֹן יוֹם שַׁבַּת קֹדֶשׁ,
עַל־כֵּן כָּל־אִישׁ בְּיֵינוֹ יְקַדֵּשׁ,
עַל־שְׁתֵּי לֶחֶם יִבְצְעוּ תְמִימִים
יום זה . . .

אֱכוֹל מַשְׁמַנִּים, שְׁתֵה מַמְתַּקִּים,
כִּי אֵל יִתֵּן לְכָל־בּוֹ דְבֵקִים
בֶּגֶד לִלְבּוֹשׁ, לֶחֶם חֻקִּים,
בָּשָׂר וְדָגִים וְכָל־מַטְעַמִּים.
יום זה . . .

לֹא תֶחְסַר כֹּל בּוֹ וְאָכַלְתָּ
וְשָׂבַעְתָּ וּבֵרַכְתָּ
אֶת־ה׳ אֱלֹהֶיךָ אֲשֶׁר אָהַבְתָּ,
כִּי בֵרַכְךָ מִכָּל הָעַמִּים.
יום זה . . .

הַשָּׁמַיִם מְסַפְּרִים כְּבוֹדוֹ,

וְגַם הָאָרֶץ מָלְאָה חַסְדּוֹ.

רְאוּ כִּי כָל־אֵלֶּה עָשְׂתָה יָדוֹ

כִּי הוּא הַצּוּר פָּעֳלוֹ תָמִים

יום זה . . .

YOM ZEH MECHUBOD

(Translated by HERBERT LOEWE)

Crown of days, above all blest,
The Rock of Ages chose thee for His rest.

Six days are for toil created
But the seventh God has consecrated.
Do no labour! Thus He bade us;
In six days a world He made us.
Crown of days, above all blest,
The Rock of Ages chose thee for His rest.

First of all His feasts renowned,
Holy Sabbath day, with glory crowned,
With our cup we speak thy blessing,
With twin loaves His grace confessing.
Crown of days, above all blest,
The Rock of Ages chose thee for His rest.

Eat thy fill, then drink thy pleasure,
For he granteth of His richest treasure
Gifts to all His word believing,
To His faithful promise cleaving.
Crown of days, above all blest,
The Rock of Ages chose thee for His rest.

Lacking naught, give thanks abounding,
Satisfied, then let thy praise be sounding.
Love the Eternal thy God Who loved thee.
From all nations He approved thee.
Crown of days, above all blest,
The Rock of Ages chose thee for His rest.

Hark, the heavens His praise are singing;
With His mercy, hark, the spheres are ringing!
Look, He wrought these works enduring,
True His word our weal assuring.
Crown of days, above all blest,
The Rock of Ages chose thee for His rest.

שַׁבָּת הַיּוֹם לַיְיָ

שַׁבָּת הַיּוֹם לַיְיָ,
מְאֹד צַהֲלוּ בְרִנּוּנִי,
וְגַם הַרְבּוּ מַעֲדָנַי
אוֹתוֹ לִשְׁמוֹר כְּמִצְוַת יְיָ —
שַׁבָּת הַיּוֹם לַיְיָ.

———

מֵעֲבוֹר דֶּרֶךְ וּגְבוּלִים,
מֵעֲשׂוֹת הַיּוֹם פְּעָלִים,
לֶאֱכוֹל וְלִשְׁתּוֹת בְּהִלּוּלִים.
זֶה הַיּוֹם עָשָׂה יְיָ —
שַׁבָּת הַיּוֹם לַיְיָ.

———

וְאִם תִּשְׁמְרֶנּוּ, יָהּ יִנְצָרְךָ כְּבָבַת,
אַתָּה וּבִנְךָ וְגַם־הַבַּת,
וְקָרָאתָ עֹנֶג לַשַּׁבָּת,
אָז תִּתְעַנַּג עַל־יְיָ —
שַׁבָּת הַיּוֹם לַיְיָ.

———

אֱכוֹל מַשְׁמַנִּים וּמַעֲדַנִּים,
וּמַטְעַמִּים הַרְבֵּה מִינִים,
אֱגוֹזֵי פֶרֶךְ וְרִמּוֹנִים,
וְאָכַלְתָּ וְשָׂבָעְתָּ וּבֵרַכְתָּ אֶת־יְיָ —
שַׁבָּת הַיּוֹם לַיְיָ.

———

לַעֲרוֹךְ הַשֻּׁלְחָן לֶחֶם חֲמוּדוֹת,
לַעֲשׂוֹת הַיּוֹם שָׁלֹשׁ סְעוּדוֹת,
אֶת־הַשֵּׁם הַנִּכְבָּד לְבָרֵךְ וּלְהוֹדוֹת,
שְׁקְדוּ וְשִׁמְרוּ וַעֲשׂוּ בָנַי —
שַׁבָּת הַיּוֹם לַיְיָ.

SHABBOS HAYOM L'ADONOY

(Translated from the Hebrew by HERBERT LOEWE)

Keep ye holy Sabbath rest before your God today.

Come, cry out with joyful shout, exulting in your play:
Pleasure mine, treasures fine, take with laughter gay.
Yet be mindful, God's command obey:
Day of rest, God hath blest Israel's Sabbath day.

Cease thy weary journey, stay and rest beside the road.
Toil is past, thy burden cast, for I will bear thy load:
Sweetmeats I bring thee, eat thy fill and say:
Day of rest, God hath blest Israel's Sabbath day.

Keep me safe and God will ever guard thee in His sight.
Thou, with all thy tender ones, shalt find in me delight.
Joyful, in chorus, raise the festive lay,
Day of rest, God hath blest Israel's Sabbath day.

Bring me finest dainties, bring me sweets and spices rare:
Crispest nuts and ripest fruit shall be our Sabbath fare.
Raisins and comfits, see their choice array,
Day of rest, God hath blest Israel's Sabbath day.

Set twin loaves beside thy cup, so He will bless thy bread.
Feast our guest and with thy best, thrice let thy board be spread.
Praise Him who fed thee, turn to Him and pray,
Day of rest, God hath blest Israel's Sabbath day.

יִשְׂמָחוּ

יִשְׂמְחוּ בְמַלְכוּתְךָ שֹׁמְרֵי שַׁבָּת וְקוֹרְאֵי עֹנֶג. עַם מְקַדְּשֵׁי
שְׁבִיעִי. כֻּלָּם יִשְׂבְּעוּ וְיִתְעַנְּגוּ מִטּוּבֶךָ. וְהַשְּׁבִיעִי רָצִיתָ בּוֹ וְקִדַּשְׁתּוֹ.
חֶמְדַּת יָמִים אוֹתוֹ קָרָאתָ זֵכֶר לְמַעֲשֵׂה בְרֵאשִׁית:

YISMECHU

They that keep the Sabbath and call it a delight shall
rejoice in Thy kingdom; the people that hallow the seventh
day, even all of them shall be satiated and delighted with
Thy goodness, seeing that Thou didst find pleasure in the
seventh day, and didst hallow it; Thou didst call it the
desirable of days, in remembrance of the creation.

YISMECHU — יִשְׂמְחוּ.

COME, O SABBATH DAY

Gustav Gottheil

Come, O Sabbath day, and bring
Peace and healing on thy wing;
And to ev'ry troubled breast
Speak of the divine behest:
Thou shalt rest! Thou shalt rest!

Earthly longings bid retire,
Quench the passions' hurtful fire;
To the wayward, sin-oppressed,
Bring thou thy divine behest:
Thou shalt rest! Thou shalt rest!

Wipe from ev'ry cheek the tear,
Banish care and silence fear;
All things working for the best,
Teach us the divine behest:
Thou shalt rest! Thou shalt rest!

COME, O SABBATH DAY

1. Come, O Sab-bath day, and bring Peace and heal-ing
2. Earth-ly long-ings bid re - tire, Quench the pas-sions'
3. Wipe from ev - 'ry cheek the tear, Ban - ish care and

on thy wing; And to ev - 'ry troub-led breast Speak of the di -
hurt - ful fire; To the way-ward, sin oppressed, Bring Thou Thy di -
si - lence fear; All things working for the best, Teach us the di -

vine be-hest: Thou shalt rest, Thou shalt rest!
vine be-hest: Thou shalt rest, Thou shalt rest!
vine be-hest: Thou shalt rest, Thou shalt rest!

IV

HABDALAH SERVICE FOR USHERING OUT
THE SABBATH

1. THE HABDALAH SERVICE

When the Sabbath is over, the head of the household
recites the following benedictions over wine, spices, and
light, the youngest child holding a lighted candle during
the ceremony. If spices are not available the benediction
over spices is omitted.

הִנֵּה אֵל יְשׁוּעָתִי אֶבְטַח וְלֹא אֶפְחָד כִּי עָזִּי וְזִמְרָת יָהּ יְיָ
וַיְהִי־לִי לִישׁוּעָה: וּשְׁאַבְתֶּם מַיִם בְּשָׂשׂוֹן מִמַּעַיְנֵי הַיְשׁוּעָה: לַיְיָ
הַיְשׁוּעָה עַל־עַמְּךָ בִרְכָתֶךָ סֶּלָה: יְיָ צְבָאוֹת עִמָּנוּ מִשְׂגָּב־לָנוּ
אֱלֹהֵי יַעֲקֹב סֶלָה: יְיָ צְבָאוֹת אַשְׁרֵי אָדָם בּוֹטֵחַ בָּךְ: יְיָ הוֹשִׁיעָה
הַמֶּלֶךְ יַעֲנֵנוּ בְיוֹם קָרְאֵנוּ: לַיְּהוּדִים הָיְתָה אוֹרָה וְשִׂמְחָה וְשָׂשׂוֹן
וִיקָר: כֵּן תִּהְיֶה לָנוּ: כּוֹס יְשׁוּעוֹת אֶשָּׂא וּבְשֵׁם יְיָ אֶקְרָא:

(Over the Wine)

בָּרוּךְ אַתָּה יְיָ אֱלֹהֵינוּ מֶלֶךְ הָעוֹלָם. בּוֹרֵא פְּרִי הַגָּפֶן:

(Over the Spices)

בָּרוּךְ אַתָּה יְיָ אֱלֹהֵינוּ מֶלֶךְ הָעוֹלָם. בּוֹרֵא מִינֵי בְשָׂמִים:

(Over the Light)

בָּרוּךְ אַתָּה יְיָ אֱלֹהֵינוּ מֶלֶךְ הָעוֹלָם. בּוֹרֵא מְאוֹרֵי הָאֵשׁ:

(The cup is again taken in the right hand, and the following is said:)

בָּרוּךְ אַתָּה יְיָ אֱלֹהֵינוּ מֶלֶךְ הָעוֹלָם. הַמַּבְדִּיל בֵּין קֹדֶשׁ
לְחוֹל בֵּין אוֹר לְחֹשֶׁךְ בֵּין יִשְׂרָאֵל לָעַמִּים. בֵּין יוֹם הַשְּׁבִיעִי
לְשֵׁשֶׁת יְמֵי הַמַּעֲשֶׂה. בָּרוּךְ אַתָּה יְיָ. הַמַּבְדִּיל בֵּין־קֹדֶשׁ לְחוֹל:

THE HABDALAH SERVICE

shĕm a-dō-noy ek-ro. Bo - ruch a-toh a-dō-noy e-lō-

he - nu me-lech ho-ō-lom bō-rĕ p' - rī ha-go— fen. Bo -
                  bō-rĕ me - o-rĕ, no— ĕsh
                  bō-rĕ mī - nĕ b'-so—, mīm

ruch a-toh a-dō-noy e-lō-hĕ-nu me-lech ho-ō-lam há-

mav-dīl bĕn kō-desh l'-chōl bĕn ōr l'-chō-shech bĕn yis-ro-

ĕl lo-a-mīm bĕn yōm hash-vī-ī l'-shĕ-shes ye-mĕ ha-ma-seh.

Bo - ruch a-toh a-dō-noy ha-mav-dīl bĕn kō-desh l'-chōl.

1. THE "HABDALAH" SERVICE

When the Sabbath is over, the head of the household recites the following benedictions over wine, spices, and light, the youngest child holding a lighted candle during the ceremony. If spices are not available the benediction over spices is omitted.

Behold, God is my salvation; I will trust, and will not be afraid: for the Lord is my strength and song, and He is become my salvation. Therefore with joy shall ye draw water out of the wells of salvation. Salvation belongeth unto the Lord: Thy blessing be upon Thy people. (Selah.) The Lord of hosts is with us; the God of Jacob is our refuge. (Selah.) The Jews had light and joy and gladness and honor. So be it with us. I will lift the cup of salvation, and call upon the name of the Lord.

(Over the Wine)

Blessed art Thou, O Lord our God, King of the universe, who createst the fruit of the vine.

(Over the Spices)

Blessed art Thou, O Lord our God, King of the universe, who createst different kinds of spices.

(Over the Light)

Blessed art Thou, O Lord our God, King of the universe, who createst the light of the fire.

(The cup is again taken in the right hand, and the following is said:)

Blessed art Thou, O Lord our God, King of the universe, who makest a distinction between holy and profane, between light and darkness, between Israel and other nations, between the seventh day and the six working days. Blessed art Thou, O Lord, who makest a distinction between holy and profane.

2. HYMNS FOR THE CONCLUSION OF THE SABBATH

הַמַּבְדִּיל

הַמַּבְדִּיל בֵּין קֹדֶשׁ לְחוֹל. חַטֹּאתֵינוּ יִמְחֹל. זַרְעֵנוּ וְכַסְפֵּנוּ
יַרְבֶּה כַחוֹל. וְכַכּוֹכָבִים בַּלָּיְלָה:

יוֹם פָּנָה כְּצֵל תֹּמֶר. אֶקְרָא לָאֵל עָלַי גֹּמֵר. אָמַר שׁוֹמֵר.
אָתָא בֹקֶר וְגַם־לָיְלָה:

צִדְקָתְךָ כְּהַר תָּבוֹר. עַל חֲטָאַי עָבוֹר תַּעֲבוֹר. כְּיוֹם אֶתְמוֹל
כִּי יַעֲבוֹר. וְאַשְׁמוּרָה בַלָּיְלָה:

חָלְפָה עוֹנַת מִנְחָתִי. מִי יִתֵּן מְנוּחָתִי. יָגַעְתִּי בְאַנְחָתִי. אַשְׂחֶה
בְכָל לָיְלָה:

קוֹלִי שִׁמְעָה בַּל יָנָטַל. פְּתַח לִי שַׁעַר הַמְּנֻטָּל. שֶׁרֹאשִׁי נִמְלָא
טָל. קְוֻצּוֹתַי רְסִיסֵי לָיְלָה:

הֵעָתֵר נוֹרָא וְאָיוֹם. אֲשַׁוֵּעַ תְּנָה פִדְיוֹם. בְּנֶשֶׁף בְּעֶרֶב יוֹם.
בְּאִישׁוֹן לָיְלָה:

קְרָאתִיךָ יָהּ הוֹשִׁיעֵנִי. אֹרַח חַיִּים תּוֹדִיעֵנִי. מִדַּלָּה תְבַצְּעֵנִי.
מִיּוֹם עַד לָיְלָה:

טַהֵר טִנּוּף מַעֲשַׂי. פֶּן יֹאמְרוּ מַכְעִיסַי. אַיֵּה נָא אֱלוֹהַּ עֹשַׂי.
נֹתֵן זְמִירוֹת בַּלָּיְלָה:

נַחְנוּ בְיָדְךָ כַּחֹמֶר. סְלַח נָא עַל קַל וָחֹמֶר. יוֹם לְיוֹם יַבִּיעַ
אֹמֶר. וְלַיְלָה לְלָיְלָה:

הַמַּבְדִּיל בֵּין קֹדֶשׁ לְחוֹל. חַטֹּאתֵינוּ יִמְחֹל. זַרְעֵנוּ וְכַסְפֵּנוּ
יַרְבֶּה כַחוֹל. וְכַכּוֹכָבִים בַּלָּיְלָה:

HYMNS FOR THE CONCLUSION OF THE SABBATH

1

HA-MAVDIL

(Translated from the Hebrew by ALICE LUCAS)

May He who sets the holy and profane
Apart, blot out our sins before His sight,
And make our numbers as the sand again,
    And as the stars of night.

The day declineth like the palm-tree's shade,
I call on God, who leadeth me aright.
The morning cometh — thus the watchman said —
    Although it now be night.

Thy righteousness is like Mount Tabor vast;
O let my sins be wholly put to flight,
Be they as yesterday, for ever past,
    And as a watch at night.

The peaceful season of my prayers is o'er,
Would that again had rest my soul contrite,
Weary am I of groaning evermore,
    I melt in tears each night.

Hear Thou my voice, be it not vainly sped,
Open to me the gates of lofty height;
For with the evening dew is filled my head,
    My locks with drops of night.

O grant me Thy redemption, while I pray
Be Thou entreated, Lord of power and might,
In twilight, in the evening of the day,
    Yea, in the gloom of night.

Save me, O Lord, my God, I call on Thee!
Make me to know the path of life aright,
From sore and wasting sickness snatch Thou me,
    Lead me from day to night.

We are like clay within Thy hand, O Lord,
Forgive us all our sins both grave and light,
And day shall unto day pour forth Thy word,
    And night declare to night.

May He who sets the holy and profane
Apart, blot out our sins before His sight,
And make our numbers as the sand again,
    And as the stars of night.

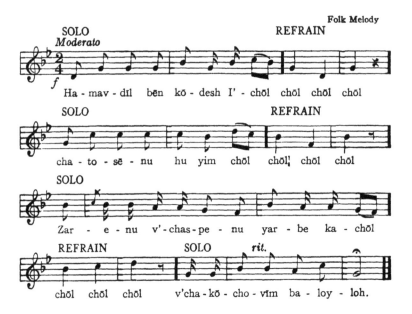

Folk Melody

SOLO — Moderato
Ha - mav - dil ben kō - desh I' - chōl chōl chōl chōl
REFRAIN

SOLO
cha - to - sē - nu hu yim chōl chōl! chōl chōl
REFRAIN

SOLO
Zar - e - nu v' - chas - pe - nu yar - be ka - chōl

REFRAIN   SOLO   rit.
chōl chōl chōl v'cha - kō - cho - vīm ba - loy - loh.

2

ELIYOHU HA-NAVI

אֵלִיָּהוּ הַנָּבִיא

Elijah the Prophet,
Elijah the Tishbite,
Elijah the Gileadite.

אֵלִיָּהוּ הַנָּבִיא, אֵלִיָּהוּ הַתִּשְׁבִּי,

אֵלִיָּהוּ, אֵלִיָּהוּ, אֵלִיָּהוּ הַגִּלְעָדִי.

May he come unto us,
Quickly in our own days,
With the Messiah, son of David.

בִּמְהֵרָה בְיָמֵינוּ, יָבוֹא אֵלֵינוּ,

יָבֹא אֵלֵינוּ עִם מָשִׁיחַ בֶּן דָּוִד.

3

כִּי בְשִׂמְחָה

כִּי בְשִׂמְחָה תֵצֵאוּ וּבְשָׁלוֹם תּוּבָלוּן,
הֶהָרִים וְהַגְּבָעוֹת יִפְצְחוּ רִנָּה.
וּשְׁאַבְתֶּם מַיִם בְּשָׂשׂוֹן מִמַּעַיְנֵי הַיְשׁוּעָה.
צַהֲלִי, צַהֲלִי, וָרֹנִּי, יוֹשֶׁבֶת צִיּוֹן, יוֹשֶׁבֶת צִיּוֹן
הַלְלוּיָהּ, הַלְלוּיָהּ.

KI V'SIMCHOH — כִּי בְשִׂמְחָה

1 Ki v'-sim-chah tē - tsē - u   u - v'-sho-lōm tu - vo - lun

2 He - ho - rim   v' - ha-g'vo - ōs,   yif - ts' - chu   ri - noh.

U - sh'-av-tem ma - yim b' - so - sōn—— mi - ma-ai - nē   ha -

y'—shu - oh—— Tsa - ha - lī,   tsa - ha - lī   vo - rō - nī   yō -

she - ves Tsi - yōn,   yō - she - ves   Tsi - yōn.

Ha - l' - lu - - yoh!   Ha - l' - lu - - yoh!

KI V'SIMCHOH

For ye shall go out with joy, and be led forth with peace,
The mountains and the hills shall break forth into singing
Therefore with joy shall ye draw water out of the wells (
    salvation.
Cry aloud and shout, thou inhabitant of Zion.
           Hallelujah, Hallelujah.

CHAPTER IV

SABBATH HOUR FOR CHILDREN

בֻּלָּם יִשְׂבְּעוּ וְיִתְעַנְּגוּ מִטּוּבֶךְ

(תפלת מוסף לשבת)

Even all of them shall find serenity and
delight in Thy goodness.
(From the Sabbath *Musaf* Service)

THE observant Jew finds delight in the Sabbath not
only by putting on his best garments, by providing
himself with the best food and by refraining from all labor,
but also by engaging in spiritual activities so that his soul,
too, may be refreshed. He participates in the synagogue
services, listens to a sermon by the rabbi, and, in the long
summer afternoons, reads a chapter of the ethical treatise,
Pirke Abot, The Ethics of the Fathers.

These spiritual and intellectual activities, however, are
not suitable for the young. Children need spiritual food
which is more palatable and more digestible. The rabbi's
sermon, however eloquent, and *The Ethics of the Fathers,*
however edifying, are usually beyond the child's compre-
hension, and are therefore anything but a "Sabbath delight."
Consequently, some parents have found it advisable to set
aside a "children's Sabbath hour," when they read to or
tell the children suitable stories. The purpose of such a
Sabbath hour for children is not necessarily to teach religion
or morals. It is rather to provide the children with an *'Oneg
Shabbat,* a delightful Sabbath experience. The practice has

99

resulted in a number of books in several languages, designed to achieve this purpose. One need only mention such
familiar titles as *Friday Night Stories*, *The Friday Nigh,*
Book, *Shabbes Schmus*, and *Matinées du Samedi*.

This Sabbath book, too, would be incomplete if it did
not provide for a children's Sabbath story hour. Although
stories for a children's Sabbath hour need not necessarily
deal with the Sabbath, it was thought advisable to include
only such stories as have the Sabbath for their theme.
Such stories make more timely Sabbath reading and serve
one of the general purposes of this book, that of publishing as much literary material dealing with the Sabbath
as can be practicably included in one volume. This procedure has necessarily limited the choice, particularly in
the field of Sabbath stories for the very young.

To further the usefulness of this chapter, the compiler
graded the stories to suit the needs of children of different
age levels. While the first few stories are suitable for very
young children, the last stories are suitable for boys and
girls of junior high school age. The parent is thus enabled
to choose the stories most appropriate for his child.

Parents of younger children need not limit themselves
to a single reading of a story. Whereas adults want novelty
in their reading, children prefer the familiar, and their
enjoyment of a story increases with repetition. The few
stories chosen for the very young will serve a surprisingly
long time. But parents should not limit themselves to the
few stories in this chapter. They should develop a library
of Jewish story books and should use these books for the
Sabbath hour. Parents may also take advantage of such
Jewish periodicals as *The Young Israel Magazine*, *The Young
Judaean*, and *Haboneh*, all of which contain much useful
material for a children's Sabbath hour.

HOW DANNY HELPED FOR SHABBOS[1]

SADIE R. WEILERSTEIN

(age level four to six)

You never saw such a busy boy as Daniel. It was Friday afternoon and he was helping Mother get ready for *Shabbos*. First he dusted all the furniture. Whisk! went the cloth!

"Hi, you speck of dust, away!
There's no room for you today:
Don't you know on Friday night
All the house is clean and bright?"

Daniel worked until you couldn't have found a bit of dust in that room, even if you had the sharpest eyes, you couldn't.

Then, "All through, Mother!" he called. "Now I'll shine the candlesticks!"

Mother lifted the candlesticks down from the shelf and gave Daniel a wooly cloth.

"Rub, rub, rub," Daniel began,

"Rub, rub, rub!
Soon you'll be as bright as new:
Rub, rub, rub!
Ho! I see my face in you."

"I do, Mother," he said. "I really do see my face in them."

Mother picked up a shining candlestick. Sure enough! There was Daniel's face smiling out at her and there was *her* face too.

"Good for you," said Mother.

"Now they're clean and gleaming bright,
Ready for the *Shabbos* light."

And now it was bath time. Off went Daniel's clothes and

> Into the tub
>
> He went for a scrub!

Such a scrub as it was!

> He scrubbed his ears,
>
> He scrubbed his nose,
>
> He scrubbed his teeth,
>
> He scrubbed his toes;

He even said,

> "For *Shabbos* dear,
>
> I think I'll scrub *behind* the ear."

And he did. He scrubbed his *neck* too. He was so shining bright when he jumped out of the tub that Mother said, "Gracious! I thought you were a *Shabbos* light."

So Mother helped Daniel into his Sabbath suit, and off they went to set the table. On the snowy cloth they put the two shining candlesticks, at Daddy's seat two big *Hallahs* covered with a beautiful cloth.

"That's for Daddy's *Kiddush*," said Daniel.

At Daniel's place — what do you suppose they put at Daniel's place? Two tiny *little Hallahs* covered with a *little* cloth.

"That's for *my Kiddush*," said Daniel.

And now it was almost dark. Daniel stood as still as still could be, while Mother lit the candles and covered her eyes.

There was a dancing *Shabbos* light at the tip of each candle, and there was Mother saying a *Berakah* over them and holding up her hands before the flame.

"Amen!" said Daniel to Mother's *Berakah*.

"Good *Shabbos*! Good *Shabbos*!" cried Mother and Daniel together.

Then Mother bent down and kissed Daniel softly on his forehead. And Daniel?

> He looked at the room all clean and bright,
> He looked at the table snowy white;
> He looked at the candles' dancing light;
> And he said, "The best time's Friday Night."

HOW K'TONTON TOOK A RIDE ON A CHOPPING-KNIFE AND WISHED HE HADN'T[2]

SADIE R. WEILERSTEIN

(age level four to six)

It was Friday, and K'tonton (the Jewish Tom Thumb) sat cross-legged on the kitchen table, watching his mother chop the fish for the Sabbath. Up and down, up and down went the chopping-knife in the wooden bowl, chip, chop, chip, chop!

Now if there was one thing K'tonton loved it was a ride.

"If I could just reach that chopping-knife," he thought, "I could sit down in the center of it with a leg on each side. It would be like riding horseback."

"Tap! Tap!" came a sound at the door. K'tonton's mother laid down the knife. "Sit still until I get back, K'tonton. Don't get into mischief," she called as she went off to see who was knocking.

But K'tonton was too busy looking about him to hear her. How could he reach the top of that chopping bowl? Ah, there was a bag of sugar tied with a string! In a moment K'tonton had taken hold of the string and was climbing up, up to the very top. Then he sprang lightly to the wooden bowl, slid down the inner side and landed right in the center of the chopping-knife. Just as he seated himself astride the blade, his mother returned. A neighbor's wife was with her. They were so busy talking that K'tonton's mother picked up the knife and began chopping away without even noticing that her little son was on it.

Up and down, up and down went the chopping-knife, chip, chop, chip, chop! Up and down went K'tonton, holding fast to the blade.

"Gee-ap!" he shouted. "Gee-ap!" But the chop-chop of the knife was so loud, his mother didn't hear him.

"This is a good ride! This is a jolly ride," thought K'tonton bouncing up and down. "Why didn't I think of it before?" Suddenly, down on his head came a shower of pepper.

"Ketchoo!" sneezed K'tonton. "Ketchoo!"

Up to his nose went his hands and down into the bowl of fish went K'tonton. Ugh, how sticky it was! But the stickiness was the least part of his trouble. Up and down, up and down the knife was going; and up and down and in and out jumped K'tonton, dodging the sharp blade.

"Help! Help!" he called, but his mother was still talking to the neighbor and didn't hear him.

"This is the end of me," thought K'tonton. "I know that Jonah was saved from the inside of a fish, but I never heard of anyone being saved from a bowl of chopped fish."

He was all covered with fish by this time. His legs were so tired he could hardly jump any more.

"I'd better say my *Shema*'," said K'tonton.

But at that moment the chopping-knife was lifted out of the bowl and K'tonton's mother was looking down into it.

"Ugh! There's a fly in the fish."

Down into the bowl went her spoon and — up came

K'tonton! Such a sputtering, struggling, sorry-looking K'tonton!

"K'tonton!" cried his mother, "what have you been doing to yourself?"

"Taking a ride, Mother, a ride on the chopping-knife."

"A ride? A ride on the chopping-knife? God be thanked who preserves the simple!"

Then she picked K'tonton up in her two fingers, and held him under the faucet until there wasn't a bit of sticky fish left.

You may be sure K'tonton never rode on a chopping-knife again.

THE SABBATH TASTE[1]

SADIE R. WEILERSTEIN

(age level four to six)

Every Friday Ruth and Debby carried a bowl of chicken soup to Mrs. O'Keefe, their neighbor. Mrs. O'Keefe had been sick in bed for a long time.

"Bless your hearts," she would say. "If it isn't soup again! No one can make chicken soup like your mother. It puts marrow into these old bones."

Debby told Mother about it.

"Mrs. O'Keefe thinks your soup is DELICIOUS, Mother," she said.

"Does she?" said Mother. "It will be even more delicious tonight. The Sabbath Queen will drop a special spice into it."

"Will she really?" asked Ruthie.

"Taste it and see," said Mother.

Ruth and Debby had never thought much about Mother's Sabbath soup. They just ate it. But now when *Kiddush* was over and the soup was brought to the table, they looked at it carefully. It was clear and golden, with noodles swimming inside. They put a spoonful to their lips. It DID have a wonderful taste. It wasn't like weekday soup at all.

"Maybe the chicken is different, too," thought Debby. She tried it. It was DE-LI-CIOUS.

That was the beginning of Ruth's and Debby's discovery. EVERYTHING on the Sabbath had a different taste, the fish, the twisted Ḥallah, the pudding. Ruth and Debby were so pleased with their discovery, they had to tell Daddy about it. But Daddy wasn't surprised at all.

"Of course, Sabbath food has a special taste," he told them. "There's a story about it."

He sat down in the big armchair with Ruth and Debby at his feet.

"The story is about Joshua ben Hananiah and the Emperor," he told them. "An Emperor is a kind of king. You remember Rabbi Joshua don't you? The one whose Mother brought him to school when he was just a baby?"

Ruth and Debby nodded. Of course they knew Rabbi Joshua. Their baby doll was named after him.

"Rabbi Joshua was so wise when he grew up that everybody wanted him for a friend, even the Emperor. He was often invited to the palace.

"One day the Emperor happened to be walking through the Jewish streets. He wasn't dressed like an Emperor, so no one knew who he was. He passed through the street of the cobblers and the street of the goldsmiths, the street of the charcoal burners and the street of the weavers. It was Sabbath. The shops were closed. The houses were scrubbed and shining. Their doors were open and the Emperor could see inside. The Jews were having their Sabbath meal.

" 'It must be a wonderful kind of food they are eating,' thought the Emperor. 'They enjoy it so much. You couldn't enjoy a common meal as much as that.'

"So next day he sent for Rabbi Joshua.

" 'Rabbi,' he said, 'Will you tell me how the Jews prepare their Sabbath food? I want my cooks to prepare a meal for me just like theirs.'

" 'I will tell you gladly,' said Rabbi Joshua.

"So the Emperor sent word to the royal kitchen and up came all the cooks, the Head Cook, the First Helper to the Cook, the Second Helper to the Cook, the Pudding Maker and the Baker.

"They bowed to the Emperor. Then they turned to Rabbi Joshua and listened carefully. And Rabbi Joshua told them exactly how the Jews prepared their Sabbath food.

" 'O Emperor,' said the Head Cook when Joshua had finished, 'tomorrow you shall have a meal exactly like the Sabbath meal of the Jews.'

" 'Exactly!' said the First Helper to the Cook, the Second Helper, the Pudding Maker and the Baker. Then they bowed again and went back to the royal kitchen.

"Next day the Emperor could hardly wait for dinner to begin. A servant appeared. He set a platter of fish before the Emperor. The Emperor tasted it. He looked puzzled. It didn't have a special taste at all. It was just fish.

"A second servant came in. He set a golden bowl of soup before the Emperor. The bowl was golden and the soup was golden. There were noodles in it, fine as thread. The Emperor tried a spoonful. 'Take it away,' he ordered. 'It's the kind of soup I get every day.'

"The Head Cook came in. He carried a huge platter on his head. There was roast chicken on the platter with a pudding on one side and carrot stew with dumplings on the other. The Emperor's mouth watered.

" 'Now surely,' he said, 'I shall taste the wonderful taste.' He picked up a chicken leg and put it to his mouth. Then he pushed back his plate and left the table.

" 'Send for Rabbi Joshua,' he cried to his servants. 'Send for the Royal Cooks!'

"The cooks filed into the throne room. Rabbi Joshua followed them.

" 'Cooks,' asked the Emperor, 'did you prepare the food exactly as Rabbi Joshua told you to?'

" 'Exactly!' said the Head Cook.

" 'Exactly!' said the First Helper to the Cook, the Second Helper, the Pudding Maker and the Baker.

" 'But Sabbath food MUST have a special taste,' the Emperor insisted. 'I saw the Jews when they ate it. They sang with every bite. You couldn't enjoy everyday food like that.'

" 'O Emperor,' said Rabbi Joshua, and he smiled. 'The Sabbath food HAS a special taste. The taste comes from a certain spice that is in it, a spice called Sabbath.'

" 'Why didn't you say so before? Give me that spice,' cried the Emperor.

" 'O Emperor,' said Rabbi Joshua again, 'the spice cannot be given. It comes of itself — to those who love the Sabbath.' "

Daddy looked down at Ruth and Debby. "So the Emperor never tasted the wonderful taste after all," he said, "but YOU taste it every week."

JOSEPH THE SABBATH LOVER⁴

JUDAH STEINBERG

Translated from the Hebrew
(age level seven to nine)

On one of the estates of a rich Edomite there lived a poor man whose name was Joseph. He labored in the fields and vineyards of the Edomite who was an evil, hard-hearted man. The Edomite worked Joseph at hard labor from sunrise to sunset and in addition he regularly cheated the poor man in every possible way. Joseph lived a life of dire poverty. During the weekdays he sustained himself and his family on mere bread and water; but the Sabbath he honored with fish and meat and beautiful clothes like one of the rich men. All who knew him therefore called him Joseph the Sabbath Lover.

Joseph worked for his master faithfully, and the Edomite became wealthy and grew richer from day to day.

Once the Edomite dreamed a dream, and behold an old man, white-bearded and robed in white, came into his palace and rebuked him for exploiting Joseph. "All your wealth and your possessions have come to you from Joseph," said the old man, "and to Joseph they will return!"

The Edomite awoke in fear and trembling. "How can I save my possessions from the hands of this Jew?" he thought. He sat up in bed a long time, feverishly casting about in his mind for ways to keep his wealth. At last he said, "I shall sell my possessions, and shall purchase one precious article which I can watch all the time."

And he did as he planned. He sold everything he had and with the money he bought a very precious stone which he hid in his turban.

"Now let Joseph sit and wait until my wealth comes into his possession!" So thought the Edomite and he rejoiced.

Once the Edomite was crossing a bridge when suddenly a strong gust of wind blew off his turban and carried it into the river below. The Edomite ran up and down, shouted for help, but it was too late. The turban sank to the bottom of the river, and there it lay for a long time until it rotted and the precious stone fell out. A large fish happened to come by and swallowed the stone. The same day, which happened to be *Erev Shabbos,* a fisherman came to the river, threw in his line and caught the fish.

The fisherman took the fish to town to sell. But no one would buy it because it was too big and the fisherman demanded a high price.

Then thought the fisherman, "I shall go to Joseph the Sabbath Lover. This poor man usually buys the best fish for the Sabbath, and he is not stingy."

Sure enough, Joseph bought the fish. When he opened it in order to prepare it for *Shabbos*, he was amazed to find inside a precious stone so dazzling, he had never seen the like before. He greatly rejoiced at his fortune, and when the Sabbath was over, he sold the stone and became a very rich man.

ARIEL[6]

B. S. LEVIN

(age level seven to nine)

Many years ago, while the Jewish community of Palestine was still poor and small in numbers, the Jews of Jerusalem once sent a *Shaliaḥ* (messenger) to Egypt to collect alms for the support of the poor of the Holy City. The *Shaliaḥ* was a famous rabbi, a man who was known far and wide for his piety and great learning. After completing his preparations for the journey, he left Jerusalem one morning for Hebron where he was to join a caravan bound for Suez, on the shore of the Red Sea. In those days people did not cross the desert alone; it was too dangerous. They traveled in caravans, the men well armed for defense. And the desert journey was not a mere day's travel, but took a whole fortnight. The rabbi reached Hebron safely enough. There he hired a mule and approached the sheik, who was to lead the caravan, with the request that when the Sabbath came he would halt his caravan wherever he happened to be, and that he would not resume the journey until the

close of the sacred day. At first the sheik refused, saying
he could not enter into any such arrangement. But when
the rabbi promised to pay him a handsome sum for his
trouble, the leader of the caravan agreed to the terms.
And so the rabbi paid him ten pieces of gold — a large
sum in those days — and clapped his hands as a sign that
the matter had been settled. The following morning the
caravan was made up and started on its way across the
sea of sand.

On Friday afternoon, just before sunset, the rabbi went
up to the sheik and said: "Our day of rest is now at hand.
The sun is already low in the heavens. According to our
contract, it is time for me as well as the other travelers in
this caravan to halt and pitch camp. Will you therefore
give the order to your camel drivers to stop behind those
stones and to put up our tents."

But the sheik thought otherwise. "What?" he said
angrily, "make the whole caravan halt here just for your
sake! Who ever heard of such a thing! What will my men
do? Why should they lose a whole day? Certainly not...."

In vain the rabbi pleaded. In vain he pointed to his
written contract. In vain he appealed to the camel driver's
sense of justice. The sheik merely nodded his head and
said firmly, "No." Then by way of emphasis he added
dryly: "If the Jew troubles us further we shall cast him
off."

The rabbi was in despair. What should he do? Break
the Sabbath and continue with the rest of the caravan, or
leave them and stay alone in the wilderness?

Once again he attempted to persuade the sheik to call a
halt. He reminded him again of the agreement they had
drawn up in Hebron. He offered to pay him more money
if he would only call a halt for one day. But the sheik was

obdurate. No! he would not camp in that place for all the jewels in Mohammed's sword, for all the gold in Allah's paradise.

Seeing that he had no alternative, the rabbi quietly slid off his mule, slung his little bag over his shoulder and left the caravan.

"This fellow must be crazy," said the other travelers, some pitying him for his stubbornness, others ridiculing him for being so foolhardy.

* * *

As the sun sank in the west the rabbi turned his face toward Jerusalem to welcome the Sabbath. He chanted the evening prayer in a pleasant voice, took a little bottle of wine out of his bag and blessed the Sabbath, as he was accustomed to do every week. He took out some bread and fruit, dipped his hands in a vessel of water that he had brought with him, and recited the blessing over the bread. Then he sat down to eat his lonely meal. At its conclusion he sang the sweet Sabbath songs just as he was wont to do at his home in the company of his wife and children.

As he was about to lie down to rest he suddenly became aware of the presence of another living being near him. He looked around cautiously. With a shock he saw behind him a desert lion.

"Ah," thought the rabbi, "how foolish of me to have left the caravan!"

But the lion did not approach a step nearer. He merely crouched on the sand opposite the rabbi, at whom he gazed steadfastly.

Then the rabbi remembered the miracle of Daniel in the lion's den. Perhaps here, too, a miracle would be per-

formed. At any rate, he had set out for a worthy purpose —
to bring help and comfort to his stricken brethren in the
Holy City — and this journey he had undertaken without
thought of personal reward.

For an hour or two he remained in the sitting position
he had assumed when he had first beheld the lion. He was
still too frightened to lie down. But gradually his eyes
grew tired, his head drooped, and in a little while he was
in deep sleep.

*   *   *

The following morning he awoke with a start. The sun
was already high in the heavens scorching the sand with
its fierce rays. He rubbed his eyes to see where he was.
In a moment he recalled his adventures of the night before.
He looked about to see whether his unwelcome visitor was
still there. Sure enough, directly in front of him crouched the
lion, watching his every motion with steadfast gaze. Seeing
that the lion meant no harm, the rabbi gathered courage.
He rose, washed his hands and face with the little water
still left in his flask, and recited with devotion the usual
morning prayer. After this, he chanted the morning *Kiddush*
and ate his food, leaving just enough for the third meal.
Then he sat down behind a great rock and watched to see
what the lion would do. But all that the beast did was to
wag its tail contentedly and keep silent watch.

Then an anxious thought occurred to him: now that the
bread and water would soon be gone, how would he escape
death in this desert? But he immediately dismissed these
thoughts. Once more there came back to him his faith in
his ultimate deliverance. Surely after the miracle of the
preceding night, God would not let him die of hunger and
thirst! Surely he was to be spared for a happier future!

The day gradually drew to an end — the longest day he had ever experienced. As the sun sank below the sand dunes, he arose, said the evening prayer, recited the *Habdalah*, and smelled the spices which he had with him. And lo, just as the last words of the service were ended, the lion arose, and wagging his tail like a dog, came up to the rabbi, licked his hands, and pawed the sand at his feet. Mutely he seemed to beg the rabbi to get on his back. The rabbi was quick to take the suggestion. He grasped the animal's mane, mounted upon its back, and in a moment they were off.

All night they traveled through the wilderness. All night they saw neither man nor beast in the vast desert.

At dawn the lion brought the rabbi to where the caravan had stopped for a rest. At the sight of the lion and his rider the caravan set up a shout of joy. Then the lion fell to his knees until the rabbi dismounted. In a trice the lion rose again, shook his royal mane and disappeared.

*   *   *

The sheik ran over to the rabbi and prostrated himself before him. "The offense I committed by abandoning you in the desert is too serious to be pardoned. Nevertheless, knowing your goodness of heart, I ask you to have mercy on me. Please forgive me and do not deal with me according to my deserts but according to the goodness of your own kind heart."

The rabbi forgave him, and the caravan leader became his devoted friend and staunch supporter. Whenever the rabbi had occasion to go on a journey he called upon this sheik to assemble the camels and to arrange the details of the journey. And whenever the rabbi had need to send a message, he would permit no one to take it except this caravan driver. This rabbi became known as Rabbi *Ariel*, or the Rabbi of God's Lion, and his descendants retained this name long after his death. Indeed, some members of the Ariel family still live in Hebron.

BEYOND THE SAMBATYON[6]

JOSEPH GAER

(age level seven to nine)

This story is about an evil king called Nebuchadnezzar. Like so many other kings before him and so many rulers since, the Chaldean King Nebuchadnezzar wished he could own the entire earth. He went East and he went West. He went North and he went South. And when his soldiers reached as far as the Dead Sea, they reduced the Kingdom of Judah to a heap of ruins, and carried its people captive to far Babylonia.

That is remembered by the Jews to this day as *The Babylonian Captivity*.

Before the multitudes of Captive Israel rode King Nebuchadnezzar and his victorious army, carrying as trophies the gold and silver vessels from the Temple of Solomon. And behind the sorrowful Judeans followed the guards who prodded them on without mercy.

Week after week the heartbroken captives, bearing heavy burdens on their backs, trudged on over the mountains of Syria, over the dreary plains of Babylonia, and down the long valley of the Euphrates.

King Nebuchadnezzar came riding down the line one day to review his prisoners of war, and noticed a small group of Judeans chained like the rest, but their shoulders free of any burden.

"Nebuzaradan!" the King called to the leader of the armies. "Who are these men?"

"These are the Princes of Judah," Nebuzaradan replied.

"Why are they allowed to go without any burden?" the King demanded.

"I really do not know," the leader of the armies admitted shamefacedly. "But I'll find out."

He immediately sent a messenger to Marshal Rabsaris, asking:

"Why are the Princes of Israel allowed to go into captivity without burdens on their backs?"

"I really do not know," Marshal Rabsaris replied greatly flustered. "But I'll find out."

He sent a messenger to General Sharazar, demanding:

"Explain without delay why the Princes of Judah are allowed to march to Babylon without burdens upon their shoulders!"

"This is the first time I've heard of it," General Sharazar flushed. "I'll find out at once."

His messenger hurried to Major Rambag.

"Report at once the cause and reason for letting the accursed Princes of Judah go into captivity without any burdens to carry!"

"I shall find out this very minute," said Major Rambag, red with rage.

His messenger ran to Captain Nebo:

"Report at once to your superior officer the reason for your shameful neglect to impose burdens upon the Princes of Judah!"

Captain Nebo coolly reported:

"We did not impose burdens on the Princes of Judah because we had nothing for them to carry."

"O!" said Major Rambag, and sent the message back to the General.

"O!" said General Sharazar, and sent the message back to the Marshal.

"O!" said Marshal Rabsaris, and the message was sent back to the Head of the Armies.

"O!" said Nebuzaradan, and took the message back to the King.

"If you have no burdens for them to carry," said the King, "then take their Holy Scrolls and cut them up into strips; sew the strips together into sacks; fill the sacks with sand; and let the Princes of Judah carry those sacks to Babylon."

When the King's commands were carried out, all the captives began to weep. But the guards ordered them to be silent, and prodded them on.

Near Babylon the victorious King was greeted by many of the people of that city, who had prepared a great feast for him and his officers.

At the feast the King said to his people:

"I have brought back with me such musicians as are not to be found in our land. These are the far-famed Levites of the Temple of Solomon." And to his messengers he said: "Go and bring the Levites here to entertain us!"

When the message reached the Levites, they whispered to each other:

"The walls of Jerusalem are in ruins and the Holy Temple lies in ashes. How can we play upon the holy instruments of the Temple to amuse the King?"

"Rather die than do such a thing!" they all decided.

They hung their harps upon the willows near the camp, and cut their fingers with sharp knives. Then they went before the King and stretched out their bleeding hands.

"Look upon our hands," they said. "How can we play upon our harps with them?"

The King's face darkened with rage, and he shouted:

"O you stiffnecked sons of a stiffnecked race! Because
you have tried to humble me before my people I shall have
you all executed tomorrow at sunrise!"

The hearts of the Levites were filled with sorrow, but
their faith remained unshaken. All through the night they
prayed, and prepared themselves for death in the morning.
And as they prayed, a heavy fog, thick as a cloud and wet
as a fine drizzle, slowly descended upon them.

Toward dawn, as the Levites chanted the Morning
Prayers before the executioners came for them, the thick
fog began to lift.

To their great astonishment, the Levites could see neither executioners, nor guards, nor anything that had sur-
rounded them when the preceding night had descended
upon them.

Instead of the dreary plains of sunbeaten Babylon, they
saw before them softly rolling hills of green, with patches
of flowers upon them.

The Levites looked about them as full of wonder now as
they had been full of sorrow the night before. They rubbed
their eyes and looked again. They were not dreaming.

The Levites raised their voices and sang, as they had
often sung in the Temple of Solomon:

> "Great is our God,
> And greatly to be praised:
> Of His greatness there is no end!"

Then they fell upon each other's necks and wept with
joy.

"Surely this is the land beyond the power of our enemies,
and here we can live according to the Holy Law!" they said
to each other.

In that beautiful land the Levites settled, and there

their offspring live to this day. Their domain is called the Land of the Red Jews; and it is unlike any other land in the world.

Their trees bloom twice each year, and twice each year bear fruit. The unkindness of winter winds and of summer storms are unknown to them. Their plains are always full of sunshine, and their valleys full of peace. And in all the length and breadth of their country there is to be found no poisonous reptile or poisonous plant.

Nor can any outsider ever disturb them. For on three sides they are protected by stormy seas and inaccessible mountains; and on the fourth side, reaching from sea to sea and safeguarding them forever, flows the River Sambatyon.

Six days each week, every week in the year, the River Sambatyon throws out mighty boulders along its entire length, making an approach to it utterly impossible. On Friday evening, when the Sabbath nears, the river becomes calm and peaceful. But a heavy fog descends to blind those who might try to cross on the Sabbath. In that way the Sambatyon protects the Red Jews, offspring of the Levites, from invaders.

Undisturbed by enemies from within and from without, they live a peaceful, happy life.

Because all the people there are equal, they have no kings or princes among them.

Because they never go to war, they have neither soldiers nor firearms.

Because the people are never ill, doctors are unknown to them.

Neither judges nor Courts of Justice nor lawyers are to be found there, for they have no thieves and no murderers.

Because they have no murderers and no thieves, they have no detectives.

But because they have no detectives, alas, they also have no Detective Stories!

THE PRINCESS SABBATH[7]

JEHUDI

(Translated from the German by MERVIN ISAACS)

(age level seven to nine)

There were once two boys, named Moses and Isaac, who started out to look for a fairy. Where to find her they could not tell, for fairies' names were not in their address book. They knew, however, that they would have to go through large, thick woods, for fairies always lived in woods.

They sought the thickest woods in their neighborhood and walked bravely in. No fairies were in sight and Isaac wanted to turn back; but Moses, standing in front of him, said:

"Don't be a dunce! Do you think fairies come out one. two, three? They come only when you're asleep."

They therefore went to sleep and were soon snoring lustily. In a short time a dwarf appeared from one of the bushes. He took a blade of grass and tickled the noses of the sleeping boys. "Atchoo! Atchoo!" they sneezed and jumped up.

"*Leḥayyim*," called out the dwarf, swinging on a branch of a tree. The boys looked at him stupidly. "They want to see a fairy," he tittered, "and lie down and snore." He seemed almost bursting with laughter.

"How do you know?" asked Isaac astonished.

"Oh, a dwarf can read you through and through! And especially one who is so clever as Sir *Lekah Dodi*."

"Sir *Lekah Dodi*? Are you mocking me?" called out Isaac.
The dwarf drew a card from his pocket and handed it
to the youngster. It read:

> LEKAH DODI
>
> Minister to Her Holiness
> The Princess Sabbath
> Knight of the Order
> SHIR HA-MA'ALOT

Although neither had heard of the princess, her minister,
or his Order, they at once became respectful toward the
little man.

"But tell me, Sir Minister, what are you doing around
here? Does your Princess not need you?" asked Isaac.

"She has sent me to bring you to her palace. Will you
follow me?"

"Most gladly, Sir Minister," replied Moses, making his
grandest bow.

"Lead on, little Minister," cried Isaac, who had again
become insolent. The dwarf went on and our friends followed. At the back of a neighboring oak stood a guard as
tall as the giant Goliath. He wore a bearskin cap and
carried a musket and a sword. He roared in a fearful voice,
"Halt! Give the password."

"*Sheshet yamim ta'avod*" (Six days shalt thou labor),
cried out the dwarf.

"What does that mean?" asked Isaac of Moses. The
little man drew near, and threatening him with his finger,
said:

"That comes, little boy, of not going to *Ḥeder*, or falling
asleep there! Don't you know the Fourth Commandment?"
Then to Moses: "Whoever wants to go to the Princess
Sabbath must pass her six guards, one for each day of the

week. The giant we just passed is the guard of the first day. He will stop any who do not know the password."

In a little while, a beautiful woman wearing a long flowing robe appeared. She called herself "Lady *Zedakah*" (Charity) and asked for a toll. Isaac answerd loudly:

"Madam, we have nothing but empty stomachs." Then Lady *Zedakah* took from her robe bread and meat, and handed them to the hungry lads.

"A very good toll-collector," thought Isaac, biting into his bread. Moses, however, broke off a piece and gave it to a bird that came hopping up to him. Lady *Zedakah* said nothing, but disappeared smiling.

They went on and came to a large open place where all the tools of the world were heaped up — everything that was needed to give occupation to diligent hands. Over it hung a shield: "Here one may work."

Isaac laughed over the queer inscription and sat down watching Moses take a goose quill and parchment to make a Torah for the Princess Sabbath. The little minister said nothing, but stroked his beard thoughtfully.

They went on and came to the guard of the second day of the week, who was a little smaller than the first, and all went as before. Lady *Zedakah* gave food and drink, the bird received a share from Moses, Isaac remained lazy, and Sir *Lekah Dodi*, full of dignity, stroked his beard. And so they went on to the other guards of the remaining four days of the week. Each guard was a little smaller than the one ahead, the last being no larger than Sir *Lekah Dodi*.

At the end of the road stood the great palace of the princess, and at its gate stood a beautiful young man in festive garments. Sir *Lekah Dodi* called him "My dear Sir *'Erev Shabbat*" (Sabbath Eve). He led them to the throne of the princess who was so beautiful that she cannot be described. The two boys kneeled before her, but looking angrily at Isaac, she cried:

"Whoever will not work during the six days of the week shall not see Princess Sabbath! Away with him!"

Oh, how quickly Isaac snatched a long knife and cut one piece of wood from another as if his life depended on it! But it was of no use. Sir 'Erev Shabbat forbade him to work in the presence of the Princess Sabbath, and when he would not cease, they pushed him back out of sight.

Then the minister began to sing a beautiful song of praise to the Princess Sabbath. And Moses lived with the princess a whole day in splendor and joy. Even lazy Isaac shared in the joy, for, like all good fairies, the Princess Sabbath was kind to all men.

At the very end of the day she drank to their health out of a golden cup, and letting them smell the fragrance of her spice-box, blew out the candles she held in her hand.

In a moment the two boys stood again in front of the palace. Here stood their old friend, the giant guard of the first day of the week, smiling. A man passed by who knew the guard well and greeted him with:

"Good morning, *Yom Ri'shon*" (Sunday).

ELIJAH, A FRIEND OF THE POOR[8]

SAMUEL M. SEGAL

(A Story for Saturday Night)*

(age level seven to nine)

The sages tell a story of a very poor man who had a wife and five sons. One day he felt extremely distressed because of his poverty, and sat about the house in deep gloom.

---

* This story is traditionally associated with Saturday night when it is customary to pray for the coming of Elijah with the good tidings of redemption for Israel and all mankind.

His wife advised him to go to the market place where God might put something in his way and thus save the family from starvation. The husband asked blankly, "Where can I go? I have no relatives, no friends, no one except God." The good woman could not insist, for she realized how hopeless things were. But when the children in their hunger cried for bread, the mother again urged her husband to go to the market place and try to find some kind of work. To this plea the man answered: "How can I go? I have nothing to cover my nakedness." The woman then found a torn garment and gave it to him that he might protect his body.

The man wandered mutely and aimlessly about the city. He lifted his eyes to heaven and prayed, "Master of the Universe, Thou knowest that there is no one to look upon my poverty or to take pity on me, neither brother nor relative nor friend. My children are hungry and cry for bread. O God, have pity upon us, or gather us into Thine arms, that our suffering may cease."

His prayer went up to heaven, and behold, Elijah appeared unto the man. "Why do you weep?" he asked. The man recited the story of his suffering. Elijah then said, "Do not be afraid. Keep calm. Take me and sell me as a slave in the market place and you will have money to live on." The man returned: "My lord, how can I sell you as a slave when people know that I never have possessed slaves of my own? I fear that people will say that you are the master and I am your slave." Elijah assured him: "Do as I tell you. But when you have sold me, give me but one silver coin."

The poor man took Elijah to the market place, and indeed the people took Elijah to be the master and the other the slave. But when Elijah was asked about it, he insisted that he was the slave and the poor man his master. Then one of the king's princes happened to pass by, and was impressed by Elijah. He offered eighty thousand golden denars for him. The poor man accepted the offer and, following the instruction of Elijah, gave one silver coin of the purchase price to him. Elijah returned the coin to the man, saying, "Keep it, and with it you will support your family. You will know no more of want or suffering."

Elijah went away with the prince, while the man returned home to his famished dear ones. He brought them bread and wine and they ate and drank and had food in abundance. The wife asked her husband how all this bounty had come to him, and he told her all that had happened. In true womanish fashion she said, "It is good that you followed my advice and went to the market place. Had you remained moping about the house we would all have died of hunger." From this day on God blessed that man, and he and his family knew no more want and suffering all their days.

As for Elijah, the prince brought him before the king who at that time was planning to build a luxurious palace outside the city. The king had bought many slaves to move rocks, cut wood, and prepare other materials for the building. The king asked Elijah what his trade was. Elijah answered that he specialized in the building of large and difficult structures. The king was delighted with this news and commissioned Elijah to build a magnificent palace for him, and to have sole charge of everything that pertained to the work. He promised Elijah that if the palace was completed at the end of six months Elijah would have his freedom. Elijah then asked the king to order the workers to have in readiness all the necessary building materials. The next morning he arose and prayed to God that the palace might be built as the king desired. God granted his prayer and the palace, exactly as the king wished it, was built in one brief second. The palace completed, Elijah went on his mysterious way.

The king was informed of this amazing feat and rushed

to see the miracle. He was much impressed by it, and al-together delighted. But he wondered much how it had all happened in so short a time. He looked for Elijah but could not find him, so he assumed that Elijah was an angel and not a man.

Elijah now appeared to the man by whom he had been sold as a slave and the man asked Elijah what he had done for the prince. Elijah answered: "I did all he asked me to do. I did not want him to lose the money he paid for me, so I built him a palace which was worth far more." The man blessed Elijah and thanked him for all that he had done for him.

Elijah protested. "Thank God, for He has done all this for you."

_____

"REMEMBER THE SABBATH DAY"⁹

(age level ten to twelve)

In a small village in Palestine there lived three friends, a Mohammedan, a Christian and a Jew. The Mohammedan kept his Sabbath on Friday, the Christian on Sunday, and the Jew, of course, on Saturday.

On Friday the Jew and the Christian set out for their fields. When the Jew saw that the Arab's field was but half ploughed, he said: "Today my friend can do no work. It is his Sabbath day. Tomorrow it may rain, and he may not have his field ploughed in time for the sowing. I shall plough his field a little, and thereby it may be that his work will be easier for him." In the meantime the Christian had said much the same thing to himself, so that, unaware of the presence of one another, each of them ploughed the Arab's field; one from the east, the other from the west.

On the next day when the Arab came and found his field all ploughed he wondered, saying to himself, "Who could have ploughed my field? It must be that God has sent His angels to help me."

Months passed by, and the time of reaping came. It was Sunday. The Jew and the Arab had gone to their fields, and the Christian remained at home to keep his Sabbath. When the Jew saw that his Christian friend's corn was full and ready to be cut, he said: "Today my neighbor cannot cut his grain, tomorrow a wind may come and scatter his seeds. I shall cut a little for him while I have the time." Now, strange to say, while the Jew was thinking of his Christian friend's corn, the Arab had the same thought, so that, unseen by one another, they cut the Christian's grain, the Jew from the south, the Arab from the north.

Next day the Christian went out to cut his corn and found it all done. He was so surprised that he could not explain it. "It must be that God has sent His good angels to cut my corn for me," he mused.

Reaping time passed and the season of threshing approached. It was Saturday. The Jew remembered his Sabbath day "to keep it holy." The Christian and the Arab were at work. Looking up at the clouded sky the Arab thought to himself: "Ah, the rain is coming, and it is the day of rest of our Jewish friend. Alas! the rain will wash his grain away," and going to his Christian neighbor he said, "Come, neighbor, let us thresh the grain for our friend, the Jew." To this the Christian gladly agreed, and after threshing the grain they bound it up and covered it with straw to protect it from the rain.

When Sunday came and the Jew set out for his field, he found his grain not only well threshed, but dry under the straw. Then, lifting up his eyes to Heaven, he exclaimed, "Blessed art Thou, O Lord, who dost send Thy angels to help those who remember Thy Sabbath day 'to keep it holy.'"

A STORY ABOUT A COIN[10]

S. J. AGNON

(Translated from the Hebrew by JACOB KATZMAN)
(age level ten to twelve)

On his way home from the synagogue one Sabbath eve, a poor Jew saw a coin lying in the road. "What luck!" he exclaims, only to remember that it is already Sabbath and that the carrying of money on the Sabbath is forbidden. "Oh," he thinks, "if only it were a little earlier in the day! I could take this coin and buy raisins to make wine for *Kiddush*, or a nice white Ḥallah, or something else fitting for the Sabbath. Too bad, too bad!" He shakes his head and continues on his way home to welcome the Sabbath without wine, without Ḥallah and without any other of the Sabbath dainties.

Sabbath morning, on his way to synagogue, he says to himself, "I must look and see if the coin is still there." In his heart he hopes that the *Sabbath Goy* has not noticed it. He walks to the place, and lo and behold! Instead of the copper coin of the night before he now sees a silver coin. "There's luck for you!" he exclaims inwardly. "I thought that it was only a farthing and instead it's a real silver coin. My, oh my! What I couldn't do with it! But then again," he admonishes himself, "watch your step; who knows, maybe the Lord wants to test you . . ." He shoves his hands deep into his pockets and marches straight off to synagogue.

After the Sabbath services he starts for home again, confident that the coin is no longer there to tempt him. "After all," he thinks, "many people have passed that way and no doubt must have seen it. And yet they may not have noticed it. It may still be there. Let's have another look. If no one has taken it I will make sure that it is really a silver coin as it seemed to be this morning. And if it is no longer there I will be able to rid myself of evil thoughts."

He walks briskly to the spot and, sure enough, the coin is still there. But wonder of wonders! Instead of the copper coin he had seen yesterday, the silver coin he had seen that morning, the coin he now sees is of gold! "What sort of magic is this?" he wonders, and stares in amazement. But then it occurs to him that the golden glitter may be nothing more than the reflection of the afternoon sun. "So what?" he ruminates. "What if it is only a *silver* coin? A silver coin is no trifle either."

Thus the poor man thinks and is sorely tempted to pick up the coin. In his imagination he sees all the luxuries that he could purchase with this coin — white *Hallah*, a glass of wine, a herring, and so many other delicacies to enhance the joy of the Sabbath and tickle the palate as well. He stoops to pick up the coin, but at once straightens himself up. He bends down a second time and almost has it in his fingers. But the awe of Sabbath is great in his heart and wins this time, too. Empty-handed he slowly wends his way home.

*   *   *

On his way to the synagogue for late afternoon prayers he takes another path. "Who knows whether I will be able to resist temptation this time? In the afternoon when the stores were closed and I could buy nothing anyhow, I was able to talk myself out of it. But now, when the stores are about to open and the smell of good things comes to me on the evening breeze, I am afraid I may yield and break the holy Sabbath commandment."

But the demon of the evil in every man is strong-willed. The poor man argues piously against the demon of temptation, but the latter advances his subtle arguments, too. "Who says that you must pick up the coin with your hand?" the demon whispers.

"Just shove it to one side with your foot. Push it into a corner where no one will see it, or cover it with a stone so that no one can find it . . ."

As soon as he has finished his late afternoon prayers, the poor man decides to look at the coin again. Surely there is no sin in just looking . . . It is already dusk; the sun is setting. Its golden rays spread fan-wise on the horizon. The poor man trudges along the road and soon finds the spot where he had seen the coin. But lo and behold! Instead of a single coin there is now a whole heap of gold coins. He cannot believe his own eyes. Surely it is only an illusion caused by the coin's reflection of the sun's rays! "And suppose it is no more than one coin?" he thinks. "A *single* gold coin is also something." And this time he can hardly resist the temptation to bend down and pick it up. How much it would mean to him! He could live on it for at least three or four weeks! After all, how much does a poor man need? Yet here he stands in the road not even bothering to go home for the third meal because there is nothing at home for the third meal anyway . . .

He tries to change his line of thinking. "What fool of a man goes about throwing his money in the mud? One would think that money grows on trees! Now, if I had that money I would carry it in a little bag right next to my heart and every time my wife or children cry for food I would say to them, 'So, you want to eat, do you? Here you are, my hearties!' and I would take a coin out of my little bag and throw it to them."

Hardly aware of what he is doing the poor man bends down to pick up the coin, when suddenly a thought flashes through his mind. "What if this is a trick of the Devil! What if the Devil left this money to tempt me from the righteous path!" He straightens himself up, muttering, "Why, of course it's the Devil's work. Who else but *he* would stand in the mud mocking a poor Jew? What else has *he* got to occupy himself with? *He* doesn't have to go to synagogue. *He* doesn't have to pray . . . But I've got to hurry or else I'll be late for evening prayer." And he hastens off to synagogue.

*   *   *

After evening prayers he is loath to go back to the coins again. "Enough is enough," he says to himself. "They have mocked me all day. But then again," he thinks, "now that the holy Sabbath is over what harm can there be in going to look at what shone so in the mud?"

So he goes once more, and when he bends down to look he beholds a small miracle of miracles . . . There before him is a pile of gold that literally takes his breath away. So he stuffs his pockets full of coins until they bulge and can hold no more (and you may be sure that his pockets were wide and deep). And when he has filled them to over-flowing he marches off to the nearest shop, and for a single gold coin buys wine for *Habdalah*, white bread, herring and all the luxuries that are good for the body and not bad for the soul.

That night his wife spread a meal fit for a king. And from that day on he never lacked for anything. And in his household Sabbath was Sabbath, and was always greeted with the preparations befitting a Queen.

THE SABBATH GUEST[11]

RUFUS LEARSI

(age level ten to twelve)

Rob Sender, the merchant, was the richest and most important man in the town of Zolotka. He lived in the finest house on the finest street; the clothes he wore seemed

to be always new; and his face bore a proud and command-
ing expression. In the synagogue he sat right next to the
rabbi, and after services, if there happened to be a poor
stranger in the House of Worship, the much envied honor
of entertaining him for the Sabbath would be sure to fall
to Reb Sender.

A happy man was Reb Sender the merchant. He believed that nothing he desired could ever fail to come to
pass. He had triumphed over all his enemies, and all men,
although they did not love him, were anxious to be his
friends. They smiled to him and flattered him, and Reb
Sender asked for nothing more.

Now, at the other end of the town there lived a very
humble and poor old man called Isaac the shoemaker. He
earned enough by his cobbling for himself and his old wife,
and there was nothing more in the world that he desired.
And although his seat in the synagogue was right near
the door, he was one of the very few who never flattered
Reb Sender the merchant. The rich man hated him, but
considered him too low to appear to notice him.

Was there really nothing more that Isaac the shoemaker
desired? Alas, Isaac the shoemaker did have one great
wish, one hope that he nourished in his soul. Isaac felt
that his years were nearing their fullness, and yet throughout his life he had never been able to obey the divine law
of hospitality: he had never had the honor of entertaining
at his board a poor guest over the Sabbath. For how could
he ever induce one of these much-desired poor guests to
come and eat at his table when he had for competitors men
like Reb Sender the merchant? The poor guests, of course,
preferred the tables of the rich.

Isaac the shoemaker continued to hope that this only
wish of his might some day be realized. He confided his
hope to some of his neighbors, but they laughed at him.

"Old Isaac has rich man's taste and poor man's trousers," they said.

*   *   *

Something out of the ordinary seems to have come over the synagogue of Zolotka. It is Friday night and the place is full of Sabbath holiness. But is it the usual Sabbath that has brought in this unusual hush, this feeling of awe which stirs in every heart and may be read on every face? Even the face of Reb Sender the merchant is without its usual haughty expression, while that of Isaac the shoemaker seems to be transfigured with a strange ecstasy.

The synagogue is as though filled with the divine presence. And yet, only the usual worshippers are there, with the exception of a stranger in shabby clothes. He wears a large cap which almost covers his face, and stands near the door, not far from Isaac the shoemaker — evidently a poor guest.

The services seem to have taken longer than usual, but now they are over. There is a note of sincerity and real friendliness in the Sabbath greetings. Everybody feels happy. Everybody would like to invite the stranger to be his guest for the Sabbath. Reb Sender is especially anxious to have him and feels sure of him already.

"You will be kind enough to come with me for the Sabbath," says Reb Sender to the stranger.

The latter raises his head, and his cap falls back revealing his countenance. A youthful black-bearded face looks out upon the men of Zolotka. And the eyes express so much tranquillity and majesty that Reb Sender and the others can scarcely hold up their own eyes under his gaze.

"And what have you to offer me in your home?" asked the stranger.

"Offer you?" repeated Reb Sender, smiling uneasily.

Then his pride was pricked. "What a strange question for a poor guest to ask!" he declared.

"How strange of you to invite me when all you have to offer me is bread and meat!" retorted the other.

Reb Sender was puzzled.

"And is not that enough for you?" he asked.

"No," answered the stranger. "That is not enough for me."

"He must be out of his senses to talk like that," thought Reb Sender, and he answered in a tone of light mockery: "I am sorry, but I am afraid you will not suit your taste in this town."

"That remains to be seen," said the stranger. Then turning to the others, he asked:

"Is there no one else here who would invite a poor guest for the Sabbath?"

But the others, puzzled by the strange conduct of the poor guest, and afraid, moreover, to enter into competition with Reb Sender the merchant, remained silent.

But suddenly there stepped forth old Isaac the shoe-maker. He was never able to account for the boldness that urged him to speak.

"I invite you," he said, "come with me."

The crowd was amused but silent. "Isaac, too," they thought, "must have gone out of his mind."

But the stranger stepped forth and took Isaac by the hand.

"Come," he said quietly, "let us go."

And together they left the synagogue.

A feeling of disquiet fell upon those who stayed behind. Reb Sender tried to shake it off.

"The shoemaker will certainly suit his taste," said he.

But strange to relate, the others, who usually fawned on him, just looked at one another with an expression of astonishment on their faces.

* * *

Reb Sender the merchant sat down to his table that night, but found it impossible to put his red wine to his lips, or to touch a morsel of his white bread or tender meat. The calm, majestic face of the black-bearded stranger refused to leave his mind for a moment. Reb Sender rose from his table and went out, hoping to find peace in the solitude of the night.

The stars hung low in the sky and never had they appeared to him so big. And each one of them pierced into his soul like the eyes of the poor guest.

Reb Sender walked straight on, and before he knew it he found himself in the poor section of the town. Rarely did he visit that section. Then why did he go there now? He asked himself that question, but was unable to answer it.

Then suddenly the answer flashed on his mind.

"Why, of course," said he to himself, "I am going to Isaac the shoemaker," just as though that had been his object from the moment he left his home.

He came to a crooked street with scattered tumble-down houses. Behind one of these, in a straw-thatched hut, he knew that Isaac had his home. He turned the dark corner of the house and stopped before Isaac's hut in amazement.

Through the only window of Isaac's dwelling a wonderfully brilliant light issued and illumined all the surrounding spaces. Inside the hut, on a shelf, he could see the two

Sabbath candles, but the light they shed was as brilliant as if it came from a hundred lamps.

"How marvellous!" thought Reb Sender. "And yet people don't seem to have noticed the light. Is it possible they don't see it?"

Stealthily he approached the window and looked in.

Could this be the home of Isaac the shoemaker? How strange! How beautiful! The cloth that covered the table was spotlessly white, the dishes — knives, forks, and spoons — shone and flashed like the purest silver; and the wine in the large crystal bottle sparkled like a heap of liquid rubies. On the table were foods of all sorts, white bread, fish, meat, steaming soup, and all kinds of delicacies.

At the head of the table sat the stranger of the synagogue, the "poor guest," and opposite him sat old Isaac and his wife. The face of the stranger shone like the sun of the heavens so that Reb Sender had to turn away his eyes from that radiance. And the faces of Isaac and his wife reflected the glory of the Presence.

Afraid of being discovered, Reb Sender quietly hastened away. But he had seen enough. And the vision had passed over him like a cleansing wave. As he hastened to his home, the low-hanging stars, like the eyes of the "poor guest," continued to look down on him, but now they seemed to look with cheer and pity. For the first time tears came to his eyes and fell on the street of the poor. Reb Sender the merchant understood at last.

Next morning, when all the people were gathered in the synagogue, Reb Sender refused to take his old place of honor at the East Wall, but stayed near the door by the side of Isaac the shoemaker, and prayed together with him.

A FALSE TURN[12]

Louis Schnabel

(age level thirteen to fifteen)

The people of Bumsle are, strictly speaking, no fools. But should some sort of folly meet them halfway, they would be more apt to run after it than step aside.

Sam Passy, a good-natured but narrow-minded sort of fellow, had never crossed the boundaries of his little native place, although spring had, at its yearly appearance, more than fifty times invited him to visit the surrounding fields and meadows. He stubbornly clung to his lane and to his little shop on the market place.

He had a thousand-and-one excuses. He was no migratory bird; he did not like a change; he was afraid of getting homesick; he favored the very dust of his lane; and last, but not least, he considered it ungrateful to absent himself even for a few hours from his birthplace. Spring might have come and gone fifty times more without having the least effect upon him. And Sam Passy might have gone to his fathers in peace and been buried at a good old age, without ever having seen Prague, the capital of his province.

But it happened one Sabbath, while in the synagogue, that he had in his pew a man from Prague, a *shnorrer* on a tour through Bohemia and Moravia. Despite the fact that preaching on a common Sabbath had not yet been introduced, the *Musaf* service still lasted more than two hours. Now, I ask, is it possible to pray with devotion for two consecutive hours? The guest quite naturally devoted some time to talking to our Sam Passy. He entertained him most pleasantly, relating many a legend of the "great Rabbi Loeb" of Prague, and of the *Golem* into whose nostrils the rabbi breathed the spirit of life, and how he slew him again on Sabbath eve and flung him into the garden of the *Altneuschul* where to this day he still lies, and may be seen changed into a heap of mud.

From that moment Sam had nothing but the *Golem* in his mind.

Coming home from *Schul* in feverish excitement, he ate twice as much as on an ordinary Sabbath: half a *Kugel* plus half a *Zwetschenbobele*. After his Sabbath nap he felt as if his stomach could enjoy a rest of forty days and forty nights. And like the Prophet Elijah, he felt that he could undertake a very, very long journey and courageously meet any adventure. And were the *Golem* resuscitated from his mud-heap, running wild in the streets of Prague, he would not fare any better under his, Sam's, hands than the priests of Baal under the mighty blows of the Prophet Elijah.

"Leah, my dear," said he to his wife, "this evening, as soon as the *Habdalah* light is smothered in the wine, you will bring down my stick and lantern, for I have a long journey before me. I am starting out on foot to Prague that I may get there tomorrow morning.

"To Prague, afoot? Are you, God forbid, out of your senses?" exclaimed Leah, quite beside herself. "Why just now? One would think you were a messenger hired to deliver a message in Prague in the morning. If you wish to see Prague, why not select a weekday when you can either get a free ride or travel in a stagecoach?"

"Let other people talk reason to women, I will not," replied Sam, angrily. "Had I told you, Leah, that I would start tomorrow, you would have said: 'why not rather start immediately after *Habdalah*, so that you could have the whole Sunday for yourself?' Pray do not disturb my 'Oneg Shabbat (Sabbath delight). No more objections, if you please, for it is my firm wish to be in Prague tomorrow morning."

Leah was silent. Another objection would have produced

the effect of a red flag on a fighting bull. She was silent even when Sam, cleaning his lantern in a hurry, knocked out one of the panes (a very ominous sign for a Sabbath evening undertaking). She stood on her door sill and repeated the *Yebarekeka* (blessing) until her husband was out of sight.

Until midnight everything went well with our traveler. He passed his time pleasantly, singing liturgical songs.

Midnight came, and with it an unexpected perplexity. He had arrived where the road branched like a fork, one path leading to the right, the other to the left.

Which way now? He deliberated a little while, and setting his lantern on the ground, he looked now in one, now in the other direction. "All ways lead to Rome," he soliloquized in the words of the old proverb. He lifted his lantern with the intention of taking the road to the right, when all of a sudden a draught blew out his light. Quickly he turned about to protect his lantern against the wind and to try to revive his light by blowing into the fainting glow of the wick. In vain. All his efforts were fruitless.

This little mishap made him entirely forget that he had turned "about face." And carrying his lantern under his arm, he marched forward, looking neither to right nor left. Did I say "forward?" I beg pardon. I should have said he marched back, straight back to Bumsle.

"All ways lead to Rome," he comforted himself once more. "And suppose I arrive an hour or two later?" Cheerfully he marched on through the second half of the night, following the road that led him direct to Bumsle.

Morning dawned. A cool breeze fanned his face with the sweet fragrance ascending from the meadows, and the merry songs of the birds made the world appear bright and glad. Over the horizon lay a dense fog.

"Perhaps I am nearer Prague than I think," he said to himself. "This fog appears to me like a huge, gray, silk nightcap drawn over the head of the city which sleeps late in the day. On my arrival I may be the first to wake her from her sleep."

And when the first rays of the sun had frightened away the mist, a city did lie before him, and Sam Passy could not find words to express his admiration of the beautiful steeple which, like a slender oak, rose above the church.

"How great are Thy works, O Lord!" he exclaimed, agreeably surprised. "Just the same as in Bumsle! Isn't it wonderful! Our steeple and this one are as like as two peas."

Arrived in the middle of the market place, his eyes fell on the statue of St. John Nepomuk (the Bohemian St. Patrick). Amazed, he halted before the huge stone figure.

"Wonders never cease!" he cried out. "I could swear that the Bumsle Nepomuk and this are twin brothers."

But the Jews' lane with the little synagogue utterly disappointed him.

"And this is the famous *Altneuschul* all the world talks so much about, this little structure, which is not a bit larger than our own? Is it not just like the one in Bumsle? Really they ought to be ashamed of themselves, these Jewish nabobs of Prague, who spend no more money on their synagogue than we in Bumsle."

Not far from the synagogue he stopped in front of a house that called to mind his own cosy little abode in Bumsle. He could not resist the temptation of entering, and ran up one flight of stairs.

Leah Passy was an excellent housekeeper as well as a very pious woman. Even at that early hour, her room was already in perfect order. She was reading her morning prayers out of a goodly sized *Tefillah*, at the same time watching a porringer in which the milk for her breakfast was boiling — thus devoting soul and body jointly to the fear of the Lord and the fear lest the milk run over.

At the unexpected sight of her husband she was unable to find words to express her surprise. But had she found any, she could not have uttered them at the moment without committing a grave offense, that of interrupting herself in the middle of the *Eighteen Benedictions.*

This circumstance gave her husband the chance to give vent to his angry feelings. But the blow of his fist on the table, having tumbled over the porringer and spilt the milk, softened his temper.

"Wife," said he, "I do not wish to quarrel over spilt milk. But tell me one thing, is Bumsle not good enough for you anymore that you must run after me to Prague?"

THE KIDDUSH CUP[13]

MARTHA WOLFENSTEIN

(age level thirteen to fifteen)

Of all the stories that Maryam told, Shimmele, her grandchild, liked best the one that was logically connected in his mind with the Sabbath eve. It was the story of the *Kiddush* cup, a beautiful cup of silver which stood in solitary grandeur on Maryam's Sabbath table. It was the one story that was delivered to him without an appendage, and contained but few moral reflections. And Maryam had a way of telling it, with many gestures and ejaculations, that Shimmele never tired of it, and the shudders were none the less delightful because he knew just when they were coming.

It was usually in the evening when Maryam was fondly rubbing the cup with her apron, before putting it aside on the shelf, that she would begin:

"Five and forty years next Purim —"

"The French were then in the land," Shimmele would prompt encouragingly.

"That they were," said Maryam. "It was a dreadful time that, the time of the French, when a single man — his name was Napoleon — took for himself the whole world, and left nothing for anyone else. In those days, many a one who sat one day good and secure on his inherited estate, was next day a beggar with wife and child. And thy grandfather — he rests in Paradise — lost all we had, and though he was a learned man, a great *Talmid Ḥaḳam*, he had to tramp through the country with a big pack of flax on his back. From one farm to the other he trudged, buying flax and bringing it to town to sell. It was hard, bitter bread he earned, for he was, *nebbich*, a poor businessman — may he forgive me for saying it, but it is true — and when he should have been thinking of a bargain, his head was full of learned things.

"Well, one day — the French had then overrun the whole land, and were as far as Vienna — thy grandfather was walking with his pack on his back just at the branching of the roads, when suddenly six men came dashing out of the bush. They had neither hats nor shoes, and their faces and hands were scratched and bleeding.

" 'Save us, for Christ's sake!' they cried —" (Here Shimmele would look with breathless admiration at Maryam, for few in the *Gass* [Ghetto] dared pronounce the dreadful name of the Christian Messiah; but Maryam was an intrepid soul.) " 'We are Austrian soldiers, prisoners of the enemy. They are upon us,' they cried.

"Thou canst imagine thy grandfather's fright, Shimmele. What was to be done? He had just come from the farm of his friend, Salme Randar, and to Salme he directed them.

" 'Tell him Hayyim Prager sent you,' he said, 'and Salme

will hide and take care of you,' and as a sign that they were not lying, he gave them his *Tefillin* bag to give to Salme —"

Here Shimmele's eyes would rove knowingly to the *Kist* (chest), and Maryam would say, "Yes, 'tis the same one, of velvet, with the *Magen David* worked in it, that lies with my grave-clothes — I made it for my Hayyim when we were betrothed.

"So off they rushed, and hardly had they disappeared in the bush when thy grandfather heard hoof-beats on the road. He quickly pulled out his prayer book, for he was in great agony of soul, and they were upon him, a great company, twenty men on horseback.

"At the branching of the roads, which go out like a three-pronged fork from there, they stopped, for they did not know which way to go. Then only thy grandfather saw what a fearful thing he had done. He had brought his friend Salme Randar with wife and child to destruction; for that French captain, if he had any *Sekel* (sense), would surely divide his company in three, each to follow one of the roads.

"*Wai geschrieen!* What was to be done? With all his soul thy grandfather prayed to God to let *him* die, if need be, but to save Salme and his family; but all the while his mind was not idle, for he knew, if *he* did not help, how should God? Was he Moses that God should do a miracle for him?

"Now, thy grandfather in his travels had often gone as far as the Frenchmen's borders, and he knew their language, but at that moment fright drove every word out of his head. It was the work of God, though thy grandfather did not then know it.

"He went up to them anyhow, and asked in German what they sought.

"There was one among them who could speak German, and he translated to the captain what thy grandfather said.

" 'Ask him if he saw any runaway soldiers pass this way,' the captain said to this man, whom they called something like Michele. But thy grandfather did not reply, for he saw at once that no matter what he said they would not believe him, he being an Austrian and they the enemy.

In any case they would divide in three, and destroy not only the runaways, but also Salme Randar.

"*Shema*'! 'tis God's wonder thy grandfather did not drop dead on the spot with fright.

"Then, while he hesitated, one of the soldiers, who perhaps noticed his prayer book, cried:

" 'Offer him money. He'll sell his soul for money, he's a dog of a Jew,' and more such, as is their manner.

"Now, wilt thou believe it, Shimmele, my life, even as he spoke a light went up in thy grandfather's head. Then he knew that God meant it well with him, and had answered his prayer. Nothing is too insignificant to hold the word of God. Here it was contained in this mean soldier's words. Now thy grandfather saw, too, that it was a blessing from God that he had not spoken in French, for they thought that he did not understand them. So he made himself very sly and said to this man, this Michele:

" 'Ask your captain how much he will give me, if I show him the way they went.'

"When Michele translated this, they all set up a great roar of laughter, and thy grandfather knew that he had them.

"It was a great blessing, Shimmele, that those Frenchmen were such a pack of idiots, for thy grandfather, who rests out there in the 'good place' (cemetery), was but a poor hand at tricks.

"They soon struck a bargain, and thy grandfather told them a pack of lies — how that the runaways had taken the forest road to Rodow, how that the way was hard to find, and he would show it if they paid five gulden extra.

"*Nu*, why should I tell a long story? In the Black Marsh he led them astray, and when their horses stood shoulder-deep in water, and they could go no further, thy grandfather turned around and said in good French:

" 'I'm afraid, Mr. Captain,' he said, 'I'm afraid we've lost the way.'

" 'Tis the truth I'm telling thee, Shimmele — there was not a man among them that did not turn white as chalk, and out jumps the captain's sword ready to run thy grandfather through. But he had no fear; he had been saying his prayers all along the road, and was prepared to die. So he said:

" 'What do you think, Mr. Captain!' he said. 'You have come to steal my Emperor's land, and now you want to shoot down his soldiers. But I tell you, I will not *allow* it.'

"Then they began to laugh, and the captain made a deep bow and said to thy grandfather:

" 'I hope Your Worship will *allow* that we leave this place; 'tis a trifle damp.'

"My word, Shimmele, thy grandfather did not feel at all like joking, and he said to the captain:

" 'No, Mr. Captain, that also I cannot allow. With God's help I shall take you out again, but not until tomorrow morning, for I have calculated that those escaped soldiers will need at least six hours' start to get to safety. By that time it will be dark, and,' says he, 'many a one has ventured through the Black Marsh after dark, but none has yet come out alive.'

"When the captain heard this, he became entirely *Meshugga*'. 'You are my prisoner,' he yelled, 'I command — forward!'

"Thy grandfather did not budge.

" 'Shoot him down, fellows!' bawled the captain.

"Wilt believe it, Shimmele, thy grandfather only laughed.

" 'Look here, Mr. Captain,' he said, 'you are a clever captain, and I am only a poor Jew, yet I tell you that one of us is a fool, and it is not I. If I will not, I will not; if I am dead, I cannot — well, then! And this also I tell you, without me to guide you back you will all perish here like rats in a trap. Do I wish that? God forbid! Do I not know that you also are human beings and have wife and child at home? Find your way out if you can, and I promise you may shoot me the moment your foot touches dry ground.'

"Well, after two of their men's horses were drowned, and the men barely escaped drowning also, they were glad enough to follow thy grandfather to a high, dry place he knew of, and there they passed the night. And grandfather built a fire and boiled water for their whiskey in his little cooking pot that they might have something warm in their stomachs, and they called him no more vile names, and drank together like comrades.

"Then thy grandfather prepared himself for death. He knew they would take him prisoner to the French camp next day, where he would be shot. He wrote me a long letter which the captain, who had a heart of gold in him, promised to send me — thanks and praise be to God, I never got it! Then they sat and talked together all night, and Hayyim told him how hard it went with the poor Jews in those troubled times, and how he could hardly make a living for his wife and two young children — thy father, Shimmele, was then a new-born babe — and the captain told him that he, too, had a wife and a little baby at home. And so they talked together like brothers. And the next day he led them safely out of the marsh, and they went back the way they had come.

"Well, after a while they stopped at a field to feed their horses, and as they stood there on the road, thy grandfather with his hands tied behind his back, they suddenly heard the rolling of drums. The captain started, listened, then quickly cried:

" 'The Austrians! Mount—forward—gallop—' and before thy grandfather could catch his breath he found himself standing alone in the road, his pack lying a little way off.

"Thy grandfather knew at once that this drumming was but the children of the last hamlet playing at war — in those days even the children had the war-fever — but the soldiers were gone. All that was left was a cloud of dust rolling down the road.

"Shimmele, to the day of his death thy grandfather could not decide whether or not that captain did it on purpose.

"It was long after, the French had already left the country — they had, alas, humbled the Kaiser, and he had to buy peace with heavy gold — when, one day, six soldiers appeared in the *Gass* and asked to be shown to our house.

"Yossel Kummer — he was then a lad — ran so that the people cried 'Where is the fire?' and ran after him, and when they got to our house, half of the *Gass* was at their heels.

"Imagine the fright, Shimmele, my life! Thy grandfather had just come home for the Sabbath, and all thought that he was to be arrested and brought to destruction, but it turned out that those soldiers were the same ones thy grandfather had sent to Salme Randar's. They knew all the rest he had done, and they carried a green leather box, and in it was this same *Kiddush* cup that stands here on the table.

"One of them made him a speech — it was, alas, a foolish speech — he said a lot about a noble Christian deed, and more such nonsense. The people said, 'With one hand they fondle, and with the other they smite him'— but they meant well, and, *nebbich*, knew no better. And thy grandfather was not insulted, and when he saw what the present was then he knew *how* well they meant it.

"They might have given him half a dukedom and he could not have been happier with it. Not because it was beautiful and of silver, but because the *Goyim* gave it to him, gave him a *Kiddush* cup with Hebrew letters engraved on it.

" 'It must always remain in the family,' he used to say, 'and go from father to son, to be a sign and a hope in dark days that the Jew shall some day have justice.'

"It was to him a sign of the coming of that day when God will be One and His Name One."

SABBATH POEMS FOR CHILDREN

SABBATH EVE[14]

ELMA EHRLICH LEVINGER

My mother cleaned the house to-day,
     Till all was shining bright;
For Sabbath Queen is on her way,
     And she will come to-night.

Said mother: "Little son of mine,
     The house is clean and sweet.
I've blessed the candles that will shine
     To guide Queen Sabbath's feet.

"But, little son, have you swept clean
     Your heart, and set a light
Within your soul for Sabbath Queen
     When she comes here to-night?"

STARS AND CANDLES[15]

SHULAMITH ISH-KISHOR

It seems to me on Friday night,
The stars come out more big and bright,
And many more I seem to see,
As if each one had turned to three —
Are angels walking through the air
And lighting *Shabbos* candles there?

THE TWIN STARS[16]

JOEL BLAU

Up above me star and star —
Side by side like twins they are:
Like the eyes of God they seem,
As in Heaven's height they gleam.

Like on Sabbath light and light,
By my mother twinkle bright.
Are there eyes that watch on high?
Are there Sabbaths in the sky?

If Almighty's eyes they be,
Do they fondly look at me?
But if lights for Sabbath-day —
Who'll the Blessing o'er them say?

SABBATH CANDLES

SHIRLEY LABOVICH

When mother lights the candles
I'm always standing near;
I love to see the candle lights
First flicker, then grow clear.

The flames are just like fireflies
Which in the dark glow best.
I'm glad that on our candlesticks
Is where they chose to rest.

SABBATH BLESSING[17]

JESSIE E. SAMPTER

The Sabbath light is burning bright;
Our prettiest cloth is clean and white,
With wine and bread for Friday night.

At set of sun our work is done;
The happy Sabbath has begun;
Now bless us, Father, every one.

O Sabbath guest, dear Sabbath guest,
Come, share the blessing with the rest,
For all our house tonight is blest.

A JEWISH HOME[18]

(Abridged)

JESSIE E. SAMPTER

I think that it is very fine
To have a Jewish home like mine,
Where every Friday evening shine
    The lovely Sabbath lights.
To bless them, mother hides her face;
And loaves and wine at father's place
For *Kiddush* stand, and books for grace
    That each of us recites.

When I am grown and married, too,
I know exactly what I'll do,
Because, you see, I am a Jew,
    And mother teaches me.
I, too, shall bless the Sabbath light,
And keep my dishes clean and bright,
And teach my children what is right
    And what a home should be.

A SABBATH CHANT[19]

S. Benzion (A. Gutman)

(Translated from the Hebrew by Harry H. Fein)

To the market mother went
    To buy some food for Sabbath;
From the market mother came
    And brought some food for Sabbath.
            What?
Flour and meat and fish and fruit,
To honor Sabbath, to honor Sabbath.

Mother kindled a fire to make
    Dainty food for Sabbath;
Mother worked all day and made
    Dainty food for Sabbath.
            How?
She baked and cooked and broiled and fried
Dainty food for Sabbath, dainty food for Sabbath.

Father went to the synagogue
    To welcome the Queen Sabbath;
Father came back from the synagogue,
    And we honored the Queen Sabbath.
            With what?
With food and drink and chants and praise,
We honored Sabbath, we honored Sabbath.

WELCOME, QUEEN SABBATH[20]

ZALMAN SHNEIUR

(Translated from the Hebrew by HARRY H. FEIN)

Oh, come let us welcome sweet Sabbath the Queen!

The cobbler abandoned his awl and his thread,
The tailor's brisk needle now sleeps in its bed.
Father has bathed, washed his hair, and he says:
   Sweet Sabbath is near,
   Sweet Sabbath is here,
Oh, come let us welcome sweet Sabbath the Queen!

The storekeeper locked and bolted his store,
The teamster unbridled his horse at the door,
The sexton runs hither and thither and says:
   The sun sets in the sky,
   Sweet Sabbath is nigh,
Oh, come let us welcome sweet Sabbath the Queen!

The white-bearded cantor has hastened along
To welcome the Sabbath with blessing and song,
Dear mother is lighting the candles and prays:
   Day of holiness, rest,
   Forever be blest,
Oh, come let us welcome sweet Sabbath the Queen!

A DEED OF DARING[21]

A. M. KLEIN

This is a tale of a deed of daring;
How Samson got the rabbi a herring,
The rabbi who ate for his Sabbath supper
A herring's parts, lower, middle, and upper.

So Samson the brave, his pennies sparing,
Into the market went wayfaring,
And bought, and got, and brought the herring;
This is a tale of a deed of daring.

THE SHABBOS-KUGEL[22]

SHULAMITH ISH-KISHOR

When the *Shabbos-kugel*'s hot,
Steaming in the big round pot,
And my grandpa comes to look,
And he says, the finest cook
Ever lived, is our grandma,
And what lucky boys we are, —
Then I think I just can't wait
Till it's lying on my plate;
And I wonder what boys do,
When their papa's not a Jew,
And their grandma doesn't make
Such a splendid *Shabbos*-cake!

SABBATH THOUGHT[23]

SHULAMITH ISH-KISHOR

I wonder why the faithful sun
    Must always work so long;
He never has a Sabbath day;
    It seems to me that's wrong.

But then perhaps, God lets him stay
    And keep his shining mark,
Because if he should go away,
    'Twould make our Sabbath dark!

THE SABBATH VISIT[24]

JESSIE E. SAMPTER

I always go to Grandpa's house
    On Sabbaths — I am never missing —
And stand as quiet as a mouse
    To get my Sabbath blessing.

At Grandma's Sabbath cap I look,
    And touch its edges, frilled and beaded;
And Grandpa holds a holy book,
    And lets me try to read it.

MY SABBATH CALL

SHIRLEY LABOVICH

Oh, Sabbath, I think, is the best day of all,
'Cause that's when I pay my grandma a call!

I knock on the door, and she says, "Who is it?
Who can be coming to pay me a visit?"

That's when I call out, "There's nobody here."
Then she opens the door, and looks far and near.

And though I am wearing my very best clothes,
She can't even see me right under her nose!

"That's funny," she says, "I thought there would be
A little boy calling, but there's no one, I see!"

And quietly I giggle at grandma's mistake,
Till she says, "What will I do with my beautiful cake?"

Then, "Grandma," I cry, "look down and see,
There's nobody here excepting just me!"

Grandma looks so surprised with her eyes open wide
That both of us laugh, and we both go inside.

Then she tells Sabbath stories and treats me to cake.
And what I can't finish to mother I take.

Oh, my Saturday visits I like best of all.
I have the most fun paying grandma a call!

HABDALAH[25]

JESSIE E. SAMPTER

Blessed be He that gave us days
For work and rest, to serve and praise
In orderly and seemly ways.

That set the bounds of day and night
With fine distinctions in His sight,
And bade us honor them with light.

Blessed be He whose Sabbath rest
With song and wine and light expressed,
Shall make the days of labor blest.

CHAPTER V

THE SABBATH IN THE SYNAGOGUE

וּמִדֵּי שַׁבָּת בְּשַׁבַּתּוֹ יָבוֹא כָל בָּשָׂר
לְהִשְׁתַּחֲוֹת לְפָנַי אָמַר ה' (ישע' ס"ו, כ"ג)

And from one sabbath to another,
Shall all flesh come to worship before Me,
Saith the Lord (Isa. 66.23).

THE TRADITIONAL SABBATH SERVICES

SABBATH services in the synagogue are not only important religious exercises; they are an integral part of Sabbath observance. Without the synagogue services the Sabbath is an empty shell. That is why the Sabbath prayers have been so chosen as to reflect the Sabbath spirit by their deliberate disregard of personal needs and mundane worries. Only such prayers are included as sing the praise of God and glorify the Sabbath. They abound in hymns of thanksgiving for God's loving-kindness, especially as it has revealed itself in the selection of Israel for the greatest of divine gifts — the Sabbath.

Like all the festive days, the Sabbath is honored by an additional service, called *Musaf*. But the Sabbath services differ from the festival services in that they teach the Torah to the congregation. On all holidays a portion of the Torah is read during the morning and afternoon services for the purpose of teaching the significance of the holiday. On the Sabbath the portion of the Torah is read solely for the pur-

157

pose of public instruction. The Pentateuch is divided into fifty-four portions, one or more of which is read consecutively at each Sabbath morning service, thus annually completing the Five Books of Moses. A few congregations follow the triennial cycle. In such synagogues the weekly portion is much shorter, and the Pentateuch is completed once in three years.

The Sabbath afternoons were utilized for private study and additional public instruction. It used to be the practice of almost every Jew to spend most of the Sabbath afternoon in the synagogue where he either listened to a sermon by a *Maggid* (a preacher), or studied the Bible or the Talmud. During the long summer afternoons it was also the custom to read or study a chapter of the treatise of the Mishna Pirke Abot, *The Ethics of the Fathers*. This treatise, containing five chapters to which a sixth was subsequently added, was originally studied only during the six Sabbaths between Passover and the Feast of Weeks. But the ethical contents of the Pirke Abot proved so popular that it became customary to read a chapter every Sabbath afternoon throughout the summer. Every Jew therefore reread this ethical work several times annually. In the winter months, when afternoons are short, the study of *The Ethics of the Fathers* was replaced by the reading of Psalms 104, 120–134.

The Sabbath as a day of prayer and instruction is an old institution. The biblical account of the Shunamite woman (II Kings 4.23) clearly indicates that visiting the prophet on the Sabbath was an established custom in the days of the prophet Elisha. It may also be assumed that these visits were of a religious nature, consisting of worship and instruction. That it was also a very common practice to visit the Temple in Jerusalem on the Sabbath is borne out by Isaiah's bitter denunciation of his contemporaries who disregarded the spirit of the law yet trampled the courts of the Temple

on the Sabbath (Isa. 1.12). The systematic reading of the
Torah as part of the Sabbath services is likewise an ancient
custom attributed by tradition to Ezra the Scribe who lived
in the fifth century B. C. E.

Sabbath service attendance became a universal practice
even before the destruction of the Temple in Jerusalem.
By the beginning of the Middle Ages absence from synagogue
on Friday at sunset, and more particularly on Saturday
morning, was inconceivable. Not only did public opinion
and religious convictions compel universal attendance, but
the Sabbath services satisfied the Jew's social needs. The
Sabbath services were closely tied up with his most vital
social experiences. It was during the Sabbath services that
the community officially took note of such dramatic events
as birth, coming of age, marriage, and death. When a child
was born, the father was called up to the reading of the
Torah and a special prayer was offered for the recovery of
the mother and the well-being of the child. If the newly
born child was a daughter the naming of the child took place
while the father stood at the Torah. When a boy became
thirteen years old, he was officially and ceremoniously presented to the congregation as a member of the religious
community. On such an occasion, the boy was called up to
the Torah where he recited the customary benedictions,
chanted the *Haftarah* and, at times, read the entire portion
of the Torah. This appearance of the boy on the pulpit is
still one of the thrilling and memorable experiences of every
Jewish lad. When a young man was about to be married,
he and his family, and indeed the whole community, celebrated this event in the synagogue. On the Sabbath
immediately preceding the wedding the bridegroom was
called up to the Torah. The *Aufrufung*, as this celebration
was called, was always an event of importance. When a
Jew escaped from grave danger his deliverance was publicly

noted in the synagogue. On the Sabbath following this experience, the person concerned was called up to the Torah where he pronounced a special benediction, the *Birkat ha-Gomel*, in which he publicly thanked God for His mercy and loving-kindness. And finally, the synagogue played an important part in the life of the Jew when death invaded his home. On the first Sabbath after the burial the mourners came to the synagogue to pour out their grief. In some localities, the congregation expressed its sympathy by rising as the mourners entered. Thus every vital aspect of life had its point of contact with the synagogue.

Nor was the Sabbath service itself a monotonous weekly repetition of an old established ritual. In addition to the family events which rendered the services especially attrac tive to the whole community, there were fourteen Special Sabbaths listed in the Jewish calendar. Each of these Special Sabbaths brought an element of novelty into the services in the form of special prayers and, in some cases, special musical renditions. On *Shabbat Mebarakim*, the Sabbath preceding the New Moon, the congregation pleaded and the women prayerfully wept for a month "of life, of good, of blessing, of sustenance, of bodily vigor, of fear of Heaven and dread of sin." On *Shabbat Ḥazon*, the Sabbath preceding the Fast of Ab, the congregation heard the mournful tunes of the book of Lamentations (though not the book itself) as a reminder of the fall of Jerusalem and the dispersion of the Jewish people. On the following Sabbath, known as *Shabbat Naḥamu*, the comforting promise of redemption replaced the words of doom read the week before. Thus the yearly cycle with its Special Sabbaths rolled on, "and from one Sabbath to another" the Jew came to worship and to study in the synagogue. He found in it spiritual and social satisfaction, and, best of all, consolation and hope.

THE DECLINE OF SABBATH SERVICE ATTENDANCE

That Sabbath services today are poorly attended is generally acknowledged. The reasons are not hard to discover. The world has undergone several interrelated revolutions which have had their effects on Jewish life. Scientific progress has brought with it a widespread skepticism that has tended to undermine religious authority. Scientific discoveries have challenged the biblical story of creation and have deprived the Sabbath of a vital sanction. Biblical criticism coupled with the concept of evolution have weakened the accepted belief in the divine origin of the Sabbath institution, and have made service attendance an "elective" in Jewish life. Non-Jews, too, have felt the effect of these forces. Attendance at Sunday services has decreased considerably. Only fifty per cent of the Christians in America are affiliated with the church, and only one third of those affiliated attend services, except on Christmas and Easter.[1] The record is only a little better in the Catholic Church, where Sunday attendance is about forty per cent.[2]

But Sabbath services in the synagogue have suffered an additional blow. The Industrial Revolution has made Sabbath synagogue attendance almost an impossibility. The present-day economic system is in direct conflict with the observance of the Jewish Sabbath. Prior to the Industrial Revolution the Jew was an independent economic agent. Today he is part of the complicated economic life of the western Christian world. Friday at sunset and Saturday mornings he is usually in the factory, store, or office. To stop all economic activities in order to attend Sabbath services may mean bankruptcy or loss of employment. Only in an all-Jewish city like Tel Aviv can the Jew drop his tools and close his shop when the trumpet is blown at sunset on Friday. In America the accepted weekly routine can hardly be altered to suit Jewish religious scruples.

Yet despite this almost insuperable obstacle, the Jew cannot abandon synagogue services on the Sabbath without crippling the Sabbath institution. Sabbath observance must continue to be linked with synagogue services just as it must continue to be tied up with the home. To meet the challenge the synagogue has already made several adjustments and is still hopeful of successfully overcoming the serious obstacles that modern life has put in its way.

THE LATE FRIDAY EVENING SERVICES

The first serious problem facing the synagogue has been that of the Friday evening services. The traditional sunset service has always been brief — a preliminary activity to the family observance of the Sabbath at home. It consisted of an evening service (*Ma'ariv*), preceded by the *Kabbalat Shabbat*³ recited in honor of the incoming Sabbath. But sunset in winter comes as early as four o'clock in the afternoon. At that hour most people are still at work. As a result the sunset service attendance dropped so precipitously that many synagogues were forced to abandon it altogether. Had there been compensation through a deepening of Sabbath observance at home, there would have been some consolation for the loss. Unfortunately, it soon became evident that Friday evening had become a popular night for secular amusement.

Faced with this unhappy situation, many American Jews met the problem in a simple but untraditional manner. They moved the Friday evening service to a later hour, after the Sabbath meal. The change was contrary to tradition because the *Kabbalat Shabbat* (the Welcoming of the Sabbath) late in the evening, after the Sabbath meal, is self-contradictory. It means welcoming the Bride long after her arrival. Besides, Friday evening after dinner had always been reserved for the home, for the weekly family reunion.

A challenge to this innovation was expected from the camp of the Orthodox. But this opposition was headed off by a simple compromise. Instead of displacing or duplicating the early sunset service, some synagogues arranged for additional religious assemblies after the Friday evening Sabbath meal. At these assemblies the people would sing hymns, join in the reading of a few psalms, and listen to a religious discourse by the rabbi.[4] What was unexpected was the strong opposition that developed within the Reform group — this despite the fact that Rabbi Isaac M. Wise, the father of the American Reform movement, instituted late Friday evening assemblies as early as 1866. Thus, Dr. K. Kohler, president of the Hebrew Union College, said, "I wish to inform you that the late Friday evening services are altogether an innovation, an innovation of a dubious character, in so far as they make those who attend them feel that they have done their duty toward the Sabbath."[5] At another convention of the Central Conference of American Rabbis, Dr. Joseph Silverman, in his "Discussion of the Sabbath Question," warned, "I claim that the institution of a late Friday night service does more harm to the Sabbath than the institution of Sunday services, or Sunday lectures, because by some peculiar reasoning people believe that if they attend synagogue for thirty minutes Friday evening, they are then keeping the Sabbath . . . ."[6]

Life, however, proved stronger than logic and tradition, and American Jews have evolved a solution which has proved to be quite satisfactory. The late Friday evening services are now almost universally accepted and are generally the

best attended of all Sabbath services. The tradition of the
sunset service has not been cast off. The few who are able
and willing to attend such a service are usually given the
opportunity to do so. And the incongruity of a *Kabbalat
Shabbat* at the late Friday evening services has either been
disregarded or removed by the elimination of this part of
the services.

Another innovation calculated to make the Friday evening
services more attractive and more meaningful is the *'Oneg
Shabbat* immediately after the services. This latest development, which is fully discussed in the next chapter, is still
in the experimental stage. But it has already proved of
considerable value, and will probably do much to enrich the
Sabbath experience for the American Jew.

Despite these adjustments, the problem of Sabbath observance in the synagogue is still far from a final solution.
The late Friday evening services are successful enough
to be the best attended of the Sabbath religious assemblies
and to tempt almost every organization to use them as a
means of "bringing its message" to the people. But they
are not successful enough to fill the synagogue, or to compete
with important non-synagogue attractions or even with
inclement weather. And far worse than the Friday evening
services are the Sabbath morning services, which in many
places are struggling for a *Minyan* — this despite the fact
that women and children have always been free to attend,
and despite the fact that now many men are free because of
the five-day work-week. It is therefore clear that, if American Jewry is to revitalize the Sabbath, it must give the
problem serious and immediate attention. It has been said
that the poet Bialik evinced more creative genius by reviv-
ing the Sabbath spirit in Palestine than by all the exalted
poems that he wrote. It will take even greater genius to

revive the Sabbath spirit in America. Indeed, so great is the task that no single person can possibly undertake it. Only the collective will of American Jewry may prove equal to it. With valiant effort it may be possible to awaken the traditional Jewish genius for religious creativity and thus make for a revitalized and vigorous Jewish religious life in America.

CHAPTER VI

THE 'ONEG SHABBAT

וְקָרָאתָ לַשַּׁבָּת עֹנֶג (ישע' נ'ח. י'ג)

And thou shalt call the
sabbath a delight (Isa. 58.13).

WHEN Aḥad Ha-'Am defined the primary function of the Jewish Homeland in Palestine as a spiritual and cultural center for the Jewish people, he surely did not expect that one of the first practical demonstrations of his ideal would take the form of a Sabbath gathering known as the *'Oneg Shabbat*. According to Aḥad Ha-'Am, the Jewish Homeland was to serve the scattered Jewish communities as the heart serves the organs of the body. Palestine as a cultural and spiritual center was to strengthen and quicken the spirit of the Jew everywhere by disseminating a stimulating and creative influence. Strangely enough, the first direct spiritual influence to emanate from Palestine and reach an appreciable part of the American Jewish community was not through an academy of learning but through the *'Oneg Shabbat*. This institution has spread among the Jewish communities outside of Palestine and has come to be the first direct, visible influence of Palestine on world Jewry.

The phrase *'Oneg Shabbat*, which means "Sabbath delight," is not a recent addition to the Hebrew language. It is as old as the Bible, for the prophet Isaiah urged the Hebrews to "call the Sabbath a delight." The phrase referred

to the joy and cheer pervading the Sabbath and to the
spiritual and intellectual activities of the day. But the
'Oneg Shabbat as a modern institution refers to a Sabbath
gathering which cultivates intellectual and spiritual activities reflecting the Sabbath spirit.

The 'Oneg Shabbat, although not a new creation, is nevertheless a direct outgrowth of the rejuvenated Jewish life in
Palestine. Whereas Jews in the Diaspora spend most of
their collective energy resisting the forces of assimilation
and staying the forces of spiritual stagnation, the new, virile
life in Palestine has directed these energies toward achieve-
ments making for spiritual and cultural growth.

Jewish life in modern Palestine, from its very outset,
discovered in the Sabbath potentialities for the dissemination of cultural and religious values. Workingmen frequently would gather in their Bate 'Am (community cen-
ters) on Saturday afternoons to discuss current problems.
These Sabbath afternoon gatherings were secular replicas
of the East European practice of gathering in the synagogue
on Saturday afternoons to hear the Maggid's sermon or to
study the Bible, Talmud, or Midrash. But it was left for
the poet Hayyim Nahman Bialik to conceive the idea of
the 'Oneg Shabbat as an established institution. He felt
that "the Sabbath is the cornerstone of Judaism." In order
to strengthen Judaism, Bialik proceeded to strengthen its
foundation — the Sabbath. He convened an assembly of
his many admirers in the Tel Aviv Bet 'Am every Saturday
afternoon. At this weekly Sabbath gathering he or his
invited guests led discussions on various subjects — literary,
religious, and sociological. After the discussions the assembly sang suitable Sabbath Zemirot, modern Hebrew
songs and hasidic melodies. As the sun slowly set and the
darkness in the hall gradually deepened, the singing assumed
a mystic tone. In the midst of the gathering darkness the

Habdalah was recited by a cantor, and as the words "the Jews had light and joy and gladness and honor" were pronounced, all the lights suddenly went on. The assembly then greeted the new week with appropriate songs.

This weekly exercise attracted thousands of Palestinian Jews and impressed every tourist as one of the most meaningful Jewish experiences. These tourists enthusiastically reported their thrilling experiences to the American Jewish communities. At first there was artificial imitation of the Palestinian procedure. Then came some experimentation for the purpose of adapting the *'Oneg Shabbat* to the American scene. In time a procedure was evolved which has proved capable of serving the needs of American Jews. The American version of the *'Oneg Shabbat* is like its Tel Aviv model in that it is neither a public lecture nor a group entertainment. It emphasizes the element of spontaneity despite the careful planning that precedes it. It stresses group participation, particularly in the singing. It insists on the Sabbath atmosphere which is created through distinctive decorations and suitable refreshments. It aims at informality and relaxation which are frequently achieved by seating the participants around tables.

The general pattern followed by American Jews is clearly illustrated by the following brief descriptions of some typical *'Oneg Shabbat* gatherings. One synagogue,[1] for example, describes its procedure as follows: "Our *'Oneg Shabbat* is a Sabbath afternoon get-together, at which we have coffee and cake, community singing, and a program which may be a reading from Yiddish literature, a lecture by some outside speaker, a debate by young people, a program offered by the children, or whatever else we may happen to arrange." Another synagogue[2] describes its *'Oneg Shabbat* as follows: "Although our program varies from time to time, the core remains unchanged .... After the [Friday evening] service

the group moves to the auditorium where the tables have
been set for the Sabbath . . . . The group sings the *Shalom
'Alekem* and then the *Kiddush* is recited. Wine and cake
are served and community singing follows immediately
thereafter. The rest of the program is usually a talk and a
discussion. The fact that the people are seated around the
tables makes for a more intimate and more vivacious discussion. On one occasion we dispensed with the formal talk.
The rabbi presided and the group was at liberty to ask him
any question whatsoever. It turned out to be an exceedingly
interesting evening. Occasionally the formal talk and discussion was replaced by a "quiz bee" on Jewish holidays
or on Jewish history, with the members of the audience
participating. On other evenings the dramatic reading of a
play or the presentation of an original play were featured.
One iron-clad rule is always followed, namely, that the
subject of the speaker or of the play must be Jewish in
content."

A Jewish children's summer camp[3] describes its procedure
in terms of the following six rules:

1. The *'Oneg Shabbat* is conducted every Friday evening.
2. Each week a different bunk is responsible for the
   'Oneg Shabbat.
3. The outward arrangements are an important part of
   the *'Oneg Shabbat.* It is always conducted around
   tables covered with white cloths, candles, fruit, etc.
4. The *'Oneg Shabbat* should not last more than one hour.
   This hour should be divided as follows:
   A talk, discussion, or story (15 to 20 minutes).
   Readings from the Bible or literature — not continuous (15 minutes).
   Singing — both solos and group singing (balance of
   hour).
5. Everything must be well prepared, the reading should
   be done with taste. Every song must be ready. *Do
   not wait for the last moment.*

The above quotations illustrate the general nature of the *'Oneg Shabbat* as it has developed in America. But the synagogue and the children's camp are not the only places where an *'Oneg Shabbat* can be arranged. It can be utilized effectively in the Hebrew School, where *'Oneg Shabbat* clubs can meet Saturday afternoons. School graduations can be held on Friday evenings immediately after the services in the form of an *'Oneg Shabbat*. Indeed, it has been done with telling effect by one of the outstanding synagogues in America. All Jewish organizations, such as Women's Associations, Men's Clubs, Young People's Leagues, Lodges, Boy and Girl Scouts, can and should take advantage of the opportunities for the joint intellectual and spiritual joy which are offered by the *'Oneg Shabbat*.

If an organization is to hold a successful *'Oneg Shabbat* it should observe the following rules:

I. The *'Oneg Shabbat* must be planned carefully.
  1. If the group is small, the ideal place is a home. If the group is large, an informal atmosphere can be achieved by seating the participants around tables.
  2. Careful attention must be given to the decorations. The tables should be covered with white table cloths; candlesticks or menorahs should be placed on the tables.
  3. Song sheets should be prepared, and a capable music leader should conduct the singing.
  4. Light refreshments should be served.

II. The program might feature any of the following:
  1. An invited speaker.
  2. A book review.
  3. A digest of a published tract.
  4. A summary of Jewish and general current events.
  5. A quiz on Jewish history or Jewish holidays.

6. A symposium with several members participating.
7. Readings from Yiddish or Hebrew literature in English translation.
8. A playlet dealing with an approaching holiday, or with some other suitable theme.
9. An exhibit of Jewish art, or a recital of Jewish music.
10. Informal questions by members of the group to be answered by a well-informed leader.

III. Group singing must never be relegated to a secondary role. It may take much time and persistence to break down the reserve characteristic of adults, and it may take much effort and planning to teach the participants the *Zemirot* and the Hebrew songs that are suitable for an *'Oneg Shabbat*. But unless the group sings with enthusiasm and abandon, the gathering is not an *'Oneg Shabbat*. If one cannot get a capable music leader to volunteer his services, it is advisable to pay for such leadership. Too much should not be expected from the first few *'Oneg Shabbat* gatherings. But after the group learns the songs and learns to enjoy the singing, the Sabbath gatherings will prove truly delightful.

The *'Oneg Shabbat* as an American institution is still in its infancy. Techniques for its effective use are still in the process of development. Before long, however, there are bound to develop not only tested procedures, but many useful aids for its effective utilization as a medium for the intellectual and spiritual quickening of organized Jewish life in America.*

---

* *'Oneg Shabbat* songs will be found in the music supplement below. The *Zemirot* on pp. 39–57; 75–90; 93–98 are also suitable for *'Oneg Shabbat* gatherings.

CHAPTER VII

THE LAW OF THE SABBATH

הַשַּׁבָּת שְׁקוּלָה כְּנֶגֶד כָּל הַמִּצְווֹת

שֶׁבַּתּוֹרָה (ירוש' נדר' פ' ג')

The observance of the Sabbath outweighs all the
commandments of the Torah (Yer. Ned. 3.9).

NON-JEWS frequently describe the law of the Sabbath as harsh and burdensome. They usually point
to the innumerable minutiae which suggest rigidity and
pettiness. But the impression given by an enumeration of
the many Sabbath prohibitions is altogether misleading.
In practice, the observance of the Sabbath was always a
joyful experience which led the Jew to regard the Sabbath
as the greatest of divine gifts to Israel. The Sabbath was a
day of physical relaxation and spiritual stimulation. The
devout Jew, although he observed all the minute details of
the Sabbath law, was conscious solely of the cheerful aspects
of the Sabbath. To him the Sabbath laws were not burdensome. On the contrary, so great and unique was the joy
which he reaped from their observance that he found it
necessary to explain his delightful experience in terms of
possessing an additional soul on the Sabbath. The numerous
laws of the Sabbath merely reflected the Jew's high regard
for the Sabbath and his earnest desire to protect it by means
of a strong legal fence.

The Sabbath law as taught in the Bible is vague. The
Bible teaches that "in it thou shalt not do any manner of

work" (Ex. 20.10). But it was impossible to obey this injunction without an explicit definition of what constituted "work." The rabbis of the Talmud, therefore, resorted to their ingenious method of interpreting the text, and defined what constitutes work on the Sabbath. In Exodus 35, immediately after the prohibition of work on the Sabbath, are the directions for the building of the Tabernacle. Since these two biblical sections are introduced by similar phrases, the rabbis concluded that everything that went into the construction of the Tabernacle was considered work and was therefore prohibited on the Sabbath. It was thus that thirty-nine major categories of work were established. Among them are such prohibitions as kindling fire, sowing, reaping, threshing, and carrying a burden from one place to another. These thirty-nine general categories and their many derivatives constitute the negative law of the Sabbath.

The Talmud, in addition to defining the Sabbath laws, also liberalized some of them. This the rabbis achieved by means of legal fictions as well as by textual interpretation. The classic example of the rabbinic efforts at liberalizing the Sabbath law is the 'Erub. The Bible teaches, "Let no man go out of his place on the seventh day" (Ex. 16.29). A literal interpretation of the word "place" would restrict all movement on the Sabbath to one's home. Indeed, the Karaites, members of a Jewish sect that has insisted on the literal interpretation of the Bible, actually refrain from walking out of their homes on the Sabbath except to go to the synagogue. The rabbis of the Talmud, however, by interpreting the word "place" to mean "city," made it possible for one to have freedom of movement not only within his city but also as far as 2,000 cubits (half a mile) beyond the city limits.[1] This Sabbath law was further liberalized by a legal fiction. If a person had to go beyond the 2,000-cubit limit for the performance of an important religious deed, he could place at the prescribed limit sufficient food for two meals, thus technically converting that spot into his abode. He was then permitted to walk 2,000 cubits beyond this technical abode. This was known as the '*Erub*. Thus by ingenious interpretation of the laws and by occasionally resorting to legal fictions, the Talmud was able to liberalize some of the biblical restrictions without abrogating any of the laws.

Since the prohibitions of the Sabbath are frequently quoted and generally known, and since "in the last instance, not what the Jew will refrain from doing will determine the spiritual influence of the Sabbath, but the affirmative conduct which the observance of the Sabbath will elicit from him,"[2] it is more advisable to set forth some of the positive aspects of the Sabbath law. The following selections were culled from the sixteenth century code, the *Shulḥan 'Aruk*, which was compiled by Joseph Karo and has been the traditional guide for Jewish practice. The selections are set forth in the hope of conveying a more accurate knowledge of the spirit and practice of the Sabbath law.

SABBATH LAW[3]

The holy Sabbath is God's great sign and covenant by which we may know that in six days the Lord made heaven and earth, and all that is in them, and rested on the seventh day. That is the foundation of our Faith. For our rabbis, of blessed memory, said that the Sabbath is equal to all the other commandments. Observance of all the laws of the Sabbath is equivalent to the observance of the entire Torah, and the desecration of the Sabbath is like the denial of the entire Torah (Ex. Rab. 25) . . . .

Hence, the praise of the prophet: "Happy is the man that doeth this, and the son of man that holdeth fast by it: that keepeth the sabbath from profaning it" (Isa. 56.2). He who observes the Sabbath according to the law, honoring it to his utmost ability, is rewarded in this world, to say nothing of the great reward in store for him in the world to come. This too is set forth by the prophet: "If thou turn away thy foot because of the sabbath, from pursuing thy business on My holy day; and call the sabbath a delight, and the holy of the Lord honourable; and shalt honour it, not doing thy wonted ways, nor pursuing thy business, nor speaking thereof; then shalt thou delight thyself in the Lord, and I will make thee to ride upon the high places of the earth, and I will feed thee with the heritage of Jacob thy father; for the mouth of the Lord hath spoken it" (Isa. 58.13, 14).

It is mandatory upon all, even upon those who have numerous domestics, to honor the Sabbath by doing something in preparation for it. Such was the habit of the Sages. Rabbi Ḥisda, for instance, used to cut the vegetables. Rabbah and Rab Joseph used to chop wood. Rabbi Zera was in the habit of lighting the fire. Rab Naḥman put the house in order, bringing all the utensils needed for the Sabbath and disposing of the things used during the week (Shab. 119a). All men should emulate their example and not regard such work as an indignity. For it is indeed man's glory to honor the Sabbath.

One should prepare choice meat, fish, dessert, and good wines, in accordance with one's means. It is desirable to eat fish at every Sabbath meal provided it is not harmful to the health of the individual .... The table should be

covered with a white cloth which should remain upon the
table the entire Sabbath day. One should rejoice at the
coming of the Sabbath, and make his house ready as one
does for the coming of a distinguished guest . . . .

Even the poorest of Israel should endeavor with all his
might to take delight in the Sabbath. He should economize
the entire week in order to have sufficient funds wherewith
to honor the Sabbath. If one has no money he should borrow
it or pawn something in order to provide for the Sabbath.
Of such a one did our rabbis, of blessed memory, say, "My
children borrow for My sake and I will repay (saith the
Lord)" (Bezah 15b) . . . . If, however, a man is very poor,
he should be guided by this maxim of our rabbis, of blessed
memory, "Make thy Sabbath as a weekday [i. e., spend no
more for it than for a weekday] and do not require the aid
of the community." However, if at all possible, he should
do some little thing to distinguish the Sabbath from all
other days (Pes. 112a) . . . .

An effort should be made to wear fine clothes as well as
a beautiful *Tallit* (prayer shawl) in honor of the Sabbath.
For it is written, "And shalt honour it," which is expounded
by our rabbis to mean that the garments for the Sabbath
should not be the same as those worn on weekdays (Shab.
113a). Even while journeying among non-Jews, Sabbath
attire is desirable, for the festive array is not for the on-
lookers but in honor of the Sabbath.

It is forbidden to engage a non-Jew to work on the Sabbath. Even if the non-Jew is not expressly told to do the
work on the Sabbath, but it is obvious from the instructions
that at least part of the work would have to be done on the

Sabbath, it is forbidden to engage him for such a purpose. For instance, if a written message is being sent through a non-Jew who is instructed to deliver the message on a given day, and it is obvious that the messenger cannot reach his destination except by traveling on the Sabbath, it is forbidden to send such a message. If market is held on the Sabbath day, it is forbidden to give a non-Jew money beforehand in order to buy merchandise which the Jew knows cannot be obtained except on the Sabbath day. Similarly, it is forbidden to give a non-Jew merchandise which it is known he must sell on the Sabbath day....

It is obligatory upon everyone to put work aside and to light the Sabbath candles at least half an hour before the appearance of the stars ....

It is mandatory to honor the Sabbath by the lighting of many candles. Some are accustomed to light ten, others seven. One should light no less than two .... It is also desirable that women set aside money for charity before lighting the candles ....

The obligation to light candles on the Sabbath devolves upon both men and women, but it is more obligatory for women, since they are at home and attend to household matters .... But the men, too, should share the *Mizvah* by setting the candles and candlesticks on the table ....

The candles should be lighted in the dining room, to show that they are lit in honor of the Sabbath, and should not be moved except in case of necessity. For instance, when the woman is sick, she may light the candles near her bed. Afterwards they may be placed in the dining room ....

It is a positive biblical law to sanctify the Sabbath in words, for it is said: "Remember the sabbath day, to keep it holy" (Ex. 20.8). This implies an obligation to remember it at its coming in by *Kiddush* and at its going out by *Habdalah*. Hence the Sages instituted the ceremony of sanctification over the cup of wine, both at the coming in and going out of the Sabbath.

It is mandatory to recite the *Kiddush* over old wine; it is also mandatory to select good wine, and if possible red wine. Where suitable grape wine cannot be obtained, *Kiddush* may be recited over raisin wine . . . .

Kiddush is also obligatory upon women. They must listen attentively when the *Kiddush* is recited, and respond "Amen." . . . . .

The bread must be covered while the *Kiddush* is being recited. When the *Kiddush* is recited over bread, the *Hallah* should be covered throughout the recitation, since it symbolizes the manna which was covered with dew.

The Sabbath morning *Kiddush*, too, should be recited over wine, though brandy is also acceptable. This *Kiddush* consists of the benediction *Bore Peri ha-Gafen*,[4] and, like the Friday evening *Kiddush*, is also obligatory upon women . . . .

Both the evening and morning *Kiddush* should be recited where the meal is eaten, for it is written: "Thou shalt call the sabbath a delight" (Isa. 58.13). And the rabbis, of blessed memory, said that wherever you recite the *Kiddush* there you shall have the pleasure of eating. Therefore, if one recites the *Kiddush* in one house and eats in another, he has not fulfilled his obligation concerning *Kiddush*. Further, the meal should immediately follow the *Kiddush*. If not, the obligation concerning *Kiddush* has not been fulfilled . . . .

Every Israelite, man or woman, is in duty bound to partake of three meals on the Sabbath, one on Friday evening and two on the Sabbath day. And at each meal it is obligatory to break bread . . . .

It is obligatory to break bread at every meal upon two whole loaves. Both loaves should be held while saying the *Ha-Mozi'*,[5] but only one need be broken . . . .

Grieving on the Sabbath is forbidden, but one may pray for God's mercy.

It is mandatory to take delight on the Sabbath in everything that gives pleasure, as it is written: "And thou shalt call the sabbath a delight" (Isa. 58.13).

Time should be set aside during the Sabbath for the study of the Torah. For relating to the Sabbath it is written: "And Moses assembled all the congregation of the children of Israel" (Ex. 35.1). And our rabbis, of blessed memory, said: "Why does it say 'And he assembled' in this particular portion and not in all the rest of the Torah? God said to Moses: 'Go down and make assemblies on the Sabbath, so that the generations to come may learn to make assemblies to study the Torah in public' " (*Yalkut Shime'oni, Vayakhel*). And again our rabbis, of blessed memory, said: "Sabbaths and festivals were given to Israel solely to devote themselves to the study of the Torah, since there are many who are too

busy during the week and have no time to study the Torah
regularly. But on Sabbaths and festivals, being free from
work, they can study the Torah properly" (*Pesikta Rab-
bati*, '*Aseret ha-Dibrot*). Hence all those who do not study
the Torah the entire week are all the more obligated to study
the Torah on the holy Sabbath, each according to his conception and capacity.

Whatever an Israelite is himself forbidden to do he must
not relegate to a non-Jew. But in the wintertime a non-
Jew is permitted to light the stove for the purpose of heating
the house. The Sabbath food may be warmed, provided the
non-Jew places it upon the stove before lighting the fire . . . .

It is written: "That thine ox and thine ass may have
rest" (Ex. 23.12). Thus has the Torah admonished us that
the cattle in the jurisdiction of an Israelite must also rest.
And not only the cattle, but all the animals as well . . . .

The words "from pursuing thy business" (Isa. 58.13) our
rabbis, of blessed memory, have expounded to mean "thy
business is forbidden thee even if thou doest no work."
Thus one is forbidden to examine his property in order to
see what must be done on the morrow. It is also forbidden
to walk through the town for the purpose of finding a horse,
a ship or a wagon in order to hire them after the Sabbath . . .

Inasmuch as it is written "thy business," our rabbis, of
blessed memory, have inferred that only the business of
man is forbidden, but not matters of Heaven . . . . Hence,
one may attend to matters of public interest on the Sabbath.
For instance, one may visit a governor or an assembly of
officers to plead for the people; for the needs of the public

are tantamount to Heavenly matters. Also, it is permissible
to inquire of a teacher whether he is willing to teach a child
Scripture or even a trade. For teaching a trade is a religious
duty, because the lack of a trade wherewith to earn a
livelihood often leads to theft (Shab. 150a) . . . .

The precept to observe the Sabbath may be disregarded
when there is danger to human life. And that is the case
with all the precepts of the Torah. Hence it is mandatory
to desecrate the Sabbath for the sake of one who is dangerously ill . . . . If the sick person will not allow such desecration, he should be compelled to submit. For it is very
iniquitous to be over-pious and refuse to be cured because
the cure necessitates the violation of a prohibition. Concerning such a person it is said: "And surely your blood of
your lives will I require" (Gen. 9.5). Indeed, violating the
Sabbath under such circumstances is not only permissible
but praiseworthy. Even if a non-Jew is present, the work
should be done by an Israelite. And he who disregards the
Sabbath for the sake of one dangerously ill, even if his
exertions prove fruitless, has earned a reward. Thus if the
physician orders a fig, and nine men run and each plucks a
fig, they have all earned a reward from the Lord, blessed
be His name, though the patient recovers from the very
first one. Even when it is doubtful that life is at stake, it is
mandatory to disregard the Sabbath and perform all
necessary work. There is nothing that supersedes the
importance of human life, for the Torah was given only for
life, as it is said, "He shall live by them" (Lev. 18.5). This
is explained to mean that man is to live by the laws and not
die on account of them. The only exceptions to this rule
are the laws prohibiting idolatry, adultery, and murder.
Not to violate these, man is asked to give his life.

Just as it is mandatory to sanctify the coming of the Sabbath over a cup of wine, the *Kiddush,* so is it mandatory to sanctify its going out over a cup of wine, the *Habdalah.* Benedictions should also be pronounced over spices and over the light. Women are in duty bound to hear the *Habdalah* .... When wine cannot be procured, the *Habdalah* may be pronounced over any other beverage except water.

The conclusion of the Sabbath should be celebrated with appropriate hymns and bright lights so that the Sabbath may depart as befits a queen. The name of Elijah the Prophet should be invoked, and prayers recited for his coming with the glad tidings of redemption ....

CHAPTER VIII

SABBATH SPICE[1]

תַּבְלִין לְשַׁבָּת

ERNEST RENAN claimed that the Hebrews had no sense of humor. He based his assertion on a study of biblical literature which contains little that is calculated to evoke laughter. Whether this negative evidence is sufficient ground for Renan's conclusion is questionable. Modern Jewish literature, however, both Hebrew and Yiddish, contains ample evidence that the Jew of today is not lacking in a sense of humor. So universal is the appreciation of the comic and the ludicrous among modern Jews that many collections of humorous Jewish anecdotes are current.

A cursory reading of the finest of these collections, the *Sefer ha-Bedihah veha-Hidud*,[2] reveals that one of the significant aspects of Jewish humor is the capacity to laugh even at those things which are generally regarded as holy, to laugh heartily yet not irreverently. The Sabbath, which is one of the holiest institutions in Judaism, has not escaped its share of banter. A number of such humorous anecdotes have been selected from the *Sefer ha-Bedihah veha-Hidud* and translated for this volume. These Sabbath anecdotes along with the "Sabbath Curiosities" will render this book more truly representative of the Jewish concept of holiness without sanctimoniousness.

SABBATH HUMOR

THE *REBBI* WORKS WONDERS

Two *Ḥasidim* were boasting of the miracles of their respective *rebbis*. Said one: "My *rebbi* is a wonder. He can perform miracles like no other. Take this miracle, for instance. It happened once that my *rebbi* was traveling to a distant town. While he was on the highway a storm suddenly gathered. Lightning flashed; thunder rent the heavens; and the rain came down in torrents. The *rebbi* stood in danger, God forbid, of drowning. Whereupon he performed a miracle. He put forth his hands and, lo! the rain fell to the right of him; and the rain fell to the left of him; but in the middle, where the *rebbi* was riding, it was perfectly dry."

"Oh, that's nothing," said the other *Ḥasid.* "Let me tell you of a miracle that my *rebbi* performed. It happened once that my *rebbi* was traveling to a distant town. It was on a Friday, and the *rebbi* had expected to reach town long before sundown. But the driver had miscalculated the distance, and suddenly the *rebbi* realized that dusk had fallen and that night was quickly coming on. He saw that he was in danger, God forbid, of violating the holy Sabbath. Whereupon the *rebbi* performed a great miracle. He put forth his hands, and, lo! it was Sabbath to the right of him and Sabbath to the left of him, but in the center, where the *rebbi* was driving, it was the middle of the week."

HOW TO SUPPORT A SON-IN-LAW

Friday evening after services one of the well-to-do members of the congregation invited a poor wayfarer to be his Sabbath guest. On the way home, the host noticed that another poor Jew was following them. Turning to his Sabbath guest he asked: "Who is that following us?"

The Sabbath guest answered: "It is all right. I invited him. He is my son-in-law and I promised him five years' support."

A SMALL JEW WITH A BIG STOMACH

Friday evening after the services a wealthy man invited a poor man to be his Sabbath guest. This poor Sabbath guest happened to be a puny fellow, but he ate voraciously. The host, observing the fellow's voracious appetite, remarked:

"I am surprised that so small a man should have so big a stomach."

"That's not surprising," said the Sabbath guest. "It is just because I am so small that I have so big a stomach. You see, when a man is about to be born an angel suspends before him a line of stomachs — some short, some long — and tells him to pick his own. A tall chap can reach up to the short ones, while a little fellow, like me, can reach only the long ones. That's why the stomach of a short man is so much bigger than the stomach of a tall man."

FULFILLING A COMMANDMENT

A poor man was the Sabbath guest of a rich one. At the table he ate so voraciously and with such vigor that perspiration streamed down his face. The host, noticing the beads of sweat on the fellow's brow, said: "My dear guest, why do you work so hard?"

"Because," answered the Sabbath guest, "I am trying to fulfill the Commandment 'In the sweat of thy face shalt thou eat bread' " (Gen. 3.19).

WINE FOR *KIDDUSH* AND *HABDALAH*

Beryl complained to his friend Shmeryl:

"Every Friday I buy a whole bottle of wine for *Shabbos*. There is enough for *Kiddush*, but I run short for *Habdalah*." Thereupon Shmeryl advised him to buy two bottles.

Next week Beryl again complained: "I bought two bottles. I had enough for *Kiddush* and again ran short for *Habdalah*." Whereupon Shmeryl advised him to buy three bottles.

Sometime later, when the two friends met, Shmeryl asked: "Well, Beryl, do you find the three bottles enough?"

"Yes," said Beryl, "I make the three do. But I do not wait with the *Habdalah* till Saturday night. I recite the *Habdalah* right after the *Kiddush*."

THE SUPERSTITION OF SABBATH OBSERVANCE

A former East-Side Jew, newly rich and relieved of his orthodoxy, rushed into a Jewish bookshop to buy an amulet for his new-born child.

"Sorry," said the storekeeper's wife, "the store is closed on *Shabbos*, and my husband is in the synagogue."

The Jew hastened to the synagogue, ferreted out the storekeeper, and demanded that an amulet be sold to him.

"I am very sorry," replied the storekeeper; "I transact no business on *Shabbos*."

"What!" shouted our freethinking brother, "because of your superstition of Sabbath observance my child is to go without an amulet for a whole day?"

A SUCCESSFUL SERMON

A *Maggid* (preacher) once delivered a fiery sermon against Sabbath-breakers, warning them of the dire punishment that awaited them in the next world. On the following day he went from house to house for the contributions he was wont to collect for his preaching. In one such house there lived the most notorious of the Sabbath-breakers. He kept his store open every Sabbath day. To the *Maggid*'s surprise the man welcomed him heartily and gave him a large contribution.

"God be praised," said the *Maggid*, "that He has turned your heart toward repentance, and that you are turning from the evil of desecrating God's holy day."

"Oh, no," answered the storekeeper. "My generosity is not born of repentance. I am grateful to you for your sermon because it will induce other storekeepers to close shop on the Sabbath, and I'll have at least one day in the week without business competition."

THE THREE WHO FORGOT

Three "emancipated" young Jews were surreptitiously enjoying a cigarette on a Sabbath afternoon, and were caught in the act by a pious old neighbor.

"My sons," said the old man, deeply hurt, "have you forgotten that today is the Sabbath?"

"Yes," said one, "I did forget that today is the Sabbath."

"And you," demanded the old man of the second one, "did you, too, forget?"

"No," replied the offender, "I remembered that today is the Sabbath, but I forgot that it is forbidden to smoke on the Sabbath."

"And how about you?" asked the old man of the third. "What did you forget?"

"I forgot to pull down the shades," answered the third.

SMOKING PROHIBITED

A small-town talmudic student, a freethinker, stole forth beyond the city gates one Sabbath afternoon to enjoy a *Shabbos* cigarette. While passing a soldiers' barracks, the sentinel called to him:

"Hey, there, smoking is forbidden!"

"Oh, yes, we know those Orthodox views," replied the student, "but I am emancipated!"

YOU CALL THAT BUSINESS?

A small-town Jew was visiting a large city. While on his way to the synagogue on Saturday morning he noticed with bitterness that Jewish stores were open. And as he passed one of the stores a "puller" called to him:

"Suits at half price, Mister, at half price."

The pious Jew retorted in anger: "Isn't it enough that you are doing business on the Sabbath? Must you shout it in public?"

"Doing business, did you say?" shouted the storekeeper. "I'm losing five dollars on each suit, and you call it 'doing business'?"

FOOLISH MERCHANTS

A small-town Jew, coming home from a visit to a large city, was telling of the marvels he had seen, concluding with the comment:

"The Jews in the city are all Sabbath-breakers. I spent five Sabbaths there and on all of them the stores were open."

"The fools!" laughed a simpleton. "What's the good of keeping the stores open when trading on the Sabbath is forbidden?"

CARRYING A BURDEN ON *SHABBOS*

An over-pious Jew, taking a Sabbath afternoon stroll, observed another Jew drawing a handkerchief out of his pocket. He walked up to him and indignantly exclaimed: "How dare you carry a handkerchief on *Shabbos*?"

"And how dare you," replied the *Apikoros* (freethinker), "carry a donkey's head on your shoulders both on *Shabbos* and weekdays?"

SABBATH CURIOSITIES

1

The commandment to observe the Sabbath is repeated in the Pentateuch twelve times.

Rabbi Jacob, called the *Ba'al ha-Turim*, points out that the Sabbath Commandment deals with the seventh day of the week, begins with the seventh verse in the Ten Commandments, begins with the seventh letter of the alphabet, and legislates rest for seven categories of creatures (Ex. 20.8–11).

2

According to an ancient rabbinic tradition, ghosts and spirits, both good and evil, owe their disembodied existence to the Sabbath. They were created late Friday afternoon, and before their creation was completed the Sabbath arrived. Hence they remained unfinished — without bodies.

3

Abraham, Isaac, and Jacob observed the Sabbath although they lived prior to the giving of the Torah at Mount Sinai. That is why we read in the Sabbath afternoon service "Abraham was glad, Isaac rejoiced, and Jacob and his sons rested thereon."

4

The Day of Atonement never falls on a Friday or a Sunday because it would greatly inconvenience people by making it necessary to prepare food both for the Sabbath and for the breaking of the fast.

5

Hosha'nah Rabbah (seventh day of *Sukkot*) never falls on the Sabbath.

6

The Greeks called the Jews lazy because they abstained from work every seventh day.

7

Apion, the notorious Alexandrian anti-Semite, who lived in the first century of the Common Era, explained the origin of the Sabbath as follows: "When the Jews had traveled a six days' journey, they had buboes in their groins; and on this account it was that they rested on the seventh day . . . and called that day the Sabbath, for that malady of buboes on their groin was named Sabbatosis by the Egyptians."[3]

8

"It was a common belief among the ancient Romans that the Jews fasted on the Sabbath, because no smoke was seen from their houses on that day."[4]

9

"Marcion[5] proclaimed a fast on the Sabbath in opposition to the God of the Jews who created this evil world of matter, because this God rested on the seventh day."[6]

10

One of the privileges that King James I of Aragon conferred upon the Jews of Valencia in 1262 provided that "Jews who were imprisoned for non-payment of taxes were to be set free on . . . Fridays at nightfall and be allowed full freedom on the day and night of the Sabbath . . ., on condition that they gave formal assurance of their return to the place of detention the following morning."[7]

11

"In the Ballot Act of 1872 special provision is made to enable voters 'of the Jewish persuasion' who object on religious grounds to mark the ballot paper on the Jewish Sabbath to have, 'if the poll be taken on Saturday,' their votes recorded by the presiding officer in the same way as votes given by persons incapacitated by blindness or other physical cause."[8]

12

Dr. David G. Mandelbaum, in his article "The Jewish Way of Life in Cochin,"[9] records the following tradition current among the Jews of Cochin, India: "While the Jews could scarcely defend themselves against great armies of marauders, it is clear that they were proficient in arms. The two great opponents of the Malabar coast, the Raja of Cochin and the Zamorin of Calicut, each had a brigade of Jewish soldiers in their forces. In 1550, the allied Portuguese and Cochin armies fought against the Raja of Vatakkenkur. The Portuguese captain planned to attack the enemy on a Saturday, but the Raja of Cochin objected, because on that day the Jews would not fight and they 'were the best warriors he had raised'."

13

The story of the Sabbath river, Sambatyon, that casts up stones on the six days of the week but rests on the seventh, is corroborated by the historian Josephus. The only

difficulty with this corroboration is that the river, according
to Josephus, rests on the six days of the week and flows
only on the Sabbath. Furthermore, his evidence is based
on hearsay.[10]

There is also a legend regarding a certain fish that rests
on the Sabbath. Rabbi David Kimḥi, called the *ReDaK*,
says in his commentary on the Bible: "It is claimed that
there is a certain fish in the ocean that does not swim on
the Sabbath, and rests all the day near the dry land or
near a rock."

14

One rabbinic tradition has it that the *Ma'ariv* service on
Saturday night is prolonged as an act of pity for the souls
of the wicked who are free on the Sabbath from their
expiatory suffering and resume their expiation at the end
of the Sabbath. The service is deliberately prolonged so as
to delay their return to suffering.

15

The Roman Catholic Church, sixteen centuries after the
Nicaean Council, still retains the Sabbath of the Decalogue
on its calendar, marking Sunday as the Lord's Day and
Saturday as the Sabbath.

16

"SHAMBAT"[11]

A Soviet newspaper, which reached me quite by accident
more than a year after its appearance, contains the news
item that Prof. Yegiazaroff recently died in Kazan at a ripe
old age. He was widely known in the field of jurisprudence
(for fifty years he was a professor of Roman Law in various

Russian universities), but in my mind his name is linked with a conversation I had with him years ago, a conversation which left me with a lasting impression of mystery and romance.

I used to see Prof. Yegiazaroff quite frequently in Kiev in 1920. Although his appearance was somewhat Oriental, I seldom thought about his national origin. He intimated to me several times, half-jokingly, that he had a secret to tell me. He was not certain whether the occasion for revealing it would ever arise. This remark, accompanied as it was by a foxy grin, used to arouse an inner disquiet in me in those nerve-wracking days of the Civil War. In my heart of hearts I bore him a secret grudge. It was a brutal form of humor, unbefitting a man of his age and position, to tell someone that you had a secret to tell him, but that you might have to take it along to the grave with you.

Towards the end of the year I had occasion to visit him in his office at the University on a matter of business. I had succeeded in persuading the University — may the God of Social Revolution spare my soul! — that it should "draft" me for a scientific investigation in Podolia. The scientific mission was 90% pure fiction, and for the 10% which had some substance, I was eminently unprepared. What I was really after was a chance to visit several towns in Podolia where contrabandists would smuggle me across the Dniester into Rumania. Yegiazaroff was one of the members of the academic committee that had to pass on the value of the scientific project. Otherwise, as a member of the Red Army, I would not be allowed to leave the city. I came to him for his signature.

Yegiazaroff, I recall clearly, read the document over two or three times, thought for a while, then took up his pen and signed his name in one quick stroke. He handed me the paper and said, laughing heartily:

"Now that you have my signature I can speak frankly. You are, if you will forgive me, a faker. This hoax of a scientific mission may sound convincing to the ears of the gullible Russian boobs, but you can't put this over on me. I'm an Asiatic, too. I know, my good friend, that you're running away. The climate of the Socialist Fatherland doesn't seem to suit you. You're succumbing to the lure of the decayed West. To tell the truth, I too would gladly rot for the rest of my days in the 'Capitalist Quagmire,' but a man of my age is no longer fit to steal across frontiers.... Now that I have consciously committed a sin against His Majesty the Proletariat in Power, you must promise to visit me this week, so that we may spend an evening together before you start out on your dangerous journey."

* * *

The house, comfortably furnished in the old style (why the authorities did not requisition it I still do not know), had a spacious dining room heavily hung with hairy Caucasian tapestry. On the table stood a round, smartly polished *samovar*, steam pouring from it and filling the room with a tempting aroma, and all sorts of delicacies, which had long disappeared from everyday consumption: three different kinds of jelly, sheep's cheese, freshly baked rolls, made of the best-grade flour, a whole salami, a bottle of aged wine....

After the table was cleared, late in the evening, we were finally alone. My host sat me down in a comfortable drawing-room chair, and began his "inquisition."

"Are you a Jew?"

"Of course I am. You know that."

"Do you remember the Bible?"

"Yes, I do."

"I believe you know Hebrew, too?"

"Yes, I can read the Hebrew texts."

"Well, tell me, then, what happened to the Ten Tribes of Israel?"

"I'm sure I don't know. Some believe that the English are the ten lost tribes. Others maintain that the American Indians are. I have even heard it suggested that the Japanese are Israelites gone astray."

"Then you admit that you don't know the answer to my question . . . ."

"No, I'm afraid that belongs to the many things I don't know."

"Well, then, I'll ask you a simpler question. I know you have some knowledge of philology. Perhaps you can tell me the linguistic origin of my name, Yegiazaroff? I'll give you five minutes. If I don't get an answer in five minutes, I'll know that you're not much of a philologist. A philologist, my good friend, is above all a detective. If you don't have the nose of a secret agent or of a bloodhound, you'll never get anywhere in that field."

The five tense minutes passed. I felt confused and quite foolish. His harsh examiner's tone left me completely bewildered.

"You should be ashamed of yourself, you, a Hebrew scholar," he suddenly said, breaking the oppressive silence. "It probably didn't even occur to you, that I bear a Hebrew name. The suffix '-off' is obviously Russian: if Napoleon Bonaparte had settled in Russia, the name in his passport would probably have been 'Bonapartoff.' My real name is *Yehi-'Ezer* (in Hebrew: 'May salvation come'). In Armenian it became 'Yehiazr,' or 'Yehiazar.' Since in Russian there is no letter 'h' and every 'h' is pronounced 'g,' the name became 'Yegiazar'."

Here, I thought, was the beginning of the secret that he had been teasing me with for some time. I said:

"You mean to say, then, that you are an Armenian?"

"How do you like that," he burst out laughing and slapped my back with the broad gesture of a friend and teacher. "Because I have a Hebrew name, I am an Armenian. And why not a Jew, one of the seed of Abraham?" (He uttered the last phrase in its Hebrew original.)

He then began telling me things, each stranger than the other.... He rose from his seat, stood as erect as his plumpish figure would allow and went through the motions of a formal presentation:

"I am a Shambat, a true, full-blooded Shambat. Don't you know what this means? I'm sure you're familiar with the word *Sambatyon*, which appears so frequently in Jewish folklore. A Shambat is an Armenian of Hebrew origin, a descendant of a Hebrew tribe which settled in Armenia back in the days of the Assyrian King Sennacherib. It lived on the banks of a river which was later called Shambat, or Sambatyon, because the inhabitants of its shores were known for their weekly observance of the *Shabbat*."

He stepped over to the bookcase, took out a book, which he himself had written, and pointed to two parallel columns: "Here you have, in one column, the agrarian laws in the Code of Moses, and in the other column — the parallel laws of the Armenian pagans. It is the very same code. These are Jewish laws which the Armenians took over and formulated in their own manner. Remember, these laws were adopted centuries before the Christian era. Remember, too, that the first signs of Christianity appeared among the Armenians only in the Third Century. How then, does the Bible come to pagan Armenia? How did they get to know the agrarian laws in the Mosaic code?

Through the tribe of the Shambats, whom Sennacherib exiled from Palestine!

"Does it sound fantastic? Read the story of the noble family Bagratuni in the works of our classical historian, Moses of Horen. Generation after generation, the Bagratuni family enjoyed the privilege of crowning the Armenian kings. Moses of Horen proves that they were descended from Jews — from the Shambats. But the Shambats all turned Christian, when Christianity engulfed Armenia. I don't know whether they did it of their own free will, or out of compulsion. It may well be that the first Jewish Marranos lived in Armenia in the days of Gregory. But Christianity betrays more Old Testament influence in Armenia than anywhere else . . . .

"I've told you already," he continued, "that I'm a Shambat, a Christian Armenian of Jewish origin. If I were to use your terminology, I would say that the Shambats *did not assimilate*. We don't advertise the fact — it is one of our family secrets — that a Shambat always marries another Shambat. Racially we are perhaps the purest Jews in the world. There are special, hardly visible signs, by means of which one Shambat recognizes another. We are a community within a community, with traditions of our own. Many Shambat families secretly teach their children Hebrew. We have no special teachers for that purpose, but every father who knows the language makes it his ambition to teach his children the Bible in the original. My father, for example, knew even the Talmud. He possessed a fine library of Hebrew theological books. In my childhood days, I remember, a rabbi from Persia would visit us from time to time and would spend long hours studying from those books. My mother used to prepare kosher meals, whenever a guest deserved particular respect. It is a pity that the library was destroyed: a band of Kurds once attacked our country home, and put fire to it together with all of its contents . . ."

It was getting late. I rose to take leave. He clasped my hand for a long time, and would not let me go. He had a request to make:

"First, please take along my book about the agrarian legislation in pagan Armenia. If you succeed in getting it across the border with you, please send it as my modest gift to the National Library in Jerusalem. And secondly: a university will probably soon be established in Jerusalem. Please bear me in mind. One of these days I will most likely go back to Armenia and become a professor in the Armenian University . . . . I'm an Asiatic, and my oriental blood is calling me back to Armenia, even to Persia. What do Kiev, Kazan or Moscow mean to me? My place is in Echmiajin, in Nahishevan. Spiritually I'm an Armenian, but somewhere in my mental make-up is hidden a Jew, an ancient Hebrew, and it seems to me at times that if I were placed somewhere between Jerusalem and Bethlehem, familiar scents of homeland would come to my nostrils. What is it? Blood? Imagination? Self-delusion? Are the Shambats victims of hypnosis? I don't know what it is, but I know that I'm really of double nationality: Armenian and Jewish . . . . If ever I succeed in escaping to Armenia and if the University of Jerusalem is established, I would like to be considered for a position there. I would then divide my academic year into two: one semester in the Armenian and the other in the Hebrew University . . . ."

* * *

I started on my "scientific" mission about a week after my visit with Professor Yegiazaroff.

I have never heard from him during all these years. I had good reason not to write to him, for my letters would

certainly have caused him much trouble. As I think of
the "secret" he told me, I find it hard to determine where
fact ends and fiction begins .... I know that whenever I
meet an Armenian, I want to look into his eyes in search
of some hidden secret. Sometimes I am even tempted to
ask him, discreetly: "Are you perhaps a Shambat?"

How old was Yegiazaroff when he died? Very old, probably near ninety. But it seems he never went back to
Armenia. Nor did he ever go "back" to Palestine ....

BOOK TWO

THE SABBATH IN LITERATURE, ART AND MUSIC

CHAPTER IX

THE SABBATH IN THE BIBLE

BIBLICAL commentators frequently point out that the command to observe the Sabbath is repeated in the Bible twelve times, the most important being in the Decalogue. The Sabbath is thus singled out in the Bible as the most important of all holy days. It is described not only as a memorial of Creation and of the exodus from Egypt, but as the "sign of the covenant between God and Israel."

The biblical references to the Sabbath are either in the form of legislation such as the command not to kindle a fire on the Sabbath, or exhortations such as the prophet Jeremiah's repeated pleas for Sabbath observance, or historical accounts such as Nehemiah's enforcement of Sabbath observance. All these references reveal the Sabbath as an old institution, generally recognized and widely honored, but still in a state of development, still far from the form it assumed in rabbinic times. It is only toward the end of the Bible, in the books of Ezra and Nehemiah, that we discover a tendency to associate the Sabbath with complete physical rest and general intellectual stimulation.

Although most of the details of Sabbath observance are post-biblical in origin, the general nature it was destined to assume, and the central role it was destined to play in Jewish life are fully rooted in the Bible, as the few excerpts in this chapter amply illustrate.

GOD RESTED ON THE SEVENTH DAY AND HALLOWED IT[1]

And the heaven and the earth were finished, and all the host of them. And on the seventh day God finished His work which He had made; and He rested on the seventh day from all His work which He had made. And God blessed the seventh day, and hallowed it; because that in it He rested from all His work which God in creating had made (Gen. 2.1–3).

THE FOURTH COMMANDMENT

Remember the sabbath day, to keep it holy. Six days shalt thou labour, and do all thy work; but the seventh day is a sabbath unto the Lord thy God, in it thou shalt not do any manner of work, thou, nor thy son, nor thy daughter, nor thy man-servant, nor thy maid-servant, nor thy cattle, nor thy stranger that is within thy gates; for in six days the Lord made heaven and earth, the sea, and all that in them is, and rested on the seventh day; wherefore the Lord blessed the sabbath day, and hallowed it (Ex. 20.8–11).

Observe the sabbath day, to keep it holy, as the Lord thy God commanded thee. Six days shalt thou labour, and do all thy work; but the seventh day is a sabbath unto the Lord thy God, in it thou shalt not do any manner of work, thou, nor thy son, nor thy daugher, nor thy man-servant, nor thy maid-servant, nor thine ox, nor thine ass, nor any of thy cattle, nor thy stranger that is within thy gates; that thy man-servant and thy maid-servant may rest as well as thou. And thou shalt remember that thou wast a servant in the land of Egypt, and the Lord thy God brought thee out thence by a mighty hand and by an outstretched arm; therefore the Lord thy God commanded thee to keep the sabbath day (Deut. 5.12–15).

FOOD FOR THE SABBATH MUST BE PREPARED
ON FRIDAY

And it came to pass that on the sixth day they gathered twice as much bread (manna), two omers for each one; and all the rulers of the congregation came and told Moses. And he said unto them: "This is that which the Lord hath spoken: To-morrow is a solemn rest, a holy sabbath unto the Lord. Bake that which ye will bake, and seethe that which ye will seethe; and all that remaineth over lay up for you to be kept until the morning." And they laid it up till the morning, as Moses bade; and it did not rot, neither was there any worm therein. And Moses said: "Eat that to-day; for to-day is a sabbath unto the Lord; to-day ye shall not find it in the field. Six days ye shall gather it; but on the seventh day is the sabbath, in it there shall be none." And it came to pass on the seventh day, that there went out some of the people to gather, and they found none. And the Lord said unto Moses: "How long refuse ye to keep My commandments and My laws? See that the Lord hath given you the sabbath; therefore He giveth you on the sixth day the bread of two days; abide ye every man in his place, let no man go out of his place on the seventh day." So the people rested on the seventh day (Ex. 16.22–30).

THE SABBATH, A SIGN BETWEEN GOD AND
ISRAEL

Wherefore the children of Israel shall keep the sabbath, to observe the sabbath throughout their generations, for a perpetual covenant. It is a sign between Me and the children of Israel for ever; for in six days the Lord made heaven and earth, and on the seventh day He ceased from work and rested (Ex. 31.16–17).

NO FIRE TO BE KINDLED ON THE SABBATH

And Moses assembled all the congregation of the children of Israel, and said unto them: "These are the words which the Lord hath commanded, that ye should do them. Six days shall work be done, but on the seventh day there shall be to you a holy day, a sabbath of solemn rest to the Lord; whosoever doeth any work therein shall be put to death. Ye shall kindle no fire throughout your habitations upon the sabbath day" (Ex. 35.1–3).

THE SABBATH, A DAY OF SOLEMN REST AND HOLY CONVOCATION

And the Lord spoke unto Moses, saying: Speak unto the children of Israel, and say unto them:

The appointed seasons of the Lord, which ye shall proclaim to be holy convocations, even these are My appointed seasons. Six days shall work be done; but on the seventh day is a sabbath of solemn rest, a holy convocation; ye shall do no manner of work; it is a sabbath unto the Lord in all your dwellings (Lev. 23.1–3).

INIQUITY ALONG WITH SOLEMN ASSEMBLY GOD HATETH

When ye come to appear before Me,
Who hath required this at your hand,
To trample My courts?
Bring no more vain oblations;

It is an offering of abomination unto Me;
New moon and sabbath, the holding of convocations —
I cannot endure iniquity along with the solemn assembly
(Isa. 1.12–13).

THE REWARD OF HONORING THE SABBATH

If thou turn away thy foot because of the sabbath,
From pursuing thy business on My holy day;
And call the sabbath a delight,
And the holy of the Lord honourable;
And shalt honour it, not doing thy wonted ways,
Nor pursuing thy business, nor speaking thereof;
Then shalt thou delight thyself in the Lord,
And I will make thee to ride upon the high places of the
    earth;
And I will feed thee with the heritage of Jacob thy father;
For the mouth of the Lord hath spoken it (Isa. 58.13–14).

THE SABBATH, A UNIVERSAL DAY OF WORSHIP

And it shall come to pass,
That from one new moon to another,
And from one sabbath to another,
Shall all flesh come to worship before Me,
Saith the Lord (Isa. 66.23).

JERUSALEM'S GLORY AND DOWNFALL DEPEND
ON THE HALLOWING OF THE SABBATH

And it shall come to pass, if ye diligently hearken unto
Me, saith the Lord, to bring in no burden through the gates
of this city on the sabbath day, but to hallow the sabbath

day, to do no work therein; then shall there enter in by the
gates of this city kings and princes sitting upon the throne of
David, riding in chariots and on horses, they, and their
princes, the men of Judah, and the inhabitants of Jerusalem;
and this city shall be inhabited for ever.

But if ye will not hearken unto Me to hallow the sabbath
day, and not to bear a burden and enter in at the gates of
Jerusalem on the sabbath day; then will I kindle a fire in
the gates thereof, and it shall devour the palaces of Jerusalem, and it shall not be quenched (Jer. 17.24, 25, 27).

ISRAEL'S CONTINUED PROFANATION
OF THE SABBATH

So I caused them to go forth out of the land of Egypt,
and brought them into the wilderness. And I gave them
My statutes, and taught them Mine ordinances, which if
a man do, he shall live by them. Moreover also I gave them
My sabbaths, to be a sign between Me and them, that they
might know that I am the Lord that sanctify them. But
the house of Israel rebelled against Me in the wilderness;
they walked not in My statutes, and they rejected Mine
ordinances, which if a man do, he shall live by them, and
My sabbaths they greatly profaned; then I said I would
pour out My fury upon them in the wilderness, to consume
them. Nevertheless Mine eye spared them from destroying
them, neither did I make a full end of them in the wilderness.
And I said unto their children in the wilderness: Walk ye
not in the statutes of your fathers, neither observe their
ordinances, nor defile yourselves with their idols; I am the
Lord your God; walk in My statutes, and keep Mine ordinances, and do them; and hallow My sabbaths, and they
shall be a sign between Me and you, that ye may know that

I am the Lord your God. But the children rebelled against Me; they walked not in My statutes, neither kept Mine ordinances to do them, which if a man do, he shall live by them; they profaned My sabbaths; then I said I would pour out My fury upon them, to spend My anger upon them in the wilderness. Nevertheless I withdrew My hand, and wrought for My name's sake, that it should not be profaned in the sight of the nations, in whose sight I brought them forth (Ezek. 20.10–13, 17–22).

NEHEMIAH'S ENFORCEMENT OF SABBATH OBSERVANCE

In those days saw I in Judah some treading winepresses on the sabbath, and bringing in heaps of corn, and lading asses therewith; as also wine, grapes, and figs, and all manner of burdens, which they brought into Jerusalem on the sabbath day; and I forewarned them in the day wherein they sold victuals. There dwelt men of Tyre also therein, who brought in fish, and all manner of ware, and sold on the sabbath unto the children of Judah, and in Jerusalem. Then I contended with the nobles of Judah, and said unto them: 'What evil thing is this that ye do, and profane the sabbath day? Did not your fathers thus, and did not our God bring all this evil upon us, and upon this city? yet ye bring more wrath upon Israel by profaning the sabbath.'

And it came to pass that, when the gates of Jerusalem began to be dark before the sabbath, I commanded that the doors should be shut, and commanded that they should not be opened till after the sabbath; and some of my servants set I over the gates, that there should no burden be brought in on the sabbath day. So the merchants and sellers of all

kind of ware lodged without Jerusalem once or twice. Then
I forewarned them, and said unto them: 'Why lodge ye
about the wall? if ye do so again, I will lay hands on you.'
From that time forth came they no more on the sabbath.
And I commanded the Levites that they should purify
themselves, and that they should come and keep the gates,
to sanctify the sabbath day (Nehem. 13.15–22).

CHAPTER X

THE SABBATH IN JUDAEO-HELLENISTIC LITERATURE

THE problems of modern Jewish life are not altogether modern. The Jews of 2,000 years ago were already a dispersed people faced with problems arising from their minority status. True, they were a larger minority within the Roman Empire than are the Jews of today within any state. But their strength of numbers only aroused greater suspicions in those who saw in the Jews a large alien group determined to live in accordance with alien traditions and convictions. Many Gentiles suspected, feared, and hated this alien group, and the result was that "almost every note in the cacophony of medieval and modern anti-Semitism was sounded by the ancient writers."[1]

Equally disturbing was the problem arising from the process of Hellenization of Diaspora Jewry. The Jews not only spoke Greek as their native tongue but forgot their Hebrew to such an extent that the Bible had to be translated even for synagogue use. And so much were they influenced by Greek culture that they found it necessary to give the Bible the sanction of Greek philosophy.

These problems stimulated a number of literary men among the Jews to write in defense of their people and their culture. These writers sought to deepen the Jewish faith in God, to defend the Jews against their detractors, and to demonstrate the superiority of Judaism to paganism. Among the outstanding Judaeo-Hellenistic writers was

Philo Judaeus, a pious Alexandrian Jew, who lived in the first half of the first century. In his philosophical writings Philo reinterpreted the Bible by the allegorical method, and harmonized its teachings with Greek philosophy. Equally famous was Flavius Josephus, a Palestinian Jew, who lived during the second half of the first century. Josephus played an inglorious role in the war of the Jews against Rome during the years 67-70 C. E. But his fame rests upon his historical works, and his defense of the Jews entitled *Against Apion*. Both Philo and Josephus were Pharisees by conviction, and they enthusiastically praised the Sabbath, as is evident from the excerpts chosen for this chapter.

Among the other literary works produced during the Hellenistic period—though in no sense a Hellenistic book—was the book I Maccabees which gives an account of the Jewish struggle against the Syrian Greeks who had decreed the extermination of Judaism. The Maccabees, who were the leaders of the heroic rebellion, had to decide whether it was permissible to desecrate the Sabbath in self-defense. This problem and its solution are discussed in the excerpt from I Maccabees.

These and many other Judaeo-Hellenistic writers not only scrupulously observed the Sabbath, but defended it against its detractors and extolled it for their own and for future generations.

THE MACCABEES DECIDE TO DEFEND
THEMSELVES ON THE SABBATH[1]

Then many that sought after justice and judgment went down into the wilderness, to dwell there: both they, and their children, and their wives, and their cattle; because afflictions increased sore upon them. Now when it was told the king's servants,[3] and the host that was at Jerusalem, in the city of David, that certain men, who had broken the king's commandment, were gone down into the secret places in the wilderness, they pursued after them a great number, and having overtaken them, they camped against them, and made war against them on the sabbath day. And they said unto them, "Let that which ye have done hitherto suffice; come forth, and do according to the commandment of the king, and ye shall live." But they said, "We will not come forth, neither will we do the king's commandment, to profane the sabbath day." So then they gave them the battle with all speed. Howbeit they answered them not, neither cast they a stone at them, nor stopped the places where they lay hid; but said, "Let us die all in our innocency: heaven and earth shall testify for us, that ye put us to death wrongfully." So they rose up against them in battle on the sabbath, and they slew them, with their wives and children, and their cattle, to the number of a thousand people.

Now when Mattathias and his friends understood hereof, they mourned for them right sore. And one of them said to another, "If we all do as our brethren have done, and fight not for our lives and laws against the heathen, they will now quickly root us out of the earth." At that time therefore they decreed, saying "Whosoever shall come to make battle with us on the sabbath day, we will fight against him; neither will we die all, as our brethren that were murdered in the secret places" (I Macc. 2.29-41).

THE BIRTHDAY OF THE WORLD[4]

But after the whole world had been completed according to the perfect nature of the number of six, God hallowed the day following, the seventh, praising it, and calling it holy. For that day is the festival, not of one city or one country, but of all the earth; a day which alone it is right to call the day of festival for all people, and the birthday of the world (Philo Judaeus, "On the Creation of the World," 30).

THE SABBATH, A DAY OF CONTEMPLATION
AND SELF-IMPROVEMENT

The fourth commandment has reference to the sacred seventh day, that it may be passed in a sacred and holy manner... for the sacred historian says, that the world was created in six days, and that on the seventh day God desisted from His works, and began to contemplate what He had so beautifully created; therefore He commanded the beings also who were destined to live in this state, to imitate God in this particular also,... applying themselves to their works for six days, but desisting from them and philosophizing on the seventh day, and devoting their lesiure to the contemplation of the things of nature, and considering whether in the preceding six days they have done anything which has not been holy, bringing their conduct before the judgment-seat of the soul, and subjecting it to a scrutiny, and making themselves give an account of all the things which they have said or done....

Moreover, the seventh day is also an example from which you may learn the propriety of studying philosophy; as on that day, it is said, God beheld the works which He had made; so that you also may yourself contemplate the works of nature, and all the separate circumstances which contribute towards happiness.

Let us not pass by such a model of the most excellent ways of life, the practical and the contemplative; but let us always keep our eyes fixed upon it, and stamp a visible image and representation of it on our own minds, making our mortal nature resemble, as far as possible, His immortal one, in respect of saying and doing what is proper (Philo Judaeus, "On the Ten Commandments," 20).

THE SABBATH, A DAY OF STUDY AND REFLECTION[5]

(An excerpt from the speech of Nicolaus, pleading before the Emperor Agrippa in behalf of the Jews of Ionia)

. . . And none of our customs are inhuman, but all tend to piety, and are devoted to the preservation of justice; nor do we conceal those injunctions of ours by which we govern our lives, since they are memorials of piety, and are of a friendly conversation among men. And the seventh day we set apart from labour; it is dedicated to the learning of our customs and laws because we think it proper to reflect on them, as well as on any other good thing, in order that we may avoid all sin. If any one therefore examine into our observances, he will find that they are good in themselves, and that they are also ancient (Flavius Josephus, *Antiquities of the Jews*, XVI, 2.3).

AUGUSTUS EXEMPTS THE JEWS FROM COURT DUTIES ON THE SABBATH

(An excerpt from the proclamation issued by Augustus in reply to complaints by the Jews of Asia Minor)

Caesar Augustus, high priest and tribune of the people, ordains thus: Since the nation of the Jews hath been found grateful to the Roman people, not only at this time, but in time past also, and chiefly Hyrcanus the high priest, under my father, Caesar the emperor, it seemed good to me and my counsellors, according to the sentence and oath of the people of Rome, that the Jews have liberty to make use of their own customs, according to the law of their forefathers, as they made use of them under Hyrcanus the high priest of the Almighty God; and that their sacred money be not touched, but be sent to Jerusalem, and that it be committed to the care of the receivers at Jerusalem; and that they be not obliged to go before any judge on the sabbath day, nor on the day of the preparation to it, after the ninth hour. . . (Flavius Josephus, *Antiquities of the Jews*, XVI, 6.2).

ON THE SABBATH JEWS BATTLED ONLY IN SELF-DEFENSE

(From the account of Pompey's siege of the
Temple Mount during the reign of Hyrcanus)

But Pompey himself filled up the ditch that was on the north side of the temple, and the entire valley also, the army itself being obliged to carry the materials for that purpose. And indeed it was a hard thing to fill up that valley, by reason of its immense depth, especially as the Jews used all the means possible to repel them from their superior situation; nor had the Romans succeeded in their endeavours, had not Pompey taken notice of the seventh day (on which the Jews abstain from all sorts of work on a religious account) and raised his bank, but restrained his soldiers from fighting on those days; for the Jews only acted defensively on sabbath days. But as soon as Pompey had filled up the valley, he erected high towers upon the bank, and brought those engines which they had fetched from Tyre near to the wall, and tried to batter it down (Flavius Josephus, *Wars of the Jews*, I, 7.3).

THE SABBATIC RIVER

Now Titus Caesar tarried some time at Berytus, as we told you before. He thence removed, and exhibited magnificent shows in all those cities of Syria through which he went, and made use of the captive Jews as public instances of the destruction of that nation. He then saw a river as he went along, of such a nature as deserves to be recorded in history; it runs in the middle between Arcea, belonging to Agrippa's kingdom, and Raphanea. It hath somewhat very peculiar in it; for when it runs, its current is strong, and has plenty of water; after which its springs fail for six days together, and leave its channel dry, as any one may see; after which days it runs on the seventh day as it did before, and as though it had undergone no change at all; it hath also been observed to keep this order perpetually and exactly; whence it is that they call it the Sabbatic River, that name being taken from the sacred seventh day among the Jews (Flavius Josephus, *Wars of the Jews*, VII, 5.1).

JERUSALEM SURRENDERS TO A TYRANT RATHER THAN GIVE BATTLE ON THE SABBATH

(Josephus quotes Agatharchides to prove the
nobility of the Jews)

Agatharchides gives a similar example of what was reported concerning us, and writes thus: "There are a people called Jews, and dwell in a city the strongest of all other cities, which the inhabitants call Jerusalem, and are accustomed to rest on every seventh day; on which times they make no use of their arms, nor meddle with husbandry, nor take care of any affairs of life, but spread out their hands in their holy places, and pray till the evening. Now it came to pass, that when Ptolemy, the son of Lagus, came into this city with his army, that these men, in observing this mad custom of theirs, instead of guarding the city, suffered their country to submit itself to a bitter lord. . . ." Now this our procedure seems a ridiculous thing to Agatharchides, but will appear to such as consider it without prejudice a great thing, and what deserved a great many encomiums; I mean, when certain men constantly prefer the observation of their laws, and their religion towards God, before the preservation of themselves and their country (Flavius Josephus, *Against Apion*, 2.22).

THE INSTITUTION OF THE SABBATH IS BEING ACCEPTED UNIVERSALLY

We have already demonstrated that our laws have been such as have always inspired admiration and imitation among all other men; nay, the earliest Grecian philosophers, though in appearance they observed the laws of their own countries, yet did they, in their actions and their philosophic doctrines, follow our legislator, and instructed men to live sparingly and to have friendly communication one with another. Nay, further, the multitude of mankind itself have had a great inclination of a long time to follow our religious observances; for there is not any city of the Grecians nor any of the barbarians, nor any nation whatsoever, whither our custom of resting on the seventh day hath not come, and by which our fasts and lighting up lamps, and many of our prohibitions as to our food, are not observed; they also endeavour to imitate our mutual concord with one another, and the charitable distribution of our goods, and our diligence in our trades, and our fortitude in undergoing the distresses we are in, on account of our laws; and, what is here a matter of the greatest admiration, our law hath no bait of pleasure to allure men to it, but it prevails by its own force; and as God himself pervades all the world, so hath our law passed through all the world also (Flavius Josephus, *Against Apion*, 2.40).

CHAPTER XI

THE SABBATH IN THE TALMUD
AND THE MIDRASH

DURING the biblical period Sabbath observance was
not yet a universal practice. The institution was
still in the process of development. The Bible, therefore,
in speaking of the Sabbath merely indicated the general
principles of Sabbath observance through rest and joy.
It also indicated the basic purposes of Sabbath observance,
namely, the commemoration of the Creation and the redemption of Israel. The Bible also stressed the function of the
Sabbath as a "sign" between God and Israel.

But in the post-biblical rabbinic literature, the Talmud
and the Midrash, Sabbath observance is no longer a goal
to be achieved. It is an established institution, universally
observed and treasured. General principles no longer suffice.
Merely to teach people to abstain from work, without defining what constitutes work, is to confuse the Sabbath observer. The Talmud, therefore, defines the general principles
enunciated in the Bible and applies them to the actual
situations in life. The Sabbath law as developed in the
Talmud, despite or perhaps because of its minutiae, rendered
the Jewish Sabbath not only a day of complete rest and
relaxation but a day of genuine delight.

The joyous exaltation which the Jew derived from Sabbath
observance constituted the main subject of the non-legal
talmudic discussions dealing with the Sabbath. To the rabbis the Sabbath was a weekly experience which enriched
and sanctified their lives. When they speak of the Sabbath

as a divine gift or as a foretaste of the hereafter, they are not prescribing the manner of Sabbath observance but are describing their own experiences; and their experiences reflect the traditional Jewish regard for the Sabbath for over two millennia.

THE SABBATH IS GOD'S GIFT TO ISRAEL

"That ye may *know* that I am the Lord who sanctify you" (Ex. 31.13). The Holy One, blessed be He, said unto Moses, "I have a precious gift in my treasure house, and its name is Sabbath. I wish to present it to Israel. Go and make it *known* to them" (Shab. 10b).

GOD OBSERVED AND SANCTIFIED THE SABBATH

The Holy One, blessed be He, observed and sanctified the Sabbath, and Israel is likewise obliged to observe and sanctify the Sabbath. Know that it is so! Come and see! when He gave them the manna He gave it to them for forty years on the six days of Creation; but on the Sabbath He did not give it to them . . . . When the people saw that the Sabbath was observed by Him, they also rested, as it is said, "So the people rested on the seventh day" (Ex. 16.30).

"And God blessed the seventh day, and hallowed it" (Gen. 2.3). The Holy One, blessed be He, blessed and hallowed the Sabbath day, and Israel is likewise bound to keep and to hallow the Sabbath day. Hence they said: "Whosoever pronounces benediction and sanctification over the wine on the eve of the Sabbath, his days will be increased in this world and in the world to come, as it is said, 'For by me thy days shall be multiplied' (Prov. 9.11) in this world; 'and the years of thy life shall be increased' (ibid.) in the world to come" (*Pirke de-Rabbi Eliezer*).[1]

THE SABBATH IS ISRAEL'S BRIDE

Rabbi Simeon ben Yoḥai taught: The Sabbath said unto the Holy One, blessed be He, "O Master of the Universe, every living thing created has its mate, and each day has its companion, except me, who am alone!"

The Holy One, blessed be He, answered, "The Congregation of Israel will be your mate."

When the Israelites stood at Mount Sinai, the Holy One, blessed be He, said unto them, "Remember what I said to the Sabbath — 'The Congregation of Israel will be your mate.'" It is with reference to this that the Fourth Commandment reads, "*Remember* the sabbath day, to keep it holy" (Gen. Rab. 11.8).

THE IMPORTANCE OF KEEPING THE SABBATH

The Holy One, blessed be He, said unto Israel, "If you succeed in keeping the Sabbath, I shall account it unto you as if you have kept all the commandments of the Torah. But if you profane the Sabbath, I shall account it unto you as if you have profaned all the commandments of the Torah," as it is written in the Scriptures, "He that keepeth the Sabbath from profaning it [is like unto him who] keepeth his hand from doing all evil" (Isa. 56.2). (Ex. Rab. 25.12).

SABBATH OBSERVERS ARE PARTNERS IN CREATION

Rabbi Hamnuna said, "He who prays on the eve of the Sabbath and recites the verses that begin 'And the heaven and the earth were finished' (Gen. 2.1), the Scriptures speaks of him as though he had become a partner with the Holy One, blessed be He, in the Creation; for it is said, *Va-yekullu* [and the heaven and the earth were finished]; read not *va-yekullu* but *va-yekallu* [and they[2] finished the creation of the heaven and the earth]" (Shab. 119b).

SABBATH OBSERVANCE ATONES FOR SINS

Rabbi Ḥisda said in the name of Mar Ukba, "He who prays on the eve of the Sabbath and recites the verses that begin 'And the heaven and the earth were finished' (Gen. 2.1), receives the blessing of the two ministering angels who accompany man on the Sabbath. They place their hands on his head and say to him, 'and thine iniquity is taken away, and thy sin expiated'" (Isa. 6.7). (Shab. 119b).

THE SABBATH IS AN EVERLASTING INSTITUTION

"It is a sign between Me and the children of Israel for ever" (Ex. 31.17). This implies that the Sabbath will never disappear from Israel. And you thus find that the things for which the Israelites sacrificed their lives, such as the Sabbath, circumcision, and the study of the Torah, were the things which remained with them forever. But the things for which the Israelites did not sacrifice their lives were not preserved in their midst (Mekilta, Shabbata, 1).

SABBATH OBSERVANCE WILL BRING REDEMPTION

Rabbi Johanan said in the name of Rabbi Simeon ben Yoḥai, "If the Israelites were to keep two Sabbaths according to their prescribed law, they would immediately be redeemed; for Scripture speaks concerning those 'that keep My sabbaths' (Isa. 56.4), and immediately thereafter says, 'Even them will I bring to My holy mountain'" (Isa. 56.7). (Shab. 118b).

THE SABBATH IS A DAY OF PUBLIC INSTRUCTION

"And Moses assembled all the congregation of the children of Israel" (Ex. 35.1). Our rabbis said, "From the beginning of the Torah unto its end there is no portion in which is found the phrase 'and he assembled' except here in connection with the Sabbath. This is to teach us that the Holy One, blessed be He, said to Moses, 'Gather large congregations and speak before them about the laws of the Sabbath, so that the leaders of future generations may follow your example and gather congregations every Sabbath in order to teach the words of the Torah, and to decide for the children of their children what is permissible and what is prohibited. By doing so they will glorify My great Name among My children" (Yalkut Shim'oni, Vayakhel).

MOSES INSTITUTED THE SABBATH AS A DAY OF RECUPERATION

We read in the Scriptures, "He [Moses] went out unto his brethren, and looked on their burdens" (Ex. 2.11). Moses saw that the Hebrews had no rest from their labor. He therefore went to Pharaoh and said to him, "If one has a slave and he does not allow the slave to rest at least one day in the week, the slave is apt to die from exhaustion. These Hebrews are your slaves. If you do not let them rest one day in the week, they too may die."

Thereupon Pharaoh said to Moses, "Go and do unto them as you have suggested."

So Moses went and established for them the Sabbath as a day of rest and recuperation (Ex. Rab. 1.28).

SABBATH PREPARATIONS BY HILLEL AND SHAMMAI

It used to be said concerning Shammai the Elder that everything he ate during his whole life was in honor of the Sabbath. If he came across some especially tempting food he would say, "This is for the Sabbath." If later he came

across something better, he would use the first for weekdays
and the second he would set aside for the Sabbath.

But Hillel the Elder had a different custom. All his deeds
were dedicated to Heaven in accordance with the verse
"Blessed be the Lord, day by day" (Ps. 68.20). Thus the
School of Shammai used to say, "Prepare for thy Sabbath
from the first day of the week," while the School of Hillel
used to say, "Blessed be the Lord, day by day" (Bezah 16a).

THE SABBATH ANGELS

It was taught that Rabbi Jose ben Rabbi Judah said,
"Two ministering angels escort man on the eve of Sabbath
from the synagogue to his home. One of these angels is a
good one, and the other an evil one. When the man comes
to his house and finds the Sabbath lights kindled and the
table set, the good angel says, 'May it be thus the next
Sabbath,' and the evil angel, against his will, says 'Amen.'
But if he does not find his home thus prepared, the evil
angel says, 'May it be thus the next Sabbath,' and the good
angel, against his will, says 'Amen'" (Shab. 119b).

SABBATH EXPENSES

Thus taught Rabbi Taḥlifa . . . , "Man's needs are all
apportioned to him during the Ten Days of Penitence,
except his expenditures for Sabbaths, festivals, and the
teaching of the Torah to his children. If a man diminishes
these expenditures, his income is diminished; and if he adds
to them, his income is increased" (Bezah 15b–16a).

SABBATH SPICE

The Roman Emperor [Hadrian] asked Rabbi Joshua ben
Hanania, "Why is it that Sabbath dishes have such a
fragrant scent?"

Rabbi Joshua answered, "We put in a certain spice called Sabbath."

The Emperor said, "Please give me some of that spice."

Rabbi Joshua answered, "It is effective only for those who keep the Sabbath" (Shab. 119a).

A DISCUSSION ON THE SABBATH BETWEEN RABBI AKIBA AND TURNUS RUFUS

Turnus Rufus asked Rabbi Akiba, "What makes the Sabbath more important than all the other days of the week?"

Rabbi Akiba answered, "What makes you more important than other men?"

Turnus Rufus answered, "It is because the Emperor chose to honor me."

"This is equally true of the Sabbath," said Rabbi Akiba. "It is because the King of kings wishes to honor the Sabbath" . . . .

"If God chooses to honor the Sabbath, then why does He not keep the wind from blowing, and the rain from falling, and the grass from growing on the Sabbath?" asked Turnus Rufus.

Rabbi Akiba answered, "In his own courtyard, a man is permitted by law to carry things on the Sabbath from one place to another. So is it with the Holy One, blessed be He. The whole world is His, and His glory is not shared by any other power. Hence He can permit these things even on the Sabbath" (Gen. Rab. 11.5).

THE SABBATH SOUL

Rabbi Simeon ben Lakish said, "On the eve of Sabbath the Holy One, blessed be He, gives man an extra soul. At the conclusion of the Sabbath, this extra soul is taken away from him, as it is written in the Scriptures (on the seventh day) *'Shabat vayinafash'* (Ex. 31.17), i. e., as soon as He finished the Sabbath, it is woe! because the soul is gone"[3] (Bezah 16a).

SAVING LIFE SUPERSEDES THE SABBATH

How do we know that the duty of saving life supersedes the Sabbath? Rabbi Jonathan ben Joseph said, "It is written in the Scriptures 'Ye shall keep the sabbath, for it is holy *unto you*' (Ex. 31.14). This implies that the Sabbath is committed to you, not you to the Sabbath."

Rabbi Simeon ben Menasia said, "It is written in the Scriptures, 'And the children of Israel shall keep the sabbath' (Ex. 31.16). The Torah saith, 'Desecrate for a man one Sabbath, so that he may be able to keep many Sabbaths'" (Yoma 85b).

TYPES OF WORK PERMITTED ON THE SABBATH

Rabbi Samuel ben Naḥmani said in the name of Rabbi Joḥanan, "One may visit theaters and circuses on the Sabbath for the purpose of attending to communal needs."

Moreover, the School of Menasseh taught, "One may make arrangements on the Sabbath for the betrothal of young girls, for the religious instruction of a child (even for the teaching of a trade); for it is written, 'nor pursuing thy business, nor speaking thereof' (Isa. 58.13). *Thy* business is forbidden, but the affairs of Heaven are permitted" (Shab. 150a).

THE REWARD OF HIM WHO DELIGHTS IN THE SABBATH

Rabbi Johanan said in the name of Rabbi Jose, "He who delights in the Sabbath is given an unbounded heritage; for it is written, 'Then shalt thou delight thyself in the Lord, and I will make thee to ride upon the high places of the earth, and I will feed thee with the heritage of Jacob thy father' (Isa. 58.14). Not like Abraham, of whom it is written, 'Arise, walk through the land in the length of it and in the breadth of it' (Gen. 13.17); nor like Isaac, of whom it is written, 'For unto thee, and unto thy seed, I will give all these lands' (Gen. 26.3); but like Jacob, of whom it is written, 'And thou shalt spread abroad to the west, and to the east, and to the north, and to the south' " (Gen. 28.14) . . . .

Rab Judah said in the name of Rab, "He who delights in the Sabbath is granted his heart's desires, for it is said, 'Delight thyself in the Lord; and He shall give thee the petitions of thy heart' (Ps. 37.3). We do not know what this 'delight' refers to; but since it is said, 'And thou shalt call the Sabbath a delight' (Isa. 58.13), we must conclude that it refers to the delight of the Sabbath."

Wherewith does one show his delight in the Sabbath? . . . . Rabbi Hiyya ben Ashi said in the name of Rab, "Even a trifle, if it is prepared in honor of the Sabbath, is called Sabbath delight" (Shab. 118a–118b).

KING DAVID'S SABBATH

Rabbi Judah said in the name of Rab, "What is the implication of the verse 'Lord, make me to know mine end, and the measure of my days, what it is; let me know when I cease to live' (Ps. 39.5)?

"David said to the Holy One, blessed be He, 'Master of the Universe, make me to know mine end.'

" 'It is decreed by Me not to make known to man his end' [i.e., when he is to die], God replied.

" 'And the measure of my days, what is it?' pleaded David.

" 'It is decreed by Me not to make known to man the measure of his days' [i. e., the length of his life].

" 'Let me know when I cease to live.'

" 'You will die on a Sabbath,' answered God.

" 'Let me die on the first day of the week,' pleaded David.

"God said to him, 'Solomon, thy son, is destined to start his reign on that first day of the week, and the reign of one king must not overlap the reign of another even by a thread's breadth.'

" 'Let me die on Friday,' again pleaded David.

"God said unto him, ' "A day in thy courts is better than a thousand" (Ps. 84.11). I prefer one day in which you sit and occupy yourself with the study of the Torah, to a thousand whole-burnt offerings which thy son Solomon will bring upon the altar.'

"Thereafter every Sabbath, King David sat and studied the Torah all day long. On the Sabbath, when King David was to die, the Angel of Death came to him but could not overpower him because David did not cease studying the Torah [and Death has no power over a man while he is occupied with the fulfillment of God's commandments]. The Angel of Death, therefore, resorted to cunning in order to interrupt David's continuous study of the Torah. He went into the garden which was in the rear of David's palace and shook the trees. Thereupon King David went out to see the cause of the noise. But no sooner had he set foot on the steps than they collapsed and he died" (Shab. 30a–30b).

CHAPTER XII

THE SABBATH IN MEDIEVAL
JEWISH LITERATURE

LIFE for the medieval Jew would have been utterly intolerable had he not possessed spiritual "Cities of Refuge" to which he could escape from the horrors of medieval reality. One of these "Cities of Refuge" was the *Beth ha-Midrash*, the house of study, where every Jew carried out his religious duty to "meditate in His law day and night" (Ps. 1. 2). Another was the Synagogue where every Jew prayed for redemption, and in so doing deepened his faith in the ultimate vindication of Israel's suffering. Not the least of these "Cities of Refuge" was the Sabbath when the Jew did not merely recover from the ordeals of the week, but gathered sufficient strength of body and spirit to face the trials of the coming week. On that day he was honored host to the divine Princess Sabbath; and he rejoiced in his exalted role.

Medieval Jewish literature reflected the Jew's high regard for and the deep love of the Sabbath. This is particularly evident in the literature of the Spanish Jews. The many literary works of their scholars, poets, and philosophers frequently discussed the Sabbath both in regard to its holiness and to its unique role in the life of the Jew. The excerpts in this chapter were culled from the writings of a few of the men who rank among the greatest of that era. Judah Halevi, who was born in Toledo, Spain, in 1085, was the greatest Hebrew poet of post-biblical times. He was also a philosopher of note, having written *The Cusari* in which he defended tradition and faith against the inroads of Greek philosophy. Even greater was Moses Maimonides, who was born in Cordova in 1135. He is known primarily for his monumental code, the *Mishneh Torah*, in which he systematized all Jewish learning, and for his philosophical work, *The Guide for the Perplexed*, in which he harmonized Judaism with Aristotelian philosophy. Another philosopher was Joseph Albo, who was born in Spain in 1380. He is the author of the *Book of Principles*, an apologetic work which gained great popularity among the Jews. The last of the Spanish Jews represented in this chapter is Abraham ibn Ezra. He was born in Toledo, Spain, in 1092 and was one of the most versatile men of his time. His fame, however, rests primarily on his biblical commentary and on his poetry. An altogether different type was Judah he-Ḥasid of Regensburg who lived in the latter part of the 12th and in the early part of the 13th centuries. His book, *Sefer Ḥasidim* (Book of the Pious), is one of the great Jewish classic texts in the field of ethical literature. In all these works, as well as in many other medieval Jewish writings, the Sabbath is extolled not only because it gave the Jews rest and spiritual joy, but because it was an assurance of the perfect Sabbath to come, the day when God, the Redeemer and Creator, would make their life and the life of all mankind free and creative.

THE JOYOUS OBSERVANCE OF THE SABBATH IS PREFERABLE TO MONASTIC RETIREMENT AND ASCETICISM

Judah Halevi

Our law, as a whole, is divided among *fear*, *love*, and *joy*, by each of which one can approach God. Thy contrition on a fast day does nothing to bring thee nearer to

God than thy joy on the Sabbath and holy days, if it is the outcome of a devout heart . . . .

God commanded cessation of work on Sabbath and holy days, . . . "as a remembrance of the exodus from Egypt," and "as a remembrance of the work of Creation." These two things belong together, because they are the outcome of the absolute divine will, and not the result of accident or natural phenomena . . . . The observance of the Sabbath is therefore an acknowledgment of God's omnipotence, and at the same time an acknowledgment of the Creation by the divine word. He who observes the Sabbath because the work of Creation was finished on it acknowledges the Creation itself. He who believes in the Creation believes in the Creator. He, however, who does not believe in it falls a prey to doubts of God's eternity and to doubts of the existence of the world's Creator. The observance of the Sabbath is therefore nearer to God than monastic retirement and asceticism.[1]

THE SABBATH, A MEANS OF PRESERVING ISRAEL'S STRENGTH AND LUSTRE[2]

JUDAH HALEVI

The Rabbi: ". . . No people can equal us at all. Look at the others who appointed a day of rest in the place of Sabbath. Could they contrive anything which resembles it more than statues resemble living human bodies?"

Al Khazari: "I have often reflected about you and I have come to the conclusion that God has some secret design in preserving you, and that He appointed the Sabbath and holy days among the strongest means of preserving your strength and lustre. The nations broke you up and made you their servants . . . . They would even have made you their warriors were it not for those festive seasons observed by you with so much conscientiousness . . . . Had these not been, not one of you would put on a clean garment; you would hold no congregation to remember the law, on account of your everlasting affliction and degradation. Had these not been, you would not enjoy a single day in your lives. Now, however, you are allowed to spend the sixth part of life in rest of body and soul. Even kings are unable to do likewise, as their souls have no respite on their days of rest. If the smallest business calls them on that day to work and stir, they must move and stir, complete rest being denied to them. Had these laws not been, your toil would benefit others, because it would become their prey. Whatever you spend on these days is your profit for this life and the next, because it is spent for the glory of God.[3]

INTRODUCTION TO A SABBATH EPISTLE[4]

ABRAHAM IBN EZRA

'Twas in the year 4919 (1158 C.E.) at midnight, on Sabbath eve, the 14th of Tebeth (December 7th), that I, Abraham ibn Ezra, a Spaniard, was in one of the cities of the island called "the corner of the earth" (*Angleterre*), for it is in the last of the seven divisions of the inhabited earth. And I was sleeping and my sleep was pleasant unto me. And I looked in my dream and, behold, beside me stood one with the appearance of a man and a sealed letter in his hand. And he addressed me and said, "Take this letter which the Sabbath sends thee." . . . And I laid hold of it . . . and I read it. In the beginning it was as honey for sweetness, but when I read the concluding lines my heart waxed warm within me, and my soul almost departed, so that I asked him that stood by me, "What is my trespass? What is my sin? . . . I have always loved the Sabbath, and before she

came I used to go out to meet her, and when she departed
I used to speed her with gladness and with singing . . .
Wherefore then has she sent to me this letter?" And this
is it:

I am the Sabbath, the crown of the law of the chosen ones,
the fourth among the Ten Words.
And between the Lord and his sons I am the perpetual
sign of the covenant for all generations.
In me God completed all His works and so it is written in
the beginning of the books (Gen. 2. 2).
And of old Manna did not fall on the Sabbath day that I
might be a proof to the generations.
I delight the living on earth and give repose to the multitude of the dwellers of graves.[5]
I am the joy of men and of women, old and young rejoice
in me.

I have preserved thee at all times because thou hast observed
me from the days of youth.
But in thine old age an unwitting transgression has been
found in thee, for they have brought into thy house
books
In which it is written to profane the Sabbath eve, and how
canst thou be silent and not swear vows
To compose letters in the way of truth and send them to
all sides?

And the messenger of the Sabbath answered and spoke
to me "She has been told that thy pupils brought yesterday
to thy house books of commentaries on the law, and there
is it written to profane the Sabbath eve; do thou gird up
thy loins for the honor of the Sabbath to wage the battle
of the Law with the enemies of the Sabbath and do not
treat any man with partiality" (Lev. 19.15).

And I awoke and my anger was kindled within me and my spirit was very heavy; and I arose . . . and I washed my hands and brought the books into the light of the moon⁶ and there was written an explanation of Gen. 1. "And the evening and the morning," namely, that when the morning of the second day came then one whole day had passed, for the night is reckoned as part of the preceding day. Then I almost rent my garments, . . . and I took an oath not to give sleep to mine eyes after the conclusion of the holy day till I had written a lengthy letter to explain when was the beginning of the day according to the Law, to remove every stumbling block and to clear away snare and pitfall.⁷

TWO REASONS FOR THE OBSERVANCE
OF THE SABBATH

MOSES MAIMONIDES

Two different reasons are given for this commandment (to observe the Sabbath), because of two different objects.

In the Decalogue in Exodus, the following reason is given for observing the Sabbath: "For in six days the Lord made heaven and earth, the sea, and all that in them is, and rested on the seventh day" (Ex. 20.11). But in Deuteronomy (5.15) the reason given is: "And thou shalt remember that thou wast a servant in the land of Egypt, and the Lord thy God brought thee out thence by a mighty hand and by an outstretched arm; therefore the Lord thy God commanded thee to keep the Sabbath day."

This difference can easily be explained. In the former, the cause of the *honor* and *distinction* of the *day* is given ("Therefore the Lord hath blessed the day of the Sabbath and sanctified it") . . . . But the fact that God has given us the *law* of the Sabbath and commanded us *to keep it*, is the consequence of our having been slaves; for then our work did not depend on our will, nor could we choose the time for it; and we could not rest. Thus God commanded us to abstain from work on the Sabbath, and to rest, for two purposes; namely, (1) That we might confirm the true theory, that of the Creation, which at once and clearly leads to the theory of the existence of God. (2) That we might remember how kind God has been in freeing us from the burden of the Egyptians. — The Sabbath is therefore a double blessing; it gives us correct notions, and also promotes the well-being of our bodies.[8]

A DAY OF REST

MOSES MAIMONIDES

The object of Sabbath is obvious and requires no explanation. The rest it affords to man is known; one-seventh of the life of every man, whether small or great, passes thus in comfort, and in rest from trouble and exertion. This the Sabbath effects in addition to the perpetuation and confirmation of the grand doctrine of the Creation.[9]

THE KIND OF WAR THAT MAY BE WAGED ON THE SABBATH

MOSES MAIMONIDES

If Gentiles besiege a Jewish town for mere plunder, the Sabbath may not be violated and war may not be waged against them. But if a border town is attacked, if for no other reason than to carry off a bale of hay, it is permissible to violate the Sabbath and to bear arms against the invaders. And all Israelite neighbors who can come to the rescue must do so at once. They may not wait till after the Sabbath, but must go forth without delay. . . .

This principle holds good also when there is danger of shipwreck. If no more than one life is at stake, it is mandatory to save it, even if such saving involves the violation of the Sabbath through many forbidden occupations.[10]

HOW TO HONOR THE SABBATH

JUDAH HE-ḤASID

A simple vegetable meal on the Sabbath in a home where there is love between husband, wife, and children is better than a fatted ox in a home where there is hatred. A man should not plan to honor the Sabbath with delicacies while he knows that he will quarrel with his wife, or father, or mother. Whether it be Sabbath or festival —

"Better a dry morsel and quietness therewith,
Than a house full of feasting with strife (Prov. 17. 1).

And this is the meaning of the verse, "It is an honor for a man to keep aloof (*Shebet*) from strife" (Prov. 20.3). One should honor the Sabbath (*Shabbat*) by having no strife thereon.[11]

THE SABBATH, A SYMBOL OF THE EVERLASTING PROVIDENCE OF THE CREATOR

JOSEPH ALBO

The rabbis say, "Remember" and "Keep" were pronounced in one statement.[12] The meaning is this. The Sabbath is not intended merely to signify the existence of an agent who created the world, as is indicated in the Commandment beginning with the word, "Remember." The philosopher, too, believes in the existence of such a being, and no one denies it except the sect of Epicurus.

The main reason for the Sabbath is to show that there is a being who acts with will continually, even after the Creation of the world. This is alluded to in the Commandment beginning with the word, "Keep," mentioning as it does the deliverance from Egypt, from which it became known that God acts with will and desire, and not only at the time of the Creation of the world, but even after the world has come into being. He exercises providence and changes nature, compelling it to perform His will and desire at all times, as He did in delivering Israel from Egypt, to refute the notion of those who say there is nothing new under the sun. Hence the rabbis say that the Commandment beginning, "Remember," which calls attention to the existence of a divine agent, and the Commandment beginning, "Keep," which calls attention to the existence of a divine agent who acts continuously with will and exercises providence, both were said in one word or command, i. e., in the word which commands the Sabbath. For the purpose of the Sabbath is to call attention to the existence of a divine agent continually acting with will and exercising providence, and not merely to teach the existence of a divine agent.

Consider this carefully, for it is a wonderful interpretation of the rabbinic passage, which I have not seen adequately explained by any of the commentators.[13]

CHAPTER XIII

THE SABBATH IN MODERN
JEWISH LITERATURE

THE author of Ecclesiastes, though he lived about two thousand years ago, complained that "there is no end of making many books." The same complaint is heard today when literally thousands of books are published annually, this despite the fact that whole centuries pass without the birth of a single new idea. New books, however, are valuable in that they dress old ideas in modern garb and apply them to new situations. The Sabbath is one of the old ideas that has profited from such literary renovation. Modern Jewish essays, novels, short stories, and poems have described the Sabbath in modern idiom and have rendered its basic principles relevant to modern life. Despite the widespread desecration of the Sabbath, Jewish writers of today, whether rabbis or laymen, loyalists or assimilationists, speak of the Sabbath with enthusiasm and affection and acclaim it as an institution of central importance in Judaism.

The selections in the following chapter have been chosen from the writings of men well known to Jews throughout the world. The excerpts are from the writings of the eminent religious leaders, Solomon Schechter, K. Kohler, J. H. Hertz, and Mordecai M. Kaplan; the well-known novelists, Israel Zangwill and Sholom Asch; the "father of Yiddish literature," Mendele Moker Sefarim; and the apostles of the Jewish national renaissance, Aḥad Ha-'Am and Ḥayyim Naḥman Bialik.

THE SABBATH — A DAY OF REST, PLEASURE, AND DELIGHT

SOLOMON SCHECHTER

The law of the Sabbath is one of those institutions the strict observance of which was already the object of attack in early New Testament times. Nevertheless, the doctrine proclaimed in one of the Gospels — that the son of man is Lord also of the Sabbath — was also current among the Rabbis. They, too, taught that the Sabbath had been delivered into the hand of man (to break, if necessary), and not man delivered over to the Sabbath. And they even laid down the axiom that a scholar who lived in a town, where among the Jewish population there could be the least possibility of doubt as to whether the Sabbath might be broken for the benefit of a dangerously sick person, was to be despised as a man neglecting his duty; for, as Maimonides points out, the laws of the Torah are not meant as an infliction upon mankind, "but as mercy, loving-kindness and peace."

The attacks upon the Jewish Sabbath have not abated with the lapse of time. The day is still described by almost every Christian writer on the subject in the most gloomy colors, and long lists are given of minute and easily transgressed observances connected with it, which, instead of a day of rest, would make it to be a day of sorrow and anxiety, almost worse than the Scotch Sunday as depicted by continental writers. But it so happens that we have the prayer of Rabbi Zadok, a younger contemporary of the Apostles, which runs thus: "Through the love with which Thou, O Lord our God, lovest Thy people Israel, and the mercy which Thou hast shown to the children of Thy covenant, Thou hast given unto us this great and holy Seventh Day." And another rabbi who probably flourished in the first half of the second century, expresses himself (with allusion to Ex. 31. 13: "Verily My Sabbaths ye shall keep . . . that ye may know that I am the Lord that doth sanctify you"): "The Holy One, blessed be He, said unto Moses, I have a good gift in My treasures, and Sabbath is its name, which I wish to present to Israel. Go and bring to them the good tidings." The form again of the blessing over the sanctification-cup — a ceremony known long before the destruction of the Second Temple — runs: "Blessed art Thou, O Lord our God, who hast sanctified us by Thy commandments, and hast taken pleasure in us, and in love and grace hast given us Thy holy Sabbath as an inheritance." All these rabbis evidently regarded the Sabbath as a gift from heaven, an expression of the infinite mercy and grace which God manifested to His beloved children.

And the gift was, as already said, a *good* gift. Thus the rabbis paraphrase the words in Scripture, "See that the Lord hath given you the Sabbath" (Ex. 16. 29): God said unto Israel, behold the gem I gave you, My children; I gave you the Sabbath for your good. Sanctify or honor the Sabbath by choice meals, beautiful garments; delight your soul with pleasure and I will reward you (for this very pleasure); as it is said: "And if thou wilt call the Sabbath a delight and the holy of the Lord honourable (that is, honoring the Sabbath in this way) . . . then shalt thou delight thyself in the Lord" (Isa. 58.13-14).

The delight of the Sabbath was keenly felt. Israel fell in love with the Sabbath, and in the hyperbolic language of the *Aggada*, the Sabbath is personified as the "Bride of Israel;" whilst others called it "Queen Sabbath."

Thus we are told of Rabbi Judah ben Ilai that, when the eve of the Sabbath came, "he made his ablutions, wrapped himself up in his white linen with fringed borders, looking like an angel of the Lord of hosts." Thus he prepared for the solemn reception of Queen Sabbath. Another rabbi used to put on his best clothes, and rise and invite the Sabbath with the words, "Come in Bride, come in." What the Bride brought was peace and bliss. Nay, man is provided with a super-soul for the Sabbath, enabling him to bear both the spiritual and the material delights of the day with dignity and solemnity. The very light or expression of man's face is different on Sabbath, testifying to his inward peace and rest. And when man has recited his prayers (on the eve of the Sabbath) and thus borne testimony to God's creation of the world and to the glory of the Sabbath, there appear the two angels who accompany him, lay their hands on his head and impart to him their blessing with the words: "And thine iniquity is taken away and thy sin expiated" (Isa. 6. 7). For nothing is allowed to disturb the peace of the Sabbath; not even "the sorrows of sin," though the Sabbath had such a solemn effect on people that even the worldly man would not utter an untruth on the Day of the Lord. Hence it was not only forbidden to pray on Sabbath for one's own (material) needs, but everything in the liturgy of a mournful character (as for instance the confession of sin, supplication for pardon) was carefully avoided. It was with difficulty, as the rabbis say, that they made an exception in the case of condoling with people who had suffered loss through the death of near relatives. There is no room for morbid sentiment on the Sabbath, for "the blessing of the Lord maketh rich, and he addeth no sorrow with it" (Prov. 10. 22). The burden of the Sabbath prayers is for peace, rest, sanctification and joy (through salvation) and praise of God for this ineffable bliss of the Sabbath.

Such was the Sabbath of the old rabbis and the same spirit continued through all ages. The Sabbath was and is still celebrated by the people, who did and do observe it, in hundreds of hymns which would fill volumes, as a day of rest and joy, of pleasure and delight, a day in which man enjoys some foretaste of the pure bliss and happiness which are stored up for the righteous in the world to come.[1]

THE MOST IMPORTANT INSTITUTION OF
THE SYNAGOGUE

KAUFMANN KOHLER

The most important institution of the Synagogue, and the one most fraught with blessing for all mankind, is the Sabbath. Although its name and existence point to a Babylonian origin, it is still the peculiar creation of the Jewish genius and a chief pillar of the Jewish religion. As a day of rest crowning the daily labor of the week, it testifies to the Creator of the Universe who made all that is in accordance with His divine plan of perfection. The underlying idea expressed in Scripture is that the Sabbath is a divine institution. As God Himself worked out His design for the world in absolute freedom and rested with delight at its completion, so man is to follow His example, working during six days of the week and then enjoying the rest of the Sabbath with a mind elated by higher thoughts. Moreover, the day of rest observed by Israel should recall his redemption from the slavery and continual labor of Egypt. Thereby every creature made in God's image, the slave and stranger as well as the born Israelite, is given the heavenly boon of freedom and recreation to hallow the labor of the week.[2]

THE SABBATH AS AN INSTRUMENT OF PERSONAL
AND SOCIAL SALVATION

MORDECAI M. KAPLAN

An artist cannot be continually wielding his brush. He must stop at times in his painting to freshen his vision of the object, the meaning of which he wishes to express on his canvas. Living is also an art. We dare not become absorbed in its technical processes and lose our conscious-ness of its general plan . . . The Sabbath represents those moments when we pause in our brushwork to renew our vision of this object. Having done so we take ourselves to our painting with clarified vision and renewed energy. This applies alike to the individual and to the community. For the individual the Sabbath becomes thereby an instru-ment of personal salvation; for the community an instrument of social salvation.[3]

THE THREE-FOLD MEANING OF SABBATH OBSERVANCE

Mordecai M. Kaplan

Sabbath implies an affirmation that the world is so con-stituted as to afford man the opportunity for salvation. But what is there in the world that gives us this assurance? In what aspects of life do we recognize the Power that makes for salvation? The answer to these questions is to be found in the three leading motifs enunciated in the Torah and developed by the Sages in their interpretation of the Sabbath. The first of these is the idea of creativity, for the Sabbath is associated in Jewish tradition with the completion of the task of creation, when God surveyed all that He had made and found it "very good." The second is the idea of holiness. The reference to the Sabbath in the Decalogue bids us "Remember the sabbath day, to keep it holy," and the prophetic passage from the book of Isaiah (58.13) calls the Sabbath "the holy of the Lord." The third is the idea of covenantship, which regards the Sabbath as a sign of God's covenant with Israel. These three leading ideas associated with the observance of the Sabbath play

an important part in Jewish religion generally. They therefore make the Sabbath the symbol of the most significant
elements in the Jewish conception of God.[4]

THE DIGNITY OF LABOR

Joseph H. Hertz

The recognition of the dignity of labor could not be looked
for in Athens and Rome. In these societies, labor was
relegated to the slave, who was merely 'an animated tool'
without any human claims or rights. In every such society,
work itself — even that of a physician or schoolmaster —
becomes dishonorable; and, as in Sparta, is forbidden to the
free citizen.

In sharpest contrast to the above, the Jewish Sages are
unanimous in their insistence that work ennobles and sanc-
tifies, and that idleness is the door to temptation and sin.
They were themselves toilers, earning their daily bread by
following some handicraft as masons, tailors, sandalmakers,
carpenters. The most renowned of all the rabbis, Hillel
the Elder, was a woodcutter.

In Israel, man remained master of labor; labor did not
mean the bondage of man. The Sabbath gave the laborer
every week a day of freedom and leisure. This was quite
incomprehensible to the Greeks and Romans. Their writers —
Tacitus, Juvenal, Plutarch — make merry over the idea of
presenting one day in every seven to the worker! The far-
reaching humanitarian significance of the Sabbath was, of
course, undreamt of by them; and even "our modern spirit
with all its barren theories of civic and political rights, and
its striving towards freedom and equality, has not thought
out and called into existence a single institution that, in
its beneficent effects upon the laboring classes, can in the

slightest degree be compared to the Weekly Day of Rest promulgated in the Sinaitic wilderness" (Proudhon). It was many ages before its man-redeeming implications began to be seen. The Mosaic restrictions as to the *days of weekly* work that might be demanded of the laborer, laid down a principle of immeasurable importance for the social legislation of the future. At long last, after three thousand years, humanity has taken the next step; viz., that of regulating the *hours of daily* labor. This slowness in recognizing the needs of labor is no doubt due to the fact that, till quite recent times, classical literature monopolized the education of the governing classes of the European peoples. As with the Greeks and Romans, idleness became the mark of nobility; and it was deemed to be beneath the man of gentle birth to worry over the condition of serfs or toilers (Bloch).[5]

THE SABBATH OF THE POOR

Mendele Moker Sefarim

Six days in the week Shmulik the rag-picker lives like a dog. But on the eve of the Sabbath all is changed in his house. The walls are whitewashed, the house is cleaned; a new cloth shines on the table, and the rich and yellow bread, a joy to the eyes, rests thereon. The candles burn in their copper candlesticks, burnished for the Sabbath; and a smell of good food goes out of the oven, where the dishes are covered. All week long the mother of the house has been black as coal; to-day her face is resplendent, a white kerchief is tied on her head, and a spirit of grace has breathed upon her. The little girls, with bare feet, have come back from the bath; their hair is coiled in tresses;

they linger in the corners of the room; by their faces it may
be seen that they are waiting, joyous hearted, for those
whom they love.

"*Gut Shabbos*," says Shmulik, as he enters; and he looks
with love on his wife and his children, and his face beams.
"*Gut Shabbos*," says Moishele, his son, loudly, as he too
enters hurriedly, like one who is full of good tidings, and
eager to spread them. And to and fro in the house the
father and the son go, singing, with pleasant voices, the
Shalom 'Alekem songs that greet the invisible angels that
come into every Jewish house when the father returns from
the house of prayer on the eve of the Sabbath.

The rag-picker is no longer a dog; to-day he has a new
soul. It is *Shabbos*, and Shmulik is the son of a king.
He says the *Kiddush* over the wine, and he sits down at the
table. His wife is on his right, and his children are around
them. They dip their spoons into the dish, to take a little
soup, a piece of meat, a fragment of fish, of barley, or of
the other good things that they know nothing of during
the week. The children carry these dainties to their lips
with their five fingers, so that they may lose nothing of
them. They eat carefully, as attentive to their food as the
squirrel at the top of a tree, when he crunches a nut between his teeth and all his mind and body are concentrated
on the act. . . .

Now Shmulik clears his throat and begins to intone a
song of the Sabbath. "Beautiful and holy is the Sabbath
day." And his voice becomes stronger as he goes on to the
Ma Yafit, and sings of the weary who find rest, and of the
wild river Sambatyon, which is tumultuous six days of the
week, and on the seventh rests from its rage. "Sambatyon,
Sambatyon, wild with haste every day." Sambatyon . . .
is not Sambatyon Israel? All week long Israel runs from

place to place. When the Sabbath day comes he pauses, and rests; and on the eve of the Sabbath there is no more sadness and no more sighing.[6]

ISRAEL, THOU ART A PUZZLE!

MENDELE MOKER SEFARIM

O Israel, thou art indeed a puzzle to the nations; they do not understand! The conflicts of thy soul puzzle them. Thou art a puzzle to other nations with thy shabby clothes during the week days and thy gay jewels and silks on the holidays! Thou art a puzzle to other nations in thy ways of thinking and thy ways of doing things. Thou art a slave and a king! Thou art repulsive and attractive, as the tents of Kedar, as the curtains of Solomon!

Thou art a puzzle, Israel, to the nations; they do not understand! But he who can discern the innermost depths of thy heart will find there the solution of these puzzles in thy utter devotion to God and to His teachings. Only from these wells of salvation can the Jew drink and forget his poverty, only from this source of inspiration can the Jew transcend his cares, vexations, anxieties; only through the purity of his soul can he shake off the bitterness of his painful conflicts and taste the sweetness of life. The struggles of the Jew during the week are but preparation for the finer things of the Sabbath. This is the all-pervading aim of his life and his dominating desire. To this end, the Jew strives with his whole heart and soul; in this aim he finds comfort and solace for his down-trodden and humiliated spirit. Then the Jew sings to his bride, Sabbath, the traditional Hebrew melody "Come my friend;" and the depression of his spirit passes away — his will now is submerged in the will of God.[7]

THE HEBREW'S FRIDAY NIGHT

Israel Zangwill

The rabbi was returning from the synagogue . . . He
had dropped into a delicious reverie — tasting in advance
the Sabbath peace. The work of the week was over. The
faithful Jew could enter on his rest — the narrow, miry
streets faded before the brighter image of his brain. *"Come,
my beloved, to meet the Bride, the presence of the Sabbath let
us welcome."*
Tonight his sweetheart would wear her Sabbath face,
putting off the mask of the shrew, which hid not from him
the angel countenance. Tonight he could in very truth call
his wife (like his ancestors in the Talmud) "not wife but
home." Tonight she would be in very truth *Simḥa* — rejoicing. A cheerful warmth glowed at his heart, love for
all the wonderful Creation dissolved him in tenderness. As
he approached the door, cheerful lights gleamed on him
like a heavenly smile . . . The rabbi kissed the *Mezuzah*
on the outside of the door and his daughter whom he met
on the inside. Everything was as he had pictured it — the
two tall wax candles in quaint heavy silver candlesticks,
the spotless tablecloth, the dish of fried fish made pictur-
esque with sprigs of parsley, the Sabbath loaves shaped
like boys' tip-cats, with a curious plait of crust from point
to point and thickly sprinkled with a drift of poppy-seed,
and covered with a velvet cloth embroidered with Hebrew
words; the flask of wine and the silver goblet. The sight
was familiar yet it always struck the simple old rabbi anew,
with a sense of special blessing.
"Good *Shabbos*, Simḥa," said Reb Shemuel.
"Good *Shabbos*, Shemuel," said Simḥa. The light of love
was in her eyes, and in her hair her newest comb. Her
sharp features shone with peace and good-will and the

consciousness of having duly lit the Sabbath candles and thrown the morsel of dough into the fire. Shemuel kissed her, then he laid his hands upon Hannah's head and murmured:

"May God make thee as Sarah, Rebecca, Rachel, and Leah," and upon Levi's, murmuring: "May God make thee as Ephraim and Manasseh."

Even the callous Levi felt the breath of sanctity in the air and had a vague restful sense of his Sabbath Angel hovering about and causing him to cast two shadows on the wall while his Evil Angel shivered impotent on the door step.

Then Reb Shemuel repeated three times a series of sentences commencing: *"Peace be unto you, ye ministering Angels,"* and thereupon the wonderful picture of an ideal woman from Proverbs, looking affectionately at Simḥa the while. "A woman of worth, whoso findeth her, her price is far above rubies. The heart of her husband trusteth in her; good and not evil will she do him all the days of her life . . ."

Then, washing his hands with the due benediction, he filled the goblet with wine, and while everyone reverently stood he "made *Kiddush*," in a joyous traditional recitative ". . . blessed art Thou, O Lord, our God! King of the Universe, Creator of the fruit of the vine, who doth sanctify us with His commandment and hath delighted in us . . . Thou hast chosen and sanctified us above all people and with love and favor hast made us to inherit Thy holy Sabbath . . ."

And all the household . . . answered "Amen," each sipping of the cup in due gradation, then eating a special morsel of bread cut by the father and dipped in salt; after which the good wife served the fish, and cups and saucers clattered and knives and forks rattled . . . .

When supper was over, grace was chanted and then the

Zemirot were sung — songs summing up in light and jingling
metre the very essence of holy joyousness — neither riotous
nor ascetic — the note of spiritualized common sense which
has been the keynote of historical Judaism. For to feel
"the delight of Sabbath" is a duty and to take three meals
thereon a religious obligation — the sanctification of the
sensuous by a creed to which everything is holy. The Sabbath is the hub of the Jew's universe; to protract it is a
virtue, to love it a liberal education. It cancels all mourning — even for Jerusalem. The candles may gutter out at
their own greasy will — unsnuffed, untended — is not Sabbath its own self-sufficient light?[8]

THE SAMBATYON AT REST

ISRAEL ZANGWILL

The roaring Sambatyon of life was at rest in the Ghetto;
on thousands of squalid homes the light of Sinai shone. The
Sabbath Angels whispered words of hope and comfort to
the foot-sore hawker and the aching machinist, and refreshed their parched souls with celestial anodyne and made
them kings of the hour, with leisure to dream of the golden
chairs that awaited them in Paradise.

The Ghetto welcomed the Bride with proud song and
humble feast, and sped her parting with optimistic sym-
bolisms of fire and wine, of spice and light and shadow. All
around their neighbors sought distraction in the blazing
public-houses, and their tipsy bellowings resounded through
the streets and mingled with the Hebrew hymns. Here
and there the voice of a beaten woman rose on the air. But
no Son of the Covenant was among the revellers or the wife-
beaters; they remained a chosen race, a peculiar people,
redeemed at least from the grosser vices, a little human

islet won from the waters of animalism by the genius of
ancient engineers. For while the genius of the Greek or the
Roman, the Egyptian or the Phoenician survives but in
word and stone, the Hebrew word alone was made flesh.[9]

SABBATH AT A JEWISH INN IN EIGHTEENTH CENTURY POLAND

Sholom Asch

On getting home from the bath, all clean and dressed in
clean shirts with broad white collars folded over their long
green coats, they found the inn transformed into a peaceful Sabbath nest. There was nothing in evidence which
could remind one of an inn. The kegs of brandy were
covered with white sheets, and before the shelves were
hung shawls and curtains. The inn was tidied up and transformed into a Sabbath home looking as though no buying
and selling of any sort had ever been conducted there.
Seven pure tallow candles burned in the large brass candlestick, on the base of which sparkled the words in Hebrew:
"Lights for the Sabbath." Two pairs of white loaves, one
large pair for the master of the house and one small one
for the young husband, were set upon the white linen-
covered table together with a large silver cup and a small
silver cup. And the mother with her daughter-in-law sat
by the table, both dressed in long trailing coats of green
silk and new lace head-dresses. Their white foreheads were
bound with fillets, and on their bosoms sparkled the plates
studded with jewels which they had received from their
husbands. Little Deborah, looking as though she were
disguised as a young wife, aped everything that her mother-
in-law did, and Marusha, the maid, dressed for the Sabbath
in a new apron and a new headkerchief, sat on a little stool

near the oven and gazed with pride on the young mistress. Mother and daughter sang together a song in honor of the Sabbath before the blessing of the candles:

> A pleasant song I now will sing,
> With joyful voice which loud shall ring,
> In honor of the holy Queen far-famed:
> Sabbath is the name by which she is named.
>
> God, with whom doth ever dwell the light,
> May He send unto my home the Sabbath bright;
> For her dear sake my house I purified,
> Why lingers she so long outside?
>
> Six long days she roams in sun and rain
> Like one who doth in exile suffer bitter pain;
> Even like a bird from roof to roof she flies
> Until the hour when holy Sabbath hither hies.

And when Shlomele had taken the large prayer book and was ready to go with his father to the synagogue, there was heard the noise of a big Polish equipage with many horses, which stopped in front of the inn.

"Hey there, Jew, open! His exalted Excellency, Pan Dombrowski, is knocking at your door. Open!"

"Heavens, his great Excellency Pan Dombrowski is knocking at my door! I cannot, I cannot, dear master, it is the Sabbath now."

"Jew, I will have thirty lashes given you. Open the door!"

"I must not, dear master. It is the Jew's Sabbath now!"

"How dare you, Jew? His Exalted Excellency, Pan Dombrowski, desires a glass of whiskey."

"I cannot, dear master; I must not, dear master; it is the Sabbath now."

"Put a measure of brandy down behind the door. Not a drop to be had in the whole city."

"I cannot, dear master, my wife has already lighted the candles."

"Accursed Jew! When the Jew keeps his Sabbath all Poland must be without brandy," said a voice from the other side of the door.[10]

THE SABBATH HAS KEPT ISRAEL

AḤAD HA-'AM

A Jew who feels a real tie with the life of his people throughout the generations will find it utterly impossible to think of the existence of Israel without the Sabbath. One can say without exaggeration that more than Israel has kept the Sabbath, the Sabbath has kept Israel. Had it not been for the Sabbath, which weekly restored to the people their "soul" and weekly renewed their spirit, the weekday afflictions would have pulled them farther and farther downward until they sank to the lowest depths of materialism as well as ethical and intellectual poverty. Therefore one need not be a Zionist in order to feel all the traditional sacred grandeur that hovers over this "good gift," and to rise up with might against all who seek to destroy it.[11]

THE SABBATH IS THE CORNERSTONE OF JUDAISM

ḤAYYIM NAḤMAN BIALIK

I wish to explain the concept of 'Oneg Shabbat. We are coming to Eretz Israel to renew our life, to create for ourselves a distinctive life, with features and characteristics uniquely our own. And in order to create forms of life that are rooted and genuine, that are true to the character of the nation, the founders of the 'Oneg Shabbat movement felt that they must use for their creative work only such material as is derived from the foundation stones of the original forms of life. They felt that they must dig down to the strongest of all foundations, to the very cornerstone of Jewish life. And in their search they found no form loftier or more profound than the Sabbath, which preceded the giving of the Torah and was observed by the Children of Israel while they were still in Egypt. The Sabbath is indeed the cornerstone of Judaism, and it is not without cause that it is called the "sign of the covenant" between God and the Children of Israel. In the Sabbath are enfolded many national and social concepts. If in the Ten Commandments is enfolded the whole Torah, then in the Sabbath are probably enfolded all the Ten Commandments.[12]

THE SABBATH, A PRODUCT OF *HALAKAH* AND *HAGGADAH*

Ḥayyim Naḥman Bialik

The Jews have a beautiful creation of their own — a holy day — the "Princess Sabbath," whom the imagination of the people endowed with a living soul, with a body and form, perfect in beauty and splendor. She is the Sabbath given by God to the world after six days of creation, so that the "embroidered and brocaded canopy shall not want for a bride." She was the treasure guarded by God in His chambers, the bride for whom He found no proper mate except Israel. According to the folk-tale she sits, the daughter of the king, "as a bride set among her maids" hidden in the place of Eden, in the innermost of seven chambers, her six handmaids, the six workdays, in attendance upon her. When she enters the town, all turn their faces to the gate and greet her with a joyful blessing, "Enter, O Bride, enter, O Bride, thou Princess Sabbath," while the early *Ḥasidim* went out into the fields to receive her. Once she appeared in a dream to Ibn Ezra and sent through him a pathetic letter to her mate, Israel; the well-known "Sabbath Epistle" (see pp. 231–3).

All poets of Israel, from Judah Halevi to Heinrich Heine, dedicated to her their poems and songs. Is she not, then, a perfect haggadic ideal? Is she not in herself a fountain of life and holiness for an entire people, a spring welling copious inspiration for poets and singers? And yet who can say, or who will determine, whose handiwork she is and by what means she came to be what she is, *Halakah* or *Haggadah*?

Tractate Sabbath contains one hundred and fifty-seven folios; *'Erubin,* one hundred and five, and the haggadic passages in these tractates are few indeed. They dwell mostly on elaborate investigations into the thirty-nine forms of forbidden labor and their branches and offshoots, the fixing of *Teḥumin* (boundaries) for the Sabbath and the holidays and the like subjects. "With what may one light his house for Sabbath?" "With what may a beast go out?" "How may a partnership in *Teḥumin* be effected?" and such. What a weariness of the mind; what a squandering of earnest thinking on every jot and dot. And yet, as I peruse these folios and watch groups upon groups of *Tanna'im* and *Amora'im* at work, I exclaim, "Artists of life are these men; artists of life at work in the potter's house, at the potter's wheel." Such a tremendous labor of the mind — dwarfish and gigantic at the same time — done for its own sake, can come only out of a faith and love unbounded, and is quite impossible without the aid of the Holy Spirit in its full manifestation. Each of these individuals did his work according to his individual character and natural propensities; yet all of them bowed their heads in submission to a higher will that controlled them all. It cannot have happened otherwise than that one sublime idea, one divine and ideal form of Sabbath, was before the eyes of all these different individuals, which coordinated their work through many generations and made them co-partners in its creation and final perfection.

Each "point of objection," each "point of contradiction," each "fence" and definition is nothing else but a new line, a new phase of the old form, both of them necessary to complete and perfect it. And what is the result of all this wearisome labor of the *Halakah*? A day that is an idyl of haggadic splendor and beauty![13]

CHAPTER XIV

THE SABBATH IN THE SHORT STORY

DOMESTIC HAPPINESS[1]

Isaac Loeb Perez

HAYYIM is a street porter.

When he goes through the town stooping beneath his case of wares, one can hardly make him out — it looks as if the box were walking along on two feet of its own. Listen to the heavy breathing! One can hear it quite a long way off.

But now he lays down his load, and is given a few pence. He straightens himself, wipes the sweat off his face, draws a deep breath, goes to the fountain and takes a drink of water, and then runs into the court.

He stands close to the wall and lifts his huge head till the point of his chin and the tip of his nose and the brim of his hat are all on a level.

"Hannah," he calls.

A little window opens just below the eaves, and a small female head in a white kerchief answers, "Hayyim!"

The two look at each other very contentedly.

The neighbors say they are "lovering."

Hayyim tosses up his earnings wrapped in a piece of paper, and Hannah catches them in the air — not for the first time in her life, either!

"You're a wonder!" says Hayyim, and shows no disposition to go away.

"Off with you, Hayyim!" she says, smiling. "I daren't take my eyes off the sick child. I have placed the cradle near the fireplace, and I skim with one hand and rock with the other."

"How is it, poor little thing?"

"Better."

"God be praised! Where is Henne?"

"With the seamstress, learning to sew."

"And Yossele?"

"In *Ḥeder*."

Hayyim lowers his chin and goes away. Hannah follows him with her eyes till he disappears. Thursday and Friday it lasts longer.

"How much have you got there in the paper?" inquires Hannah.

"Twenty-two pennies."

"I am afraid it is not enough!"

"Why, what do you want, Hannah?"

"A nickel's worth of ointment for the baby, a few farthing dips — a Sabbath loaf I have — oh! meat — a pound and a half — let me see — and wine for the *Kiddush*, and a few splinters."

"Those I can get for you. There are sure to be some in the market."

"And then I want," and she makes a calculation of all she needs for the Sabbath, and it comes to this: that one can say the *Kiddush* quite well over a loaf, and that there are heaps of things one can do without.

The two important ones are: the candles to say the blessing over and the salve for the child.

And if only the children, God helping, are well, and the metal candlesticks not in pawn, and supposing there is even a pudding, they spend a cheerful Sabbath.

Hannah *is* wonderful at puddings!

She is always short of something, either meal or eggs or

suet, and the end of it all is a sweet, succulent, altogether ravishing pudding — it melts away into the very limbs!

"An angel's handiwork!" says Hannah, smiling delightedly.

"An angel's is it?" Hayyim laughs. "You think you are a little angel, do you, because you put up with me and the children? Well, they worry you enough, goodness knows! And I'm a regular crosspatch, *I* am, at times — and never a curse do I get. You're not like other women. And what a comfort I must be to you, too! I'm no good at *Kiddush* or *Habdalah* either — I can't even sing the hymns properly!"

"You're a good husband and a good father," persists Hannah. "I ask no better for myself or anyone else. God grant that we may grow old together, you and I!"

And they gaze into each other's eyes so kindly and so affectionately as it were from the very heart. It looks for all the world as if they were newly married, and the party at table grows more and more festive.

But directly after his nap Hayyim repairs to the little synagogue to hear the Law. A teacher expounds *Alshech*[2] there to simple folk like himself.

The faces still look sleepy.

One is finishing his doze; another yawns loudly. But all of a sudden, when the right moment comes, when there is talk of the other world, of *Gehenna*, where the wicked are scourged with iron rods, and of the lightsome Garden of Eden, where the just sit with golden crowns on their heads and study the Torah, then they come to life again! The mouths open, the cheeks flush, they listen breathlessly to be told what the next world will be like. Hayyim usually stands near the stove.

His eyes are full of tears, he trembles all over, he is all there, in the other world!

He suffers together with the wicked; he is immersed in

the molten pitch, he is flung away into hell, he gathers chips and splinters in gloomy woods . . . .

He goes through it all himself, and is covered with a cold sweat. But then, later on, he also shares the bliss of the righteous. The Garden of Eden, the angels, Leviathan, Behemoth, and all good things present themselves so vividly to his imagination that when the reader kisses the book before closing it, Hayyim starts as it were out of a dream, like one called back from the other world!

"Ah!" he gasps, for wonder has held him breathless. "O Lord, just a tiny bit, just a scrap, just a morsel of the world to come — for me, for my wife, and for my little children!"

And then he grows sad, wondering: After all, because of what? As a reward for what?

Once, when the reading was over, he went up to the teacher:

"Rabbi," he said, and his voice shook, "advise me! What must I do to gain the world to come?"

"Study the Law, my son!" answered the teacher.

"I can't."

"Study the *Mishnah*, or some *'En Jacob*, or even *Perek*."

"I can't."

"Recite the Psalms!"

"I haven't time!"

"Pray with devotion!"

"I don't know what the prayers mean!" The teacher looks at him with compassion.

"What are you?" he asks.

"A street porter."

"Well, then, do some service for the scholars."

"I beg pardon?"

"For instance, carry a few cans of water every day toward

evening into the house-of-study so that the students may have something to drink."

"Rabbi," he inquired further, "and my wife?"

"When a man sits on a chair in Paradise his wife is his footstool."

When Hayyim went home to say *Habdalah*, Hannah was sitting there reciting "God of Abraham." And when he saw her he felt a tug at his heart.

"No, Hannah," he flung his arms around her, "I won't have you be my footstool! I shall bend down to you and raise you and make you sit beside me. We shall sit both on one chair, just as we are doing now. We are so happy like that! Do you hear, Hannah? You and I, we are going to sit in a chair together . . . . the Almighty will *have* to allow it!"

THE TREASURE¹

ISAAC LOEB PEREZ

To sleep in summer time in a room four yards square, together with a wife and eight children, is anything but a pleasure. Even on a Friday night. So Shmerel, the wood-cutter, rises hot and gasping from his bed, and, though only half through with the night, hastily pours some water over his finger-tips, flings on his dressing gown and escapes bare-foot from the parched *Gehenna* of his dwelling. He steps into the street. All is quiet, all the shutters are closed, and over the sleeping town stretches a distant, serene, and starry sky. He feels as if he were all alone with God, blessed be He, and he says, looking up at the sky, "Now, Lord of the Universe, now is the time to hear me and to bless me with a treasure out of Thy treasure-house!"

As he says this, he sees something like a little flame coming along out of the town, and he knows that that is the treasure! He is about to pursue it when he remembers that it is Sabbath when one must not run. So he goes after it walking. And as he walks slowly along, the little flame begins to move slowly, too, so that the distance between them does not increase, though it does not decrease, either. He walks on. Now and then an inward voice calls to him: "Shmerel, don't be a fool! Take off the dressing gown, jump and throw it over the flame!" But he knows it is the Evil Inclination speaking. He throws the dressing gown onto his arm, but to spite the Evil Inclination he takes still smaller steps and rejoices to see that, as soon as he takes these smaller steps, the little flame moves more slowly, too.

Thus he follows and follows the flame till he gradually finds himself outside the town. The road twists and turns across fields and meadows, and the distance between him and the flame grows no longer, no shorter. Were he to throw the dressing gown now it would not reach the flame. Meantime the thought revolves in his mind: Were he indeed to become possessed of the treasure, he would no longer have to be a woodcutter in his old age; truly he no longer has the strength for such work. Then he would rent a seat for his wife in the women's *Shool*, so that her Sabbaths and holidays should not be spoiled by not being allowed to sit here or sit there. On New Year's Day and the Day of Atonement it is all she can do to stand through the service. Her many children have exhausted her! And he would have a new dress made for her and buy her a few strings of pearls. The children should be sent to better *Hadarim*, and he would cast about for a match for his eldest girl. As it is, the poor child carries her mother's fruit baskets and never has time so much as to comb her hair thoroughly. And she has long, long plaits, and eyes like a deer.

"It would be a meritorious act to pounce upon the treasure!"

The Evil Inclination speaks again, he thinks. If it is not to be, well, then it is not to be! If it were a weekday, he would soon know what to do! Or if his Yainkel were here he would have something to say. Children nowadays! Who knows what they don't do on the Sabbath! And the younger one is no better. He makes fun of the teacher in *Heder*. When the teacher is about to administer a blow they pull his beard. And who's going to find time to look after them — chopping and sawing the whole day through.

He sighs and walks on and on, now and then glancing up into the sky. "Lord of the Universe, of whom are you making trial? Shmerel Woodcutter? If you mean to give me the treasure, *give* it to me!" It seems to him that the flame advances more slowly. But at this moment he hears a dog barking and recognizes the bark as that of the dog in Vissoke. Vissoke is the first village you come to on leaving the town. He sees white patches twinkling in the dewy morning atmosphere. Those are the Vissoke peasant cottages. Then it occurs to him that he has gone a Sabbath day's journey and he stops short.

"Yes, I have gone a Sabbath day's journey," he thinks, and says, speaking into the air: "You won't lead me astray! It is *not* a Godsend! God does not make sport of us. It is the work of a demon." And he feels a little angry with the thing and turns and hurries toward the town, thinking: "I won't say anything about it at home, because, first, they won't believe me, and if they do, they'll laugh at me. And what have I done to be proud of? The Creator knows how it was, and that is enough for me. Besides, *she* might be angry, who can tell? The children are certainly naked and barefoot, poor little things! Why should they be

made to transgress the commandment to honor one's
father?"

No, he won't breathe a word of it. He won't even remind
the Almighty of it. If he really has been good, the Almighty
will remember without being told.

And suddenly he is conscious of a strange, inward calm,
and there is a delicious sensation in his limbs. Money is,
after all, dross. Riches may even lead a man from the
right way. And he feels inclined to thank God for not
having brought him into temptation by granting him his
wish. Now he would like to sing a song! "Our Father, our
King" is one he remembers from his early years, but he
feels ashamed and breaks off. He tries to recollect one of
the cantor's melodies, a Sinai tune, when suddenly he sees
that the little flame which he left behind him is once more
preceding him, and moving slowly townward, townward.
And the distance between them neither increases nor
diminishes, as though the flame were taking a walk, and
he were taking a walk, just taking a little walk in honor of
the Sabbath. He is glad in his heart and watches it. The
sky pales, the stars begin to fade, the east flushes, a narrow
pink stream flows lengthwise over his head, and still the
flame flickers onward into the town, enters his own street.
There is his house. The door, he sees, is open. Apparently
he forgot to shut it. And, lo and behold! the flame goes in,
the flame goes through his own house door! He follows and
sees it disappear under the bed. All are asleep. He goes
softly up to the bed, stoops down, and sees the flame spinning round underneath, like a top, always in the same
place. He takes his dressing gown, throws it under the bed,
and covers the flame. No one hears him. And now a golden
morning beam steals in through the chink in the shutter.

He sits down on the bed and makes a vow not to say a
word to anyone till Sabbath is over — not half a word, lest

it cause desecration of the Sabbath. *She* could never hold her tongue, and the children certainly could not. They would at once want to count the treasure, to know how much there was, and very soon the secret would be out of the house and in the *Shool*, the house-of-study, and all the streets. And people would talk about his treasure, about his luck. They would not say their prayers, or wash their hands, or say grace, as they should. And he would have led his household and half the town into sin. No, not a whisper! And he stretches himself out on the bed and pretends to be asleep.

And this was his reward: When, after concluding the Sabbath, he stooped down and lifted the dressing gown there lay a sack with a million gulden in it!

And he lived happily all the years of his life.

Only his wife was continually throwing it up to him: "Lord of the World, how could a man have such a heart of stone as to sit a whole summer day and not say a word, not a word, not to his own wife, not one single word! And there was I crying over my prayer as I said God of Abraham — and crying *so* — for there wasn't a penny left in the house."

Then he would console her, and say with a smile:

"Who knows? Perhaps it was all thanks to your prayer — 'God of Abraham' — that it went off so well."

THRICE HE LAUGHED[1]

(A *Ḥasidic* Story)

MEYER LEVIN

The meal of Sabbath eve was ready upon the table.

Rabbi Israel's head was sunken, and anxiety was deep upon his face. His scholars, seated about the long table, were silent.

The Baal Shem arose and began to recite the blessing over the wine. He lifted his glass.

And all at once a golden glow of joy spread over his cheeks and eyes; he raised his glass, threw back his head, and broke forth in merry laughter. He laughed until he had to wipe bright tears from his eyes.

The scholars could not understand what might have caused the rabbi's laughter. They looked one to another, they looked at the rabbi, they looked all about the room. But everything was as usual. The candles burned, casting their radiance upon the long white tablecloth and upon the plates that bore the Sabbath meal and upon the cups of Sabbath wine.

The Master had ceased laughing. But all the sadness was gone from his face. He drank his wine and set cheerily to his meal.

He began to eat the fish. Suddenly he set down his hand. His eyes looked far away. And again he broke into laughter.

During the entire Sabbath it was the custom of the scholars never to ask questions of the Baal Shem Tov. Therefore they could not ask him the cause of his strange and sudden joy. They ate, and looked one to the other, and wondered.

And when Rabbi Israel was eating the soup, he broke into laughter for the third time. And this time he laughed with the easy contentment of a father watching his children at play.

That night, and all through the Sabbath, the students gathered in groups and discussed the rabbi's laughter. Three times he had laughed. And they sought in the Torah for explanation of his joy. But they could find no certain answer.

It was the custom of Rabbi Israel, at the end of the Sabbath, to receive one of the scholars and to answer any question that might have arisen among the disciples during the day of rest.

When evening came, the scholars gathered and chose Rabbi Wolf from among themselves to go to the Master and ask why he had laughed three times during the Sabbath meal. Rabbi Wolf went to the hut in the forest, to which the Baal Shem Tov often withdrew for solitary contemplation. He knocked and entered.

Rabbi Israel asked, smiling, "What questions have the scholars today?"

"They would like to know," said Rabbi Wolf, "why the Master laughed three times during the meal on the eve of Sabbath."

"Come," said the Baal Shem Tov, "we will get into the wagon and ride, and perhaps you will find the answer to your question."

Often, on the evening after Sabbath, Rabbi Israel and his students would get into his wagon and ride on the country roads. Now they harnessed the horses, and all the scholars got into the wagon. All were silent. The night was soft and pleasant. The Baal Shem let the reins lie loosely over his knees. The horses ambled down a forgotten lane. And the Baal Shem hummed to himself, and soon all of the *Ḥasidim* were humming. Thus they rode hour after hour, and instead of turning back they rode onward, and they rode all through the night.

On Sunday morning they found themselves in a village which they had never before seen. Rabbi Israel halted the wagon in front of a tiny synagogue. He got down and called the *Shammash*.

Soon it was known among all the Jews in the village that the great Rabbi Israel, the Baal Shem Tov, was come among them. Men and women hastened to the market place, and mothers ran carrying their children to the rabbi for his blessing, while childless women sought the touch of his hand. When a great many people had assembled, he said, "Are all the Jews of the village here?"

The head of the congregation looked from one to the other and said, "All."

But Rabbi Israel looked among them as though he sought for someone; and at last he said, "Where is Sabbatai, the bookbinder?"

The *Shammash* ran at once to call the aged Sabbatai. In a moment the *Shammash* returned, followed by a small, gray-haired man, whose blue eyes shone clearly in a mild face.

"Let his wife also be called," said Rabbi Israel.

Then Sabbatai hurried and fetched his wife.

When the two of them were there, Rabbi Israel asked them to stand in the center of the market place. On one side of them were all the Jews of the town. And on the other side were Rabbi Israel's scholars.

"Now," said the Master, "tell me, Sabbatai, exactly what you did on last Sabbath eve! But tell me everything and do not be ashamed or afraid to speak!"

"Master," said Sabbatai, "I shall indeed tell you everything that happened to me, and what I did; and if it is God's will that I be punished, I am ready to accept His punishment, asking no more than to serve Him."

Then the aged bookbinder told his story:

"You must know that since my youth I have lived in this village and practiced my craft as a bookbinder. In those early years, when I was filled with vigor, I was able to manage a thriving business and I lived on all that was best in the world.

"My little wife and I loved to dress well and to have good things to eat, and this we permitted ourselves. For as long as I had enough work to do there was no lack of money.

Perhaps we were even somewhat extravagant in buying costly clothing, but my wife was the prettiest girl in the village and I wanted to see her clothed as became her beauty. And when we drove to the neighboring villages, I too had to be dressed in a way that would not put her to shame. So it happened that we spent all the money that I earned, never putting away anything for later years.

"With all that, we led honest and observant lives. From my earliest youth it was the custon in our house to observe the Sabbath strictly. On Thursday afternoon my wife would go to the market and buy fish, meat, flour, candles, and all things that were needed for the Sabbath. On Friday morning at ten o'clock I would put aside my work, close my shop, and go to the synagogue. There I would remain until night fell, when I would go home to the Sabbath meal. Coming toward the house I would see the lighted candles shining through the window, and I would know that everything was well in my house.

"But during these last years, the weakness of old age has come upon me. I have no sons to help me. And it seems that, little by little, the world is forgetting me. I no longer receive much work from the neighboring villages. And as I am not as vigorous as I was in my youth, I cannot go out to seek more work. Therefore it goes hard with me these years.

"There have been days when we did not have a penny with which to buy bread. On those days we fasted. For I said to my wife, 'The people among whom we live are kindhearted and charitable, and they would be generous toward us if they knew of our plight. But I have lived all my life without asking help of anyone but God, and so I would finish my days.'

"Last Thursday, when my wife was ready to go out to the market, she saw that there was no money in the house and no food, not even a bit of flour-dust to bake into bread. She came to me and asked me what money I had, but I had earned nothing at all that day. 'Perhaps by tomorrow morning,' I said, 'some work will come into the shop.' Then she went home and for the first time during our years of marriage my wife did not do her Sabbath marketing on Thursday afternoon.

"On Friday morning no work came. Then I said to my wife, 'Let us fast throughout the Sabbath. But above all we must not let our neighbors know that we are in need. For the neighboring women would come with meat and fish and Sabbath bread, and you would not be able to refuse their offerings.'

"Then I conceived of a plan, and said to my wife. 'I will tell you how we must manage. I will stay late in the synagogue, later than usual. I will stay until all the others have gone. Then I will be able to come home without meeting anyone who may ask me: Sabbatai, why are there no candles lit in your house? I would not know how to answer such a question. And when I come home at night we will praise God, accepting what he has given us.'

"So my good wife agreed. And at ten o'clock in the morning I closed the door of my shop and went to the synagogue.

"In our little house sat my wife, and as there was no Sabbath meal to prepare she had nothing to do. Since she did not like to sit empty-handed she began to clean the house again. She cleaned the bare table and washed the empty pots, she brushed the vacant cupboard, she swept and dusted where there was no particle of dust, and when she was finished the house was as perfect as a jewel.

"Still time hung heavy on her hands. So she began to look for other things to do. And she bethought herself of the great chest filled with old clothing. 'I will put the old clothing in order,' she said, 'and clean it, and mend what needs to be mended.'

"In the chest were all the fine clothes we had worn in our youth. And there among the garments she found a coat that I had worn when we went to the village dances, and on that coat were seven buttons covered with gold. My wife was overjoyed! She took her scissors and cut the golden buttons from the coat. She ran with them to the goldsmith. He weighed the gold and paid her the worth of it in money. Then she hastened to the market. She bought meat and fish and flour and fine tall candles, and she had enough money to buy wine for the Sabbath blessing and all the other necessities for a perfect Sabbath! Then she went home and all during the afternoon she was busy preparing the Sabbath meal.

"When darkness came and all the others had gone from the synagogue, I walked slowly toward my house. I met no one on the way, and for that at least I was grateful, for I would not have known what to say if anyone had met me and asked, 'Sabbatai, why are there no candles in your house tonight?'

"But as I came near the house, I saw the light of candles! Then I thought: my good wife has not been able to withstand this trial, and has accepted the help of neighbors.

"I came into the house. I saw the white cloth spread on the table and upon the cloth was arranged a beautiful Sabbath meal. I saw fish and meat and fresh-baked Sabbath bread, and soup and wine for the blessing.

"Then, as I did not want to break the peace and joy of the Sabbath, I said nothing to my wife. I withheld the disappointment that I felt when I thought that she had accepted gifts from our neighbors. I recited the blessing over the wine, and over the meal, and I sat down to the Sabbath table.

"But after a while I spoke to her as gently as I could, so that she would not feel hurt at my words. I said, 'My good wife, I see that you were not able to refuse the kindness of our neighbors, for you are a soft-hearted woman.'

"But she smiled in a strange joyous way and laughed at me and said, 'My honest Sabbatai, do you remember the costly coat you had when you were young, your coat with the golden buttons? Today, having nothing with which to occupy my hands, I searched in the old clothes chest and I found your coat. I cut off the buttons and took them to the goldsmith, and he gave me money with which I bought all that we needed for the Sabbath. And there is enough money left for food for another day!'

"Master! My heart was so filled with joy that I could not contain myself. Tears fell from my eyes. Once more I praised the Lord for not having forgotten His children. And I praised Him again and again, happy that it was from God Himself, and not from man, that we had received our Sabbath.

"My heart was filled with singing. I forgot the majesty of the Sabbath. And I took my wife by the hand and led her out, and we danced in our little house. Then we sat down to eat. But when she served the fish course I was so overcome with joy that I took her in my arms and danced with her again. And when we ate the soup we danced a third time, and laughed and cried for happiness. For my soul overflowed with the glory of God.

"But, Master, it came to me afterwards that perhaps our dancing and laughter had disturbed the sublimity of God's Sabbath. If we have sinned that way and you have come here to find us out, then impose penance on me and my wife, and we will do all in our power to carry it out in order once more to come into the grace of God."

So spoke the bookbinder, Sabbatai, while his wife stood by his side.

Then Rabbi Israel said to his scholars and to all who were assembled there, "Know, that all the hierarchy of Heaven sang and laughed and was joyful and danced hand in hand with this aged man and his wife when they were happy on Sabbath eve. And there was a golden joy spread all through Paradise, and joy filled the Eternal Heart. And the three times you heard my laughter, my friends, I was here with them when they went out to dance, and I danced and sang with them!"

THE SEVERE PENANCE[1]

(A *Hasidic* Story)

MARTIN BUBER

The young Rabbi Michael, the "Slotscher," had imposed hard penance on a man who had unwittingly desecrated the Sabbath. For it had happened that the man's cart had broken down, and, though journeying fast, he had not reached the town before the Sabbath had set in.

The man tried with all his might to fulfill the penance imposed upon him, but he soon became aware that his strength was failing and that he was becoming ill, and finally that his mind was weakening. Suddenly he learnt that the Baal Shem was travelling through the country, and that he was stopping at a place near by.

Summoning courage, he went to the Master and besought him to impose penance that would set him free from the sin which he had committed. "Take a pound of candles to the prayer-house," said the Baal Shem, "and have them lit for the Sabbath; that shall be thy penance." The man thought that his communication could have been only half heard, and urgently repeated his request. When the Baal Shem still persisted in his mild sentence, the man confided to him what a severe punishment had been inflicted upon him. "Only do as I bid thee," said the Master. "But let Rabbi Michael know that he is to come to the town of Chowstaw where I am keeping the next Sabbath." With a lightened heart the petitioner took his leave.

Rabbi Michael's carriage wheel broke on the way to Chowstaw and he had to proceed on foot. Although he made as much haste as he could, when he entered the town it was already dark, and when he stepped over the Baal Shem's threshold he saw that the Master had risen, goblet in hand, in order to recite the blessing over the wine in preparation for the day of rest. The Master stopped short in what he was doing and said to the man who stood dazed before him: "Good Sabbath, thou man free from sin! Thou hast not tasted the pain of the sinner, and hast never borne within thee his broken heart; thus it came easy to thee to administer harsh penance. Now taste the pain of the sinner! Good Sabbath, you sinner."

THE SABBATH QUEEN[6]

B. LEVNER

And God blessed the seventh day, and hallowed it; because that in it He rested from all His work which God in creating had made.

And the Lord God placed the Sabbath upon a throne, and all the angels of heaven came to do her honor. They danced before her and sang in chorus, "It is a Sabbath unto the Lord!"

The Sabbath was happy in their praise, and her bright beauty illumined all the Seven Heavens. When she breathed, the fragrance of Paradise was wafted from one end of the heavens to the other.

And Man saw the Sabbath in all her glory and splendor, and he asked of the angels that stood about her as a court of honor, "Tell me, O sons of Heaven, to whom hath the Sabbath been given: To you or to the sons of Man?"

The angels answered, "The Lord God hath said that one day in every week the Sabbath shall go down to mankind to comfort them for all their sorrow and their toil."

But the Man continued to question. "If that be so, O sons of Heaven, why is it that ye rejoice in her?"

And the angels answered him further: "The Sabbath is the chief of all the joys that our loving Father hath created. Therefore do we also rejoice in her."

The Sabbath left her seat of honor and went to bow down before the Divine Presence. "It is a good thing to give thanks unto the Lord," she cried out. And the cherubs took up the refrain, "And to sing praises unto Thy name, O Most High!"

When the Lord saw all the joy and rapture which the Sabbath had brought into the world, He said to her, "Hear Me now, O Queen Sabbath! Six days in every week do men labor in the sweat of their brows. Go thou down to them on the seventh day that they may rejoice in thy peace and tranquility. 'Delight' shall they call thee, and receive thee with songs of praise. Each man will cry to his neighbor, 'Come, my beloved, to meet the Bride! Let us welcome the presence of the Sabbath!' "

And the Sabbath answered, "According to Thy will be it done, O Lord. But I know not the dwelling place of the sons of men, nor the path thither. How shall I be able to go to them?"

The Lord answered and said, "Behold, my daughter, I will create angels for thee who shall guide thee in the way thou shalt go among the sons of men."

The Sabbath made obeisance before the Heavenly Throne, and went out from the presence of the Lord.

The Sabbath descended upon the earth, and went over land and sea searching for them who waited for her. She saw many peoples, but none of them called upon her name. And she went on, through forest and field, valley and mountain range until she came upon a multitude of men and women toiling. Not for a moment did they pause, nor did they give rest to their men-servants or their maid-servants, or to their cattle. They gave no sign of desire to entertain the Sabbath, nor did they pause to look up as she passed them by.

So she turned and flew back to Heaven, and in a moment she stood before the Lord.

"Hear me, O Lord, my God, I pray Thee! I have seen the sons of men, and, behold, they have no delight in me. They call not upon my name, neither do they desire my peace. I pray Thee, give me the angels of whom Thou hast spoken. Let them lead me."

"Go down to earth a second time, My daughter, and thou shalt find the sons of Abraham, Isaac and Jacob. They have sworn to honor and to sanctify thee; and, if they do as they have sworn, the angels of whom I have spoken will be created."

And the Sabbath went down to earth a second time, as the Lord had commanded. It was the evening of the sixth day of the week as she entered the Land of Israel. The sky was covered with thick clouds, a heavy rain was falling, and the roads were covered with mire.

"How evil and bitter is the lot of man," she lamented.

Soon she came to a Jewish estate. A long avenue of

acacias and fir trees led to the house, and beautiful shrubs and plants had been set out in the courtyard.

As the Sabbath entered the house, she saw that the light of the candles gleamed in every corner. The whole household was bathed in peace and joy as the mother embraced each child. The father entered and blessed each child as it ran up to him with "*Shabbat Shalom!*" "May you be as Ephraim and Manasseh," he said, as he placed his right hand upon the heads of the little boys; and "May you be as Sarah and Rebecca, as Rachel and Leah," he wished for the little girls.

The house sparkled with cleanliness, and the faces of father and mother, of boys and girls, took on a new glow in the radiance of the Sabbath.

The Sabbath was so overjoyed at what she saw that she laughed aloud in the abundance of her pleasure.

And the Lord took her laughter and created an angel from it, saying to him: "Behold, peace and contentment and purity went to thy making. Whenever thou shalt find a household where these prevail on the Sabbath, thou shalt bless it, saying, 'Let your next Sabbath be like unto this one!'"

The Sabbath returned to the Lord after the seventh day had passed. As they were flying between Heaven and Earth, the Angel said to the Sabbath, "Tell me, I pray thee, Blessed of the Lord, what is the name of that land where I was created?"

And the Sabbath answered and said, "The Land of Israel."

Many years passed. Israel went into Exile, his land lay desolate in the hands of strangers.

The wandering Jew could no longer work on the soil, but had to become an artisan and a merchant. He lost his upright bearing, and became bowed and haggard with care.

His Sabbath and festival rejoicing ceased and nothing was heard from his lips but moaning and lamentations.

When the Queen Sabbath came to the Land of Israel once more, she found it as a mother bereft of her children. The Sabbath sought but could not find them. When she turned to the newcomers to abide with them, they said surlily, "We know thee not!"

Then she said, "Woe's me! They that love and keep me have gone into Exile. Therefore will I follow them to give them comfort and solace in their affliction. I will give them strength to bear their sorrows, and put hope into their hearts for the better days that are to come."

With her escorting angel, the Sabbath turned sadly away from the Land of Israel. Over burning deserts they passed until, on the eve of the Sabbath, they came to the rivers of Babylon.

The sun burned in the heavens like a fiery furnace. The hot wind raised columns of fine dust and sand that flew into the eyes and mouths of the people. Yet they had to keep at their tasks while great drops of perspiration rolled down their faces, and the dust parched and blinded them.

At last evening came, and the Sabbath entered a Jewish house. The window-panes were so thick with dust that the sun's rays could not have come through at noon. The floor was grimy, and so were the tables and beds and chairs. The children teased and pestered each other. The slovenly mother took no notice of them, but kept groaning and wishing she were dead.

The house grew darker and the children quarreled worse than before. The woman looked up finally. "Woe is me for the Sabbaths that have ceased from my house..." she moaned.

Pleased at the mention of her name, the Sabbath called upon the wind to come and clear away the dust from the window-panes. The sunset glow lighted up the room. "Quick, children, tidy up the house," cried the woman, "and bring out the lamps! The holy Sabbath will be here in a moment!"

"O mother," called a little boy, "there's no broom to sweep with. Give me money to buy a new one."

"And mother!" added a little girl, "don't you remember that our lamps are in pawn?"

Disheartened because she could not receive the Sabbath fittingly, the woman relapsed into her gloom, the children began to cry because there was no supper, and the very walls seemed to grieve for the poverty of the household. The tender heart of the Sabbath was touched and a tear fell from her eye.

The door turned on its rusty hinges and the father came in. He was a bowed, fagged-looking man. Throwing a heavy pack from his shoulders, he sat down groaning. "There's nothing to hope for," he cried out in despair. "Times are very bad. It's harder for me to earn a living than it was for our ancestors to cross the Red Sea. I know no rest, night or day; and yet all my work brings nothing . . . . Cursed be the day wherein I was born!"

The woman made him an angry answer and in a few minutes the house resounded with curses and imprecations. The children huddled together, crying and frightened at the strife between their parents.

Satan hurried in delight to this scene. He gathered up the curses of the parents, the tears of the children, the uncleanliness of the house, and gave them wings. "Fly!" he said. "Fly unto the Lord, and tell Him that Satan follows you!"

The black host flew away and presented itself before the Lord. Realizing what mischief Satan was planning, the Sabbath and her angel flew back to Heaven.

Satan already stood before the Divine Presence. "Righteous Judge!" he cried. "Thou didst give Thy most precious gift, the Sabbath, to the Children of Israel, saying to them, 'This is your Delight! In her shall you find joy and comfort.' Yet have I found this much gloom and profanation of Thy Sabbath in a Jewish home. Shall not the True Judge take note of these curses and imprecations?"

The Lord grew wroth. The pillars of heaven trembled, the light of the stars was darkened, and the angels were mute with fear. Then Satan rejoiced exceedingly. He held up a vial filled with the tears of the children and urged the Lord to pour out His wrath upon the desecrators of the Sabbath. But in the vial the Lord saw the gleaming tear shed by the Sabbath over the poverty of that Jewish house, and He asked of Satan: "Whose tear is this?"

Satan's eyes blazed as he realized how foolish he had been to gather up with the others the tear shed by the Sabbath.

In that instant the Sabbath appeared, crying, "O Lord! Show Thy mercy and grace and lovingkindness!" And she fell prostrate upon her face.

"Arise, My daughter!" came the Divine command. "Why dost thou weep? And what are these curses that resound through the heavens?"

And the Sabbath related how bitter was the life of Israel in Exile, how deep his humiliation, how wretched his poverty. The Angels of Mercy wept as they listened, and their tears rolled even to the foot of the Throne . . . .

"Only the Exile is the cause of all this," pleaded the Sabbath. "Only the sufferings of Thy children embitter their hearts and their souls."

Satan trembled at these words, but still urged his case against Israel. "Hearken not, I pray Thee, O Lord, to the Sabbath, for she doth delight in Israel. Not poverty, but

iniquity is the cause of the profanation of the Sabbath. I
have seen a Jewish family, sunk in the depths of poverty, do
great honor to the Sabbath. Send Thy angels of peace,
O Lo:d, to bring them hither."

An Angel of Peace stepped forward.

"Bring hither the family of whom Satan hath spoken,
My son," commanded the Lord.

. . . . . .

Before the Throne of Grace stood a poor little house.
Within could be seen a man and a woman and children
sitting around a table. The cloth was snow-white, the
candlesticks were brightly polished, the light of the candles
penetrated every dark corner.

Mother and father looked at each other lovingly and
spoke gently to their children.

As the father recited the Sabbath prayers, his eyes filled
with tears of joy. And the Lord took those tears and set
them into His Crown.

"Who made all the peace and lovingkindness that I see
in this household?" asked the Lord.

And the Angel of Peace answered, "All of them. The
man helps his wife, and she helps him. The children obey
their mother, and take the teachings of their father to
heart. It is the love of each for the other that sweeps the
house and trims the lamps and draws water from the well
and cares for the babies. All of them together bring a
blessing upon their house."

The Lord asked further, "What is this man's occupation?"

The Angel of Peace made answer, "He is a bearer of
burdens. He works very hard, and all his reward is bread
and water by measure. Would that the Lord would open
up His treasure house and give him —"

The Lord cut him short. "I have given him abundance

already. He and his wife and his little ones were created with pure hearts, and I have given them contentment with their lot."

. . . . . .

The vision passed. Satan stood once more before the Lord. "Most High Judge! Thou knowest that the Sabbath hath no cause to defend that evil household. Recompense it, I pray Thee, according to the measure of its wickedness."

The Lord passed judgment: "Behold," He said, "I shall create yet another angel to accompany the Sabbath when she goes down among the sons of men. Out of the filth and strife that Satan has brought hither will I create him. And it shall come to pass that when they enter a home where peace and gladness prevail, the Good Angel shall say: 'Your next Sabbath shall be like this one.' And the Evil Angel shall say, 'Amen!'

"But if uncleanliness and strife shall be found in a Jewish home on the Sabbath, the Evil Angel shall call out in his anger, 'Your next Sabbath shall be like this one!' And then will the Good Angel be forced to say, 'Amen!' "

As these words came from the mouth of the Lord, the Evil Angel was born. He was black all over, and his mean little eyes looked about with hatred. The angels of light shuddered at his appearance, but Satan rejoiced greatly at the creation of one of his own kind.

. . . . . .

The next week, as the Sabbath turned to go down among the sons of men, the Evil Angel inquired of her, "What was the name of that land from whose mire I was created?"

The Sabbath pointed downward toward the earth and answered with a sigh, "The name of that land is the Land of Oppression."

THE SABBATH-BREAKER[7]

Israel Zangwill

The moment came near for the Polish centenarian grand-mother to die. From the doctor's statement it appeared that she had only a bad quarter of an hour to live. Her attack had been sudden, and the grandchildren she loved to scold could not be present.

She had already battled through the great wave of pain, and was drifting beyond the boundaries of her earthly refuge. The nurses, forgetting the trouble her querulousness and her overweening dietary scruples had cost them, hung over the bed on which the shrivelled entity lay. They did not know that she was again living through the one great episode of her life.

Nearly forty years back, when already hard upon seventy, she received a letter. It arrived on the eve of Sabbath on a day of rainy summer. It was from her "little boy" — her only boy — who kept a country inn seven-and-thirty miles away, and had a family. She opened the letter with feverish anxiety. Her son — her *Kaddish* — was the apple of her eye. The old woman eagerly perused the Hebrew script, from right to left. Then weakness overcame her and she nearly fell.

Embedded casually enough in the four pages was a passage that stood out for her in letters of blood: "I am not feeling very well lately; the weather is so oppressive and the nights are misty. But it is nothing serious; my digestion is a little out of order, that's all." There were roubles for her in the letter, but she let them fall to the floor unheeded. Panic fear, traveling quicker than the tardy post of those days, had brought rumor of a sudden outbreak of cholera in her son's district. Already alarm for her boy had surged about her heart all day; the letter con-

firmed her worst apprehensions. Even if the first touch of
the cholera fiend was not actually on him when he wrote,
still he was by his own confession in that condition in which
the disease takes easiest grip. By this time he was on a
bed of sickness — nay, perhaps on his death-bed, if not
dead. Even in those days the little grandmother had lived
beyond the common span; she had seen many people die,
and knew that the Angel of Death does not always go about
his work leisurely. In an epidemic his hands are too full to
enable him to devote much attention to each case. Maternal
instinct tugged at her heartstrings, drawing her towards her
boy. The end of the letter seemed impregnated with special
omen — "Come and see me soon, dear little mother. I shall
be unable to get to you for some time." Yes, she must go
at once — who knew but that it would be the last time
she would look upon his face?

But then came a terrible thought to give her pause. The
Sabbath was just "in" — a moment ago. Driving, riding or
any manner of journeying was prohibited during the next
twenty-four hours. Frantically she reviewed the situation.
Religion permitted the violation of the Sabbath on one
condition — if life was to be saved. By no stretch of logic
could she delude herself into the belief that her son's recovery hinged upon her presence — nay, analyzing the case
with the cruel remorselessness of a scrupulous conscience,
she saw his very illness was only a plausible hypothesis.
No; to go to him now were beyond question to profane the
Sabbath.

And yet, beneath all the reasoning, her conviction that
he was sick unto death, her resolve to set out at once,
never wavered. After an agonizing struggle she compromised. She could not go by cart. That would be to
make others work into the bargain, and would moreover
involve a financial transaction. She must walk! Sinful as

it was to transgress the limit of two thousand yards beyond
her village — the distance fixed by rabbinical law — there
was no help for it. And of all the forms of traveling, walking was surely the least sinful. The Holy One — blessed be
He! — would know she did not mean to work; perhaps in
His mercy He would make allowance for an old woman who
had never profaned His rest-day before.

And so, that very evening, having made a hasty meal, . . .
the little grandmother girded up her loins to walk the
seven-and-thirty miles. No staff did she take with her, for
to carry such came under the talmudical definition of work.
Neither could she carry an umbrella, though it was a season
of rain. Mile after mile she strode briskly on towards that
pallid face that lay so far beyond the horizon, and yet
ever shone before her eyes like a guiding star. "I am coming, my lamb," she muttered. "The little mother is on
the way."

It was a muggy night. The sky, flushed with a weird,
hectic glamor, seemed to hang over the earth like a pall.
The trees that lined the roadway were shrouded in a drag-
gling vapor. At midnight the mist blotted out the stars.
But the little grandmother knew the road ran straight. All
night she walked through the forest, fearless as Una, meeting neither man nor beast, though the wolf and the bear
haunted its recesses, and snakes lurked in the bushes. But
only the innocent squirrels darted across her path. The
morning found her spent, and almost lame. But she walked
on. Almost half the journey was yet to do.

She had nothing to eat with her; food, too, was an illegal
burden, nor could she buy any on the holy day. She said
her Sabbath morning prayer walking, hoping God would
forgive the disrespect. The recital gave her partial oblivion
of her pains. As she passed through a village the dreadful
rumor of cholera was confirmed; it gave wings to her feet

for ten minutes, then bodily weakness was stronger than everything else, and she had to lean against the hedges on the outskirts of the village It was nearly noon. A passing beggar gave her a piece of bread. Fortunately it was un-buttered, so she could eat it with only minor qualms lest it had touched any unclean thing. She resumed her journey, but the rest had only made her feet move more painfully and reluctantly. She would have liked to bathe them in a brook, but that, too, was forbidden . . . . Then the leaden clouds melted into sharp lines of rain which beat into her face, refreshing her for the first few moments but soon wetting her to the skin. The downpour made her sopped garments a heavier burden and reduced the pathway to mud which clogged still further her feeble footsteps. In the teeth of the wind and the driving shower she limped on. A fresh anxiety consumed her now — would she have strength to hold out? Every moment her pace lessened, she was moving like a snail. And the slower she went, the more vivid grew her prescience of what awaited her at the journey's end. Would she even hear his dying word? Perhaps — terrible thought — she would only be in time to look upon his dead face! Mayhap that was how God would punish her for her desecration of the Holy Day. "Take heart, my lamb!" she wailed. "Do not die yet. The little mother comes."

The rain stopped. The sun came out, hot and fierce, and dried her hands and face, then made them stream again with perspiration. Every inch won was torture now, but the brave feet toiled on. Bruised and swollen and crippled, they toiled on. There was a dying voice — very far off yet, alas! — that called to her, and, as she dragged herself along, she replied: "I am coming, my lamb. Take heart! The little mother is on the way. Courage! I shall look upon thy face, I shall find thee alive!"

Once a waggoner observed her plight and offered her a lift; but she shook her head steadfastly. The endless afternoon wore on — she crawled along the forest way, stumbling every now and then from sheer faintness, and tearing her hands and face in the brambles of the roadside. At last the cruel sun waned, and reeking mists rose from the forest pools. And still the long miles stretched away, and still she plodded on, torpid from over-exhaustion, scarcely conscious, and taking each step only because she had taken the preceding. From time to time her lips mumbled: "Take heart, my lamb! I am coming." The Sabbath was "out" when, broken and bleeding and all but swooning, the little grandmother crawled up to her son's inn on the border of the forest. Her heart was cold with fatal foreboding. There was none of the usual Saturday night litter of Polish peasantry about the door. The sound of many voices weirdly intoning a Hebrew hymn floated out into the night. A man in a caftan opened the door and mechanically raised his forefinger to bid her enter without noise. The little grandmother saw into the room behind. Her daughter-in-law and her grandchildren were seated on the floor — the seat of mourners.

"Blessed be the True Judge!" she said, and rent the skirt of her dress. "When did he die?"

"Yesterday. We had to bury him hastily ere the Sabbath came in."

The little grandmother lifted up her quavering voice and joined in the hymn, "I will sing a new song unto Thee, O God: upon a harp of ten strings will I sing praises unto Thee."

. . . . . .

The nurses could not understand what sudden inflow of strength and impulse raised the mummified figure into a sitting posture. The little grandmother thrust a shrivelled claw into her peaked, shrunken bosom, and drew out a paper, crumpled and yellow as herself, covered with strange crabbed hieroglyphics whose hue had long since faded. She held it close to her bleared eyes — a beautiful light came into them and illumined the million-puckered face. The lips moved faintly: "I am coming, my lamb!" she mumbled. "Courage! The little mother is on the way. I shall look on thy face. I shall find thee alive."

CHAPTER XV

THE SABBATH IN JEWISH POETRY

THE SABBATH DAY[1]

Judah Halevi

Behold it is the Sabbath day
    And I, Thy servant, come before
Thy throne, Almighty King, to pray
    That Thou Thy holy truth wilt pour
    Upon my soul, to give it rest once more.
Grant that I may Thy praise proclaim,
For my delight it is to speak Thy name.

HYMN OF WELCOME TO THE SABBATH[2]

Solomon Solis-Cohen

Come, my belovèd, with chorus of praise,
Welcome Bride Sabbath, the Queen of the days.

"Keep and Remember!"— in one divine Word
He that is One, Alone, made His will heard;
One is the name of Him, One is the Lord!
    His are the fame and the glory and praise!

Sabbath, to welcome thee, joyous we haste;
Fountain of blessing from ever thou wast —
First in God's planning, though fashioned the last,
    Crown of His handiwork, chiefest of days.

City of holiness, filled are the years;
Up from thine overthrow! Forth from thy fears!
Long hast thou dwelt in the valley of tears,
    Now shall God's tenderness shepherd thy ways.

289

Rise, O my folk, from the dust of the earth,
Garb thee in raiment beseeming thy worth;
Nigh draws the hour of the Bethlehemite's[3] birth,
    Freedom who bringeth, and glorious days.

Wake and bestir thee, for come is thy light!
Up! With thy shining, the world shall be bright;
Sing! For thy Lord is revealed in His Might —
    Thine is the splendor His Glory displays!

'Be not ashamed,' saith the Lord, 'nor distressed;
Fear not and doubt not. The people oppressed,
Zion, My city, in thee shall find rest —
    Thee, that anew on thy ruins I raise.'

Spoiled shall thy spoilers be; banished afar,
They that devoured. But in thee, evermore,
God shall take joy; as the bridegroom, what hour,
    Blushing, the bride lifts her veil to his gaze.

Stretch out thy borders to left and to right;
Fear but the Lord, Whom to fear is delight —
The man, son of Perez,[4] shall gladden our sight,
    And we shall rejoice to the fullness of days.

Come in thy joyousness, Crown of thy Lord;
Come, bringing peace to the folk of the Word;
Come where the faithful in gladsome accord,
    Hail thee as Sabbath-Bride, Queen of the days.

Come where the faithful are hymning thy praise;
Come as a bride cometh, Queen of the days!

THE SABBATH[5]

EDITH ELLA DAVIS

The Sabbath comes with subtle grace,—
    White tapers light her way;
A festive table marks her place
    With wine and silver tray.

The Sabbath comes — a solemn queen,
   From Heaven-ways she trod;
A prayer hath wreathed her soul serene,
   Her soul the gift of God.

SABBATH HYMN[6]

AARON COHEN

Descend, descend, O Sabbath Princess,
   With rays of *Shekinah* in your eyes,
Descend and bring us peaceful tidings,
   From yonder gently dreaming skies!
Behold, in darkness, and in sadness
   We wander here, we climb, we grope;
Descend and give us Faith and Gladness,
   Descend and give us light and hope!

Descend, descend, O Sabbath Princess,
   For we are weary here and blind;
Descend and lighten all the burdens
   Of dreary souls and faithless mind.
The paths of life are rough and thorny,
   Our feet are bleeding, bleeding sore;
Descend and bring us Heaven's promise,
   And Sabbath peace for evermore.

KINDLING THE SABBATH LIGHT[7]

PHILIP M. RASKIN

From memory's spring flows a vision tonight;
My mother is kindling and blessing the light.

The light of queen Sabbath, the heavenly flame
That one day in seven quells hunger and shame.

My mother is praying, and screening her face,
Too bashful to gaze at the Sabbath lights' grace.

She murmurs devoutly: "Almighty, be blessed
For sending Thy angel of joy and of rest.

And may, as the candles of Sabbath divine,
The eyes of my son in Thy Law ever shine.". . . .

Of childhood, fair childhood, the years are long fled:
Youth's candles are quenched, and my mother is dead.

And yet ev'ry Friday, when twilight arrives,
The face of my mother within me revives;

A prayer on her lips: "O Almighty, be blessed
For sending us Sabbath, the angel of rest."

And some hidden feelings I cannot control
A Sabbath light kindles deep, deep in my soul.

THE HEBREW'S FRIDAY NIGHT[8]

ISRAEL ZANGWILL

Sweet Sabbath-Bride, the Hebrew's theme of praise,
    Celestial maiden with the starry eyes,
Around thine head a sacred nimbus plays,
    Thy smile is soft as lucent summer skies,
    Before thy purity all evil dies.
In wedding-robe of stainless sunshine drest,
    Thou dawnest on life's darkness, and it dies;
The bridal-wreath is lilies Heaven-blest,
The dowry peace and love and holiness and rest.

The father from the synagogue returns
    (A singing-bird is nestling at his heart),
And from without the festive light discerns
    Which tells his faithful wife has done her part
    To welcome Sabbath with domestic art.
He enters and perceives the picture true,
    And tears unbidden from his eyelids start,
As Paradise thus opens on his view,
And then he smiles and thanks God he is a Jew.

For "Friday night" is written on his home
  In fair, white characters; his wife has spread
The snowy Sabbath-cloth; the Hebrew tome,
    The flask and cup are at the table's head;
    There's Sabbath magic in the very bread,
And royal fare the humble dishes seem;
    A holy light the Sabbath candles shed;
Around, his children's shining faces beam;
He feels the strife of every day a far-off dream.

His buxom wife he kisses; then he lays
  Upon each child's young head two loving hands
Of benediction, so in after-days,
    When they shall be afar in other lands,
    They shall be knit to God and home by bands
Of sacred memory. And then he makes
    The blessing o'er the wine, and while each stands,
The quaintly convoluted bread he breaks,
Which tastes to all tonight more sweet than honeyed cakes.

So in a thousand squalid Ghettos penned,
  Engirt yet undismayed by perils vast,
The Jew, in hymns that marked his faith, would spend
    This night, and dream of all his glorious past,
    And wait the splendors by his seers forecast.
And so, while medieval creeds at strife
    With nature die, the Jew's ideals last;
The simple love of home and child and wife,
The sweet humanities which make our higher life.

SHABBAT[9]

E. Grindell

This is it
To come from the blazing sunlight
Into the dim quiet of the synagogue.
To sit with my grandfather, his thin shoulders
Sharp against his white silk *Tallit.*

To hear the murmur of old men
And the rising, melancholy song of the cantor;
The crying song of God and of prayer.

This is the great warmth, the great at-homeness;
This is the knowledge of belonging;
The loneness merging into a strong oneness.
One lost drop of water finding its way into the sea.
The Torah gleams white and silver, and we stand
Singing and praying,
Our hearts warm with peace,
Our spirits quiet in the quietness of *Shabbat*.

This is the end of the week and its beginning.
This is the moment of pause,
The refilling of the empty vessel,
The renewing of the spirit.
This is the remembering;
The shared memory of two thousand years
And the shared embarking upon two thousand more.
This is the hearth, the gathering together;
The pain and the joy,
The tears and the gentle laughter.
This is the benign wisdom in an old man's eyes
And the hope in a boy's fresh voice,
The roots into the past
And the arms stretched forward into the future . . . .

We shall live forever and ever.
We shall wander from land to land,
From nation to nation,
Sometimes driven, sometimes tormented;
We shall suffer sharp blows and many deep-hurting wounds.
But this place will be with us
And this warmth
And this rejoicing . . . .

For this is the great, the many-faceted, the bottomless *Shalom*.

PRINCESS SABBATH[10]

Heinrich Heine

In Arabia's book of fable
We behold enchanted princes
Who at times their form recover,
Fair as first they were created.

The uncouth and shaggy monster
Has again a king for father:
Pipes his amorous ditties sweetly
On the flute in jewelled raiment.

Yet the respite from enchantment
Is but brief, and, without warning,
Lo! we see his Royal Highness
Shuffled back into a monster.

Of a prince by fate thus treated
Is my song. His name is Israel,
And a witch's spell has changed him
To the likeness of a dog.

As a dog, with dog's ideas,
All the week, a cur, he noses
Through life's filthy mire and sweepings,
Butt of mocking city Arabs;

But on every Friday evening,
On a sudden, in the twilight,
The enchantment weakens, ceases,
And the dog once more is human.

And his father's halls he enters
As a man, with man's emotions,
Head and heart alike uplifted,
Clad in pure and festal raiment.

"Be ye greeted, halls beloved,
Of my high and royal father!
Lo! I kiss your holy door-posts,
Tents of Jacob, with my mouth!"

Through the house there passes strangely
A mysterious stir and whisper,
And the hidden master's breathing
Shudders weirdly through the silence.

Golden lights of consolation,
How they sparkle, how they glimmer!
Proudly flame the candles also
On the rails of the *Almemor*.

"*Lekah dodi likrat Kallah* —
Come, beloved one, the bride
Waits already to uncover
To thine eyes her blushing face!"

Pearl and flower of all beauty
Is the princess — not more lovely
Was the famous Queen of Sheba,
Bosom friend of Solomon.

But the lovely day flits onward,
And with long, swift legs of shadow
Comes the evil hour of magic —
And the prince begins to sigh;

Seems to feel the icy fingers
Of a witch upon his heart;
Shudders, fearful of the canine
Metamorphosis that awaits him.

Then the princess hands her golden
Box of spikenard to her lover,
Who inhales it, fain to revel
Once again in pleasant odors.

And the princess tastes and offers
Next the cup of parting also —
And he drinks in haste, till only
Drops a few are in the goblet.

These he sprinkles on the table
Then he takes a little wax-light,
And he dips it in the moisture
Till it crackles and is quenched.

SUMMER SABBATH[11]

JESSIE E. SAMPTER

In Summer, in the open air,
I seek my Sabbath house of prayer
    Among the friendly trees,
Beneath a blue and shining dome
Where clouds like watchful angels roam
    To guard the lands and seas.

My prayer book open on my knee,
Another prayer is taught to me,
    A Torah without words:
I hear it sung by swinging leaves,
By every breeze that sighs and heaves,
    By all the choirs of birds.

The buzzing insects sing His praise,
And all the flowers with modest ways
    Swing silently in awe;
They praise my God that made us all:
This is my people, green and small,
    That shares my life and law.

The little shining leaves of vine
That lay their tiny hands in mine
    Are praying, every one;
The maples shimmering overhead
Remember all that God has said
    And tremble in the sun.

O Lord, that made my People hold
Thy covenant from days of old,
      Is this Thy people, too?
Though we Thy truth at Sinai saw,
Each race has its eternal law,
Each life its task to do.

SABBATH THOUGHTS[12]

GRACE AGUILAR

I bless Thee, Father, for the grace
      Thou me this day hast given,
Strengthening my soul to seek Thy face,
      And list the theme of heaven.

I bless Thee that each workday care
      Thy love hath lull'd to rest,
And every thought whose wing has prayer
      Thine answering word hath blest.

I bless Thee, Father! Those dark fears
      That linger'd round my heart,
That called for murmurs, doubts, and fears,
      Thy mercy bade depart.

O Thou alone couldst send them hence
      On this bless'd day of peace,
And with Thy spirit's pure incense
      Bid workday turmoils cease.

ABBA TACHNA[13]

ALICE LUCAS

Good Abba Tachna midst his fellows bore
The name of Pious Abba. Evermore
He strove with joyful ardour to fulfil

Each word and precept, that th' Almighty's will
Gave unto Israel in the holy law,
But most of all did he with joy and awe
Render obedience unto each behest
Pertaining to the Sabbath day of rest.
Six days he toiled for bread — then, blessing heaven,
Rested in peace from even unto even.
One Sabbath eve, when as the light of day
Was sinking slowly, on his homeward way
Abba, when passing by the city gate,
Saw, stretched upon the ground, disconsolate,
An agèd man, who, faint and helpless, cried
For one to raise him. Abba laid aside,
Hearing his prayer, the cumbrous pack he bore,
For all the coming week his scanty store,
And, moved to pity at his mournful plaint,
Raised in his arms the old man weak and faint,
And bore him, putting forth his utmost strength,
Until they reached the stranger's home at length.
"The Sabbath hour," mused Abba, "draweth nigh,
Yet to have left the agèd man to die
Had been a grievous sin. Now must I seek
My pack, else how provide throughout the week
For wife and little ones?" With this intent,
Forth to the city gate again he went.
But when, his burden bearing, through the street,
He passed with aching arms and weary feet,
The last faint rays of day had almost fled;
And those who saw him scoffed, and mocking said:
"Abba the pious bearing burdens see
On Sabbath eve! A Sabbath-breaker he.
The Sabbath-breaker be henceforth his name!"
And Abba, hearing, bowed his head in shame.
The sun had set, when lo, a miracle!
Its golden beams, but now invisible,
Shone forth anew, and bathed the world in light,
Nor did they sink again in shades of night,
Till Abba reached his home, and entering there,
With thankful heart, began his Sabbath prayer.

OUTGOING SABBATH[14]

JOSEPH LEFTWICH

The shadows are descending,
The Sabbath day is ending,
   The holy Sabbath day.
And in the silence, slowly,
With head bowed down and lowly,
   My mother starts to pray.

Oh, God of Abraham, hearken,
Send no more days that darken
   My eyes and bow my head.
Oh hear me, God in heaven,
All things by Thee are given,
   Give us our daily bread.

[Additional Sabbath poems will be found in Chap. III, pp. 38–58; 74–88; 93–98 and in Chap. IV, pp. 149 ff.]

CHAPTER XVI

THE SABBATH IN MUSIC

By

A. W. BINDER

אָשִׁיר לָךְ, שַׁבָּת, שִׁירֵי יְדִידוֹת,
כִּי יָאֲתָה לָךְ, כִּי אַתְּ יוֹם חֲמָדוֹת

(יהודה הלוי).

I will sing, O Sabbath, songs of love unto thee,
For it is fitting, O day that art precious to me.

(JUDAH HALEVI)

SABBATH MUSIC IN ANCIENT PALESTINE

EARLY in the history of the Jewish people, the Sabbath was called a delight and a day of good cheer. It was never a day of mortification or sadness, as among the Babylonians of ancient days. In the Temple at Jerusalem special sacrifices were offered, excerpts from the Bible read, and a special "Psalm for the Sabbath Day" sung by the Levites. This was Psalm 92, still recited as the Psalm of the Sabbath. Significantly, Psalm 92 is one of the ten psalms which begin with the words *Mizmor Shir*, both meaning "song." This was interpreted to mean that the Sabbath was to abound in song and praise, and so to be a delight. It was also considered significant that this psalm contains much musical terminology. In it are found such words as *'Asor*, meaning ten-stringed instrument;[1] *Navel*, large harp; *Higgayon*, meditative music; *Kinnor*, small harp; *Aranen*, "I shall sing" or "I shall be joyful."

301

Many reasons for music on the Sabbath were offered at a later time. A few typical ones are worth quoting. There are, it was said, seven gates in the head of a human being: two ears, two nostrils, two eyes, and a mouth. The last is the seventh, with which it is incumbent for the Jew to bless the seventh day.[2] Then there is a passage in the Song of Songs—"I am dark but comely"—which the Midrash interprets, "Dark am I during the six days of the week, but beautiful am I on the Sabbath with my songs and prayers." Thus music became an integral part of the celebration and of the very spirit of the Sabbath day.

It seems highly probable that more than the usual amount of singing characterized the Sabbath service in the synagogues as well as the Temple of Palestine. The prescribed portion of the Law had to be read "with a sweet tune,"[3] and this reading played an important part in the service. There was gaiety, singing and dancing on the Sabbath day in the public squares, too. Finally, Levites were permitted to play their instruments on the Sabbath and even to mend a broken string of a stringed instrument.[4] For, while the three trumpet blasts which were sounded at intervals on a Friday afternoon were a warning to cease work in preparation for the Sabbath, such prohibitions did not apply to the Temple.

ZEMIROT

After the destruction of the Temple the Jews went into mourning. Singing and instrumental music, which were a sign of joy, were prohibited. On the Sabbath, however, which was a day of rest and which was called "a delight," Israel was permitted to cast off its mourning and welcome the day in holiness and joy. אין אבלות בשבת: "Mourning on the Sabbath is prohibited!"

Music became the great aid to this principle of temporary surcease from sorrow. In the synagogue the Pentateuch and the Prophets continued to be read with a sweet
tune, as commanded. We still hear these modes in our synagogues; they are known as "cantillation modes."[5] The
ever-growing liturgy, which replaced the sacrifices, was
sung and chanted. Of this music we, today, have but
faint traces, since musical notations did not come into
existence until the 8th century. The *Kiddush* over wine,
in the synagogue as in the home, must always have been
chanted in a rather elaborate and festive style. In the home,
the Sabbath meal, too, was made to contribute to the delight of the day.

Zemirot, table songs, had begun to develop as far back
as the days of the Second Temple.[6] Thus it is believed
that *Zur mi-Shelo*,[7] one of the group of *Zemirot* for the
Sabbath eve, whose author is unknown, belongs to the
early tannaitic period, perhaps even before Jabne. The poem
is based on three benedictions of the grace: *Ha-Zan, 'Al
ha-Arez*, and *Boneh*. There is no reference at all to the Sabbath in this poem. Most of the *Zemirot*, however, are prod-
ucts of a much later day.

The idea of making the Sabbath a day of delight and
joy through music gained momentum as time went on.
Mounting persecution made the burden of the Jew increas-
ingly heavy. It became necessary to emphasize those elements in the Sabbath which could give the Jew some respite
from his troubled existence, some way of restoring his self-
respect. The Sabbath was to bring sweet peace and rest
and remind him that he was a prince of God. It is, therefore,
significant that the gayest *Zemirot* were written during the
gloomiest times.[8]

The 11th century witnessed the beginning of the great
period in the history of Hebrew poetry, both sacred and

secular. The vogue in those days was to compose religious poetry to the rhythm and melody of popular, secular songs and to imitate their phonetic sound in Hebrew.[9] At first the rabbis censured such practices; but the poets won. One rabbi, after having been persuaded of the worthwhileness of the practice, said that he saw "no reason why the Devil should have all the beautiful tunes." Many of these sacred poems became popular; some found their way into the liturgy, and a number became *Zemirot* for the Sabbath.

Another factor in the development of *Zemirot* was the growth of the Cabala, whose mystic ideas became popularly associated with the Sabbath. One cabalistic belief was that a *Neshamah Yeterah*, an additional soul or a Sabbath soul, descended upon the one who observed the Sabbath according to law. Many cabalists believed that such a soul could be attained only through song on the Sabbath. The Lurian cabalists of the 16th century laid particular stress upon the power of music. Isaac Luria himself encouraged his disciple, Shelomo Alkabetz (1505-1572), to compose the famous poem, *Lekah Dodi*. This poem, along with the Song of Songs, *Azamer bi-Shevahin* and *An'im Zemirot*, is the center of a group of love songs by which the Jew expressed his love for God and the Sabbath. *Lekah Dodi*[10] spread rapidly to all Jewish communities and, in later centuries, became a favorite text for composers of synagogue music. Isaac Luria also composed *Zemirot* for each of the three Sabbath meals: *Azamer bi-Shevahin*, *Asader li-Se'udeta*, and *Bene Hekala*.

Not only the poetry but also the tunes of certain *Zemirot* have been attributed to Isaac Luria and his cabalist followers, including Israel Najara, the composer of *Yah Ribbon 'Alam*.[11] While this may be doubted, it is clear that the Hasidim, the spiritual descendants of the Lurianic cabalists, contributed much to the music for the *Zemirot*. Hasidic tunes for *Zemirot* are almost always joyous and rhythmic. Characteristic of their method of singing is the frequent interpolation of stretches of wordless song where there is melody to spare between the phrases or verses of a poem. For the Hasidim were careless in choosing their melodies. They adapted to their needs military marches, waltzes and other popular tunes of the day and land in which they lived. Consequently, the rhythm of the song or the length of the melody did not always fit. But to Hasidim this did not seem to matter.

Among the *HaBaD* Hasidim, however, one does find melodies with mystic elements of the kind which colored their beliefs. The most mystic tunes were reserved for the Aramaic poems in the *Zemirot*, such as *Azamer bi-Shevahin*, and *Yah Ribbon*. This may have been due to the Lurianic origin of these poems.

Whether among Hasidim or Mithnagdim, *Zemirot* served as the bridge between table-talk and religious discourses, between the human and the divine, between the serious and the jocular. It has been pointed out frequently that a Jew must honor God with the beauty of his soul and the beauty of his throat:[12] "While Israel feasts, he always sings songs of praise to God."[13] The chief singers at the table were the father and the sons. Mother and daughters might join in the refrains or sing their own *Zemirot*.[14] Such were the customs as the singing of *Zemirot* gained ground during the Middle Ages, particularly in Germany and Italy.[15] The Ashkenazim sang *Zemirot* all year round, while the Sephardim sang them only in winter and summer.

There are *Zemirot* for all three meals of the Sabbath; but the most important and colorful group, from the poetic and musical points of view, are those associated with the Friday evening and Saturday midday meals. At the Sabbath eve meal the master of the home welcomes the Sabbath with the chanting of a group of prayers beginning with *Shalom 'Alekem*.[16] The *Kiddush* follows. The actual *Zemirot* are introduced with a meditative poem: *Kol Mekadesh* [17] for Friday evening and *Baruk Adonai Yom Yom*[18] for Sabbath afternoon. The tune of each of these is reminiscent of a liturgical mode: *Kol Mekadesh* is sung in the *Magen Abot* mode of the Friday evening service, suggesting the "sweet peace and rest" attitude of the Sabbath; *Baruk Adonai* is likewise associated with a Friday evening synagogue mode, that of *Adonai Malak*, suggesting Israel as the "Prince of God."

Generally the *Zemirot* melodies which follow the introductory ones are lively and bear the unquestionable stamp of the country or locality whence they stem. The Sabbath guest used to be asked to sing the *Zemirot* with the melodies customarily used in his native town. If the Sabbath guest was a good singer, his hosts and their neighbors would gather to learn his songs. This is how melodies frequently spread through Jewish communities.

It is not within the province of this discussion to speculate on the origins or authors of the poetry of the *Zemirot*; but a few remarks on this aspect of Jewish music may be in place.

Israel Najara (1550-1620), the author of the very beautiful and popular poem, *Yah Ribbon*, holds a unique place among the authors of poetry in the *Zemirot* period. He composed not only poetry but also melodies. He followed the favorite custom of his period in composing poems to existing rhythms and melodies of popular songs. He published, in 1587, in Safed, the first edition of his *divan*, *Zemirot Yisrael*, which became very popular in oriental Jewish communities. It was the first Jewish song book to be published in the Orient.

The poem in the Sabbath *Zemirot* which deserves special

mention is *Mah Yafit*,[19] which is the work of Mordecai ben Isaac, whose name is found therein in an acrostic. The melody of this poem is evidently of Polish origin and gained notoriety among the wealthy Polish *Pans* in the 17th, 18th, and 19th centuries. At their wild orgies these *Pans*, who were the Jews' landlords, frequently would compel a Jew to sing and dance to the *Mah Yafit* melody. Almost every Pole knew that a Jew could sing *Mah Yafit*. Even Chopin was led to remark, "Poor Polish airs, you do not in the least suspect how you will be interlarded with *Mah Yafit*."

Zemirot were not only sung at the Sabbath midday meal, but also at the *Shalosh Se'udot*, the third meal of the Sabbath. This meal usually took place after the Sabbath afternoon service, and almost always in the synagogue. The singing of *Zemirot* was kept up until sundown, and thus the *Zemirot* always had the character of a prelude to the outgoing of the Sabbath. The evening service usually followed and, after the *Habdalah*, which ushered in the secular days of the week, *Zemirot* again were sung. Later in the evening, at the *Melaveh Malkah*, which was to indicate the accompanying of "the Bride" back to her abode, until her return on the following Sabbath, more *Zemirot* were sung. As a matter of fact, there was always a great deal of singing at the outgoing of the Sabbath, for it was considered appropriate to chant hymns and thus fittingly to accompany the Sabbath Bride upon her departure.

The music for the various occasions had distinct character and atmosphere. For the greeting of the Sabbath and for the Sabbath day itself, joyous melodies were generally employed; but for the outgoing of the Sabbath, mystic and nostalgic tunes were sung. The post-*Habdalah* group of *Zemirot* dealt with the coming of Elijah the prophet to deliver Israel from exile. Elijah songs are, indeed, the most ancient of these *Zemirot*, since the Jew hoped and sang of his return to his Homeland from the very moment of exile. Of this group of songs *Eliyahu ha-Navi*[20] is the most ancient.

The table songs of the Sabbath comprised the Jewish song book. The Jew sang them through joy and tears. These poems and songs are the mirror of the soul-life of Universal Israel, for through them he attained the *Neshamah Yeterah* (Sabbath Over-Soul) which descended upon him on the Sabbath day.

There are very few parallels to the Jewish *Zemirot* among the nations. Other nations have their drinking songs, but we have our *Zemirot*. In them we find genial piety combined with good cheer and thankfulness which are usually separated in the table-songs which existed among the nations. They combine tragedy and joy, the material and the spiritual, changes of taste and progress of thought. All these elements are mirrored in the songs, and through it all, the general theme is "The Sabbath."

SABBATH MUSIC IN THE SYNAGOGUE

The precentor or cantor always occupied an important position in Jewish religious worship. He led the people in prayer and read portions of the Law to the congregation "with a sweet voice." His importance increased during the early centuries of the exile, when the liturgy replaced the sacrifices. This liturgy had to be chanted. Precentors were also required to know the prayers by heart, and, later on, to improvise or compose prayers for special occasions. Under these circumstances scholarly qualifications were paramount in precentors. Frequently the offices of rabbi and precentor were combined in one man. But as time went on, two conditions in the Jewish community led to the rise of the cantor who specialized only in chanting the prayers on Sabbaths and holidays. The first condition was the general development of the art of music in Western Europe which made its influence felt upon the Jewish communities who sojourned in various parts of the continent. Secondly, as part of his 'Oneg Shabbat the Jew wanted the cantor to entertain him on the Sabbath. The better the voice and the more elaborately the prayers were chanted, the better he liked it.[21]

Gradually, toward the end of the 17th and 18th centuries, the offices of rabbi and cantor were divorced from each other, and cantors and choirs began to bring joy and comfort to their communities in the synagogues on the Sabbath. Cantor, choir and musicians, in certain communities in the 18th century, would lead the congregation in the Kabbalat Shabbat (welcoming of the Sabbath).[22] The most elaborately sung part in the section of that service was the Lekah Dodi. Congregations in Eastern Europe witnessed the development of the choir and the specialized cantor toward the end of the 18th century and the beginning of the 19th century.

Solomon Sulzer (1804-1890), in Vienna, was one of the first to bring technical order in synagogue music. His rendition of the service on the Sabbath was a delight to those who came to hear him.[23] His influence penetrated into all the progressive communities in Europe. Soon Sabbath eve and Sabbath morning were anticipated with special eagerness and interest in the synagogue. Cantor and choir satisfied the great love for music which the Jew had had since the days when he lived in Palestine as a nation among nations; for a Jew was not permitted nor wanted in the opera houses or concert halls. Nor would the pious Jew have taken advantage of such a privilege even had it been granted.

The special music on Special Sabbaths of the Jewish calendar year were musically colored by the resourceful cantor and his choir with special modes and melodies. On

Shabbat Shirah[24] when the "Song of the Red Sea" was read in the weekly portion of the Torah, it was chanted by the reader elaborately, with a special tune. On *Shabbat ha-Gadol*, the Sabbath before Passover, the cantor would give the congregation a foretaste of some of the *Seder* melodies when he reached *Hasal, Va-amartem Zevaḥ Pesaḥ*. On *Shabbat Ḥazon*, the Sabbath preceding *Tish'ah be-Ab*, he would chant the *Lekah Dodi* at the welcoming of the Sabbath with the tune of *Eli Zion*[25] of the *Kinnot*, and on the Sabbath day, the focal point of the synagogue service was the reading of the *Maftir*, *Ḥazon Yesha'yahu*[26] to the cantillation mode of the Book of Lamentations,[27] which is chanted on *Tish'ah be-Ab* eve. This, as it were, set the scene for *Tish'ah be-Ab*.

On the next Sabbath, *Shabbat Naḥamu*, the Sabbath of Comfort, the heavy veil of mourning was lifted. All was cheerful and hopeful. The major mode returned to *Lekah Dodi* on the Sabbath eve, and gone was the lament from the *Haftarah*[28] on the Sabbath day. In the East European town, immediately after *Tish'ah be-Ab*, joyous strains could be heard from the rehearsal room of the cantor and choir, who would be preparing some special joyous composition to be sung on *Shabbat Naḥamu*. The town musicians, too, would be tuning up for many weddings which would take place on the Friday afternoon of *Shabbat Naḥamu* and on Saturday evening.[29]

Shabbat Mebarekim, the Sabbath on which the new moon was announced, which naturally came once a month, also had its special importance and significance. The cantor considered it the most important Sabbath of the month and on it special musical works were sung. The focal point of the service was, of course, the section which dealt with the benedictions for the new month. These were sung as follows: *Yehi Razon* (May It Be Thy Will), in the *Ahavah Rabbah* and *Seliḥah* mode; *Mi she'Asah* (He Who Wrought Miracles), the Announcement of the New Moon, and *Yeḥadshehu* (May He Renew) in the *Adonai Melek* mode.

When the new moon or *Rosh Ḥodesh* occurred on the Sabbath, the day was called *Shabbat Rosh Ḥodesh*. On it the *Hallel* (Psalms 113-118) was chanted and special changes were made in the *Musaf* prayers to conform with the character of the day. The general atmosphere in the synagogue on that Sabbath, as soon as the *Hallel* Psalms arrived, was like that of the Three Festivals— *Pesaḥ*, *Shabu'ot* and *Sukkot*. This spirit was created by the cantor who ushered in the *Hallel* Psalms with the Three-Festival cadence. From then on, all was festive.

SYNAGOGUE MUSIC

Of the enormous amount of liturgical synagogue music which was created during the 19th century, we find about eighty per cent set to the Sabbath liturgy. The reason for this abundance is the fact that cantors did not see any necessity for varying the music of the festivals and holidays, which came but once a year, but did find it necessary, for the sake of variety and interest on Sabbath after Sabbath, to have various versions of certain parts of the liturgy in their repertoire.

When the Reform movement began to flourish in Germany, it aimed to obliterate as much of the oriental color in synagogue music as possible. The cantillation modes of the Torah, the *Ahavah Rabbah* mode in the liturgy, were eliminated as a step in this direction. Solomon Sulzer in Vienna and Louis Lewandowski in Berlin were the composers who accommodated themselves to and became instruments for these theories and reforms. In their synagogue works one finds very little trace of the traditional Sabbath modes. Consequently their music cannot be considered typical of the synagogue. While larger communities in

Eastern Europe liked the musical order which Sulzer and Lewandowski brought into the synagogue, they could not accept the music itself which lacked the synagogal Sabbath spirit. We find in the works of Solomon Naumburg (1815-1880), cantor in Paris, a desire to utilize the Sulzer and Lewandowski method, but, applied to the ancient Sabbath prayer modes. However, it was left to men like Weintraub in Koenigsberg and later to the cantors and composers of Eastern Europe to start applying modern methods of musical composition to the ancient Jewish modes and melodies. Among these were Schorr, Nowakowsky, Dunaiewsky, Gerovitch, Belzer and scores of lesser known cantors.

While even these were under the influence of European form and harmony, still we find in their works a constant striving to adhere to tradition. The literature, which these cantors and choir directors created, forms part of the tremendous structure of Jewish music.

SABBATH MUSIC IN AMERICA

If it were possible to observe the Sabbath according to tradition, we would find our Sabbath music far richer than it is. But because the Sabbath is inadequately observed in our day, we find an attitude of satisfaction in a musical status quo.

In Orthodox synagogues the music of the 19th century prevails. What is laudable in the Orthodox synagogue is the fact that the cantillation modes and prayer modes are rather strictly adhered to. In the Conservative synagogue, where a mixed choir and organ are employed, the orthodox musical method is peppered with some Episcopal hymns and Unitarian anthems. The music of the Reform synagogue moved away from tradition almost entirely, until about a decade ago.

The Reform synagogues, however, have had the greatest facilities for the presentation of good music. Some Jewish musicians, who have sensed these possibilities, have tried, therefore, since the early part of this century, to create and present music which is truly representative of the synagogue. This work began with the efforts of Edward Stark (1863-1918), cantor of Temple Emanuel, San Francisco, California, and has been set forth in our own day by men such as Ernst Bloch, Jacob Weinberg, Isidore Freed, and the writer. The Reform movement has begun, though slowly, to realize its musical shortcomings and, in an effort to provide a remedy, has revised *The Union Hymnal* twice in almost half a century. The present edition contains a special Sabbath section of hymns, based on the traditional Sabbath modes and liturgy, appropriate for synagogue and home.

In the American Jewish home, music has receded into the background on the Sabbath. One may still hear *Shalom 'Alekem* and the *Kiddush* chanted on the Sabbath eve, but the *Zemirot* have vanished almost entirely. In some Jewish homes the custom of chanting the "grace after meals" still prevails. Jewish music flourishes mostly in the synagogue, where significant contributions are now being made to Sabbath music by a small group of Jewish composers.

THE SABBATH IN FOLK MUSIC

Curiously enough, we find very little folk music in Hebrew or Yiddish dealing with the Sabbath. The reason for this is that folk songs came under the classification of *Shire Hol*, "everyday songs," while on the Sabbath only *Shire Kodesh*, "sacred songs," were sung, and only in Hebrew. Whatever folklore did spring forth out of the Sabbath was sung either before Sabbath sundown or after *Habdalah*, when the Sabbath was actually over. The only exception in using the Yiddish song on the Sabbath is found in the chant *Gott fun Avrohom*, "God of Abraham,"[30] which the women recite or chant just before the *Habdalah*. The song *Shreit-Zse Yiden Shabbos*[31] (Cry Out, "Sabbath") is a marvelous assertion of the faith of the Jew inthe Sabbath; and the *Melaveh Malkah*[32] (Seeing Off the Queen) song, attributed to the hasidic Rabbi Levi Yitzchok of Berditchev, is a picture of the Jew as he returns to his regular weekday routine. *A Chazendel Oyf Shabbos*[33] (A Cantor for the Sabbath) is a satire on Jews who ran from one synagogue to another on the Sabbath, in order to hear various cantors, and on those who were the followers of certain cantors.

In the Hebrew language we find very few modern poems dealing with the Sabbath which have been set to music. Most significant are the two poems by Bialik, *Shabbat ha-Malkah*[34] (The Sabbath Queen) and *Yesh Li Gan*[35] (I Have a Garden), which have become popular folk songs. *Shabbat ha-Malkah* has even taken its place in certain Jewish communities at late Friday evening services, or at '*Oneg Shabbat* gatherings. It has even taken its place, deservedly, with the regular *Zemirot* in homes where *Zemirot* are still sung. This poem is really a paraphrase of *Shalom 'Alekem*. *Yesh Li Gan*, is an idyllic love song which undoubtedly has no place on the Sabbath proper.

It has also become the custom in this country to sing appropriate new Palestinian Hebrew folk songs, at Sabbath gatherings.

MUSIC IN THE PALESTINIAN 'ONEG SHABBAT[36]

The great poet Bialik, remembering the sacred impressions which the Sabbath had made upon him in his early youth, felt a void in the Sabbath as it developed in Palestine, and particularly in the city of his dwelling, Tel Aviv.[37] He missed the gatherings of great multitudes of Jews on the Sabbath day in the *Bet ha-Midrash* to listen to the "holy word" and to sing together the Sabbath *Zemirot*. The '*Oneg Shabbat* which he initiated in 1929 was an institution to supply this need.

About fifteen hundred to two thousand Jews gather in the *Ohel Shem* auditorium, at about five in the afternoon. They begin with the singing led by a group of men and boys who have banded together for the purpose of leading the gathering in Sabbath *Zemirot*. They always include the prayer, *Attah Eḥad*[38] (Thou Art One), an excerpt from the Sabbath afternoon liturgy, which is sung to a melody in East European style. This tune has in it the sanctity of the Sabbath and the longing which the Jew has always had for the spiritual rewards of the day. This excerpt from the afternoon service is in lieu of the afternoon service proper. The tune is at first sung by a few, and gradually it is caught up by more and more, till the tremendous voice of an entire people is carried away on the wings of song to upper levels, where dwells the Sabbath soul of the Jew.

Then a discourse takes place. When that is over there is more singing. By this time twilight has descended on the Holy Land and the holy spirit rests on this multitude as it accompanies the Sabbath upon its departure. When the first three stars have become visible, the flicker of the *Habdalah* candle appears suddenly, and a golden voice is lifted in the opening phrases of the *Habdalah*, *Hine El Yeshu-'ati* (Behold the God of My Salvation). The entire congregation is now standing. When the words *La-Yehudim Hayetah Orah* (To the Jews There Was Light) are chanted, a blaze of light suddenly goes up, for all the lights in the auditorium have been lit. When the *Habdalah* is over, there is singing of *Zemirot* in which the entire multitude participates, and that is followed by instrumental music — for the Sabbath is over.

The great Bialik realized the power of song and made it an integral part of this celebration of the Sabbath.

In the Diaspora this idea caught hold and has been instituted in many Jewish communities throughout the world. It has helped to bring the song back into the Sabbath. We are beginning to witness the realization of כי מציון תצא תורה ודבר יי מירושלים. "For out of Zion shall go forth Torah, and the word of God out of Jerusalem."

MUSICAL ILLUSTRATIONS

The following musical illustrations are supplementary to the musical selections in Chapter III, pp. 23–98. All musical selections were compiled by A. W. Binder.

1. *Kol Mekadēsh* (p. 437 in Supplement)
2. *Baruch 'Adōnai Yōm Yōm* (p. 435 in Supplement)
3. *Mah Yofis* (p. 434 in Supplement)
4. *Gott Fun Avrohom* (p. 415 in Supplement)

CANTILLATION MODES EMPLOYED ON THE SABBATH

1. Cantillation of Pentateuch (p. 471 in Supplement)
2. Cantillation of Prophets (p. 472 in Supplement)
3. Cantillation of "Song of the Sea" (p. 472 in Supplement)
4. Cantillation of The Book of Lamentations (p. 473 in Supplement)

SABBATH LITURGICAL MUSIC

1. *Lecho Dōdi* by L. Lewandowski (p. 404, no. i, in Supplement)
2. *Lecho Dōdi* by S. Sulzer (p. 404, no. ii, in Supplement)
3. *Lecho Dōdi* (p. 404, no. iii, in Supplement)
4. *Lecho Dōdi* for Sabbath Preceding *Tish'a be'Ab* (p. 405, no. iv, in Supplement)
5. *Veshomru* (pp. 408–9 in Supplement)
6. *Kadshēnu* (pp. 410–11 in Supplement)
7. *An'im Zemirōs* (p. 413 in Supplement)

YIDDISH FOLK SONGS DEALING
WITH THE SABBATH

1. *Jacob's Lied* (p. 462 in Supplement)
2. *Oy Brider Zog* (p. 463 in Supplement)
3. *Shrait Sze Yiden Shabbos* (p. 463 in Supplement)
4. *A Chazendel Oif Shabbos* (p. 464 in Supplement)

SELECTED SONGS FOR *'ONEG SHABBAT*
GATHERINGS

1. *Halleluyah*: MUSIC — p.. 457 in Supplement
2. *Na'aleh L'artsenu*: MUSIC — p. 458 in Supplement
3. *Yesh Li Gan:* MUSIC — p. 459 in Supplement
4. *Attoh Echod*: MUSIC — p. 412 in Supplement
5. *L'Dovid Boruch*: MUSIC — p. 414 in Supplement
6. *Nigun Bialik*: MUSIC — p. 460 in Supplement
7. *A Radel*: MUSIC — p. 461 in Supplement
8. *Boruch 'Elohenu*: MUSIC — p. 468 in Supplement
9. *V'taher Libenu*: MUSIC — p. 470 in Supplement

The following additional hymns are especially recommended for *'Oneg Shabbat* gatherings.

Mah Yofis, p. 434
Yismechu, p. 405
Menucho Vesimcho, p. 422
Sholōm Loch Yōm Hashvī'ī, p. 424

CHAPTER XVII

THE SABBATH IN ART

By

RACHEL WISCHNITZER-BERNSTEIN

שְׁחוֹרָה אֲנִי כָּל יְמוֹת הַשָּׁבוּעַ

וְנָאוָה אֲנִי בְּשַׁבָּת (ש׳ הש׳ רבה. א׳)

"Black am I during the weekdays,
but I am beautiful on the Sabbath."
(Cant. Rab. 1)

IT is regrettable that there is no Sabbath *Haggadah*, no single book containing both the complete Sabbath service and the pictures depicting its ceremonies. To obtain an insight into Sabbath ceremonies and usages of the past, it is necessary to refer to various types of illustrated prayer books and Bibles, to non-Jewish publications which portray Jewish rites and customs, and to ceremonial objects dedicated to Sabbath use.

KINDLING THE SABBATH LIGHTS

The ceremonial aspect of Sabbath observance, as it has evolved in the course of time, gives a conspicuous part to the wife and mother. She ushers in the Sabbath with the rite of kindling the Sabbath lights. She recites the blessing over the lights and invokes God's blessing upon the family. This scene of the woman kindling and blessing the lights on Sabbath eve is familiar from a much reproduced woodcut

319

of the *Minhagim*, printed in Amsterdam in 1707. It may be traced even further back to an excellent woodcut in the *Seder ha-Tefillot*, a Sulzbach print of about 1670. This earlier and better woodcut, reproduced in Figure 1, shows the woman, daintily dressed (in a closefitting bodice and ample skirt, a frill around her neck, a prettily embroidered apron, and her hair hidden under an elaborate headdress), standing at a table set for the Sabbath meal, her hands raised toward a lamp suspended above the table. It is an oil lamp with six radial spouts for the floating wicks and a pan below designed to catch the dripping oil. Copper and brass lamps of this type have been preserved, some with an adjustable ratchet for raising and lowering the lamp. More elaborate examples have two tiers, and are decorated with reflectors, spread-eagles, and other decorative devices. That the Sabbath lamp was still in use in the 1830s can be be inferred from the Jewish family scenes by Moritz Oppenheim. A beautiful Venetian silver lamp with eight spouts, in repoussé work, dating from about 1750, was shown in the Akiba Eger Exhibition of the Jewish Museum in Berlin in 1937 (Fig. 2). But it is not certain that the suspended oil lamp was used in Italy for the Sabbath blessing. There candles were probably used for this purpose. In a 15th century prayer book of Italian origin, in the collection of the late Baron Edmond de Rothschild, there is a Sabbath eve scene showing a two-branched candlestick standing on a table. It is quite possible that the two traditions existed side by side. Thus in the *Jüdisches Ceremoniel* by Paul Christian Kirchner, a non-Jewish publication issued in Nuremberg in 1726, there is an engraving showing a woman blessing the candles. In an engraving in the *Kirchliche Verfassung* by Johann Christoph Georg Bodenschatz, another well-known non-Jewish work issued in Erlangen in 1748, a woman is seen raising her hands toward the sus-

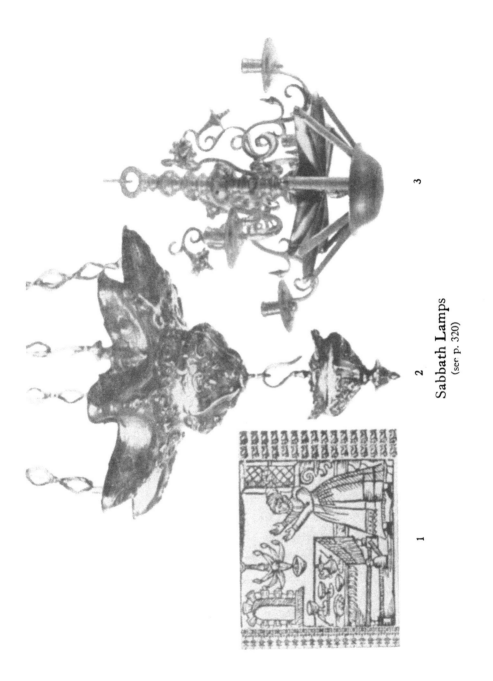

Sabbath Lamps
(see p. 320)

4

Sabbath Scenes in Synagogue and Home
(see p. 321 f.)

Sabbath Candlesticks
(see pp. 321–2)

7

8

Sabbath Candlesticks
(see p. 322)

11

Sabbath Prayers
(see p. 323)

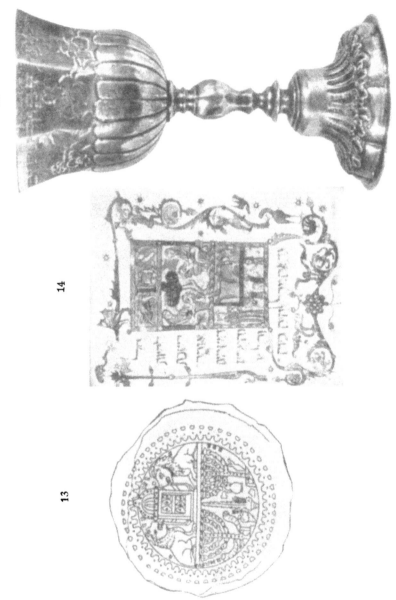

Kiddush Symbols
(see p. 325)

18

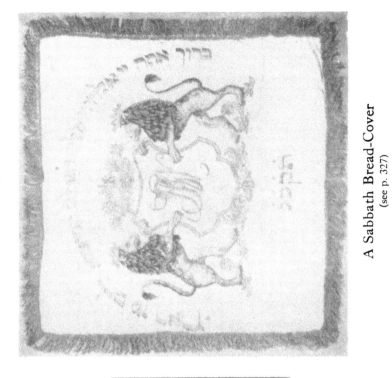

ברוך אשר...

A Sabbath Bread-Cover

(see p. 327)

16

17

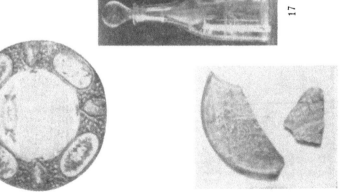

19

Utensils for Kiddush

(see pp. 326–7)

20

21

Home Scenes of the Sabbath

(see pp. 327–8)

Dishes and Cup for *Habdalah*

(see p. 328)

25   26   27

Spice Boxes for *Habdalah*
(see p. 329)

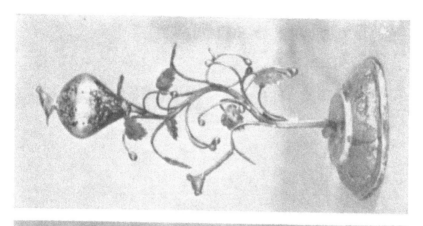

28   29   30

Spice Boxes for *Habdalah*
(see p. 329)

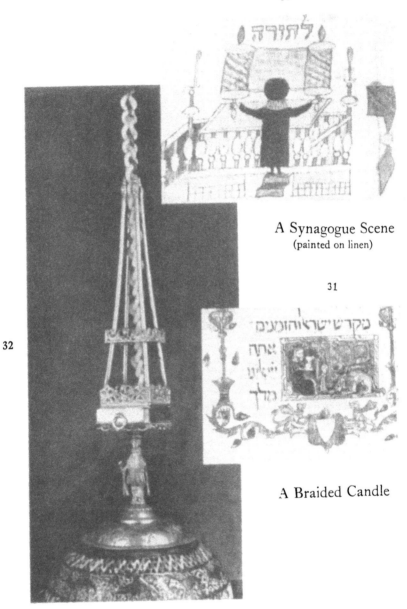

33

A Synagogue Scene
(painted on linen)

31

A Braided Candle

32

A *Habdalah* Candle

(see pp. 329–31)

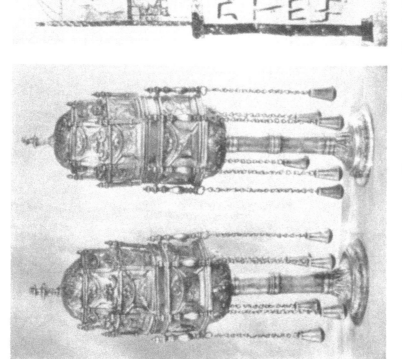

35   34

Ornaments for the Torah Scroll
(see pp. 331–2)

36

37

Ornaments for the Torah Scroll

(see p. 331)

40

39

38

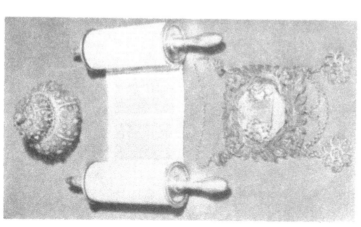

Ornaments for the Torah Scroll
(see p. 332)

41

The Torah
(oil painting)

42
Weighing the Temple Tax
(woodcut)

43
Title Page of a
Sabbath Prayer Book

(see pp. 333–4)

pended lamp (Fig. 4). Both picture sets drew in great measure upon the engravings in the *Ceremonies and Religious Customs of the Various Nations* made after the drawings by the French artist Bernard Picart. There exists an English edition under that title, but the first edition appeared in Amsterdam in 1723. In Picart's cycle the scene of "Kindling the Lights" is missing. There is only a sketch of a Sabbath lamp, and the text merely refers to the ceremony of the benediction performed by the mistress of the house. There is nothing to indicate whether or not the ceremony was meant to be performed over the suspended lamp. There may have been different traditions in France, in Holland, in various regions of Germany and in Eastern Europe.

An extremely interesting pair of 18th century silver candlesticks from Germany can be seen in the Friedman Collection in the Museum of the Jewish Theological Seminary of America (Fig. 5). A graceful upright lion, cast on a bell-shaped base, carries in his forelegs a flower twig terminating in a candleholder. The bell foot is divided into compartments with alternating ornamental fields and scenes in fine repoussé work. On one of the candlesticks are depicted "Moses Tending a Flock of Sheep" (visible on Fig. 5, left), "Jacob's Dream," and "Samson and the Lion." On the other are depicted "The Sacrifice of Isaac," "The Judgment of Solomon" (visible on Fig. 5, right) and a figure standing before a pair of candles set on a table. The figure, with its round cap on the head, looks like that of a man, not a woman. But we can ascribe the mistake to the ignorance of the gentile silversmith who made the candlesticks. The presence of that particular picture, however, indicates that the candlesticks were intended for Jewish use. There are other interesting objects cast on the horizontal plate of the base of these candlesticks. They are a lizard, a sea-shell, and a fly on one plate, and a lizard, a crawfish, and a fly on the other. The choice is not accidental. The animals are meant to symbolize the three elements. The lizard represents earth, the sea-shell and the crawfish represent water, and the fly represents air. But where is the fourth element? The reader will easily guess that the fourth element, fire, is represented by the candlestick itself.

In Eastern Europe the function of kindling the lights became so intimately associated with the mistress of the house that the Sabbath candlestick was used in the decoration of women's tombstones. A fine example is an 1832 gravestone in Sereth, Bukovina (Fig. 7). It shows, in relief, a four-branched heavy brass candlestick, specimens of which are to be found in museums and private collections. Another tombstone is decorated with a pair of candleholders and a woman's hands blessing them. Figure 8 is a wash of this tomb relief. The candlestick with two to four branches is called in some regions the Cracow Lamp. An example of this type can be seen in the Friedman Collection in the Museum of the Jewish Theological Seminary of America (Fig. 9). It displays two facing lions carrying a crown, and the spread-eagle in open-work decoration. The incised ornaments point to a rather late origin. The candlestick bears the Hebrew inscription "For kindling the Sabbath light."

With the introduction of the kerosene lamp in the 1860s, the oil lamp disappeared in Europe, and wax, tallow, or stearine candles were substituted for Sabbath use. In the more conservative Orient the oil lamp was still in use in the eighties, as is shown in an 1882 etching by Max Rapine (after a painting by Le Comte du Nouy), portraying Moroccan Jews studying Scripture on the Sabbath. The painting does not offer much *couleur locale* except for the lamps. Beside the oriental oil lamp with its glass vases for the wicks there are shown suspended oil lamps of the type discussed above.

It is interesting to note how the centuries-old subject of the Jewish woman kindling the Sabbath lights has been dealt with by a modern artist. Max Band, whose painting is reproduced in Figure 10, is a Lithuanian by birth. He lived for many years in Paris, and is now in Mexico. He is well known in the United States where he has frequently exhibited. His canvas, in the collection of Mrs. Ethel London in Johannesburg, has all the traditional characteristics. But it conveys quite a different mood. There is much less determination in the woman's gesture. She is shown with her hand only slightly raised, and her eyes are lost in meditation. The emphasis is on the delight in the tranquility of the moment rather than on the ceremonial performance itself.

THE WOMAN OF VALOR

It is not until the Sabbath lights are lit that the master of the house and his elder sons leave for the synagogue. Back home from the service he blesses the younger children (Fig. 11), and in accordance with traditional usage recites, in honor of his wife, the "Praise of the Virtuous Woman" (Prov. 31. 10-31). This song in praise of the wife seems to be an old practice as is evident from an illustration in a 13th century Rhenish Hebrew Bible in the Pavlikowski Library in Lwow, wherein this particular subject was picked out by the artist for illustration. The virtuous wife, the efficient housewife "who rises while it is yet night" and "worketh willingly with her hands" and yet finds leisure to take care of her appearance—note her "clothing is fine linen and purple"— is rendered in the Lwow Bible (Fig. 12) as a young woman gracefully leaning with her left arm on what is supposed to be a wall, and uplifting with her right hand her crimson mantle lined with ermine. Her headdress is quite a sophisticated affair, all white, with just a bit of a diadem seen in front. It also has a chin ribbon and a veil in the back. The deer hunt sketched beside her alludes most gallantly to Prov. 5.19, where "the wife of thy youth" is likened to a lovely hind.

That the biblical verses dealing with the "virtuous woman" were early associated with the Sabbath home liturgy is also be to inferred from a picture in the above mentioned 15th century prayer book of the Rothschild collection. She appears again in the Moses Mendelssohn Bible which was published by the Anton Schmid press in Vienna in 1817. An engraving in the book of Proverbs shows the virtuous woman from a somewhat different aspect. She is fashionably dressed and is giving alms to an old man, thus illustrating Prov. 31, 20, "She stretches out her hand to the poor." The moral and social approach to the subject is suggestive of the period of enlightenment.

THE *KIDDUSH*

The Sabbath ceremony following the song of praise is the *Kiddush*, or the sanctification of the Sabbath over a cup of wine. It is the master of the house who lifts the cup of wine and recites the *Kiddush*.

The Sabbath cup is one of the oldest Jewish ceremonial objects. In museums all over the world are preserved about a dozen sherds of the so-called "Jewish goldglasses," *fondi d'oro*, discovered in Jewish catacombs in Rome and dating back to the 4th century of the Common Era. These fragments are regarded as cup bottoms. They are in fact double bottoms, consisting of two glass slabs with a decoration in gold foil pressed between the two layers of glass. Similar gold glass sherds were found in Christian catacombs. These glasses bear Latin or Greek inscriptions the meaning of which can be reduced to the words "Take the sanctified drink and live." The Jewish glasses display Jewish religious symbols, mostly appurtenances of the Temple or the Synagogue, among which the wine jar occurs frequently (Fig.13).

If the gold glasses are the oldest preserved Jewish wine glasses used for Sabbath and Festivals, pictorial representations of the wine cup or jar are even earlier. They are to be found stamped on Palestinian coins of the first rebellion (67-69 C. E.), and of the second Bar Kochba rebellion (132-135 C. E.). Whether the cup depicted on the coins is meant to represent the symbolical cup of salvation or the Sabbath cup is a matter of conjecture. However, since the symbolism of the Sabbath is tied up with eschatological and messianic conceptions— Sabbath being visualized as a foretaste of the world to come—the images may be interpreted as signifying the same thing from different aspects.

The Sabbath *Kiddush* also forms part of the Passover ritual because at least one Sabbath falls on the Passover. That is why *Kiddush* scenes are depicted in the Haggadah. In the Spanish 14th century Haggadah-manuscript in the British Museum (Add. 14761) there is such a *Kiddush* scene (Fig. 14). The *pater familias* is holding the cup, a young boy is carrying the wine bottle, while another child and the mother look on. The emphasis is on the didactic value of the performance as is indicated by the two old men who are seated above the scene, pointing to the ceremony.

Medieval and Renaissance Sabbath cups have not been preserved. The favorite type is the silver standing cup with a rather high baluster-stem and a bell-shaped bowl decorated with repoussé work in the rocaille style of the 18th century. Authentic specimens of the period exist (Fig. 15). The

Renaissance type with molded six bosses, known from engravings in liturgical books, is preserved in later copies, sometimes executed in 19th century filigree work. Some of these cups have the stem cut off so that they can be held in the palm of the hand. The beaker type with cover is chiefly used as guild and brotherhood cups. The cups are occasionally engraved with the Hebrew verse "Remember the Sabbath day to keep it holy." An attempt to revive the symbolism of the Sabbath cup was made in Paris by the Polish artist, Israel Schorr (now in New York), who has produced cups in engraved and chased work. He happily combines good craftsmanship and a certain heaviness and naïveté of folk art. His Jewish liturgical silver was much noticed at the Salon d'Automne in 1938.

There are no particular stands associated with the *Kiddush* cup. However, there are some older *Kiddush* dishes in existence. There is the majolica dish from Ancona, Italy, dated 1616, in the Berson Museum in Warsaw (Fig. 16), of which there exist slightly different versions. Special bottles for Sabbath wine were common, as can be seen from a few preserved examples. One such pretty flask (about 1850), made of glass with incised decorations and Hebrew inscriptions, in Kassel, is illustrated in Figure 17.

THE FRIDAY EVENING MEAL

The white table cloth for the Sabbath meal was usually plain. Not so the square napkin for covering the two Sabbath loaves of bread. This cloth was of linen or silk, embroidered in wool, silk and beadwork. The pattern usually consisted of the heraldic lions of Judah, the crown of the Torah, the Shield of David, the Tablets of the Law, or different combinations of these pictures. The cloth was usually ïnscribed with the verse "Remember the Sabbath day to keep it holy," or with the benediction over bread. The name of the owner and the date of its manufacture and acquisition used to be embroidered on the napkin. The one in the Friedman Collection in the Museum of the Jewish Theological Seminary, reproduced in Figure 18, bears the initials of the owner in Latin letters, while the date 523 of the Hebrew Era (1763) and the benediction are in Hebrew lettering. The whole is daintily embroidered in broadstitch, brown and gold on white silk.

It is an ancient custom to have fish for the Sabbath meal. A picture of a dish with fish in it is to be found on gold glasses, confirming the assumption that these gold glasses were used as Sabbath wine cups. On the fragment in the Metropolitan Museum in New York (Fig. 19) the fish on a round dish is recognizable on the broken-off smaller fragment. The meal is concluded with a cup of wine and the recital of the grace, the *Birkat ha-Mazon.*

The Sabbath meal is illustrated in the graceful pen and ink drawing in the handwritten 18th century parchment *Mahzor,* formerly in the collection of the late Sally Kirschstein (Fig. 20).

THE SABBATH DAY AT HOME

The Sabbath morning is devoted to the synagogue services, while the afternoon for the most part is devoted to rest and study. There are numerous paintings, particularly of the 19th century, portraying Jewish men gathered on the Sabbath around a table, reading and discussing theological problems. These paintings are too numerous to be dealt with here. Instead, a drawing is reproduced (Fig. 21), showing a young boy with his teacher at a "Sabbath Test." This drawing by Regina Mundlak, made in Paris in 1911, marks a new approach to the subject. What interests the artist is the human relationship of teacher and pupil, the concentration of both on their study, emphasized by the bareness and dullness of the room in which they work.

THE *HABDALAH* SERVICE

After the evening prayers are recited at the synagogue the Sabbath is brought to a close in a farewell ceremony in synagogue and home. The symbolism of the *Habdalah* Service is meant to convey the separation or distinction of the Sabbath from the weekday. For this ceremony a wine cup on a stand is used. The stand is meant to catch the overflowing wine which symbolizes the hope for a week of plenty. Of the older *Habdalah* plates there existed one in Italian majolica in the Jewish Museum in Berlin. There are modern ones in china, pewter, silver, and brass. In the modern silver *Habdalah* plate in the Friedman Collection in the Museum of the Jewish Theological Seminary the decorative effect is obtained chiefly from the Hebrew lettering (Fig. 22).

The benediction over wine is followed by two other benedictions — one over spices and one over light. The spicebox, or *Besamim* box, often has as many as four or five compartments for different spices, such as anise, cloves, etc. But more often there is only one undivided space for the spices. The older spiceboxes are shaped like slender turrets with archbusiers shown standing at the embrasure. They portray the lower community functionaries such as the beadle (*Shammash*), the *Schulklopfer*, the *Mazzot* baker, and the butcher. Sometimes they merely represent the musicians who used to play at weddings.

A sketch of a spicebox in the form of a Gothic turret, dated 1553 and designed by a Christian artist, has been preserved in the City Archives of Frankfurt. The earliest dated spicebox is the turret-type Friedberg piece of 1651. An even earlier specimen known to have come to Kassel in 1583 is reproduced in Figure 25.

In the 18th century many new forms were introduced. These were influenced by the current forms of pepper and salt shakers which were ball-like, oval, or cylindrical containers of small size with perforated tops. An even greater influence were the nature forms favored in the manufacture of the glassware and silver plate of the period. The symbolism of the spicebox found expression in flower and fruit-like containers. Pears, apples and sunflowers were among the favored forms. The fish, skillfully made with a flexible body, and the Easter-lamb, taken over from the Christians, were also in vogue. But the turret continued to be the popular form. The H. E. Benguiat Collection in the Museum of the Jewish Theological Seminary has an elaborate silver spicebox, with a structure of several tiers, displaying the familiar repertory of forms — a crown, lions, bells, dismountable pears, a perforated sunflower, and a bowl with a round cover. This spicebox bears the names of several donors and is inscribed "Berdichev, 1775" (Fig. 26).

The *Habdalah* candle is generally braided so as to have several wicks and give a bright light. It is worth noting that a braided candle is already to be found in the *Habdalah* scene of the above-mentioned 14th century *Haggadah* of Spanish origin (Fig. 31).

At the end of the ceremony the flame of the candle is dipped into the wine which has been poured into the *Habdalah* plate. In order to prevent the candle from falling into the wine, a special candlestick was sometimes provided. This candlestick had four vertical rods fixed to the socket. The rods are topped with finials, and held together with an adjustable plate. This contrivance is similar in principle to the spiral rod in colonial candlesticks designed for a similar purpose. The candleholder is sometimes provided with a drawer-like compartment for spices, thus combining a spicebox and a candlestick in one. Such a combination is reproduced in Figure 32. It belongs to a rather early group which was described by the late Rudolf Hallo, an expert on Jewish liturgical silver. The prototype to which these candlesticks with spice drawers can be traced is a piece made in the earlier part of the 18th century by the Frankfurt master, Jeremias Zobel. They display fine 17th century ornament, and a man in the posture of Atlas supporting the candleholder. The man is carrying in his hands a cup, a spicebox, or a dish. Our specimen from the Jewish Museum in Berlin is mounted on an enameled copper bowl with a shoulder strip in open work — a sort of oriental spice burner. The Atlas-like figure has an oriental dress, and shows evidence of having been in the Orient where it underwent some transformations.

THE SABBATH SERVICES IN THE SYNAGOGUE

At the Sabbath synagogue service the weekly portion of the Torah is read. The public reading of the Torah is inaugurated or concluded with the ceremony of holding up the open scroll before the congregation. This ceremony is portrayed in a 15th century *Haggadah* manuscript. According to the inscription, the scene was intended to illustrate "Moses receiving the stone tablets on Mt. Sinai." But the medieval artist in his naïveté depicted the familiar synagogue performance instead of the historical event.

Bernard Picart portrayed the ceremony, and it was also painted and embroidered on many Torah wrappers in Germany. It was customary to give a Torah wrapper to the synagogue in the name of a son when he reached his first birthday. These Torah wrappers used to bear the inscription "May he grow up for marriage, Torah, and good deeds." The word "Torah" was usually adorned with the scene of the Reader holding up the scroll. The community of Worms possessed a valuable collection of such wrappers, some dating to the 16th century. The Jewish Community Archives in Berlin also had a large collection of Torah wrappers. One of these is reproduced in Figure 33 which shows the *Hazzan* holding up the scroll. It is painted on linen and is originally from Witzenhausen, dated 1817.

The two rods on which the scroll is rolled are topped with silver finials. The rods are called '*Aze Hayyim* (Trees of Life), and the finials are called *Rimmonim* (Pomegranates). The finials are hollow cylinders with knoblike or towerlike terminations. Our example (Fig. 34), from the Friedman Collection in the Museum of the Jewish Theological Seminary, is quite elaborate, with three superimposed drumlike tiers covered with a dome. The sides of the drums are treated so as to produce an effect of vaults seen from below. This baroque, illusionistic effect is enhanced by the framing elements, consisting of columns and balusters. Rich floral decoration alludes to the symbolism of the *Rimmonim*. The finials are of the 18th or early 19th century.

A crown is sometimes used instead of the two finials. The crown is in fact the older ornament of the Torah. Single conical headpieces surmounting the scroll may be seen in medieval illuminated manuscripts (Fig. 35). The oldest dated crown is in silver of Augsburg make (Fig. 36), engraved with the inscription "Abraham son of Hayyim, 1690." Typical of the ornaments of the Torah scroll is the bell seen suspended from the top of the crown.

The pointer (*Yad*, hand) used at the reading of the Torah terminates in a tiny hand, and is usually suspended on a chain from the dressed scroll. It is made of silver, ivory, coral or wood, and combines the form of a corporation mace and a reliquary hand. The oldest dated example is of 1611. Our Figure 39 is of the 17th or 18th century. The characteristics of the Torah pointer are the carefully executed hand with the pointing forefinger, the elaborate treatment of the sleeve or cuff, and the upper termination in a crown, a ball, or a lion.

Another important part of the outfit of the Torah scroll is the breast-plate (*Tass*). This is a shield suspended from chains on the wrapped scroll. The breastplate usually cast in silver is frequently executed in fine open work, or in repoussé. It displays in its decoration the traditional symbolical motives, floral decorations, and occasionally figure scenes. In Germany there was a Torah breastplate depicting the "Sacrifice of Isaac." Our Figure 40 shows an interesting Torah shield in the Budapest Museum of Applied Arts. According to inscriptional evidence it was made in Miklosh, Hungary, in 1845. It displays an unusual wealth of decoration, among which is Moses with the tablets of the Law, Aaron with a censer, and David with his harp, standing behind an elaborate screen in open work. On the bottom of the breastplate are depicted the spies carrying the cluster of grapes, while the upper part is decorated in the traditional manner. The decoration is in appliqué work which denotes a certain decline in workmanship. The Torah breastplates are usually provided with exchangeable little plaques with inscriptions indicating the day of the service. The little plaque on our breastplate reads "*Yom ha-Shabbat.*"

The mantle which covers the rolled-up scroll is usually of crimson silk or velvet. This is the oldest part of the Torah outfit recognizable on miniatures in medieval manuscripts (Fig. 35). These representations indicate that the medieval Jews used for the Torah-mantle silks with woven-in patterns. Our modern Torah-mantles are usually embroidered with the traditional symbols in gold and silver. Modern artists have been fascinated by the Torah crowned and wrapped in her mantle, shining in red, gold and silver. The excellent painters, Zygmunt Menkes and Mané Katz, have given us their most personal and most revealing interpretation of the subject. Mané Katz's painting (Fig. 41) was in his exhibition at Wildenstein's Gallery in New York.

THE SPECIAL SABBATHS

In the Jewish calendar there are Special Sabbaths the services of which are included in the *Maḥzor* (the prayer book for festivals for the whole year). These Special Sabbaths sometimes stirred the imagination of the medieval illustrator. Thus *Shabbat Parah*, alluding to Numbers 19.1–22, is marked in the 14th century *Maḥzor* of the Leipzig University Library with a picture of a red heifer. The motive is elaborated with more details in a woodcut in the *Minhagim* of 1707.

Shabbat Shekalim, referring to the Temple *Shekel* tax which was converted in the Middle Ages into a collection for the Palestine poor, was also illustrated in medieval *Maḥzorim*. Among these is the *Maḥzor*, dated 1272, in the Museum of the Worms Synagogue. This invaluable codex probably perished during the Nazi pogrom of November, 1938. The picture shows a tax collector weighing the *Shekalim* on a pair of scales, referring to a time when money was worth its weight. The woodcut in the *Minhagim* reproduced this motive in its basic elements — striking evidence of a continuous tradition. Our Figure 42 is a woodcut from the Amsterdam edition of *Minhagim* of 1723.

Shabbat Rosh Ḥodesh is usually illustrated with scenes of

men reciting the blessing over the New Moon. Such a scene is to be found in the 14th century *Mahzor* of the Leipzig University Library, and again in the *Minhagim* which includes a woodcut referring to *Shabbat ha-Gadol* and some other illustrations of Special Sabbaths.

In conclusion, we wish to mention the exquisite handwritten copy of the *Seder Tikune Shabbat*, containing Sabbath prayers according to the version of Isaac Luria. The title page of this volume, which was once in the Sally Kirschstein collection, is adorned with delightful tiny Bible scenes in grisaille. They depict Elijah's Ascension, King David playing the harp, King Solomon praying before the Temple, Pinhas punishing the Israelite and the Midianite woman, and the Sacrifice of Isaac. The choice of the Pinhas scene, rarely met with in Christian iconography, indicates that the pictures were designed by a Jewish artist. According to an inscription the book was produced in Vienna in 1738 (Fig. 43).

The few pictures gleaned from the still unexplored wealth of artistic material referring to the Sabbath may give some idea of the efforts that Jews made to convey the sanctity of the day of rest. They outline a distinct pattern of life, and a naïve yet poetic conception of light and dark, holy and profane. The light is kindled, the light is extinguished. This is the whole story. But it is with this ever-recurring, this eternal light that the Jew has associated his most treasured expectations of an ultimate peace for all mankind.

BOOK THREE
THE SABBATH IN HISTORY

CHAPTER XVIII

THE ORIGIN AND DEVELOPMENT
OF THE SABBATH

כִּי שֵׁשֶׁת יָמִים עָשָׂה ה' אֶת הַשָּׁמַיִם וְאֶת

הָאָרֶץ וּבַיּוֹם הַשְּׁבִיעִי שָׁבַת וַיִּנָּפַשׁ

(שמות ל"א. י"ז)

For in six days the Lord made heaven
and earth, and on the seventh day He
ceased from work and rested (Ex. 31.17).

THE seven-day week is so universally accepted and
the Sabbath as a weekly rest-day is so firmly rooted
an institution that hardly anyone questions their origin.
It is generally assumed that the seven-day week ending
with a day of rest is part of the scheme of creation, and that
like the laws of Nature it has always existed and will continue to exist forever. People rarely stop to recall that
the seven-day week is a unique Hebrew creation, and that
the Sabbath, as a universal rest-day, is one of the most
important Hebrew contributions to modern civilization.

Among the ancients the week was usually a subdivision
of the lunar month. Since the lunar cycle consists of ap-
proximately twenty-nine and a half days, any subdivision
yielded weeks of unequal length. Some peoples divided
the lunar month into four parts, obtaining three seven-day
weeks and one eight- or nine-day week in each month.
Other peoples divided the lunar months into three, five,
or six parts, giving them a ten-day, six-day, or five-day
week. In each case one week in the month was shortened

so as to adjust the weeks to the lunar cycle. One of the more common forms of the week was the ten-day week based on the division of the lunar month into three parts— (1) the waxing crescent or increase of the moon, (2) the approximate full disc or the culmination of the moon's growth, and (3) the waning crescent or the decrease of the moon. The ten-day week, adjusted to the lunar month, was prevalent among the ancient Egyptians, Greeks, Chinese, Japanese, many African tribes, and some American Indian tribes. Today the ten-day week, as well as the other forms of the week, have generally been displaced by the Semitic seven-day week, except in a few places such as French Indo-China, where some of the people still continue to divide the lunar month into three parts.[1]

The origin of the seven-day week ending with a rest-day is obscure. In the Bible the Sabbath is already an old and well established institution. In the first Decalogue we are told to "remember the sabbath day, to keep it holy" (Ex. 20.8), an injunction which by its very wording infers that an established institution is being sanctioned. The biblical versions of the origin of the Sabbath, which ascribe its beginnings either to the creation of the world (Gen. 2.2-3; Ex. 20.11) or to the Exodus from Egypt (Deut. 5.15; Ezek. 20.12; Nehem. 9.14) only substantiate its pre-biblical origin. The biblical author already knows of the seven-day week ending with the Sabbath, and he supplies two motives for the observance of this Sabbath. One motive is religious — that we are to imitate God and rest from our labor on the seventh day; and the second motive is social — that we are to remember our emancipation from Egypt and therefore provide rest from labor for ourselves, for our slaves, and for the stranger in our midst.

The Bible, however, has yielded some clues which have partly clarified the problem, but this only after the discovery of some Babylonian cuneiform tablets. In one of these tablets appears the word *Shabattum*, which is explained to mean "a day of pacification of the gods." Another cuneiform tablet made it clear that the Babylonian *Shabattum* was the day of the full moon. The original meaning of the word *Shabattum*, however, is still unknown, even as is the original meaning of the Hebrew word *Shabbat*. If we assume that the Hebrew word *Shabbat* was originally related to the Babylonian word *Shabattum*, and if we also assume that the Hebrew word *Shabbat* originally had reference to the day of the full moon, a very obscure and troublesome passage in the Bible becomes meaningful. In Lev. 23.11, 15, the Hebrews are commanded to begin the counting of the *'Omer* from "the morrow after the Sabbath." Jewish tradition has always interpreted "the morrow after the Sabbath" to mean, not the first day of the week, but the morrow after the first day of the Passover, which always falls on a day of the full moon. This biblical phrase, wherein the word *Shabbat* seemingly means "the day of the full moon," is one of the most significant literary survivals of the ancient meaning of this word, a meaning already obsolete in the Bible, where the word *Shabbat* (with the above exception) always refers to the seventh day of the week.[2]

It is also significant that the Bible frequently speaks of the new moon and the Sabbath, mentioning the new moon first. When the Shunamite woman starts out on her journey to see the Prophet Elisha, her husband asks, "Wherefore wilt thou go to him today? it is neither new moon nor sabbath" (II Kings 4.23). Amos rebukes those "that would swallow the needy, and destroy the poor of the land, saying: 'When will the new moon be gone, that we may sell grain? And the sabbath, that we may set forth corn?' " (Amos 8.4-5). Similarly does Isaiah complain, "New moon and sabbath, the holding of convocations — I cannot endure iniquity along with the solemn assembly" (Isa. 1.13). These passages, it has been suggested, are also literary survivals of an ancient pre-biblical time when the word *Shabbat* referred to the day of the full moon and not to a weekly rest-day. According to this interpretation the recurring biblical phrase "new moon and sabbath" is a survival of a very ancient time when the days of the new moon and full moon were important religious festivals. This would also render meaningful the seemingly illogical sequence in these phrases wherein the new moon precedes the Sabbath, despite the superior sanctity and greater frequency of the latter.

But these speculations, it is to be noted, do not answer the problem regarding the origin of the seven-day week with its rest day, the Sabbath. The only conclusion that might be reached from the above discussion is that there was a time, long before the Bible was written, when the Hebrew word *Shabbat* had reference to the day of the full moon. This word *Shabbat*, at a later time, was somehow transferred to another day, the weekly rest-day. The whole discussion at best only suggests that the word *Shabbat*, at an earlier period, had a different meaning. The original problem regarding the origin of the seven-day week with its weekly rest-day still remains unsolved.

A study of the Babylonian calendar, however, offers several additional clues which deserve careful study. The Babylonian calendar was based on the movements of the moon. Not only were the days of the new moon and the full moon (*Shabattum*) reverently observed as important days, but all the phases of the moon were considered as critical days which determined the fortunes of men. The Babylonians, therefore, observed the days of the moon's phases as "unlucky" or "evil days." On the seventh, the fourteenth, the twenty-first, and the twenty-eighth days of *certain* months, the king, as the representative of the gods, was forbidden to do certain things lest he arouse their anger. Some of these restrictions remotely resemble several biblical laws regarding the Hebrew Sabbath, and suggest a possible remote relationship between the two institutions. The Babylonian king, for example, was forbidden to eat meat roasted on coals, or any food touched by fire; the Hebrews were commanded "Ye shall kindle no fire throughout your habitations upon the sabbath day" (Ex. 35.3). The Babylonian king was forbidden to ride in his chariot, to change his clothes, and to discuss affairs of state; the Hebrews were instructed "Abide ye every man in his place, let no man go out of his place on the seventh day" (Ex. 16.29). The Babylonian priests and physicians were also singled out for special legislation. On these "unlucky days" of the phases of the moon the priests were not to consult the oracles, and the physicians were not to treat the sick. The nineteenth of the month was also set apart as an "unlucky day" with the same restrictions for the king, the priests, and the physicians. This nineteenth day of the month, though not associated with the phases of the moon, was nevertheless of special significance, because the addition of the nineteen days of that month to the thirty days of the preceding month made forty-nine days, or seven times seven, a very significant number for the Babylonians.

An examination of the Babylonian weeks with their "evil days" is suggestive of a very tempting hypothesis, superficially convincing but altogether incapable of accounting for the origin of the seven-day week and for the distinctive characteristics of the Hebrew Sabbath. In the first place, the Babylonian "unlucky days" were based on superstitious fear, and the restrictions were meant to appease the angry gods, while the Hebrew Sabbath was a day of social significance which prescribed rest for man and beast.

Similarly, the Hebrew Sabbath was not an "evil day" or an "unlucky day," but rather a day of joy and "a delight." Nor was the Hebrew Sabbath in any way connected with the phases of the moon. It is the end of a seven-day *periodic week* which is independent of both the lunar month and the solar year.

The original problem, therefore, is still unsolved. The question still remains — how could or how did the ancient Semitic observance of the new moon and the full moon, or the observance of the four phases of the moon as evil days, become the *periodic* week with its *humanitarian* Sabbath? This question cannot be answered satisfactorily. The only conclusion that may be drawn is that the seven-day Hebrew week, with its humanitarian rest day as we have it now, is a unique creation of the Hebrew religious genius, and is one of the most valuable Hebrew contributions to the civilization of mankind.

If the Bible provides but little information regarding the origin of the Sabbath, it does help considerably in tracing the development of the institution. In the earliest biblical codes we already find that labor on the Sabbath is forbidden. Indeed, the punishment prescribed for the desecration of the Sabbath is that "every one that profaneth it shall surely be put to death" (Ex. 31.14). But despite this rigorous legislation, and despite the recorded execution of a man who gathered wood on the Sabbath, we may be sure that the Sabbath was not always universally observed, and that the death penalty, because of the rabbinic aversion to capital punishment, was not applied.

Our best guide in tracing the development of the Sabbath, however, is not legislation, which is often no more than a recorded theory, but historical records which describe actual practice at a given time. Among the biblical passages that shed light on the Sabbath as it was observed in the prophetic period is the one wherein we are told that the husband of the Shunamite woman, seeing his wife getting ready to go to the prophet, asks: "Wherefore wilt thou go to him today? it is neither new moon nor sabbath" (II Kings 4.23). We are also told that she took along an ass and one of the servants. Her acts are described in a matter-of-fact manner, indicating that we have a description of the usual procedure when visiting a prophet. It may, therefore, be inferred that it was customary to visit the prophet on the Sabbath, and that work was suspended on that day even in harvest time. The prophet Amos, in his bitter rebuke of those "that would swallow the needy, and destroy the poor of the land, saying 'When will the new moon be gone, that we may sell grain? And the sabbath, that we may set forth corn?' " (Amos 8.4-5) also bears witness to the suspension of trade on the Sabbath.

Visiting the prophet on the Sabbath was necessarily limited to the few. But visiting the Temple on the Sabbath was a widespread custom. This conclusion is borne out in the bitter condemnation by the prophet Isaiah. "When ye come to appear before Me, who hath required this at your hand, to trample My courts?... New moon and sabbath, the holding of convocations — I cannot endure iniquity along with the solemn assembly" (Isa. 1.12,13). In his condemnation of hypocrisy, the prophet unintentionally reveals that it was a widespread practice to visit the Temple on the Sabbath. This is further borne out by the fact that two-thirds of the royal bodyguard was regularly assigned for duty in the Temple court on each Sabbath. The Sabbath was also honored in the Temple by a refilling and a rekindling of the seven-branched *Menorah*, and it was customary to place in the Temple each Sabbath twelve fresh cakes of shewbread (Lev. 24.8).

But observance of the Sabbath was far from universal. There were many who disregarded it wholly or in part. It is not surprising, therefore, that a movement to enforce Sabbath observance eventually developed under the leadership of the prophets Jeremiah and Ezekiel. One of Jeremiah's pleas in behalf of the Sabbath reads: "Thus saith the Lord: 'Take heed for the sake of your souls, and bear no burden on the sabbath day, nor bring it in by the gates of Jerusalem; neither carry forth a burden out of your houses on the sabbath day, neither do ye any work; but hallow ye the sabbath day, as I commanded your fathers'" (Jer. 17.21, 22). Ezekiel pleads more persistently and even claims that the dispersion of the Jews was in part due to the desecration of the Sabbath. "Thou hast despised My holy things, and hast profaned My sabbaths. . . .[therefore] I will scatter thee among the nations, and disperse thee through the countries" (Ezek. 22.8, 15).

These exhortations of the prophets coupled with the crushing tragedy of the exile to Babylonia brought a reawakening in regard to the Sabbath. Not only did the prophets associate the profanation of the Sabbath with the sufferings of Israel, but it so happened that the Sabbath was best adapted to the new life in exile. Whereas the celebration of the festivals of Passover, *Shabu'ot* and *Sukkot* was in part dependent on the Temple, the Sabbath was wholly independent of the shrine in Jerusalem. Adapted as it was to independent existence, the Sabbath gained from the temporary decline of the major festivals. Indeed, the Sabbath became the visible "sign" of Israel's relationship to God, a "sign" which waxed in importance with the destruction of the Temple, which had been till then the symbol of God's presence among His people.

This deepened loyalty to the Sabbath was later brought back to Palestine by Ezra and Nehemiah. The latter relates in the biblical book that bears his name that, upon his return to Palestine, he was shocked to see the widespread desecration of the holy day. On the Sabbath people labored in the fields, gathered the harvests, bought and sold publicly. Nehemiah rebuked the nobles of Judah and ordered the gates of Jerusalem closed during the Sabbath (Nehem. 13.15-22). His vigorous efforts finally led to the establishment of the Sabbath as a day of universal rest among the Jews of Palestine.

The religious revival initiated by Ezra and Nehemiah and deepened by their disciples, the *Sopherim* (Scribes), ultimately made Sabbath observance a matter of universal concern. There developed a complicated code of restrictions calculated to insure complete rest on the Sabbath. These restrictions were meant to safeguard and preserve the spirit of the Sabbath, in the same manner as the shell protects the kernel. The *Sopherim* were remarkably successful in their efforts, for the concept of the Sabbath as a day of delightful rest and as a day of spiritual and intellectual edification reached its fullest development during their era.

By the time of the Maccabees (2nd century B. C. E.), the Sabbath as an institution was so deeply rooted in Jewish consciousness, and so treasured by the individual Jews, that life itself was often not too costly a price for the privilege of observing it. Antiochus IV, in his attempt to destroy Judaism, sensed the central importance of this institution and proscribed its observance on pain of death. Little did he suspect that thousands of martyrs would choose to die rather than to desecrate the Sabbath.[3] Likewise, the Jews chose to lose many a crucial battle rather than profane the Sabbath by warlike activity.[4] The danger of this uncompromising attitude was realized by Mattathias, the leader of the revolt. He therefore ruled that in self-defense it was permissible to take up arms on the Sabbath (I Macc. 2.41).

This was the first of a number of rulings designed to liberalize some of the restrictions of Sabbath observance. Among
these was the legal fiction of the 'Erub, which, among other
things, extended the walking distance permitted on the
Sabbath. Another ruling insisted on the kindling of lights on
the Sabbath, thus negating the view of the literalists who
sat in darkness on Sabbath eve in accordance with the literal interpretation of the biblical injunction, "Ye shall
kindle no fire throughout your habitations upon the sabbath
day" (Ex. 35.3).

By the beginning of the Common Era, the Sabbath, as
we know it, had been almost fully developed both in its
theory and practice. One of the unique practices of that
time was the sounding of six *Shofar* blasts to announce the
ushering in of the Sabbath. The first sound of the *Shofar*
was a signal for the farmers in the fields to stop work and
to start for home; the second blast was for the merchants to
close their shops; the third blast was for the housewives to
kindle the Sabbath lights; and the last three blasts announced the actual arrival of the Sabbath.

The custom of initiating the Sabbath in those days was
somewhat different from our practice in still another respect. This difference was due to the fact that congregation-
al services on Friday evenings were not yet in vogue. The
family would start the meal at dusk. The lights were kindled just before that meal, and the holiness of the day
(*Kiddush*) was proclaimed over the cup of wine with which
it was customary to start the meal. It was later that there
developed the custom of gathering in the synagogue for
services before the Friday evening meal. Although the
meal was no longer eaten at the very beginning of the Sabbath, nevertheless the recital of the *Kiddush* over the wine
was retained.

The conclusion of the Sabbath, too, was different in

those ancient days. The family would gather for the meal before sundown. As it grew dark, the beadle's *Shofar* blast, announcing the conclusion of the Sabbath, would be heard. The lights would then be kindled, and the benediction over the light would be pronounced. At the conclusion of the meal, spices on burning coals would be brought into the room in accordance with the accepted custom of the day, and the benediction over spices would be recited. Grace after the meal would then be recited over a cup of wine.[5] Then came the *Habdalah* prayer. Later, when it became customary to eat the third Sabbath meal earlier in the day, the *Habdalah* was necessarily divorced from the meal. But the blessings over the light, over the spices, and over the wine continued to be part of the *Habdalah*,[6] even as they are now.

The Middle Ages left their own imprint on the Sabbath institution. Among the more significant developments that can be traced to those centuries is the custom of singing *Zemirot* at the Sabbath meals. Many of these unique table songs were composed at that time and some of them are still sung in Jewish homes. Another development, that of the *Kabbalat Shabbat* (Welcoming the Sabbath), had its beginnings in the sixteenth century. The Jewish mystics of Safed evolved an elaborate ceremony whereby the "Sabbath Bride" was officially welcomed. The worshipers would actually march to the outskirts of the city to welcome the Sabbath. They would also recite suitable psalms and sing appropriate hymns in honor of the newly arrived "guest." Psalms 95-99, 29, 92, 93 and the hymn *Lekah Dodi* are still part of the Friday evening service in most synagogues and are still read or chanted as a *Kabbalat Shabbat*, a communal reception to the "Sabbath Bride."

Among the other customs that arose during the Middle Ages is that of blessing the children on Friday evenings and of inviting poor wayfarers as Sabbath guests. These, as well as all the other characteristics of Sabbath observance, have come down to our own day. Since life has not been at a standstill, and since revolutionary changes are in the process of moulding anew the Jewish way of life, the Sabbath, too, is undergoing many transformations and readjustments. A discussion of these latest developments forms an earlier chapter in this volume

CHAPTER XIX

THE STRUGGLE FOR THE PRESERVATION OF THE SABBATH

אֵין הַשַּׁבָּת בְּטֵלָה מִיִּשְׂרָאֵל (מכילתא כי תשא)

The Sabbath will never disappear from
Israel (Mekilta, *Ki Tisa*).

"THE Sabbath will never disappear from Israel," the
Sages of the Talmud assure us. They add that
"all institutions for which Israelites have sacrificed their
lives have been firmly and everlastingly established in their
midst."[1] One such institution is the Sabbath.

That the Jews have sacrificed their lives for the Sabbath
is a known historical fact. One need only refer to the Mac-
cabean War of the second century B. C. E. when hundreds
of Jews preferred a martyr's death to desecrating the Sabbath even in self-defense.[2] Nor was this struggle in defense
of the Sabbath limited to Palestine or to any one century.
Jewish loyalty and devotion to the Sabbath have been
challenged everywhere throughout the centuries. But the
most deadly challenge of all has been that of modern times.
It has not been so dramatic as that of the ancient or medieval religious persecutions, when the Jew was given a choice
between Sabbath observance and death. But it has proved
more effective because of the modern social and economic
forces which have been acting as slow corrosives, causing
a deadly inner degeneration. This has been especially true
of the Sabbath in the American Jewish community.

349

THE ATTEMPT TO TRANSFER THE JEWISH
SABBATH TO SUNDAY

Ever since Jews settled on American soil they have faced the perplexing problem of maintaining the sanctity of the traditional Sabbath in the face of the powerful social and economic forces which have tended to undermine it. The problem, however, did not come to a head officially until the beginning of the twentieth century when the Central Conference of American Rabbis decided to deal with the question realistically. At its conference in 1902, Rabbi Jacob Voorsanger submitted a lengthy report on "The Sabbath Question."[3] The report evoked a heated discussion which was carried over to the conference of the following year.

Rabbi Voorsanger's report claimed that "the old Sabbath is gone; Saturday, for the Jew as for the rest of our citizens, is a workday."[4] We are therefore faced with the "incongruity between the theoretical profession and the radical violation" of the Sabbath. There is also "the problem of the effeminization of the synagogue, resultant from the neglect of our men to attend the services."[5] Worse still is the realization that "the feeling of the sanctity of the day has all but vanished from the consciousness of the masses. The violation of the Sabbath among us is not accompanied by the old qualms of conscience, and the rabbis are not asked for ointment to soothe the wounds of the Jewish heart."[6]

The report also discussed the causes of this unfortunate situation. "Not willfully," said Rabbi Voorsanger, "has the Jew sacrificed the ancient holiday; it has not been, as in our pessimistic moments we are apt to imagine, the immolation of an ideal upon the altar of Mammon; it has been the natural result of changed circumstances and a new mode of life."[7] Gone is the religious sanction based on the belief that God created the world in six days and rested on the seventh. This religious sanction is wholly destroyed because it is in direct conflict with the scientific concept of evolution. Also gone is the political sanction. Jewish communal organization has lost the power to legislate the observance of the Sabbath. Each Jew decides for himself the measure of his Sabbath observance, and this decision is determined largely by economic and social forces which are stronger than his most earnest desire to observe the Sabbath. For the Jew to disregard these economic forces may involve pauperization. Also, to observe the Sabbath as prescribed by tradition involves a negation of occidental life. Had they been known at the time his report was rendered, Rabbi Voorsanger might have mentioned the radio, automobile, "movies," and other forms of recreation. These exigencies of our time, the report concludes, have largely nullified Sabbath observance and have brought us to this disturbing impasse.

The report then proceeds to prescribe a possible solution — the transference of the Sabbath to Sunday. We are faced with the following choice — "whether we shall continue to fool about with homeopathic capsules, or whether the surgeon's knife shall be requisitioned, or whether we shall simply permit our patient slowly but surely to die away."[8] The choice seemed as simple as it was radical. "The only way . . . to strengthen and perpetuate the [Sabbath] idea is by infusing it into a modern institution, into our civil day of rest, by making the latter the bearer of our message, the occasion of our public worship and instruction."[9]

The report, in suggesting this seemingly simple remedy, did not fail to perceive the serious complications involved. The transfer of the Sabbath to Sunday, the report indicated, "would still further apostrophize the radical differences of faith, practice and discipline known to exist between us and our brethren, both in this country and abroad, and, from their standpoint, must necessarily be construed as a schismatic movement, which . . . would tend to our estrangement from the fraternity of our people."[10] The very thought of becoming a sectarian movement and becoming separated from Jewry like the Karaite and Samaritan sects frightened the author of the report. He therefore suggested a possible alternative. "A superficial observer . . . would merely pass judgment upon the decaying and degenerating processes that arrest his attention, and conclude that the day of the flood was nigh. But overflowing rivers have been dammed, and floods have been stayed. Is it not at least possible that by a careful analysis of causes, we may contribute some suggestion whereby the historical Sabbath may remain a part of our spiritual inheritance to our children?"[11]

The discussion was most vehement and at times vitriolic. There were some who demanded the surgical operation. One of the younger members of the Conference addressed his colleagues as follows: "To maintain an historical Sabbath is inconsistent with your whole attitude towards Judaism. Therefore you have no peace, no harmony in your religion. What is your Friday night Sabbath? It is nothing but an opportunist movement, to avoid a Sunday transference . . . . I feel that in retaining this Saturday Sabbath I have compromised my reason, that I have been inconsistent in my religion. If our religion is a religion of reason then let us not hedge and beat about the bush . . . Sabbath means rest and because there is a possibility of a Jewish rest only on Sunday, do I come out flatfooted for a Sunday Sabbath."[12]

But there were many members of the Conference who vehemently opposed this surgical operation. They claimed that "the Sabbath is not dying. There are some painful symptoms of decay — but the doctor is an alarmist, who

frightens the patient rather than encourages him."[13] Moreover, "the Jew, after four thousand years of Saturday
observance is no more able to sanctify Sunday than to
believe in a trinity or a duality."[14] One of the strongest
appeals in defense of the Sabbath was delivered by Rabbi
Rosenau. He declared: "I am in favor of maintaining the
seventh-day Sabbath because I believe it to be the symbol
of Judaism, because I do not believe it to be the right of
every separate community to legislate for itself; because I
believe in maintaining the unity of Israel; because I believe
in maintaining our historical identity; because I realize
that Judaism is not simply ethical monotheism, but that it
is monotheism plus a great quantity of ceremonialism;
because I am afraid of the results consequent upon the
institution of a Sunday service as a substitute for the Sabbath; because I believe that Israel should stand for something more than empiricism; because I realize that Sunday
services as such are nothing less than a makeshift .... And
the final reason for maintaining the historical Sabbath is
because I believe there is such a thing as development *out*
of Judaism as well as development *in* Judaism."[15]

The opposition to change, led by the late Rabbi Joseph
Silverman and fortified by the general unpopularity of the
proposition among the rank and file of the congregations,
succeeded in passing the following resolution: "This Conference declares itself in favor of maintaining the historical
Sabbath as a fundamental institution of Judaism and of
exerting every effort to improve its observance. It in-
structs the Executive Committee to appoint a commission
to study the methods of carrying this declaration into
effect and to report to the Conference whenever in the
opinion of the Executive Committee the special committee
has made an adequate report."[16]

When the problem of Sabbath observance again came up

for discussion at the Central Conference of American Rabbis, in 1937, the approach was altogether different. The report which was presented by Rabbi Israel Harburg dealt solely with the problem of the revitalization of Sabbath observance. Rabbi Harburg recommended, among other things, that we should emphasize the sacredness of the Sabbath not merely by refraining from certain actions but more so by sponsoring various spiritual activities which produce a Sabbath atmosphere. He suggested study groups and other meetings for social and cultural purposes on Saturday afternoons provided such meetings are not out of keeping with the Sabbath spirit. "Among the more educated and spiritual-minded people of our congregations, we may find a few men and women who may be taught to appreciate an intellectual late-Saturday-afternoon which may reproduce that most beautiful *Ben Minḥah le-Ma'ariv* Sabbath atmosphere of the old synagogue which has been so successfully recreated now in Palestine by the '*Oneg Shabbat* societies." The report also urged the establishment of permanent national and local Sabbath committees. "Just as we have now standing committees in our Conference for every important aspect of our work, we should also have a permanent Sabbath Committee. It shall be the task of this Committee to study the various methods that are being employed throughout the world in the strengthening of the Sabbath; to formulate literary, musical and artistic projects for the creation of a Sabbath spirit in our Temples, in our public institutions, as well as in our homes. It shall seek to cooperate with similar committees of other rabbinic bodies in an effort to enlist every Jewish organization in a common endeavor to assert the sacredness of the Sabbath in American Jewish life. Likewise, in every congregation a Sabbath Committee should be formed of our most spiritual-minded men and women whose task shall be to cooperate with this rabbinical committee in fostering as many Sabbath activities as local conditions will permit."[17]

Thus did the struggle against the well-meaning but dangerous attempt to transfer the historical seventh-day Sabbath to Sunday end with an enthusiastic reaffirmation of the traditional Sabbath. Not long after this controversy, the Reform Rabbinate was counted in the ranks of those who rose in defense of the Sabbath against the powerful forces which promoted an international movement for the simplification of the calendar, a simplification which, had it been adopted, would have proved to be the death blow to Sabbath observance.

THE PROPOSED PLANS FOR
CALENDAR REFORM

The calendar which is used in the greater part of the world is known as the Gregorian Calendar. Its disadvantages lie mainly in the inequality of the months, some having thirty-one days and others thirty days, while the month of February has only twenty-eight or twenty-nine days. Furthermore, there is no correlation between the weekly and the monthly division of time, because the week is not an exact subdivision of the month. Because of these irregularities business firms find it complicated and costly to keep their records; so much so that some firms have found it necessary to develop business calendars of their own.

In order to obviate these difficulties, several plans for calendar reform were presented to the League of Nations. One of these plans, known as the Cotsworth Plan, was chosen as the most practical. It provided for a thirteen-month year, each month to consist of four weeks or twenty-eight days. The simplicity of the plan is obvious, for the week, the month, and the year would perennially start on the same day of the week — on Sunday. Any given day of any month would always fall on the same day in the week. But the thirteen-month or fifty-two-week year would give us only three hundred and sixty-four days, which is one day short of the solar year. To remove this difficulty the plan provided for a "dies-non," or a Blank Day. After the thirteen months were completed, the next was to be a holiday and was to be known as Blank Day, Year Day, or Zero Day. The day following the Blank Day was to start the new year, and was to be known as Sunday, the first day of the week, the first day of the month, as well as the first day of the year. During a leap year when there are three hundred and sixty-six days, there would be a double holiday at the turn of the year. There would be two "dies-non" — Blank Day and Sol Day. The first day of the new year would again be called Sunday.

This plan was chosen as the most practical because all months would be equal in length, always starting on a Sunday and ending on a Saturday. It would eliminate much of the confusion caused by the present calendar wherein the months are unequal and unrelated to the week. Accountants would find it easier to systematize business records and thus save much time and expense.

The movement for the universal adoption of this calendar was headed by the originator of the plan, Mr. Moses B. Cotsworth, of London. In America, a powerful propaganda was carried on by the National Committee for Calendar Simplification, headed by Mr. George Eastman of the Eastman Kodak Co. The climax of the American campaign was reached in 1928 when a resolution recommending the calling of an international conference to consider the reform of the calendar was introduced in the House of Representatives at Washington, D. C. The resolution had a preamble specifically setting forth the Cotsworth Plan as the desirable manner of reforming the calendar.

But there was a fly in the ointment. The possible adoption of this new calendar aroused consternation among many religious people everywhere, and most of all among Jewish religious leaders. It was realized that such a calendar would put Sabbath observance in utmost confusion. The traditional seventh-day Sabbath, commonly identified with Saturday, would become a "wandering" or "shifting" Sabbath. Since the Blank Day annually shifts the days of the week, making a traditional Monday into a Sunday, the Sabbath would necessarily fall on a different day every year. One year the Sabbath would be celebrated on Tuesdays, and another year it might fall on Fridays. The economic hardships for Sabbath observers would prove unendurable. The new arrangement, though profitable to the businessman, would do violence to the conscience of the observant Jew, and would ultimately lead to the universal violation and utter abandonment of the Sabbath.

These difficulties would also affect other religious groups. The Seventh-day Adventists and the Seventh-day Baptists would find themselves in an identical situation with the Jews. Mohammedans would find their Friday Rest-Day "wandering" along with the seventh-day Sabbath. Likewise, the Christian Lord's Day would lose its permanent association with Sunday.

The opposition came largely from the League for Safeguarding the Fixity of the Sabbath, a Jewish organization, endorsed and supported by all religious groups in Judaism. The League made it clear in its memoranda to the League of Nations and to the House Committee on Calendar Reform that the Jews were not opposed to calendar reform or to any progressive act which might prove beneficial to society.

The opposition was directed only against the Blank Day feature of the proposed new calendar, a feature which would destroy the Sabbath by undoing its fixed periodicity. The League willingly conceded that the change in the calendar would bring increased monetary advantage to businessmen, but it questioned whether that would "justify forcing and foisting a change . . . which will override the religious sentiments and convictions of a law-abiding portion of the community."

The League for Safeguarding the Fixity of the Sabbath also proposed substitute plans, which, it claimed, incorporated most of the advantages of the Cotsworth Plan and at the same time did away with the disadvantages of the Blank Day feature. One of these substitute plans was an adaptation of a business calendar used by Sears, Roebuck and Company. The calendar provides for a thirteen-month year, and a twenty-eight-day month, except that one month annually has twenty-nine days. In the Sears, Roebuck and Company procedure, January first is a holiday when all books are closed. The new year opens on January second when all business accounts are reopened. January first is not counted as one of the business days, but it is not a Blank Day, and therefore does not disrupt the week.

Another substitute plan consisted of a calendar with a thirteen-month year, and a twenty-eight-day month, starting regularly on Sundays. But the extra day at the end of the year was not a Blank Day. It was allowed to accumulate until there were seven such days, when a whole week was added to the thirteenth month of that year. This plan would preserve that feature of the calendar which makes the days of the month correspond to the days of the week. It would also eliminate the Blank Day. But it would render the years unequal, because each fifth or sixth year would have an additional week. The opposition of the League for Safeguarding the Fixity of the Sabbath, aided by the active support of certain Christian groups, ultimately succeeded in the struggle. The Congressional hearings held in 1928 under the chairmanship of Representative Stephen G. Porter proved that the opposition was strong. The resolution was therefore never reported out of committee. After 1929 such a resolution was never again brought forth in either House. The League of Nations, too, after several hearings, shelved the scheme.

THE JEWISH SABBATH ALLIANCE
OF AMERICA

The precarious condition of the Sabbath, however, was in no way cured. The "incongruity between the theoretical profession and the radical violation" continued to challenge both rabbis and serious minded laymen. As early as 1892, we find the Board of Jewish Ministers of New York troubled by this disturbing situation. The Board appointed a committee consisting of Rabbis F. de Sola Mendes and Bernard Drachman and empowered that committee to publish a book entitled *Sabbath Preachings*, "being extracts from sermons preached by Jewish ministers of New York City in behalf of Sabbath observance." The preface to this volume states that "the object of the publication is . . . an earnest attempt to grapple with the great and increasing neglect of the Sinaitic Sabbath and how to restore the Sabbath to its proper place and influence in this large Jewish community."

Needless to say, the publication of *Sabbath Preachings* did not solve the problem of the widespread desecration of the Sabbath. It was only a forerunner of another attempt which was more sustained, more systematic, and more vigorous in its approach. This more practical attempt was initiated by men who "felt that a *laissez faire* policy was equivalent to definite surrender and abandonment; that to permit the ship of Judaism, as typified in its most sacred precept, the Sabbath, to drift pilotless and rudderless upon the sea of chance and individual caprice, was deliberately to wreck it and drive it to destruction on the rocks of religious indifference and economic difficulties."[18] In 1905 the Jewish Sabbath Association was organized. The name was subsequently changed to the Jewish Sabbath Alliance of America. It set for itself the task of "defending and promoting the observance of the seventh-day Sabbath in every possible way and manner." The actual program, however, has concerned itself mainly with four specific types of activity.

The first sphere of action has aimed at deepening the Sabbath convictions and loyalties among Sabbath observers. The Alliance has arranged many public meetings, printed and distributed many circulars, and stimulated the organization of similar groups in other cities.[19]

Equally important and more dramatic has been the constant struggle against legislative obstacles to Sabbath observance. In New York State, as in many other states of the Union, there are laws calculated to enforce Sunday rest on the whole population. The Alliance has therefore sought legislation exempting the Sabbath observer from enforced Sunday rest. The Alliance has logically insisted that enforcement of Sunday observance by the state is un-American, because it negates the constitutional principle of religious liberty by advancing one religious institution to the detriment of another. Such legislation also results in a gross injustice to those who observe the seventh-day Sabbath. They are forced to refrain from productive labor two days weekly and are, therefore, at a great disadvantage in relation to their competitors who observe only one rest-day. Finally, it has been argued, Sunday laws are harmful to society because the fierce economic competition makes the observance of two weekly rest-days impossible, and therefore causes Sabbath observers to abandon their religious convictions regarding the Sabbath. This is the first step leading to irreligion, a step which is not conducive to good citizenship.

The perennial legislative activity of the Alliance in New York State has not achieved the desired results. The Alliance, however, has been successful in its opposition to the annual attempt, since 1920, to introduce strict Sunday laws in the District of Columbia.

The failure to amend the Penal Code of New York State has made it necessary to defend those Sabbath observers who have found it necessary to keep their places of business open on Sunday. The Legal Department of the Alliance has therefore been constantly on the alert to defend and intervene in behalf of thousands of such arrested Sabbath observers. The Legal Department boasts that it has defended over two thousand Sabbath-observing storekeepers, and has exempted over five thousand Sabbath-observing people from paying fines for Sunday violation.

But the most useful function of the Alliance has been executed through its Employment Bureau, which has placed over forty thousand men and women in Sabbath-keeping positions. One must know the tragic plight of the Sabbath-observing workingman, to appreciate the humanitarian as well as the religious significance of this service.

As early as 1915, Dr. Bernard Drachman, the president of the Jewish Sabbath Alliance, urged the acceptance of the "Five-Day Working Week," pointing out that men need both a weekly holy day for worship and religious restfulness, and a weekly holiday for recreation and recuperation. Today this plan has largely been adopted and has therefore made it possible for workingmen and factory owners to observe the seventh-day Sabbath if they so desire. But Sabbath observance is far from strengthened by the added opportunities. Indeed, the whole struggle for the preservation of the Sabbath, whether it was against those who sought to transfer it to Sunday or against those who threatened it through calendar reform, aimed only at preserving the Sabbath from total disappearance from our midst. This limited goal has been achieved. But preservation in the past is no insurance against a mere sickly existence in the present or against total disintegration in the future. Against such possibilities the present generation must muster all its forces, for "without the observance of the Sabbath . . . the whole of Jewish life would in time disappear."[20]

CHAPTER XX

THE JEWISH SABBATH AND THE CHRISTIAN SUNDAY

"There is not one city, Greek or bar-
barian, nor a single nation, to which our
custom of abstaining from work on the
seventh day has not spread" (Flavius
Josephus, *Contra Apionem*, 2.40).

A S LONG as the Jew remained segregated in the Ghetto
or the Pale, he was not concerned with the fact that
his Christian neighbor observed the first day of the week
as his official day of rest and worship. But as soon as the
Jew was emancipated and was permitted to become part of
the political and economic life of his country, he discovered
that the Jewish week was out of step with the economic
and social order which were patterned after the Christian
tradition. Sabbath observance became a serious obstacle
in the way of earning a livelihood. Many a Jew tried to
observe the Sabbath, despite the enormous disadvantage
such observance imposed upon him, only to succumb to the
inexorable economic forces. The few who succeeded are
the proverbial exceptions that prove the rule.

The problem of the Christian Sunday has therefore become a matter of vital concern to every Jew who is troubled
by the general decline of Sabbath observance. One frequently hears the question: Why did the Christians abandon the
Sabbath? How could the Christians accept the authority
of the Bible, and more particularly the Ten Commandments,
and at the same time reject the one commandment which

is introduced by the admonition, "*Remember* the sabbath day to keep it holy"?

To answer these questions the Jew must search not so much in theology as in history, for the change from the Sabbath to Sunday was the result of a long historic process which is tied up with the formative years of Christianity. This process coincided with the drift of early Christianity from a messianic movement among the Jews to a religion of the Gentiles. When Christianity was predominantly Jewish, the Sabbath was the official Christian day of rest and worship. When Christianity finally became predominantly Gentile, the Sabbath was abandoned and Sunday became the official day of rest and worship. This change was not sudden. It was a slow process of more than three centuries' duration.

An examination of the gradual transition from the Sabbath to Sunday must begin with the realization that "the 'disciples of Jesus the Nazarene' were a conventicle within the synagogue, rather than a sect . . . . They were pious and observant Jews, who worshipped in the temple and in the synagogue like others . . . and in their observance of the Law conformed to tradition as expounded by the Scribes and Pharisees."[1] They kept the Sabbath, deviating only in a few unimportant details, and these slight deviations were not so much distinctive of the early Christians as they were of the Galilean Jews who were somewhat lax in the observance of some rituals. This observance is reflected in the admonition ascribed to Jesus, "Whosoever shall break one of these least commandments, and shall teach men so, he shall be called the least in the kingdom of heaven."[2] Even the oft-quoted statement ascribed to Jesus that "the sabbath was made for man, and not man for the sabbath"[3] can be matched by the rabbinic teaching that "the Sabbath is committed to you, not you to the Sabbath."[4]

The early Christians, however, differed from the Jews in

that they used to assemble for prayer separately, both every day and more particularly on Sunday mornings. The first day of the week was especially singled out for these prayer meetings because of the Christian belief that Jesus rose from the grave on a Sunday. Furthermore, they needed something distinctively their own, for in addition to being Jews they also believed in Jesus. These weekly prayer meetings effectively served this need. They also began to call the first day of the week the Lord's Day, i. e., the day when their Lord, Jesus, rose from the grave. This arrangement of strictly observing the Sabbath as a day of rest and worship as prescribed by the Bible and by Jewish tradition and then also gathering for prayer on the first day of the week continued as long as Jewish influence remained supreme.

The predominance of Jewish influence, however, was successfully challenged by one of the new converts to Christianity. Paul, at first a persecutor of the Christians, became the most zealous missionary, carrying the new gospel primarily to the Gentiles. Since the Sabbath with its many restrictions was a burden to those who were not trained in Jewish life, and since it was objectionable to many Gentiles who considered it, along with circumcision, as a national characteristic of the Jews, Paul abolished the Sabbath and thus opened the road of conversion to the multitude of Gentiles. This radical step was in line with his avowed policy of expediency, as he himself admits, "I am made all things to all men, that I might by all means save some."[5] He rationalized his daring action on theological grounds — namely, that the law was abolished by the death and resurrection of Jesus. Since Paul found the Sabbath objectionable, he did not institute a Christian Sabbath. He merely destroyed the Hebrew Sabbath and thus paved the way for the pagan influence which later turned Sunday into a Christian sacred day. Its immediate effect was to make the Lord's Day stand out as the significant Christian day of the week.

This radical break with Judaism did not go unchallenged. The Jewish Christians, known as the Ebionites, rejected the Epistles of Paul and even called him an apostate. They continued the original practice of observing the Sabbath and of assembling for prayer on the Lord's Day.[6] The opposition of the Ebionites, however, was ineffective because Jewish predominance in Christianity was gone. Not only were the Jewish Christians by now a small minority, but their prestige was further diminished by the crushing defeat which the Jews suffered at the hands of the Romans. The destruction of Jerusalem in the year 70 C.E. spelled the end of decisive Jewish influence on Christianity and the corresponding rise of Gentile influence.

Just as the Jews brought their traditions, including the Sabbath, into early Christianity, so did the Gentiles now bring into Christianity their own traditions, among them the sacredness of the Day of the Sun. The pagans were accustomed to regard Sunday as a sacred day because sun-worship was the central feature of many cults of that period. This was especially true of Mithraism, which was sufficiently widespread to become an official religion of the Roman Empire. The Gentiles who were converted to Christianity therefore infused into the Lord's Day the characteristics of the pagan Sunday. The Lord's Day ceased to be a mere day of prayer. It became a sacred day, thus assuming some of the characteristics of the Sabbath.

The process of completely eliminating the Sabbath and of replacing it with a sacred Sunday was furthered by the second Jewish revolt against Rome in the second century. The Hadrianic persecutions which followed the crushing defeat of the Jews proscribed Judaism on pain of death. It therefore became expedient for the Christians not to be suspected of Judaism. Since the Sabbath was one of the outstanding characteristics of Jewish life, its observance exposed one to grave dangers. It was then that the Sabbath began to disappear completely from among the Christians. We begin to hear Christians denouncing Sabbath observance as "Judaizing," and referring to the Lord's Day by the pagan name of Sunday.

The final steps that led to the transformation of the simple Christian prayer meeting on the first day of the week to the legalized "Sunday Sabbath" were not taken until the fourth century. In the year 321 C.E., the Emperor Constantine issued the following decree: "Let all the judges and town-people, and the occupations of all trades, rest on the venerable day of the sun; but let those who are situated in the country freely and at full liberty attend to the business of agriculture, because it often happens that no other day is so fit for sowing corn and planting vines, lest the critical moment being let slip, men should lose the commodities granted by the providence of Heaven." Although this decree affected only the markets and the courts, it nevertheless consummated the process that had begun during the days of Paul. With the decree of Constantine, Sunday was officially legalized as the Christian sacred day of rest. Later decrees, especially that of the Council of Laodicea, further defined the nature of the Christian Sunday but added little of consequence. Neither did the curious notion that Jesus transferred the Sabbath to the Lord's Day in any way affect the situation. Early Christianity had run its course of development. Changes, if any, could now be made only through the medium of the Church, and the Church was slow to change.

With the coming of the Reformation the Bible again became an open book, at least to many of the Protestants. Upon reading the Bible some people discovered discrepancies between the Sabbath of the Bible and the Sunday of the Christians. This discovery led to the Sabbatarian movements which resulted in the Puritan Sunday and the American blue laws. The Sabbatarians officially made Sunday into a Sabbath, and insisted that it should be observed as prescribed in the Bible. Since the Bible prohibits "all manner of work," the Puritan Sunday exceeded the Hebrew Sabbath in its restrictions. An example of the rigors imposed by the Puritan Sunday is the list of some of the laws contained in the oft-quoted code of Connecticut:

> No one shall run on the Sabbath day, or walk in his garden, or elsewhere, except reverently to and from meeting.
> No one shall travel, cook victuals, make beds, sweep house, cut hair or shave, on the Sabbath day.
> No woman shall kiss her child on the Sabbath or fasting day.
> The Sabbath shall begin at sunset on Saturday.
> If any man shall kiss his wife, or wife her husband on the Lord's day, the party in fault shall be punished at the discretion of the court of magistrates."[7]

The Sabbatarians not only prescribed the exact manner of observing the "Sunday Sabbath" for themselves, but they insisted that it was the duty of the government to protect their sacred day from desecration. Blue laws were therefore written into the statutes of most of the states, forcing everybody to abstain from work on Sunday irrespective of religious conviction.

Another by-product of the Reformation was the appearance of a different type of Sabbatarian who not only wanted to observe the Sabbath laws, but insisted that they be observed on the seventh day, as prescribed in the Bible and as practiced by Jesus and his disciples. Some of these seventh-day observers, known as the Seventh-day Baptists, were found among the followers of Oliver Cromwell. They held to the doctrines of the Calvinistic Baptists, but observed the seventh day as the Sabbath. Some of these Seventh-day Baptists migrated to America and in 1761 they established in Rhode Island their first American church.

More important and more vigorous is the younger sect, known as the Seventh-day Adventists. They came into existence about one hundred years ago when many Christians, on the basis of esoteric calculations, expected the return of Jesus in 1844. When that year passed without the advent of Jesus, one group, later known as the Seventh-day Adventists, established itself as a distinct Christian fundamentalist sect. They adhere to the belief that the coming of Jesus is imminent and that everyone should prepare himself for his advent. One of the methods of this preparation is the acceptance of the true Sabbath as the day of rest and worship. The adherents of this doctrine have been very zealous for their cause. They claim that they contribute to their church per capita "ten times as much as the Protestant average in America." Their zeal is matched by their uncompromising stand on Sabbath observance. An official statement recently issued by the Autumn Council of the General Assembly contains, among many items, the following principles regarding Sabbath observance:

> We counsel the ministry to even greater carefulness in admitting to membership in the church of God such as hold positions where it seems to them necessary to work on the Sabbath day, even though such work be minimized and made as light as possible. While it is not possible to lay down rules that will cover every case and all conditions, we warn against the tendency to let down the bars and admit and retain as members any who are unwilling to take a decided stand for the Sabbath of the

Lord. Our members should not enter into entangling business alliances or perform on the Sabbath government or community service which compromises sacred principles. The seventh day is the Sabbath of the Lord. In it we are not to do that which is forbidden by the law of God.

How can anyone think that he is observing the Sabbath as God would have it observed when he is working on that day? How can a Seventh-day Adventist attend school on that day, or prepare lessons, or write examinations, or attend public exhibitions or games? How can he listen to secular radio programs or dramas, or go to social gatherings or picnics, or habitually neglect divine service? How can he engage in or plan business ventures, read secular literature, do odd jobs around the house, go shopping, spend an undue amount of time in physical rest, go pleasure riding for selfish purposes, or do any of the many things forbidden both by God and by the enlightened conscience of the Christian? The answer, of course, must be that true Christians can do none of these things.

Despite the steady increase in the ranks of the Seventh-day Adventists, Christianity is permanently committed to Sunday as the Christian day of worship and rest. The Sabbath remains, as it has always been, distinctive of Judaism, "an everlasting covenant," "a sign between Me and the children of Israel for ever."

CHAPTER XXI

SABBATH OBSERVANCE IN THE FAR-FLUNG JEWISH COMMUNITIES

שַׁבָּת הוּא לַה' בְּכֹל מוֹשְׁבֹתֵיכֶם (ויקרא כ"ג ג')

It is a sabbath unto the Lord in all your dwellings (Lev. 23.3).

SABBATH observance in the scattered Jewish communities of the world is not uniform. Many communities have their own distinctive local customs which reflect their peculiar history and environment. In addition, there are Jewish sects with a Sabbath ritual all their own. Among the latter only two have been sufficiently numerous and vigorous to survive. These sects, the Samaritans and the Karaites, have insisted on a literal interpretation of the Bible, so that their Sabbath observance is in many respects different from ours. There are, moreover, several Jewish communities which were completely cut off from intercourse with the main body of the Jewish people. The peculiar customs of the Falashas in Ethiopia, the Bene Israel in India, and the Marranos in Portugal are the result of a self-sacrificing but unenlightened devotion to a tradition. Thus the Marranos, who were forced into baptism and were carefully watched by the Inquisition, necessarily limited their Sabbath observance to a few obscure rituals.

But sects and segregated communities are rare exceptions in Jewish life. The main body of Israel observes the Sabbath in the traditional manner. Though the recognized principles of Sabbath observance have been adjusted to

371

local conditions and often reflect the customs peculiar to a given land, the common denominator that unites all Sabbath observers is the traditional law of the Sabbath. That law is accepted not merely as a religious duty but as a unique privilege. For in the Sabbath the Jews of the world, however far apart, have always found the same precious gift—joyful rest, and intellectual and spiritual delight.

THE SABBATH AMONG THE SAMARITANS

In their strict observance of the Sabbath they go beyond the tradition of the Jews and refuse to allow a light to be kindled, sitting in darkness. They put a greater restriction upon the distance they are allowed to walk on the Sabbath, and also refuse to accept the principle of the 'Erub. Further, they forbid the drinking of wine or any intoxicating liquor on the Sabbath and festivals, for they assert that the observance of these days is equivalent to the service in the Temple, and according to Lev. 10.9 no priest was allowed to drink before approaching the altar. This is in contradistinction to the Jews who do precisely the reverse, and celebrate the Sabbath and festivals by the blessing over a cup of wine.

MOSES GASTER[1]

THE SABBATH AMONG THE KARAITES

The [Karaite] Ḥakam said that it was prohibited to desecrate the Sabbath in behalf of a dangerously sick person. If the patient recovered, then the Sabbath was desecrated in vain since the patient would have recovered anyway. And if the patient died, then the Sabbath was surely desecrated in vain.

He also forbade the Karaites to enter the house of a Rabbinite [Jew] on the Sabbath, because the Rabbinites kindle lights for the Sabbath, and the Bible says, "Ye shall kindle no fire throughout your habitations upon the sabbath day" (Ex. 35.3), i.e., where you dwell there must be no light. And he told me similar nonsense without end.

On the Sabbath the Karaites read the portion of the Torah in a printed Bible. Only when there is a distinguished guest of their own sect do they take out the scroll in his honor. . .

Of the art of music they know nothing, and they have one tune for Sabbath and holiday, for mourning and rejoicing. They never change it.

On Sabbath eve and on the Day of Atonement they do not kindle lights in the synagogue, and they recite their prayers in the dark. After the service the cantor turns his face to the congregation and blesses them, "May your prayers be accepted." He repeats the blessing three times and the congregation answers, "Amen!"

The Karaites, like the Samaritans, have interpreted the Sabbath law very harshly, according to the literal reading of the text. Like the Samaritans, they do not kindle lights on Friday nights, and, like them, they forbid going out of the house during the Sabbath, except for services, because they interpret literally the verse, "Let no man go out of his place on the seventh day" (Ex. 16.30).

EPHRAIM DEINARD[2]

The Karaites are a Jewish sect which came into being in Babylonia at the beginning of the eighth century. They deny the authority of the Oral Law, the Mishnah, and the Talmud, and they accept only the authority of the Bible. They number today only about ten thousand souls, most of whom dwell in Russia. Some of them are also to be found in Poland, Turkey, Egypt, Iraq, and a few in Palestine.

They are stricter than the Jews in regard to Sabbath observance. . . . Since the Karaites do not depend on tradition, they try to support all their Sabbath regulations with biblical texts. Work which is started on Friday and automatically continues on the Sabbath is prohibited among them. For example, a light or a fire which was kindled on Friday afternoon must not be allowed to continue to burn on the Sabbath. Such a light or fire must be extinguished before sunset, a practice similar to that of the Samaritans and the Falashas. But now there are some among the Karaites who permit the kindling of a light on Friday afternoon for Sabbath eve in order to avoid sitting in darkness.

It is also forbidden to cut food with a knife, such as bread or meat, but it may be broken by hand.

The Karaites are now divided into two groups, known as "Lovers of Light" and "Despisers of Light" according to their attitude to the Sabbath light. . . .

Carrying a burden on the Sabbath is also forbidden among them, but they do not accept the 'Erub whereby the Rabbis made this prohibition less burdensome.

M. ZOBEL [3]

THE SABBATH AMONG THE FALASHAS

We [the Falashas] celebrate the Sabbath in accordance with the teaching of the Scriptures where it is written, "For in six days the Lord made heaven and earth, and on the seventh day He ceased from work and rested" (Ex. 31.17). We do not kindle a fire from Friday evening until the end of the Sabbath.

* * *

They enjoy themselves with all sorts of good food in honor of the Sabbath. Any fast day that falls on the Sabbath is postponed. If the Day of Atonement falls on a Sabbath, they do not eat to satiety as on an ordinary Sabbath, but they taste a little food in order to demonstrate that the Sabbath is even greater than the Day of Atonement. . . Once they saw two Jewish tourists arrive on the Sabbath. They fell upon Dr. Faitlovitch[4] and said, "You are liars, not Jews. According to the letters of your rabbis, you wish to make our children loyal to Judaism. Aren't these tourists, your brethren, Jews? Why did they travel on the Sabbath? What do you wish to teach our children? Do you wish to teach our children to desecrate the Sabbath? Do you want to convert them to Christianity?"

It is customary among the Falashas especially to honor and sanctify every seventh Sabbath. On the eve of the Sabbath they all gather in the synagogue to pray. They stop just for the meal, and then reassemble and pray and sing hymns throughout the night and throughout the day.

J. FAITLOVITCH[5]

They [the Falashas] entertain the most rigid notions as to the sanctity of the Sabbath. The preparations for the due celebration of this sacred day commence on Friday at noon, when every one, who is not prevented by illness, repairs to an adjacent river to bathe and change his garb. This task accomplished, the majority lazily saunter about in the fields, or indolently recline on the grassy margin of some sparkling stream till sunset summons to the *Mesquid* (house of worship). The service, which consists of chanting Psalms and hymns relieved by allegorical stories, and of a few verses or a chapter of the book of Leviticus, lasts a considerable time, and in some places the plaintive notes of the worshippers may even be heard across the quiet valley and around the lonely hill throughout the night. This extreme religious fervor is the exclusive monopoly of the priests. Nor do their flocks envy them a privilege which would rob them after six days' toil of that very rest and physical health which the Sabbath was designed to promote.

Early on the following morning, knots of figures enveloped in the graceful folds of a white cotton dress are again seen trooping up the narrow lane and over the green sward towards the humble building dedicated to the worship of God. The service of the *Mesquid* having been duly celebrated, the people again repair to their huts, where, after a cold and frugal repast, they either indulge in a nap, or meet together for social intercourse. Most of the priests remain in the house of prayer from Friday night till Saturday evening, and no trifling circumstance could induce the few whom sickness or age forces to retire to transgress the misinterpreted command: "Let no man go out of his place on the seventh day."

Some of the prayers used in the *Mesquid* are full of devotional sentiments and impressive ejaculations. Thus, on Saturday morning, they begin:–

"Thou, O Lord, hearest in heaven the worship of Thy saints; hear us also when we cry unto Thee in Thy holy temple. O Lord, be not angry with us, nor suffer us to be destroyed. Remember the covenant of our fathers, whom Thou didst redeem out of Egypt's bondage, and forgive us our sins, and blot out our transgressions, which have separated us from Thee.

"God of our fathers, turn unto us, and cause us to live.

"God of Abraham, turn unto us, and cause us to live.

"God of Isaac, turn unto us, and cause us to live.

"God of Jacob, turn unto us, and cause us to live.

"God of angels, turn unto us, and cause us to live.

"O Lord, lead us into the right way, and give peace unto Zion, and salvation unto Jerusalem." . . .

Ignorant as the priests and their people are of the con-

tents of God's Word, they possess a most familiar knowledge of those chapters in Leviticus that treat of the laws of
purification. Saturday after Saturday the Falasha congregations throughout Abyssinia, hear in their *Mesquids*
an exposition or discourse on that edifying topic; even a
stranger, whom the officiating ministers deign to honor, is
condemned to listen amidst the melodious *la la la's* of the
women to a chapter describing leprosy, plague, or other
ills which sin and dirt, vice and ungodliness have entailed
on offending humanity.

HENRY. A. STERN[6]

THE SABBATH AMONG THE "BENE ISRAEL" OF INDIA

In Bombay there are about three hundred families of
the Bene Israel. They have two synagogues and two ritual
slaughterers. . . .

The poor who support themselves by the labor of their
hands refuse to leave their work on the Sabbath, saying
that if they miss one day's work they will be unable to support themselves. Their leaders have therefore not been
able to induce them to rest on the Sabbath. But these men
are not considered sectaries, and they too do everything in
their power to show that they sanctify the Sabbath by
word of mouth and devotion of the heart. Like the Sabbath observers, they return to their homes on Fridays at
four o'clock in the afternoon. They wash, put on their
best clothes, and go to the synagogue where they receive
the Sabbath with joy. After the services the cantor sings
Sabbath hymns and then recites the *Kiddush* over a cup of
raisin wine. The cantor drinks his cup of wine and every
worshipper receives a small cup for himself. Then they go

home in a happy mood, partake of their meals — bread, wine and fruits — and sing hymns for a long time.

In the morning they rise early to go to the synagogue. To the reading of the Torah are called only those who strictly observe the Sabbath. Those who do not properly observe the Sabbath go home to make the *Kiddush* and to eat, and at ten o'clock they go to work.

SOLOMON RINMAN[7]

SABBATH AMONG THE MARRANOS

The commandment of Sabbath observance has always been known to the Marranos, although now they are not strict in it. In former days they all refrained from desecrating the Sabbath, and because of this many of them were burned at the stake or put to the torture by the Inquisition. Today, they are careful to observe the Sabbath strictly only during the forty days preceding the Passover and the forty days preceding the Day of Atonement. There are, however, many businessmen and workingmen who refrain from all labor on the Sabbath. . . .

On Friday they clean and sweep the house, and before sunset the women kindle a light by placing an especially prepared woolen wick in a container of pure olive oil. The following is the benediction they recite: "Blessed be my God, my Lord, who commanded us and cautioned us through His holy commandments to kindle this holy light, to make bright and festive this holy Night of God, in order that God may enlighten our souls and save us from suffering, punishment, and sin."

The Sabbath light is called "God's Light," and in some places, especially in the north of Portugal, it is placed in a jar because this was the custom in former times when it was done to hide the Sabbath light from the spies of the

Inquisition. It is forbidden to extinguish the Sabbath light.

On the Sabbath day the members of the family and their relatives get together and recite the Saturday morning service and other suitable prayers three times. The food is prepared on Friday, and generally only fish and vegetables are eaten in order to avoid forbidden foods on the holy day. They are surprised when told that Jews eat meat on the Sabbath.

NAHUM SLOUSCHZ[8]

It was only by the most stringent caution that existence could be maintained under these conditions [under the implacable vigilance of the Inquisition]. Gaspar de Campos ... gives, in his confession, some account of the devices adopted for concealment. On the Sabbath the mother and girls would sit with reels or spinning wheels before them and, if anyone came in, would pretend to be at work. On fast days the servant-girl would be sent out on an errand; during her absence food would be taken out of the *Olla* (casserole), and plates and spoons would be greased, they would then go to the house of a neighbor Jewess and, when the servant followed them, she would be sent back to get her dinner, telling her that they had dined, and then the neighbor would do the same. . . .

Living thus scattered in small groups or isolated families, concealing their secret faith with the utmost care, and perpetual dread of betrayal, it is not surprising that distinctive Jewish observances were gradually reduced to a minimum, and were becoming to a great degree forgotten. . . . There was an attempt to fast on the day of Queen Esther, when that was known, and perhaps on other days of no special note, as a spiritual exercise; we hear of washing the hands before meals and giving thanks to the God of Israel;

lamps might be lighted on Friday night, but it sufficed to light one and let it burn till it went out. The Sabbath was to be kept by cessation from work, but even this was not always observed, and the changing of body-linen is rarely alluded to. Angela Núñez Marques said that Ana de Niebes and Maria de Murcía had taught her the Law of Moses and its ceremonies, which were to rest on the Sabbath and to observe fasts of four and twenty hours without food or drink, yet, during the twenty years of her residence in Pastrana, she had kept only fifteen Sabbaths, for fear of discovery by her husband and servants. Isabel Mendes Correa, who appeared in the Madrid auto-da-fé of 1680, when sick some years before, had vowed that, if she recovered, she would rest on Saturdays and light lamps on Fridays, for she deemed her illness a punishment for neglecting the Law of Moses. In short, Judaism seems to have resolved itself into Sabbath-keeping with occasional fasting, and into hoping to be saved in the Law of Moses and denying Christ and Christian doctrine.

HENRY CHARLES LEA[9]

THE SABBATH AMONG THE ARABIAN JEWS IN THE FIFTEENTH CENTURY

The following is the arrangement of the Sabbath meal customary to Jews in all Arabian countries. They sit in a circle on a carpet, the cupbearer standing near them, near a small cloth which is spread on this carpet; all kinds of fruit which are in season are brought and laid on the cloth. The host now takes a glass of wine, pronounces the blessing of sanctification (*Kiddush*), and empties the cup completely. The cupbearer then takes it from the host and hands it successively to the whole company, always refilled, and each one empties it. Then the host takes two or three pieces of fruit, eats some, and drinks a second glass, while the company say, "Health and life." Whoever sits next also takes some fruit, and the cupbearer fills a second glass for him, saying, "To your pleasure," the company join in with the words, "Health and life," and so it goes round. Then a second kind of fruit is partaken of, another glass is filled, and this is continued until each one has emptied at least six or seven glasses. Sometimes they even drink when they smell flowers which are provided for the occasion; these flowers are the *Duda'im*, which Rashi translates into Arabic by "jasmine;" it is a plant bearing only blossoms which have a delightful and invigorating fragrance. The wine is unusually strong, and this is especially the case in Jerusalem, where it is drunk unmixed. After all have drunk to their heart's content, a large dish of meat is brought, each one stretches forth his hand, takes what he wants, and eats quickly, for they are not very big eaters. Rabbi Moses brought us confectionery, fresh ginger, dates, raisins, almonds and confectionery of coriander seeds; a glass of wine is drunk with each kind. Then followed raisin wine, which was very good, then malmsey wine from Candia, and again native wine. I drank with them and was exhilarated.

There is another custom in the country of the Arabs: On Friday all go to bathe, and on their return the women bring them wine, of which they drink copiously; word is then brought that the supper is ready, and it is eaten in the daytime, before evening. Then they all come to the synagogue, cleanly and neatly dressed. They begin with psalms and thanksgiving and evening prayer is read until two hours after dusk. On their return home they repeat the *Kiddush*, eat only a piece of bread of the size of an olive, and recite the grace after meals. In this whole district the Afternoon Prayer is read on Friday in private, except in Jerusalem, where the *Ashkenazim* (Germans) have done away with the custom, and the afternoon and evening prayer are said with *Minyan* as with us, and they eat at night; the evening prayer is not begun, however, until the stars are visible. In these parts the Sabbath is more strictly kept than in any other; nobody leaves his house on the Sabbath, except to go to the synagogue or to the *Bet ha-Midrash* (house of study). I need scarcely mention that nobody kindles a fire on the Sabbath, or has a light that has been extinguished rekindled, even by a Gentile. All who are able to read the Holy Scriptures read the whole day, after having slept off the effect of their wine.

OBADIAH YAREH DA BERTINORO[10]

A SUMMER SABBATH IN A LITHUANIAN VILLAGE

The selfsame maidens looked altogether different on Sabbath eve, at the blessing of the candles, when their fathers returned from the public bath with wet temple-locks and dripping beards, their faces red and steamy. Their mothers had closed the shops on the market-place. When the young ladies had tidied up the home, ready for the Holy Sabbath — had stored the evening meal away at the back of the oven, had hidden the Sabbath soup under a pillow to keep it warm, had sprinkled the floor with a "golden" sand, decked the table with a white cloth, set upon one end of the table a pair of shining candlesticks with the candles in their places, and at the other end two loaves of home-made white bread under a white towel, and had lighted the lamps — then the maidens too cast off the weekday spirit. Their faces were washed, their eyes sparkled more freely, and into the braids of their combed hair were woven gaily-colored ribbons; in their starched dresses many of them looked as if they were indeed possessed of a new soul — the soul of the Day of Rest.

The sun goes down .... In the Jewish homes the women are reciting the blessing over the candles. After this prayer, while the parents and brothers of the girls are still at the synagogue, the maidens appear upon the street, stand about their houses, chat with their companions or play with a small brother or sister. Their bearing and even their gait is different, and if a young man acquaintance passes by, they look at him more boldly, and their voices ring more freely, louder than ever. For they are in their Sabbath, holiday mood; they feel it, and they look it. The entire landscape has assumed a Sabbatical air. All the houses are illumined, and through the windows may be seen the bright, cheery beams of the candles, which seem to escape into the street and engage in combat with the dark shadows that the summer evening casts over the village. The thicker and darker the shadows become, the more strongly and brightly shine the beams of the Sabbath lights through the windows of the Jewish homes, and the more cheerful and exalted are the eyes of the Queen Sabbath that gaze through the windows.

Over the market-place, too, hovers the Holy Sabbath. Everything is so quiet, so peaceful. The shops are closed, the tables removed. No care-worn Jewish face is visible, nor can a Jewish groan be heard. Quiet and peace. The market-place is asleep, resting from its weekday cares. The hens of the Gentile peasants, and their brood; the Gentile geese and ducks that were pecking all day about the shops and tables, left the place before nightfall. Only "Jewish" goats wander now among the closed stalls; nobody drives them away, so that they, too, feel the spirit of the Sabbath and strut about calmly, undisturbed, free. And when the desire moves them, they stop short before a shop and peacefully rub their beards against the door.

Night has fallen. Stars have been lighted in the sky.

They, too, sparkle differently than on weekday nights. Jews come forth from the synagogue. They walk along at ease, their wives and sons at their sides — one with his coat slung across his shoulders, another with both hands thrust into his sleeves, a third with his hands folded behind his back. Step by step, ever so leisurely, they walk along, as nonchalantly as if there were no cares upon earth. "Good Sabbath!" echoes the street with cheery voices. "Good Sabbath!" echoes in the houses . . . .

And soon every Jew has welcomed to his home the benevolent spirits of the Holy Sabbath. The wife softly hums the chant of the prayers as her husband intones them, and the pious daughter hums it, too. And the raisin-wine, or the sweet mead, poured from the Sabbath beaker and tasted by everybody in the house, contains every flavor. And later, when the head of the house sings the Sabbath songs, his voice sounds so free! His sons join him, and the wife and daughter chime in, humming softly or accompanying the melody in their thoughts. All sorrows are forgotten when the Sabbath comes to the village. The Jewish street, the Jewish home, the Jewish soul — all rest when Sabbath comes.

The day is particularly eventful for the girls, since every Saturday they go walking in the woods. They walk in pairs, and reaching the forest sit down upon the green carpet in the shade of the trees. Through the trees comes the noise of young men acquaintances, playing at "butter-tarts." Older men and women, who have come hither on a walk, sit on the grass, facing the young men and laughing at their antics. The girls begin to sing a Jewish folksong, whereupon the young men grow silent, soon appearing from behind the trees, looking upon the maidens and smiling foolishly. The girls turn their eyes away, arrange their hair more becomingly, glance down upon their bosoms, pluck the grass aimlessly and sing, sing.

All at once one of the young men takes up the tune, then a second, and a third, and soon all sing in chorus. The voices of the girls and the youths blend, intertwine, caress and kiss. The older folk join in the tune with a nasal humming, and the blue sky over the dark crowns of the trees seems to sing with them. Thus it continues till the evening meal. Then the groups break up and go homeward.

They cross the market-place in pairs, in threes, and even in fours; boys and girls separately, and both the youths and the maidens are still under the spell of the forest. All the way home they keep sending signals — the girls to the boys, the boys to the girls — letting themselves be heard or their presence felt, casting glances, making grimaces, uttering sudden screams, shrieks, bursting into laughter and dashing about.

The market-place is still at rest; the shops are still closed, as the Jewish boys and girls come home from the woods with their noisy chatter.

From an open window yonder peers a Jew in a skull-cap, covered with feathers from the bed from which he has very evidently just arisen. He strokes his beard in leisurely fashion, yawns in the same carefree manner and wrinkles his forehead. Another Jew with a yellow matted beard, wearing a winter coat from beneath which may be seen the yellow, grimy edges of his fringed scarf, is standing at the gate of his home, scratching himself with his left hand under his right arm-pit, making grimaces and complaining: "Ay-va! Such hot weather! Good heavens!" A Jewish woman in her Sabbath bonnet runs out of the house and shouts to her unwilling son to come right in and do his reading from the *Dicta of the Fathers*. And there on a turf-mound sits a mother with her children, telling them tales about ghosts and spirits, about miracle-workers and the thirty-six saints . . . .

Two elders come by, obviously engrossed in a deep problem. Both walk slowly, their beards clutched in their fists, their foreheads furrowed in thought. Perhaps they are discussing "politics" — Bismarck and Beaconsfield — or perhaps some knotty problem in the *Gemara* . . . . Small children with washed faces and combed hair are playing before their houses. The shirt-tails that stick out of the urchins' trousers are still white and clean; the little girls' dresses have not yet had time to be soiled.

As soon as the children spy their elder brothers and sisters returning from their stroll, they dash toward them with a glad shout, surround them and press close to their knees. The faces of the older brothers and sisters shine with a certain zest, and are covered with perspiration; their eyes glow happily. And the father, seeing this, scolds his son.

"The idea of such a husky chap running about all day long. Better stay home and do your Sabbath studying in the *Dicta of the Fathers!*"

The mother looks at her boy and sighs. "How ruddy, how healthy! He'll surely be taken as one of the Czar's soldiers!"

The sun sinks lower in the west. Soon it will set. The village folk gather in the synagogue to say the sunset prayer. The daughter remains at home, puts an apron over her Sabbath dress, and prepares the table for the closing Sabbath meal. She prepares the table and dreams her maiden's dream.

And now the men have returned home from the sunset prayer. All sit around the table and eat the closing meal of the Sabbath. The father begins to sing the Sabbath songs. The sun has set. Suddenly there resounds through the village a metallic ringing — Ding, Dong! — that trembles through the air in a long monotone. The Sabbath Spirit of Rest among the Jews shudders, and a melancholy yearning descends upon them.

The church bell rings and reverberates through the village with its alternate long and short tones: Ding, Dong! Ding, Dong! And its solemn, metallic notes mingle with the deepening shadows that night scatters through the village. They penetrate into the Jewish homes, into the Jewish souls, and rouse within them an even greater melancholy, a greater yearning — the thought of their weekday cares. The Jewish father begins to sigh; the mother looks worried anew; the sons are distraught; the daughters are sad.

Later the men return to the synagogue to say the evening prayers. All the Jewish homes are dark; the Jewish daughters cast off their Sabbath finery, remove the colored ribbons from their hair and sigh into the darkness. The church bell booms again, and how mournfully its tones vibrate through the gloom, with what soulful melancholy they echo in the dark Jewish homes out of which the Holy Sabbath has departed!

The stars have begun to twinkle in the sky. But they do not sparkle as joyfully as they did on Sabbath eve.

In the windows of the Jewish homes lonely little lights have begun to appear. Voices are heard upon the street. "Good week to you! Good week!" The voices, however, echo with cares. And soon from every house arise the prayers that end the Sabbath and call upon the Lord's blessing for the coming week. A few moments later may be heard the hoarse rattling of keys on the market-place, where the Jewish men and women are opening their shops. Here and there sound a Jewish groan. Sabbath is over.

The Spirit of Rest has departed. The weekday soul alone remains. Care has awakened, care and worries. Sabbath is over!

LEON KOBRIN[11]

(Trans. from the Yiddish by ISAAC GOLDBERG)

THE SABBATH AMONG RABBINICAL STUDENTS OF EASTERN EUROPE

The industry of the *Baḥurim* [rabbinical students] was phenomenal. They knew too well that there are no short cuts to knowledge. Many of them did not sleep in a bed except during the night from Friday to the Sabbath. All other nights of the week they spent in the *Yeshibah*, permitting themselves only a short nap as they sat over their folios.

The needy student received his meals free of charge in the Students' Refectory, the "*Baḥurim* Room," which was maintained by contributions from the local and outlying communities. Very frequently the rector of the academy, the *Rosh Yeshibah*, lodged with the students, permitting his wife and children to live elsewhere, so that he might establish the intimate relations with his disciples which are a characteristic feature of Jewish student life. On Friday evening, as a rule, all the students dined with the rector, each one being provided with a beaker of wine while the host recited the *Kiddush*. This Friday evening meal was graced by the presence of the married students as well as the others. Those who had already established households were in the habit of first consecrating the beginning of the Sabbath at home, in the circle of their families, and then they would repair to the *Baḥurim* Room for the common meal. And as the Sabbath was welcomed by teachers and disciples assembled together, so it was ushered out in the same way. *Habdalah* was recited by the rector in the presence of the students, who all drank from the chalice of the master.

LOUIS GINZBERG[12]

THE SABBATH AMONG THE ḤASIDIM

On the Sabbath and on festivals the Ḥasidim take the "sacred meals" at the table of the *Zaddik*. While they eat there is complete silence. Sometimes the *Zaddik* "speaks" Torah, that is to say, he explains a part of the Bible which is fitting to the day. All listen with respect. The *Zaddik* tastes only a little of each course. The *Shirayyim* (the remainder) is divided among the guests. The table of the *Zaddik* is termed by the Ḥasidim the "Altar of God," and the meal is "the sacrifice of God." While the *Zaddik* is taking the food, he is the High Priest making the offering to God . . . .

The third meal at the end of the Sabbath day is a particularly solemn ritual. When the late afternoon prayer (*Minḥah*) has been said, the Ḥasidim come together to join the *Zaddik* in the final Sabbath meal. They eat very little. There is only one course, fish, which has played a great part in Jewish mysticism since the time of the Talmud. The Ḥasidim sit at the table in the dark and there is a feeling of holiness. The *Zaddik* with his eyes closed and in a melancholy voice recites some mystic hymns, verse by verse, and all the Ḥasidim repeat them in chorus, verse by verse.

And they sit together like this till night.

After the evening prayer (*Ma'ariv*) has been said, the *Zaddik* recites the *Habdalah*, which is the farewell to the Sabbath and a prayer to God who distinguishes "between

holy and profane, between light and darkness, between
Israel and other peoples, between the Sabbath and the
weekdays." Before the *Habdalah*, the *Zaddik* repeats a
Yiddish prayer which was popularized in the Ukraine by
the celebrated *Zaddik*, Rabbi Levi-Yizhak of Berditchev.
The essence of this is as follows: "God of Abraham, Isaac
and Jacob, guard Thy people Israel from every evil. The
holy Sabbath is passing away; grant that the week may
bring a pure faith, love for our neighbors, reconciliation
with God, a speedy redemption and the resurrection of the
dead."

This prayer is pronounced by the *Zaddik* with much
fervor and ecstasy. The Hasidim sitting around repeat it
in a subdued voice, word for word. When it is finished, the
Hasidim stay on, to talk about their *Zaddik*. They weigh
each of his words, find a meaning in every nod of his head,
in every twinkle of his eyes. They all sit close together;
one speaks and the others listen. Every difference between
them has gone, they are no longer rich and poor, great and
small. They are just Hasidim.

S. A. HORODEZKY[13]

THE SABBATH IN PALESTINE

In Tel Aviv and in Haifa, in Jerusalem and Tiberias, in
in Rehobot and in Tel Hai, wherever I have sojourned or
dwelt for a time, I have felt the light of grace that enfolds
the world on the Sabbath.

Tel Aviv is a secular city, an altogether modern city, but
on Friday afternoon, the Sabbath becomes mistress of every
corner. The stream of life halts, peace descends on the noisy
streets. Wagons are gone from the roads, and the noise of
automobiles is silenced. The streets seem new-washed and

widened. On the down-slope of Allenby Road, near the
seashore, the Square, which will soon be filled with Sabbath
strollers, is emptied for a while, and gleams all white, as if
floodlighted from some mysterious source. Pure sunset
clouds, like transparent blue-embroidered Sabbath curtains,
hang over the sea. Like a thin partition they stretch from
the sky down to the calm waters. The sea basks in its
Sabbath rest. And whoever then sits by the sea, feels in
the air, in the lovely quiet, in the murmuring of the waters,
a tenderness of Sabbath. How sweet they are, the Sabbath
eves, on the shores of my Homeland seas!

Greater still is the impression of the welcoming of the
Sabbath in Old Jerusalem. Through narrow alleys, under
dark stone archways, companies of Jews walk in a long
procession down to the Wailing Wall, there to meet the
Sabbath. Tremblingly these Jews, washed and new-clothed,
walk towards the holy relic, fearful lest they lose a single
drop of the great Influence which they bear along with them
as a gift of thanksgiving to the Queen. All the way from
the Tower of David down to the bottom of the road, they
stream in colored garments, seeming like the delegates of a
great embassy; and whoever sees them, may deem that they
have just now come from a faraway land, and are marching
to the Wall to meet God's Presence, in the form of Sabbath
the Bride.

When the hour of the Sabbath-welcome arrives, there is
felt a kind of foretaste of the promised Redemption, even
as with every outgoing of the Sabbath there is a feeling of
the renewal of the enslavement, of the gloom ahead.

Nowhere is the forefeeling of Redemption stronger than
in Safed, in Tiberias, in the entire landscape of Galilee.
Sabbath in Galilee is overhung with a mystic sublimity, with
longings for the Messiah. The hymn *Lekah Dodi*, composed
by the Safed poet Rabbi Shelomo Alkabetz, is not merely

a song of Sabbath-welcome, but is also a messianic hymn, an announcement of Redemption.

The students of Cabala saw in this hour of Sabbath-welcome the great opportunity, the time when Redemption is ripe to come. They attached all their hopes to this hour of grace, in which all hearts are purified and united in one feeling of joy and exultation. Here is the great hour — the great opportunity for self-redemption by the power of faith, which is poured on them out of the glory of Sabbath. If only Israel would know how to use this opportunity and not miss it!

Only one who has breathed the pure air of Safed on Sabbath-nights, one who has seen the Sabbath-candles reflected tremblingly in the waters of Lake Kinnereth, may know all the charm of the Sabbath in Galilee. The blowing winds here bespeak the "Sabbath of Sabbaths," the "peace of peace." The stars, aglitter with Sabbath beams, proclaim: Redemption has come into the world!

JACOB FICHMAN[14]
(Trans. from the Hebrew by ABRAHAM REGELSON)

THE SABBATH AT MERCAHVIAH
(Abridged)

...... I remembered
Nehama and her horror of their Sabbath.
I told him. "Is it true you wash and cook
And ride upon the Sabbath?"
                    He's a "radical,"
Makes no pretence at what is called "religion."

"It's true, the women cook as much as they find needful;
There is no formalism. But the washing
Is never done on Sabbath. No, we rest
With all our might. Yet if a girl should care
To wash her blouse or rinse some handkerchief,

We make no inquisition. As for riding,
We sometimes take our wagons out on Sabbaths
To pay calls at the neighbouring settlements,
And singing, whistling, trundle down the roads.
But once there came a tourist, very urgent —
A Jew — and begged on Sabbath for the hire
Of a wagon to take him on to Ein Harod.
'No, Sir,' we said, 'we don't do business
On Sabbath.' No, Sir, we are not *goyim*."

On Friday evening there is singing, chanting
Of Hebrew ecstasies about our God
That would in other lands be called a prayer.
Here it is not a prayer, here it is re-creation.
Hands join in circle, feet begin to beat,
The circle sways, the feet and hands
And heads and bodies sing and dance,
The Hora turns now right now left,
With swaying, praying, playing forms,
Faster and faster, lighter, lighter,
Leaping, laughing, clapping, chanting,
Circle within the circle panting,
Dancing with passion, dancing with power,
With love and joy till the midnight hour.

Long sleep and tender rest
While the fields rest, and the beasts;
Singing again, and books and quiet talk,
And time for courtship and gay visiting,
And time for thought and speechless thanksgiving,
The mystic ease of muscles taut and tired.

JESSIE E. SAMPTER[15]

TIME CHART FOR KINDLING THE SABBATH LIGHTS IN THE U. S. A.[1]

This chart is valid for every year. Find the column that applies
to your geographic location and then find the nearest date.

		Lat. 44° North	Lat. 42° North	Lat. 40° North	Lat. 38°-36° North	Lat. 34°-32° North	Lat. 30°-28° North
		(Portland, Me.)	(Boston, Mass.)	(New York City, Chicago, Ill.)	(Washington,D.C. Norfolk, Va.)	(Savannah, Ga., Charleston, S. C.)	(Pensacola, Fla., New Orleans, La.)
Day of Month		For Maine, Nova Scotia, No. New York, No. Michigan, No. Wisconsin, Minnesota, N. Dakota, S. Dakota, Montana, Washington, No. Oregon, No. Idaho.	For Massachusetts, New Hampshire, Vermont, Central N. Y., So. Michigan, So. Wisconsin, No. Iowa, Wyoming, So. Idaho, So. Oregon.	For So. New York, Connecticut, Rhode Island, Pennsylvania, New Jersey, No. Ohio, No. Indiana, No. Illinois, So. Iowa, No. Nebraska, No. Colorado, No. Utah, Nevada, No. California.	For Dist. of Columbia, Delaware, Maryland, Virginia, West Virginia, So. Ohio, So. Indiana, So. Illinois, No. Missouri, Kansas, Central Colorado, Central Utah, Central Nebraska, Central California	For South Carolina, No. Georgia, No. Alabama, So. Missouri, No. Mississippi, No. Louisiana, No. Texas, So. New Mexico, So. Arizona, So. California.	For Florida, So. Georgia, So. Alabama, So. Mississippi So. Louisiana, So. Texas.
Jan.	1	4.21	4.28	4.33	4.39	4.55	5.01
	10	4.30	4.36	4.41	4.47	5.03	5.08
	20	4.43	4.48	4.53	4.58	5.10	5.15
Feb.	1	4.59	5.04	5.08	5.12	5.22	5.27
	10	5.12	5.16	5.19	5.21	5.31	5.35
	20	5.26	5.28	5.30	5.32	5.40	5.42
Mar.	1	5.38	5.40	5.41	5.42	5.47	5.49
	10	5.50	5.51	5.51	5.51	5.54	5.55
	20	6.02	6.02	6.01	6.01	6.01	6.02
Apr.	1	6.17	6.16	6.14	6.12	6.10	6.09
	10	6.29	6.25	6.23	6.20	6.16	6.14
	20	6.41	6.35	6.33	6.30	6.23	6.20
May	1	6.55	6.49	6.45	6.42	6.31	6.27
	10	7.05	6.58	6.54	6.50	6.38	6.34
	20	7.16	7.08	7.04	6.59	6.44	6.40
June	1	7.28	7.19	7.14	7.08	6.51	6.45
	10	7.34	7.25	7.19	7.13	6.55	6.49
	20	7.39	7.29	7.24	7.18	7.00	6.54
July	1	7.39	7.30	7.25	7.09	7.01	6.55
	10	7.36	7.28	7.23	7.17	7.00	6.53
	20	7.29	7.22	7.17	7.11	6.57	6.50
Aug.	1	7.16	7.10	7.06	7.02	6.48	6.43
	10	7.04	6.59	6.56	6.52	6.39	6.35
	20	6.48	6.45	6.43	6.39	6.29	6.26
Sep.	1	6.27	6.26	6.23	6.21	6.15	6.13
	10	6.10	6.11	6.09	6.08	6.04	6.02
	20	5.51	5.54	5.52	5.52	5.51	5.51
Oct.	1	5.31	5.33	5.33	5.33	5.35	5.36
	10	5.15	5.19	5.21	5.21	5.25	5.26
	20	4.57	5.03	5.06	5.06	5.13	5.15
Nov.	1	4.39	4.45	4.49	4.51	5.01	5.04
	10	4.28	4.34	4.39	4.42	4.53	4.58
	20	4.18	4.25	4.29	4.34	4.47	4.51
Dec.	1	4.11	4.19	4.24	4.30	4.45	4.50
	10	4.10	4.18	4.23	4.28	4.45	4.51
	20	4.13	4.20	4.26	4.30	4.48	4.54

[1] Adapted from "Table I" in *The Jewish Encyclopedia*, Vol. XI, pp. 593–4, Funk and Wagnalls Company, New York, 1905.

MUSIC SUPPLEMENT

I. THE SABBATH SERVICES

1. KINDLING THE SABBATH LIGHTS

בָּרוּךְ אַתָּה יְיָ אֱלֹהֵינוּ מֶלֶךְ הָעוֹלָם. אֲשֶׁר קִדְּשָׁנוּ
בְּמִצְוֹתָיו וְצִוָּנוּ לְהַדְלִיק נֵר שֶׁל־שַׁבָּת:

Bo-ruch a-toh a-dō-noy e-lō-hē-nu me-lech ho-ō - - lom a-sher ki-'d'-sho-nu b'-mitz-vō-sov v'-tsi-vo-nu l'-had-līk nēr l'-had-līk nēr shel shab-bos.

2. HYMN OF WELCOME TO THE SABBATH
ANGELS OF PEACE

SHALOM ALEKEM — שָׁלוֹם עֲלֵיכֶם

שָׁלוֹם עֲלֵיכֶם מַלְאֲכֵי הַשָּׁרֵת מַלְאֲכֵי עֶלְיוֹן
מִמֶּלֶךְ מַלְכֵי הַמְּלָכִים הַקָּדוֹשׁ בָּרוּךְ הוּא.

בּוֹאֲכֶם לְשָׁלוֹם מַלְאֲכֵי הַשָּׁלוֹם מַלְאֲכֵי עֶלְיוֹן
מִמֶּלֶךְ מַלְכֵי הַמְּלָכִים הַקָּדוֹשׁ בָּרוּךְ הוּא.

בָּרְכוּנִי לְשָׁלוֹם מַלְאֲכֵי הַשָּׁלוֹם מַלְאֲכֵי עֶלְיוֹן
מִמֶּלֶךְ מַלְכֵי הַמְּלָכִים הַקָּדוֹשׁ בָּרוּךְ הוּא:

צֵאתְכֶם לְשָׁלוֹם מַלְאֲכֵי הַשָּׁלוֹם מַלְאֲכֵי עֶלְיוֹן
מִמֶּלֶךְ מַלְכֵי הַמְּלָכִים הַקָּדוֹשׁ בָּרוּךְ הוּא.

I. GOLDFARB, arr. by A. W. B.

mf Andantino

1. Sho - lōm a - lĕ - chem mal a - chĕ ha - sho - rēs mal -
4. Tsĕs - chem l' - sho - lōm mal a - chĕ ha - sho - lōm, mal -

a - chĕ el - yōn;   mi - me - lech
a - chĕ el - yōn;   mi - me - lech

FINE

mal - chĕ ham - lo - chim, ha - ko-dōsh bo - ruch hu.
mal - chĕ ham - lo - chim, ha - ko-dōsh bo - ruch hu.

FINE

2. Bŏ - a - chem l' - sho - lŏm mal - a - chĕ ha - sho - lŏm,
3. Bor chu - nĭ l' - sho - lŏm mal - a - chĕ ha - sho - lŏm,

mal - a - chĕ el - yŏn, mi - me - lech
mal - a - chĕ el - yŏn,

D. C. al Fine

mal - chĕ ham - lo - chĭm ha - ko - dŏsh bo - ruch hu. Bor' hu.

3. A TRIBUTE TO THE MISTRESS OF THE HOUSE

A WOMAN OF VALOR — אֵשֶׁת חַיִל

(Recited by the Husband before the *Kiddush*.)

וְרָחֹק מִפְּנִינִים מִכְרָהּ:	אֵשֶׁת חַיִל מִי יִמְצָא.
וְשָׁלָל לֹא יֶחְסָר:	בָּטַח בָּהּ לֵב בַּעְלָהּ.
כֹּל יְמֵי חַיֶּיהָ:	גְּמָלַתְהוּ טוֹב וְלֹא רָע.
וַתַּעַשׂ בְּחֵפֶץ כַּפֶּיהָ:	דָּרְשָׁה צֶמֶר וּפִשְׁתִּים.
מִמֶּרְחָק תָּבִיא לַחְמָהּ:	הָיְתָה כָּאֳנִיּוֹת סוֹחֵר.
וַתִּתֵּן טֶרֶף לְבֵיתָהּ וְחֹק לְנַעֲרֹתֶיהָ:	וַתָּקָם בְּעוֹד לַיְלָה.
מִפְּרִי כַפֶּיהָ נָטְעָה כָּרֶם:	זָמְמָה שָׂדֶה וַתִּקָּחֵהוּ.
וַתְּאַמֵּץ זְרוֹעֹתֶיהָ:	חָגְרָה בְעוֹז מָתְנֶיהָ.
לֹא יִכְבֶּה בַלַּיְלָה נֵרָהּ:	טָעֲמָה כִּי טוֹב סַחְרָהּ.
וְכַפֶּיהָ תָּמְכוּ פָלֶךְ:	יָדֶיהָ שִׁלְּחָה בַכִּישׁוֹר.
וְיָדֶיהָ שִׁלְּחָה לָאֶבְיוֹן:	כַּפָּהּ פָּרְשָׂה לֶעָנִי.
כִּי כָל בֵּיתָהּ לָבֻשׁ שָׁנִים:	לֹא תִירָא לְבֵיתָהּ מִשָּׁלֶג.
שֵׁשׁ וְאַרְגָּמָן לְבוּשָׁהּ:	מַרְבַדִּים עָשְׂתָה לָּהּ.
בְּשִׁבְתּוֹ עִם זִקְנֵי אָרֶץ:	נוֹדָע בַּשְּׁעָרִים בַּעְלָהּ.
וַחֲגוֹר נָתְנָה לַכְּנַעֲנִי:	סָדִין עָשְׂתָה וַתִּמְכֹּר.
וַתִּשְׂחַק לְיוֹם אַחֲרוֹן:	עוֹז וְהָדָר לְבוּשָׁהּ.
וְתוֹרַת חֶסֶד עַל לְשׁוֹנָהּ:	פִּיהָ פָּתְחָה בְחָכְמָה.
וְלֶחֶם עַצְלוּת לֹא תֹאכֵל:	צוֹפִיָּה הֲלִיכוֹת בֵּיתָהּ.

קָמוּ בָנֶיהָ וַיְאַשְּׁרוּהָ.   בַּעֲלָהּ וַיְהַלְלָהּ:

רַבּוֹת בָּנוֹת עָשׂוּ חָיִל.   וְאַתְּ עָלִית עַל כֻּלָּנָה:

שֶׁקֶר הַחֵן וְהֶבֶל הַיֹּפִי.   אִשָּׁה יִרְאַת יְיָ הִיא תִתְהַלָּל:

תְּנוּ לָהּ מִפְּרִי יָדֶיהָ.   וִיהַלְלוּהָ בַשְּׁעָרִים מַעֲשֶׂיהָ:

(משלי ל"א י'–ל"א)

4. KIDDUSH FOR FRIDAY EVENING*

וַיְהִי עֶרֶב וַיְהִי בֹקֶר:

יוֹם הַשִּׁשִּׁי: וַיְכֻלּוּ הַשָּׁמַיִם וְהָאָרֶץ וְכָל צְבָאָם: וַיְכַל אֱלֹהִים
בַּיּוֹם הַשְּׁבִיעִי מְלַאכְתּוֹ אֲשֶׁר עָשָׂה וַיִּשְׁבֹּת בַּיּוֹם הַשְּׁבִיעִי מִכָּל־
מְלַאכְתּוֹ אֲשֶׁר עָשָׂה: וַיְבָרֶךְ אֱלֹהִים אֶת־יוֹם הַשְּׁבִיעִי וַיְקַדֵּשׁ
אֹתוֹ. כִּי בוֹ שָׁבַת מִכָּל־מְלַאכְתּוֹ אֲשֶׁר־בָּרָא אֱלֹהִים לַעֲשׂוֹת:

בָּרוּךְ אַתָּה יְיָ אֱלֹהֵינוּ מֶלֶךְ הָעוֹלָם בּוֹרֵא פְּרִי הַגָּפֶן:

בָּרוּךְ אַתָּה יְיָ אֱלֹהֵינוּ מֶלֶךְ הָעוֹלָם אֲשֶׁר קִדְּשָׁנוּ בְּמִצְוֹתָיו
וְרָצָה בָנוּ וְשַׁבַּת קָדְשׁוֹ בְּאַהֲבָה וּבְרָצוֹן הִנְחִילָנוּ זִכָּרוֹן לְמַעֲשֵׂה
בְרֵאשִׁית. כִּי הוּא יוֹם תְּחִלָּה לְמִקְרָאֵי קֹדֶשׁ זֵכֶר לִיצִיאַת
מִצְרָיִם. כִּי־בָנוּ בָחַרְתָּ וְאוֹתָנוּ קִדַּשְׁתָּ מִכָּל־הָעַמִּים וְשַׁבַּת קָדְשֶׁךָ
בְּאַהֲבָה וּבְרָצוֹן הִנְחַלְתָּנוּ. בָּרוּךְ אַתָּה יְיָ מְקַדֵּשׁ הַשַּׁבָּת:

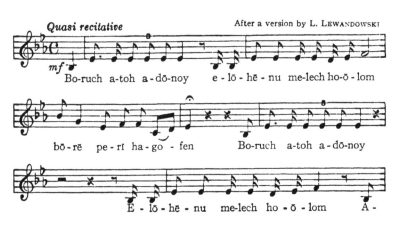

*Complete with piano acc., in A. W. B., *Kabbalath Shabbath*, Bloch Pub. Co., N.Y.

sher ki-d'-sho-nu b'-mitz-vō-sov v'-ro-tsoh vo-nu v'-sha-

bas ko-d'-shō b'-a-ha-voh ur-ro-tsōn hin-chī

lo-nu zi-ko-rōn— l'-ma-a-sēh v'-rē-

_shīs. Kī hu yōm t'-chi-loh l'-mik-ro-ē kō-desh, zē-cher

lī-tsī-as mitz-rŏ-yīm. Kī vo-no vo-char-to v'ō-

so-nu kī-dash-to mi-kol ho-a-mim v'-

sha-bas kod-sh' cho b'-a-ha-voh uv-ro-tsōn

hin-chal-to-nu. Bo-ruch a-toh a-dō-noy

allarg.

m-ka-dēsh ha-sha-bos.

5. LEKAH DODI — לְכָה דוֹדִי

לְכָה דוֹדִי לִקְרַאת כַּלָּה פְּנֵי שַׁבָּת נְקַבְּלָה.

*Complete for cantor, mixed choir and organ, in L. Lewandowski, *Todah v'Zimrah* I, J. Kaufmann, Frankfort.

**Complete for cantor and mixed choir in S. Sulzer, *Schir Zion*, S. W. Kaufmann, Leipzig.

iv

For the Sabbath preceding *Tishe'a be'Ab*

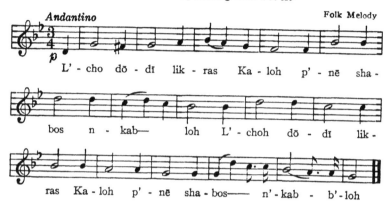

L' - cho dŏ - dĭ lik - ras Ka - loh p' - nē sha -
bos n - kab— loh L' - choh dŏ - dĭ lik -
ras Ka - loh p' - nē sha - bos—— n' - kab - b' - loh

6. YISMECHU — יִשְׂמְחוּ

יִשְׂמְחוּ בְמַלְכוּתְךָ שֹׁמְרֵי שַׁבָּת וְקוֹרְאֵי עֹנֶג. עַם מְקַדְּשֵׁי
שְׁבִיעִי. כֻּלָּם יִשְׂבְּעוּ וְיִתְעַנְּגוּ מִטּוּבֶךָ. וְהַשְּׁבִיעִי רָצִיתָ בּוֹ וְקִדַּשְׁתּוֹ.
חֶמְדַּת יָמִים אוֹתוֹ קָרָאתָ זֵכֶר לְמַעֲשֵׂה בְרֵאשִׁית:

7. V'SHOMRU — וְשָׁמְרוּ

וְשָׁמְרוּ בְנֵי־יִשְׂרָאֵל אֶת־הַשַּׁבָּת. לַעֲשׂוֹת אֶת־הַשַּׁבָּת לְדֹרֹתָם
בְּרִית עוֹלָם: בֵּינִי וּבֵין בְּנֵי יִשְׂרָאֵל אוֹת הִיא לְעֹלָם. כִּי־שֵׁשֶׁת
יָמִים עָשָׂה יְיָ אֶת־הַשָּׁמַיִם וְאֶת־הָאָרֶץ וּבַיּוֹם הַשְּׁבִיעִי שָׁבַת
וַיִּנָּפַשׁ:

Traditional, arr. by A. W. B.

8. KADSHENU – קַדְּשֵׁנוּ

אֱלֹהֵינוּ וֵאלֹהֵי אֲבוֹתֵינוּ רְצֵה בִמְנוּחָתֵנוּ. קַדְּשֵׁנוּ בְּמִצְוֹתֶיךָ
וְתֵן חֶלְקֵנוּ בְּתוֹרָתֶךָ. שַׂבְּעֵנוּ מִטּוּבֶךָ וְשַׂמְּחֵנוּ בִּישׁוּעָתֶךָ. וְטַהֵר
לִבֵּנוּ לְעָבְדְּךָ בֶּאֱמֶת. וְהַנְחִילֵנוּ יְיָ אֱלֹהֵינוּ בְּאַהֲבָה וּבְרָצוֹן שַׁבַּת
קָדְשֶׁךָ. וְיָנוּחוּ בוֹ יִשְׂרָאֵל מְקַדְּשֵׁי שְׁמֶךָ. בָּרוּךְ אַתָּה יְיָ מְקַדֵּשׁ
הַשַּׁבָּת.

ta - her li - be - nu l' - ov - de - cho b' -

e - - mes. V' - han - chi - - le - nu a - do -

noy e - lo - he - nu b' - a - ha - voh uv -

ro - tson shab - bos kod - she - cho v' - yo -

nu - chu vo yis - ro - el m' - kad - she sh-

(CANTOR)

me - cho. Bo - ruch a - toh a - do -

(CONGR.)

noy——— M' - ka - - desh ha - shab - bos.

9. ATTOH ECHOD – אַתָּה אֶחָד

אַתָּה אֶחָד וְשִׁמְךָ אֶחָד. וּמִי כְּעַמְּךָ יִשְׂרָאֵל גּוֹי אֶחָד בָּאָרֶץ.
תִּפְאֶרֶת גְּדֻלָּה וַעֲטֶרֶת יְשׁוּעָה. יוֹם מְנוּחָה וּקְדֻשָּׁה לְעַמְּךָ נָתַתָּ.
אַבְרָהָם יָגֵל. יִצְחָק יְרַנֵּן. יַעֲקֹב וּבָנָיו יָנוּחוּ בוֹ.

*Complete with piano acc., in A. W. B., *Shabbos beim Shalosh S'udos*, Metro Music Co., N. Y.

10. AN'IM Z'MĪRŌS – אַנְעִים זְמִירוֹת

אַנְעִים זְמִירוֹת וְשִׁירִים אֶאֱרוֹג
כִּי אֵלֶיךָ נַפְשִׁי תַעֲרוֹג.

נַפְשִׁי חָמְדָה בְּצֵל יָדֶיךָ
לָדַעַת כָּל רָז סוֹדֶךָ.

מִדֵּי דַבְּרִי בִּכְבוֹדֶךָ
הוֹמֶה לִבִּי אֶל דּוֹדֶיךָ.

עַל כֵּן אֲדַבֵּר בְּךָ נִכְבָּדוֹת
וְשִׁמְךָ אֲכַבֵּד בְּשִׁירֵי יְדִידוֹת.

11. L'DOVID BORUCH – לְדָוִד בָּרוּךְ

Introductory Prayer to the Saturday Evening Service

לְדָוִד בָּרוּךְ יְיָ צוּרִי. הַמְלַמֵּד יָדַי לַקְרָב אֶצְבְּעוֹתַי
לַמִּלְחָמָה: חַסְדִּי וּמְצוּדָתִי מִשְׂגַּבִּי וּמְפַלְטִי־לִי, מָגִנִּי וּבוֹ חָסִיתִי,
הָרוֹדֵד עַמִּי תַחְתָּי: יְיָ, מָה־אָדָם וַתֵּדָעֵהוּ, בֶּן־אֱנוֹשׁ וַתְּחַשְּׁבֵהוּ:
אָדָם לַהֶבֶל דָּמָה, יָמָיו כְּצֵל עוֹבֵר:

12. GOTT FUN AVROHOM – גאָט פון אברהם

(Introductory Prayer to *Habdalah* Service)

Words attributed to RABBI LEVI-ISAAC

Ad libitum　　　　　　　　　　　　　　　　A. W. B.

p Gott fun av - ro - hom fun yitz-chok un fun ya - a - koiv

ba - hit dein hei - lib folk yis - ro - el fun a - lem bei - zen,

az der li - ber hei - li - ger sha-bes koi-desh geht a - vek

und die voch und der choi - desh und dos yohr vos kumt on,

soll zein tsu ma - zel und tsu bro - cho tsu oy-sher undt tsu

ko - vod, tsu par - no - so toi - vo, tsu

ma - sim toi - vim un tsu b' - su - ros

toi - vois und tsu a - lem gu - ten A - - men.

13. THE HABDALAH SERVICE

shĕm a-dō-noy ek - ro. Bo - ruch a-toh a-dŏ-noy e - lŏ-

hĕ - nu me-lech ho - ŏ-lom bō - rĕ p' - rĭ ha - go— fen. Bo -
bō - rĕ me - o - rĕ, no— ĕsh
bō - rĕ mĭ - nĕ b' - so—, mĭm

ruch a-toh a-dō-noy e - lŏ - hĕ - nu me-lech ho-ŏ - lam hă-

mav-dĭl bĕn kō-desh l'-chōl bĕn ōr l'-chō-shech bĕn yis-ro-

ĕl lo - a-mĭm bĕn yōm hash-vĭ - ĭ l'-shĕ-shes ye-mĕ ha - ma-seh.

Bo - ruch a-toh a - dō-noy ha-mav-dĭl bĕn kō-desh l' - chōl.

הַמַּבְדִּיל

הַמַּבְדִּיל בֵּין קֹדֶשׁ לְחוֹל. חַטֹּאתֵינוּ יִמְחֹל. זַרְעֵנוּ וְכַסְפֵּנוּ
יַרְבֶּה כַחוֹל. וְכַכּוֹכָבִים בַּלָּיְלָה:

יוֹם פָּנָה כְּצֵל תֹּמֶר. אֶקְרָא לָאֵל עָלַי גֹּמֵר. אָמַר שׁוֹמֵר.
אָתָא בֹקֶר וְגַם־לָיְלָה:

נַחְנוּ בְיָדְךָ כַּחֹמֶר. סְלַח נָא עַל קַל וָחֹמֶר. יוֹם לְיוֹם יַבִּיעַ
אֹמֶר. וְלַיְלָה לְלָיְלָה: נהמבדיל

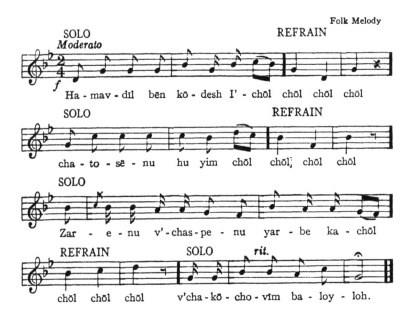

Folk Melody

ELIYOHU HA-NAVI – אֵלִיָּהוּ הַנָּבִיא

אֵלִיָּהוּ הַנָּבִיא, אֵלִיָּהוּ הַתִּשְׁבִּי,
אֵלִיָּהוּ, אֵלִיָּהוּ, אֵלִיָּהוּ הַגִּלְעָדִי.
בִּמְהֵרָה בְיָמֵינוּ, יָבוֹא אֵלֵינוּ,
יָבֹא אֵלֵינוּ עִם מָשִׁיחַ בֶּן דָּוִד.

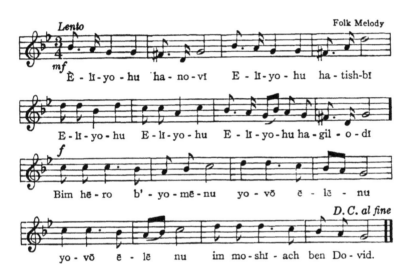

II. ZEMIROT

1. YOH RIBBON*—יָהּ רְבּוֹן

יָהּ רְבּוֹן עָלַם וְעָלְמַיָּא, אַנְתְּ הוּא מַלְכָּא מֶלֶךְ מַלְכַיָּא.

עוֹבַד גְּבוּרְתֵּךְ וְתִמְהַיָּא, שַׁפִּיר קֳדָמָךְ לְהַחֲוָיָה: ניה רבון

לְמִקְדָּשָׁךְ תּוּב וּלְקֹדֶשׁ קֻדְשִׁין, אֲתַר דִּי בֵהּ יֶחֱדוּן רוּחִין וְנַפְשִׁין.

וִיזַמְּרוּן שִׁירִין וְרַחֲשִׁין, בִּירוּשְׁלֵם קַרְתָּא דִי־שֻׁפְרַיָּא: ניה רבון

1

Yoh ri-bōn o - lam ve - ol - ma - yo ve - ol - ma - yo——

ant hu mal- ko me-lech mal-cha - yo me - lech mal-cha - yo.

ō - vad ge - vur - tĕch v' - sim - ha - yo——

sh'far—— ko - do - moch le - hach - va - yoh.

*Complete with piano acc., in S. and I. Goldfarb, *Jewish Songster*, I, N. Y·

2

Moderato   I. GOLDFARB

Yoh ri - bōn o - lam v' - ol - ma - yo

ant hu mal - ko—— me-lech mal' - cha - yoh,—— ō -

vad g' - vur - tĕch v' - sim - ha - yo.... shap -

pir — ko - do - moch l' - hach' - va - yoh————

REFRAIN

Yoh ri - bōn o - lam v' - ol - ma - yo.........

ant.... hu.... mal - ko.... me-lech mal - cha.... yo.——

2. M'NUCHOH V'SIMCHOH — מְנוּחָה וְשִׂמְחָה

מְנוּחָה וְשִׂמְחָה, אוֹר לַיְהוּדִים.
יוֹם שַׁבָּתוֹן יוֹם מַחֲמַדִּים.
שׁוֹמְרָיו וְזוֹכְרָיו הֵמָּה מְעִידִים.
כִּי לְשִׁשָּׁה כֹּל בְּרוּאִים וְעוֹמְדִים:

שְׁמֵי שָׁמַיִם אֶרֶץ וְיַמִּים.
כָּל צְבָא מָרוֹם גְּבוֹהִים וְרָמִים.
תַּנִּין וְאָדָם וְחַיַּת רְאֵמִים.
כִּי בְּיָהּ יְיָ צוּר עוֹלָמִים:

3. TSUR MISHELO — צוּר מִשֶּׁלּוֹ

צוּר מִשֶּׁלּוֹ אָכַלְנוּ, בָּרְכוּ אֱמוּנַי.
שָׂבַעְנוּ וְהוֹתַרְנוּ כִּדְבַר יְיָ: נצור]

הַזָּן אֶת עוֹלָמוֹ, רוֹעֵנוּ, אָבִינוּ.
אָכַלְנוּ אֶת לַחְמוֹ וְיֵינוֹ שָׁתִינוּ.
עַל כֵּן נוֹדֶה לִשְׁמוֹ וּנְהַלְלוֹ בְּפִינוּ.
אָמַרְנוּ וְעָנִינוּ, אֵין קָדוֹשׁ כַּיְיָ: נצור]

4. SHOLOM LOCH YOM HA-SHEVI-I — שָׁלוֹם לָךְ יוֹם הַשְּׁבִיעִי

עַל־אַהֲבָתֶךְ אֶשְׁתֶּה גְבִיעִי,
שָׁלוֹם לָךְ שָׁלוֹם, יוֹם הַשְּׁבִיעִי!

שֵׁשֶׁת יְמֵי מַעֲשֶׂה לָךְ כַּעֲבָדִים,
אִם אֶעֱבֹד בָּהֶם, אֶשְׁבַּע נְדוּדִים.
כֻּלָּם בְּעֵינַי הֵם יָמִים אֲחָדִים.
מֵאַהֲבָתִי בָךְ, יוֹם שַׁעֲשׁוּעָי. [שלום]

אֵצֵא בְּיוֹם רִאשׁוֹן לַעֲשׂוֹת מְלָאכָה,
לַעֲרֹךְ לְיוֹם שַׁבָּת הַמַּעֲרָכָה,
כִּי הָאֱלֹהִים שָׁם שָׂם הַבְּרָכָה,
אַתָּה לְבַד חֶלְקִי מִכָּל יְגִיעִי. [שלום]

Solomon Lampart, arr. by A. W. B.

lom b'-e - nay hem yo - mim a - cho - dim, Me-
hu - e - lo - him shom—— som ha - b'ro—choh,' A -

a - ha - vo - si b' - cho— yom ma - r'go - i.
toh l' - vad chel - ki mi - kol y' - gi - i.

Sho - lom l' - cho   Sho - lom l' - cho,

Sho - lom l' - cho—— yom ha - sh'vi - i.

5. SHABBOS HA-MALKOH* — שַׁבָּת הַמַּלְכָּה

הַחַמָּה מֵרֹאשׁ הָאִילָנוֹת נִסְתַּלְקָה —

בֹּאוּ וְנֵצֵא לִקְרַאת שַׁבָּת הַמַּלְכָּה,

הִנֵּה הִיא יוֹרֶדֶת, הַקְּדוֹשָׁה, הַבְּרוּכָה,

וְעִמָּהּ מַלְאָכִים צְבָא שָׁלוֹם וּמְנוּחָה,

בֹּאִי בֹאִי, הַמַּלְכָּה!

בֹּאִי בֹאִי, הַמַּלְכָּה! —

שָׁלוֹם עֲלֵיכֶם, מַלְאֲכֵי הַשָּׁלוֹם!

———————

קִבַּלְנוּ פְּנֵי שַׁבָּת בִּרְנָנָה וּתְפִלָּה,

הַבַּיְתָה נָשׁוּבָה בְּלֵב מָלֵא גִילָה;

שָׁם עָרוּךְ הַשֻּׁלְחָן, הַגֵּרוֹת יָאִירוּ,

כָּל־פִּנּוֹת הַבַּיִת יִזְרָחוּ, יַזְהִירוּ.

שַׁבָּת שָׁלוֹם וּבְרָכָה,

שַׁבָּת שָׁלוֹם וּמְנוּחָה —

בּוֹאֲכֶם לְשָׁלוֹם, מַלְאֲכֵי הַשָּׁלוֹם!

———————

*Complete with piano acc., in A. W. B.; *Jewish Year in Song*; G. Schrimer, N. Y.

Andantino — P. Minkowsky

Ha-cham-moh mĕ - rōsh ho - i - lo - nōs nis - tal-koh Bō-
Ki - bal - nu p'nĕ shab-bos bir - no-noh u - s' fi-loh, Ha -

uh - v' - nĕ - tse lik - ras sha-bos ha - mal - koh. Hi - neh
bay-so no - shu - vo b'- lĕv mo - lēh v' - gil loh. Shom

hi— yō - re - des hak - dō - shoh ha - b'ru - cho v' -
o - ruch ha - shul-chon ha - nĕ - rōs yo - i - ru. Kol

im - moh mal - o - chim ts'vo sho - lōm um - nu - choh.
pi - nōs ha - ba - yis yiz - ro - chu yaz - hi - ru.

Bō - i, bō - i, ha - mal - - koh, bō - i, bō - i ha -
Sha - bos sho - lōm u - m'vō - - roch, Sha - bas Sho-lōm u -

kal - - loh, Sho - lōm a - lĕ-chem mal - a-chĕ ha - sho-lōm.
m'vo - - roch, Bō - a-chem l' - sho-lōm mal - a-chĕ ha - sho-lōm.

6. SABBATH BLESSING

JESSIE E. SAMPTER

The Sabbath light is burning bright;
Our prettiest cloth is clean and white,
   With wine and bread for Friday night.

At set of sun our work is done;
The happy Sabbath has begun;
   Now bless us, Father, ev'ry one.

O Sabbath guest, dear Sabbath guest,
Come, share the blessing with the rest,
   For all our house tonight is blest.

A. W. B.

mf Andante

1. The   Sab-bath light is   burn-ing bright; Our   pret-tiest cloth is
2. At   set of   sun our   work is   done; The   hap-py   Sab-bath
3. O   Sab-bath guest, dear Sab-bath guest, Come, share the bless-ing

clean and white, With wine   and   bread   for   Fri - day   night.
has   be - gun;   Now bless   us,   Fa - ther,   ev - 'ry   one.
with   the   rest,   For   all   our 'house   to - night   is   blest.

7. YOM ZEH L'YISROEL — יוֹם זֶה לְיִשְׂרָאֵל

יוֹם זֶה לְיִשְׂרָאֵל, אוֹרָה וְשִׂמְחָה, שַׁבַּת מְנוּחָה.

צִוִּיתָ פִּקּוּדִים, בְּמַעֲמַד סִינַי,
שַׁבָּת וּמוֹעֲדִים, לִשְׁמוֹר בְּכָל־שָׁנַי,
לַעֲרוֹךְ לְפָנַי,
מַשְׂאֵת וַאֲרֻחָה, שַׁבַּת מְנוּחָה.

(יוֹם זֶה)

8. SHABBOS HAYYOM L'ADONOI — שַׁבָּת הַיּוֹם לַיְיָ

שַׁבָּת הַיּוֹם לַיְיָ,
מְאֹד צַהֲלוּ בְרִנּוּנִי,
וְגַם הַרְבּוּ מַעֲדָנִי
אוֹתוֹ לִשְׁמוֹר כְּמִצְוַת יְיָ —
שַׁבָּת הַיּוֹם לַיְיָ.

9. COME, O SABBATH DAY

A. W. B.

1. Come, O Sab-bath day, and bring Peace and heal-ing
2. Earth-ly long-ings bid re - tire, Quench the pas-sions'
3. Wipe from ev - 'ry cheek the tear, Ban - ish care and

on thy wing; And to ev - 'ry troub-led breast Speak of the di -
hurt - ful fire; To the way-ward, sin oppressed, Bring Thou Thy di -
si - lence fear; All things working for the best, Teach us the di -

vine be - hest: Thou shalt rest, Thou shalt rest!
vine be - hest: Thou shalt rest, Thou shalt rest!
vine be - hest: Thou shalt rest, Thou shalt rest!

10. SHIMRU SHABSOSAI — שִׁמְרוּ שַׁבְּתוֹתַי

שִׁמְרוּ שַׁבְּתוֹתַי לְמַעַן תִּינָקוּ וּשְׂבַעְתֶּם מִזִּיו בִּרְכֹותִי.

אֵל הַמְּנוּחָה כִּי בָאתֶם וּלְווּ עָלַי בָּנַי וְעֶדְנוּ מַעֲדָנִי.

שַׁבָּת הַיֹּום לַיְיָ.

חֲזַק קְרִיָּתִי אֵל אֱלֹהִים עֶלְיֹון וְהָשֵׁב אֶת נְוָתִי בְּשִׂמְחָה וּבְהִגָּיֹון.

יְשׁוֹרְרוּ שָׁם רְנָנַי לְוִיַּי וְכֹהֲנַי. אָז תִּתְעַנַּג עַל יְיָ.

שַׁבָּת הַיֹּום לַיְיָ.

11. YOM ZEH M'CHUBOD — יוֹם זֶה מְכֻבָּד

יוֹם זֶה מְכֻבָּד מִכָּל יָמִים,
כִּי בוֹ שָׁבַת צוּר עוֹלָמִים.

שֵׁשֶׁת יָמִים תַּעֲשֶׂה מְלַאכְתֶּךָ
וְיוֹם הַשְּׁבִיעִי לֵאלֹהֶיךָ,
שַׁבָּת לֹא תַעֲשֶׂה בוֹ מְלָאכָה,
כִּי כֹל עָשָׂה שֵׁשֶׁת יָמִים

יום זה . . .

12. MAH YOFIS — מַה יָּפִית

מַה יָּפִית וּמַה נָּעַמְתְּ אַהֲבָה בְּתַעֲנוּגִים
אַתְּ שַׁבָּת מְשׂוֹשׂ נוּגִים
לְךָ בָּשָׂר וְגַם דָּגִים
נְכוֹנִים מִבְּעוֹד יוֹם.

מֵעֶרֶב עַד עֶרֶב לֵב חָדִים
בְּבֹא עִתֵּךְ, עֵת דּוֹדִים
גִּיל וְשָׂשׂוֹן לַיְּהוּדִים
לִמְצֹא פִדְיוֹם.

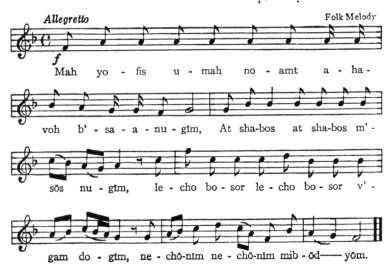

13. BORUCH ADONOY YOM YOM — בָּרוּךְ יְיָ יוֹם יוֹם

בָּרוּךְ יְיָ יוֹם יוֹם. יַעֲמָס לָנוּ יֶשַׁע וּפִדְיוֹם.

וּבִשְׁמוֹ נָגִיל כָּל הַיּוֹם.

וּבִישׁוּעָתוֹ נָרִים רֹאשׁ עֶלְיוֹן.

כִּי הוּא מָעוֹז לַדָּל וּמַחֲסֶה לְאֶבְיוֹן.

שֶׁהַשָּׁלוֹם שֶׁלּוֹ יָשִׂים עָלֵינוּ בְּרָכָה וְשָׁלוֹם.

מִשְּׂמֹאל וּמִיָּמִין עַל יִשְׂרָאֵל שָׁלוֹם.

הָרַחֲמָן הוּא יְבָרֵךְ אֶת עַמּוֹ בַשָּׁלוֹם.

וְיִזְכּוּ לִרְאוֹת בָּנִים [וּבְנֵי בָנִים עוֹסְקִים

בַּתּוֹרָה וּבְמִצְוֹת] עַל יִשְׂרָאֵל שָׁלוֹם.

14. BORUCH EL ELYON — בָּרוּךְ אֵל עֶלְיוֹן

בָּרוּךְ אֵל עֶלְיוֹן אֲשֶׁר נָתַן מְנוּחָה
לְנַפְשֵׁנוּ פִּדְיוֹם מִשֵּׁאת וַאֲנָחָה.
וְהוּא יִדְרוֹשׁ לְצִיּוֹן עִיר הַנִּדָּחָה,
עַד אָנָה תּוּגְיוֹן נֶפֶשׁ נֶאֱנָחָה.
הַשּׁוֹמֵר שַׁבָּת, הַבֵּן עִם הַבַּת,
לָאֵל יֵרָצוּ כְּמִנְחָה עַל מַחֲבַת.

15. KOL M'KADESH SHEVI-I — כָּל מְקַדֵּשׁ שְׁבִיעִי

כָּל מְקַדֵּשׁ שְׁבִיעִי כָּרָאוּי לוֹ,
כָּל שׁוֹמֵר שַׁבָּת כַּדָּת מֵחַלְּלוֹ,
שְׂכָרוֹ הַרְבֵּה מְאֹד עַל פִּי פָעֳלוֹ,
אִישׁ עַל מַחֲנֵהוּ וְאִישׁ עַל דִּגְלוֹ.

אוֹהֲבֵי יְיָ הַמְחַכִּים בְּבִנְיַן אֲרִיאֵל,
בְּיוֹם הַשַּׁבָּת שִׂישׂוּ וְשִׂמְחוּ כִּמְקַבְּלֵי מַתַּן נַחֲלִיאֵל.
גַּם שְׂאוּ יְדֵיכֶם קֹדֶשׁ וְאִמְרוּ לָאֵל,
בָּרוּךְ אֲשֶׁר נָתַן מְנוּחָה לְעַמּוֹ יִשְׂרָאֵל.

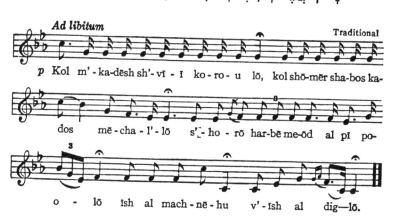

III.　GRACE AFTER MEALS

INTRODUCTORY PSALM

Psalm 126

שִׁיר הַמַּעֲלוֹת.

בְּשׁוּב יְיָ אֶת־שִׁיבַת צִיוֹן הָיִינוּ כְּחֹלְמִים:

אָז יִמָּלֵא שְׂחֹק פִּינוּ וּלְשׁוֹנֵנוּ רִנָּה

אָז יֹאמְרוּ בַגּוֹיִם הִגְדִּיל יְיָ לַעֲשׂוֹת עִם־אֵלֶּה:

הִגְדִּיל יְיָ לַעֲשׂוֹת עִמָּנוּ הָיִינוּ שְׂמֵחִים:

שׁוּבָה יְיָ אֶת־שְׁבִיתֵנוּ כַּאֲפִיקִים בַּנֶּגֶב:

הַזֹּרְעִים בְּדִמְעָה בְּרִנָּה יִקְצֹרוּ:

הָלוֹךְ יֵלֵךְ וּבָכֹה נֹשֵׂא מֶשֶׁךְ־הַזָּרַע

בֹּא־יָבֹא בְרִנָּה נֹשֵׂא אֲלֻמֹּתָיו:

GRACE AFTER MEALS

INTRODUCTORY PSALM

SHIR HAMA‘ALOS — שִׁיר הַמַּעֲלוֹת

1 Shir—— ha-ma - lŏs b' - shuv a - dŏ-noy es
2 Shu - vo a - dŏ - noy es sh - vi - sē - nu

shi - vas tsi - yŏn ho - yi - nu k'-chŏl - mim. Oz— yi-mo - lĕ
ka - a - fi - kim ba - - ne - gev. Hazŏr - im

s'chŏk pi - nu ul - shŏ - nē - nu ri - - noh.
b'dim - - oh b'ri - - noh—— yik - tsŏ - ru.

A SONG OF ASCENTS

When the Lord brought back those that returned to Zion,
We were like unto them that dream.
Then was our mouth filled with laughter,
And our tongue with singing;
Then said they among the nations:
'The Lord hath done great things with these.'
The Lord hath done great things with us;
We are rejoiced.

Turn our captivity, O Lord,
As the streams in the dry land.
They that sow in tears
Shall reap in joy.
Though he goeth on his way weeping that beareth the measure
    of seed,
He shall come home with joy, bearing his sheaves.

CALL TO GRACE AFTER MEALS

This is recited only if there are at least three men over
the age of thirteen. If ten are present, include the words
in the parentheses.

Reader

רַבּוֹתַי נְבָרֵךְ:

Assembly

יְהִי שֵׁם יְיָ מְבֹרָךְ מֵעַתָּה וְעַד עוֹלָם:

Reader

יְהִי שֵׁם יְיָ מְבֹרָךְ מֵעַתָּה וְעַד עוֹלָם:
בִּרְשׁוּת רַבּוֹתַי נְבָרֵךְ (אֱלֹהֵינוּ) שֶׁאָכַלְנוּ מִשֶּׁלּוֹ:

Assembly

בָּרוּךְ (אֱלֹהֵינוּ) שֶׁאָכַלְנוּ מִשֶּׁלּוֹ וּבְטוּבוֹ חָיִינוּ:

GRACE AFTER MEALS

If fewer than three men over the age of thirteen are present, begin here:—

בָּרוּךְ אַתָּה יְיָ אֱלֹהֵינוּ מֶלֶךְ הָעוֹלָם הַזָּן אֶת הָעוֹלָם כֻּלּוֹ
בְּטוּבוֹ בְּחֵן בְּחֶסֶד וּבְרַחֲמִים הוּא נוֹתֵן לֶחֶם לְכָל בָּשָׂר כִּי
לְעוֹלָם חַסְדּוֹ. וּבְטוּבוֹ הַגָּדוֹל תָּמִיד לֹא חָסַר לָנוּ וְאַל יֶחְסַר לָנוּ
מָזוֹן לְעוֹלָם וָעֶד: בַּעֲבוּר שְׁמוֹ הַגָּדוֹל כִּי הוּא אֵל זָן וּמְפַרְנֵס
לַכֹּל וּמֵטִיב לַכֹּל וּמֵכִין מָזוֹן לְכָל בְּרִיּוֹתָיו אֲשֶׁר בָּרָא: בָּרוּךְ
אַתָּה יְיָ הַזָּן אֶת הַכֹּל:

Bo - ruch   a - toh a - dō - noy   ha - zon— es ha - kōl.

CALL TO GRACE AFTER MEALS

This is recited only if there are at least three men over the age of thirteen. If ten are present, include the words in the parentheses.

Reader

Friends, let us say grace.

Assembly

Blessed be the name of the Lord from this time forth and for ever.

Reader

Blessed be the name of the Lord from this time forth and for ever. With the sanction of those present, we will bless Him (our God) of whose bounty we have partaken.

Assembly

Blessed be He (our God) of whose bounty we have partaken, and through whose goodness we live.

GRACE AFTER MEALS

If fewer than three men over the age of thirteen are present, begin here:—

Blessed art Thou, O Lord our God, King of the universe, who feedest the whole world with Thy goodness, with grace, with loving kindness and tender mercy; Thou givest food to all flesh, for Thy loving kindness endureth for ever. Through Thy great goodness food hath never failed us: O may it not fail us for ever and ever for Thy great name's sake, since Thou nourishest and sustainest all beings, and doest good unto all, and providest food for Thy creatures whom Thou has created. Blessed art Thou, O Lord, who givest food unto all.

נוֹדֶה לְּךָ יְיָ אֱלֹהֵינוּ עַל שֶׁהִנְחַלְתָּ לַאֲבוֹתֵינוּ אֶרֶץ חֶמְדָּה
טוֹבָה וּרְחָבָה. וְעַל שֶׁהוֹצֵאתָנוּ יְיָ אֱלֹהֵינוּ מֵאֶרֶץ מִצְרַיִם וּפְדִיתָנוּ
מִבֵּית עֲבָדִים וְעַל בְּרִיתְךָ שֶׁחָתַמְתָּ בִּבְשָׂרֵנוּ וְעַל תּוֹרָתְךָ
שֶׁלִּמַּדְתָּנוּ וְעַל חֻקֶּיךָ שֶׁהוֹדַעְתָּנוּ וְעַל חַיִּים חֵן וָחֶסֶד שֶׁחוֹנַנְתָּנוּ
וְעַל אֲכִילַת מָזוֹן שָׁאַתָּה זָן וּמְפַרְנֵס אוֹתָנוּ תָּמִיד בְּכָל יוֹם וּבְכָל
עֵת וּבְכָל שָׁעָה:

B' chol   yom,   uv - chol   es   uv'-chol   sho— oh

(On the Sabbath of Ḥanukkah add the following:)

עַל הַנִּסִּים וְעַל הַפֻּרְקָן וְעַל הַגְּבוּרוֹת וְעַל הַתְּשׁוּעוֹת וְעַל הַמִּלְחָמוֹת
שֶׁעָשִׂיתָ לַאֲבוֹתֵינוּ בַּיָּמִים הָהֵם בַּזְּמַן הַזֶּה:

בִּימֵי מַתִּתְיָהוּ בֶּן יוֹחָנָן כֹּהֵן גָּדוֹל חַשְׁמוֹנַאי וּבָנָיו כְּשֶׁעָמְדָה מַלְכוּת יָוָן
הָרְשָׁעָה עַל עַמְּךָ יִשְׂרָאֵל לְהַשְׁכִּיחָם תּוֹרָתֶךָ וּלְהַעֲבִירָם מֵחֻקֵּי רְצוֹנֶךָ.
וְאַתָּה בְּרַחֲמֶיךָ הָרַבִּים עָמַדְתָּ לָהֶם בְּעֵת צָרָתָם רַבְתָּ אֶת רִיבָם דַּנְתָּ אֶת
דִּינָם נָקַמְתָּ אֶת נִקְמָתָם מָסַרְתָּ גִּבּוֹרִים בְּיַד חַלָּשִׁים וְרַבִּים בְּיַד מְעַטִּים
וּטְמֵאִים בְּיַד טְהוֹרִים וּרְשָׁעִים בְּיַד צַדִּיקִים וְזֵדִים בְּיַד עוֹסְקַי תוֹרָתֶךָ וּלְךָ
עָשִׂיתָ שֵׁם גָּדוֹל וְקָדוֹשׁ בְּעוֹלָמֶךָ וּלְעַמְּךָ יִשְׂרָאֵל עָשִׂיתָ תְּשׁוּעָה גְדוֹלָה וּפֻרְקָן
כְּהַיּוֹם הַזֶּה. וְאַחַר כֵּן בָּאוּ בָנֶיךָ לִדְבִיר בֵּיתֶךָ וּפִנּוּ אֶת הֵיכָלֶךָ וְטִהֲרוּ אֶת
מִקְדָּשֶׁךָ וְהִדְלִיקוּ נֵרוֹת בְּחַצְרוֹת קָדְשֶׁךָ וְקָבְעוּ שְׁמוֹנַת יְמֵי חֲנֻכָּה אֵלּוּ
לְהוֹדוֹת וּלְהַלֵּל לְשִׁמְךָ הַגָּדוֹל:

We thank Thee, O Lord our God, because Thou didst give as a heritage unto our fathers a desirable, good and ample land, and because Thou didst bring us forth, O Lord our God, from the land of Egypt, and didst deliver us from the house of bondage; as well as for Thy covenant which Thou hast sealed in our flesh, Thy Law which Thou hast taught us, Thy statutes which Thou hast made known unto us, the life, grace and loving kindness which Thou hast vouchsafed unto us, and for the food wherewith Thou dost constantly feed and sustain us every day, in every season, at every hour.

(On the Sabbath of Hanukkah add the following:)

We thank Thee also for the miracles, for the redemption, for the mighty deeds and saving acts, wrought by Thee, also for the wars which Thou didst wage for our fathers in days of old, at this season.

In the days of the Hasmonean, Mattathias son of Johanan, the High Priest, and his sons, when the iniquitous power of Greece rose up against Thy people Israel to make them forgetful of Thy Law, and to force them to transgress Thy statutes, then didst Thou in Thine abundant mercy rise up for them in the time of their trouble; Thou didst plead their cause, Thou didst judge their suit, Thou didst avenge their wrong; Thou deliveredst the strong into the hands of the weak, the many into the hands of the few, the impure into the hands of the pure, the wicked into the hands of the righteous, and the arrogant into the hands of them that occupied themselves with Thy Law: for Thyself Thou didst make a great and holy name in Thy world, and for Thy people Israel Thou didst work a great deliverance and redemption as at this day. And thereupon Thy children came into the halls of Thy house, cleansed Thy temple, purified Thy sanctuary, kindled lights in Thy holy courts, and appointed these eight days of Hanukkah in order to give thanks and praises unto Thy great name.

וְעַל הַכֹּל יְיָ אֱלֹהֵינוּ אֲנַחְנוּ מוֹדִים לָךְ וּמְבָרְכִים אוֹתָךְ
יִתְבָּרַךְ שִׁמְךָ בְּפִי כָּל חַי תָּמִיד לְעוֹלָם וָעֶד:

כַּכָּתוּב וְאָכַלְתָּ וְשָׂבָעְתָּ וּבֵרַכְתָּ אֶת יְיָ אֱלֹהֶיךָ עַל הָאָרֶץ
הַטּוֹבָה אֲשֶׁר נָתַן לָךְ: בָּרוּךְ אַתָּה יְיָ עַל הָאָרֶץ וְעַל הַמָּזוֹן:

Ka - ko - suv   v'— o - chal - to   v' - so - vo - toh.

Bo - ruch   a - toh   a - do - noy   al ho -

o - retz   v'al ha - mo - - zon.

רַחֵם יְיָ אֱלֹהֵינוּ עַל יִשְׂרָאֵל עַמֶּךָ וְעַל יְרוּשָׁלַיִם עִירֶךָ וְעַל
צִיּוֹן מִשְׁכַּן כְּבוֹדֶךָ וְעַל מַלְכוּת בֵּית דָּוִד מְשִׁיחֶךָ וְעַל הַבַּיִת
הַגָּדוֹל וְהַקָּדוֹשׁ שֶׁנִּקְרָא שִׁמְךָ עָלָיו:

אֱלֹהֵינוּ אָבִינוּ רְעֵנוּ זוּנֵנוּ פַרְנְסֵנוּ וְכַלְכְּלֵנוּ וְהַרְוִיחֵנוּ וְהַרְוַח
לָנוּ יְיָ אֱלֹהֵינוּ מְהֵרָה מִכָּל צָרוֹתֵינוּ. וְנָא אַל תַּצְרִיכֵנוּ יְיָ אֱלֹהֵינוּ
לֹא לִידֵי מַתְּנַת בָּשָׂר וָדָם וְלֹא לִידֵי הַלְוָאָתָם כִּי אִם לְיָדְךָ
הַמְּלֵאָה הַפְּתוּחָה הַקְּדוֹשָׁה וְהָרְחָבָה שֶׁלֹּא נֵבוֹשׁ וְלֹא נִכָּלֵם
לְעוֹלָם וָעֶד:

For all this, O Lord our God, we thank and bless Thee. Blessed be Thy name by the mouth ·of all living always and for ever, even as it is written: And thou shalt eat and be satisfied, and thou shalt bless the Lord thy God for the good land which He hath given thee. Blessed art Thou, O Lord, for the land and for the food.

Have mercy, O Lord our God, upon Israel Thy people, upon Jerusalem Thy city, upon Zion the abiding place of Thy glory, upon the kingdom of the house of David Thine anointed, and upon the great and holy house that was called by Thy name. O our God, our Father, feed us, nourish us, sustain, support and relieve us, and speedily, O Lord our God, grant us relief from all our troubles. We beseech Thee, O Lord our God, let us not be in need either of the gifts of flesh and blood or of their loans, but only of Thy helping hand, which is full, open, holy and ample, so that we may not be ashamed nor confounded for ever and ever.

E - lo - he - nu   o - vi - nu   re - e - nu   zu - ne - nu

par - n'-se - nu   v'-chal - ke - le - nu   v' - har - vi - che - nu.

She-lŏ ne-vŏsh   v' - lŏ niko-lĕm   l' - ŏ - lom   vo - ed.

רְצֵה וְהַחֲלִיצֵנוּ יְיָ אֱלֹהֵינוּ בְּמִצְוֹתֶיךָ וּבְמִצְוַת יוֹם הַשְּׁבִיעִי
הַשַּׁבָּת הַגָּדוֹל וְהַקָּדוֹשׁ הַזֶּה כִּי יוֹם זֶה גָּדוֹל וְקָדוֹשׁ הוּא לְפָנֶיךָ
לִשְׁבָּת בּוֹ וְלָנוּחַ בּוֹ בְּאַהֲבָה כְּמִצְוַת רְצוֹנֶךָ וּבִרְצוֹנְךָ הָנִיחַ לָנוּ
יְיָ אֱלֹהֵינוּ שֶׁלֹּא תְהֵא צָרָה וְיָגוֹן וַאֲנָחָה בְּיוֹם מְנוּחָתֵנוּ. וְהַרְאֵנוּ יְיָ
אֱלֹהֵינוּ בְּנֶחָמַת צִיּוֹן עִירֶךָ וּבְבִנְיַן יְרוּשָׁלַיִם עִיר קָדְשֶׁךָ כִּי אַתָּה
הוּא בַּעַל הַיְשׁוּעוֹת וּבַעַל הַנֶּחָמוֹת:

(On New Moons and Festivals add the following:)

אֱלֹהֵינוּ וֵאלֹהֵי אֲבוֹתֵינוּ יַעֲלֶה וְיָבֹא וְיַגִּיעַ וְיֵרָאֶה וְיֵרָצֶה וְיִשָּׁמַע וְיִפָּקֵד
וְיִזָּכֵר זִכְרוֹנֵנוּ וּפִקְדוֹנֵנוּ וְזִכְרוֹן אֲבוֹתֵינוּ וְזִכְרוֹן מָשִׁיחַ בֶּן דָּוִד עַבְדֶּךָ וְזִכְרוֹן
יְרוּשָׁלַיִם עִיר קָדְשֶׁךָ וְזִכְרוֹן כָּל עַמְּךָ בֵּית יִשְׂרָאֵל לְפָנֶיךָ לִפְלֵיטָה לְטוֹבָה
לְחֵן וּלְחֶסֶד וּלְרַחֲמִים לְחַיִּים וּלְשָׁלוֹם בְּיוֹם

לראש חדש	רֹאשׁ הַחֹדֶשׁ הַזֶּה:
לפסח	חַג הַמַּצּוֹת הַזֶּה:
לראש השנה	הַזִּכָּרוֹן הַזֶּה:
לשבועות	חַג הַשָּׁבוּעוֹת הַזֶּה:
לסוכות	חַג הַסֻּכּוֹת הַזֶּה:
לשמ"ע	הַשְּׁמִינִי חַג הָעֲצֶרֶת הַזֶּה:

זָכְרֵנוּ יְיָ אֱלֹהֵינוּ בּוֹ לְטוֹבָה. וּפָקְדֵנוּ בּוֹ לִבְרָכָה וְהוֹשִׁיעֵנוּ בּוֹ לְחַיִּים.
וּבִדְבַר יְשׁוּעָה וְרַחֲמִים חוּס וְחָנֵּנוּ. וְרַחֵם עָלֵינוּ וְהוֹשִׁיעֵנוּ. כִּי אֵלֶיךָ עֵינֵינוּ.
כִּי אֵל (לר"ה מֶלֶךְ) חַנּוּן וְרַחוּם אָתָּה:

וּבְנֵה יְרוּשָׁלַיִם עִיר הַקֹּדֶשׁ בִּמְהֵרָה בְיָמֵינוּ: בָּרוּךְ אַתָּה יְיָ
בּוֹנֵה בְרַחֲמָיו יְרוּשָׁלָיִם. אָמֵן:

Bō - nēh   b' - ra - cha - mov   y' - ru - sho - la - yĭm   o - men.

Be pleased, O Lord our God, to fortify us by Thy commandments, and especially by the commandment of the seventh day, this great and holy Sabbath, since this day is great and holy before Thee, that we may rest and repose thereon in love in accordance with the precept of Thy will. In Thy favor, O Lord our God, grant us such repose that there be no trouble, grief or lamenting on the day of our rest. Let us, O Lord our God, behold the consolation of Zion Thy city, and the rebuilding of Jerusalem Thy holy city, for Thou art the Lord of salvation and of consolation.

(On New Moons and Festivals add the following:)

Our God and God of our fathers! May our remembrance rise and come and be accepted before Thee, with the remembrance of our fathers, of Messiah the son of David Thy servant, of Jerusalem Thy holy city, and of all Thy people the house of Israel, bringing deliverance and well-being, grace, lovingkindness and mercy, life and peace on this day of—

*On New Moon say—*The New Moon

*On Passover—*The Feast of Unleavened Bread

*On New Year—*Memorial

*On Pentecost—*The Feast of Weeks

*On Tabernacles—*The Feast of Tabernacles

*On the Eighth Day of Solemn Assembly—*The Eighth-Day Feast of Solemn Assembly

Remember us, O Lord our God, thereon for our well-being; be mindful of us for blessing, and save us unto life: by Thy promise of salvation and mercy, spare us and be gracious unto us; have mercy upon us and save us; for our eyes are bent upon Thee, because Thou art a gracious and merciful God and King.

And rebuild Jerusalem the holy city speedily in our days. Blessed art Thou, O Lord, who in Thy compassion rebuildest Jerusalem. Amen.

בָּרוּךְ אַתָּה יְיָ אֱלֹהֵינוּ מֶלֶךְ הָעוֹלָם הָאֵל אָבִינוּ מַלְכֵּנוּ
אַדִּירֵנוּ בּוֹרְאֵנוּ גּוֹאֲלֵנוּ יוֹצְרֵנוּ קְדוֹשֵׁנוּ קְדוֹשׁ יַעֲקֹב רוֹעֵנוּ רוֹעֵה
יִשְׂרָאֵל. הַמֶּלֶךְ הַטּוֹב וְהַמֵּטִיב לַכֹּל שֶׁבְּכָל יוֹם וָיוֹם הוּא הֵטִיב
הוּא מֵטִיב הוּא יֵיטִיב לָנוּ.

Blessed art Thou, O Lord our God, King of the universe,
O God, our Father, our King, our Mighty One, our Creator, our
Redeemer, our Maker, our Holy One, the Holy One of Jacob,
our Shepherd, the Shepherd of Israel, O King, who art kind and
dealest kindly with all; day by day Thou hast dealt kindly, dost
deal kindly, and wilt deal kindly with us; Thou hast bestowed,
Thou dost bestow, Thou wilt ever bestow benefits upon us,
yielding us grace, loving kindness, mercy and relief, deliverance
and prosperity, blessing and salvation, consolation, sustenance
and support, mercy, life, peace and all good: of no manner of
good let us be in want. The All-merciful shall reign over us for
ever and ever. The All-merciful shall be blessed in heaven and
on earth. The All-merciful shall be praised throughout all generations, glorified amongst us to all eternity and honored amongst
us for everlasting. May the All-merciful grant us an honorable
livelihood. May the All-merciful break the yoke from off our
neck, and lead us upright to our land. May the All-merciful send
a plentiful blessing upon this house, and upon this table at which
we have eaten. May the All-merciful send us Elijah the prophet
(let him be remembered for good), who shall give us good tidings,
salvation and consolation. May the All-merciful bless (my
honored father) the master of this house, and (my honored
mother) the mistress of this house, them, their household, their

yōm   vo - yōm   hu   hē - tīv   hu   mē -

tīv   hu   yē - tīv   lo - nu.

הוּא גְמָלָנוּ הוּא גוֹמְלֵנוּ הוּא יִגְמְלֵנוּ לָעַד לְחֵן וּלְחֶסֶד
וּלְרַחֲמִים וּלְרֶוַח הַצָּלָה וְהַצְלָחָה בְּרָכָה וִישׁוּעָה נֶחָמָה פַּרְנָסָה
וְכַלְכָּלָה וְרַחֲמִים וְחַיִּים וְשָׁלוֹם וְכָל טוֹב וּמִכָּל טוּב לְעוֹלָם אַל
יְחַסְּרֵנוּ: הָרַחֲמָן הוּא יִמְלֹךְ עָלֵינוּ לְעוֹלָם וָעֶד: הָרַחֲמָן הוּא
יִתְבָּרַךְ בַּשָּׁמַיִם וּבָאָרֶץ: הָרַחֲמָן הוּא יִשְׁתַּבַּח לְדוֹר דּוֹרִים
וְיִתְפָּאַר בָּנוּ לָעַד וּלְנֵצַח נְצָחִים וְיִתְהַדַּר בָּנוּ לָעַד וּלְעוֹלְמֵי
עוֹלָמִים: הָרַחֲמָן הוּא יְפַרְנְסֵנוּ בְּכָבוֹד: הָרַחֲמָן הוּא יִשְׁבּוֹר עֻלֵּנוּ
מֵעַל צַוָּארֵנוּ וְהוּא יוֹלִיכֵנוּ קוֹמְמִיּוּת לְאַרְצֵנוּ: הָרַחֲמָן הוּא יִשְׁלַח
לָנוּ בְּרָכָה מְרֻבָּה בַּבַּיִת הַזֶּה וְעַל שֻׁלְחָן זֶה שֶׁאָכַלְנוּ עָלָיו:
הָרַחֲמָן הוּא יִשְׁלַח לָנוּ אֶת אֵלִיָּהוּ הַנָּבִיא זָכוּר לַטּוֹב וִיבַשֶּׂר לָנוּ
בְּשׂוֹרוֹת טוֹבוֹת יְשׁוּעוֹת וְנֶחָמוֹת: הָרַחֲמָן הוּא יְבָרֵךְ

וְאֶת ‹אָבִי מוֹרִי› בַּעַל הַבַּיִת הַזֶּה וְאֶת ‹אִמִּי מוֹרָתִי› בַּעֲלַת הַבַּיִת הַזֶּה.
אוֹתָם וְאֶת בֵּיתָם וְאֶת זַרְעָם וְאֶת כָּל אֲשֶׁר לָהֶם.

אוֹתָנוּ וְאֶת כָּל אֲשֶׁר לָנוּ כְּמוֹ שֶׁנִּתְבָּרְכוּ אֲבוֹתֵינוּ אַבְרָהָם
יִצְחָק וְיַעֲקֹב בַּכֹּל מִכֹּל כֹּל כֵּן יְבָרֵךְ אוֹתָנוּ כֻּלָּנוּ יַחַד בִּבְרָכָה
שְׁלֵמָה וְנֹאמַר אָמֵן:

בַּמָּרוֹם יְלַמְּדוּ עֲלֵיהֶם וְעָלֵינוּ זְכוּת שֶׁתְּהֵא לְמִשְׁמֶרֶת שָׁלוֹם
וְנִשָּׂא בְרָכָה מֵאֵת יְיָ וּצְדָקָה מֵאֱלֹהֵי יִשְׁעֵנוּ וְנִמְצָא חֵן וְשֵׂכֶל טוֹב
בְּעֵינֵי אֱלֹהִים וְאָדָם:

seed and all that is theirs, us and all that is ours, as our fathers Abraham, Isaac and Jacob were blessed each with his own comprehensive blessing; even thus may He bless all of us together with a perfect blessing, and let us say, Amen.

Both on their and on our behalf may there be such advocacy on high as shall lead to enduring peace; and may we receive a blessing from the Lord, and righteousness from the God of our salvation and may we find grace and good understanding in the sight of God and man.

V'-nim - tso   chēn   v' - sē - chel
tōv b' - ē - nē e lō - him v'o - dom.

הָרַחֲמָן. הוא יַנְחִילֵנוּ יוֹם שֶׁכֻּלוֹ שַׁבָּת וּמְנוּחָה לְחַיֵּי הָעוֹלָמִים:

On New Moon Day:—

הָרַחֲמָן. הוא יְחַדֵּשׁ עָלֵינוּ אֶת־הַחֹדֶשׁ הַזֶּה לְטוֹבָה וְלִבְרָכָה:

On Festivals:—

הָרַחֲמָן. הוא יַנְחִילֵנוּ יוֹם שֶׁכֻּלוֹ טוֹב:

On New Year:—

הָרַחֲמָן. הוא יְחַדֵּשׁ עָלֵינוּ אֶת־הַשָּׁנָה הַזֹּאת לְטוֹבָה וְלִבְרָכָה:

On the Feast of Tabernacles:—

הָרַחֲמָן. הוא יָקִים לָנוּ אֶת־סֻכַּת דָּוִיד הַנֹּפֶלֶת:

הָרַחֲמָן. הוא יְזַכֵּנוּ לִימוֹת הַמָּשִׁיחַ וּלְחַיֵּי הָעוֹלָם הַבָּא:

מִגְדּוֹל יְשׁוּעוֹת מַלְכּוֹ וְעֹשֶׂה חֶסֶד לִמְשִׁיחוֹ לְדָוִד וּלְזַרְעוֹ
עַד־עוֹלָם: עֹשֶׂה שָׁלוֹם בִּמְרוֹמָיו הוא יַעֲשֶׂה שָׁלוֹם עָלֵינוּ וְעַל
כָּל־יִשְׂרָאֵל וְאִמְרוּ אָמֵן:

May the All-merciful let us inherit the day which shall be wholly a Sabbath and rest in the life everlasting.

On New Moon Day:—

May the All-merciful renew unto us this month for good and for blessing.

On Festivals:—

May the All-merciful let us inherit the day which is altogether good.

On New Year:—

May the All-merciful renew unto us this year for good and for blessing.

On the Feast of Tabernacles:—

May the All-merciful raise up for us the fallen Tabernacle of David.

May the All-merciful make us worthy of the days of the Messiah and of the life of the world to come.

He is a tower of salvation to His king; and showeth loving kindness to His anointed, to David and to his seed, for evermore. He who maketh peace in His high places, may He make peace for us and for all Israel, and say ye, Amen.

The Lord will give strength unto His people: the Lord will bless His people with peace.

bim - rŏ - mov Hu ya - aseh sho - lŏm o -
lĕ - nu v'al kol yis - ro - ĕl v'-im - ru o - men.

יְיָ עֹז לְעַמּוֹ יִתֵּן. יְיָ יְבָרֵךְ אֶת־עַמּוֹ בַשָׁלוֹם:

IV. 'ONEG SHABBAT SONGS

1. HALLELU-YOH*— הַלְלוּיָהּ

הַלְלוּהוּ הַלְלוּהוּ בְּצִלְצְלֵי שָׁמַע,
הַלְלוּהוּ הַלְלוּהוּ בְּצִלְצְלֵי תְרוּעָה.
כֹּל הַנְּשָׁמָה תְּהַלֵּל יָהּ הַלְלוּיָהּ.

*Complete with piano acc.. in A. W. B., *New Palestinian Songs*, I. Bloch, N. Y.

2. NA'ALEH L'ARTSENU*—נַעֲלֶה לְאַרְצֵנוּ

נַעֲלֶה לְאַרְצֵנוּ בְּרִנָּה.
יוֹם גִּילָה, יוֹם רִנָּה,
יוֹם קְדוּשָׁה, יוֹם מְנוּחָה.

*Complete with piano acc., in A. W. B., *New Palestinian Songs*, I, Bloch, N. Y.

3. YESH LI GAN*— יֵשׁ לִי גַּן

יֵשׁ לִי גַּן וּבְאֵר יֵשׁ לִי   וְהַדְלִי כָּלְבָבִי עֵר,
וּמָן הַבְּאֵר תָּלוּי דְלִי.   נוֹטֵף פָּז אֶל פִּי הַבְּאֵר,
מִדֵּי שַׁבָּת בָּא מַחֲמַדִי   נוֹטֵף פָּז, נוֹטֵף בְּדוֹלַח.
מַיִם זַכִּים יֵשְׁתְּ מִן הַדְלִי.   דּוֹדִי הוֹלֵךְ, דּוֹדִי הוֹלֵךְ

*Complete with piano acc., in A. W. B., *Pioneer Songs of Palestine*, E. B. Marks
Co., N. Y.

4. NIGGUN BIALIK*

*Complete with piano acc., in A. W. B., *New Palestinian Songs*, I, Bloch, N. Y.

5. A MELODY OF A HASIDIC RABBI

(A Radel fun'm Libavitcher Rebbe)

La   la   la   la

6. JACOB'S SONG — (יעקב'ס ליעד)

Andante   Folk Song

O - mar a - doi - shem le - ya - kŏv yoh ta - te yoh

host doch uns tsu - ge - zogt al tI - ro av - di ya - kŏv,

oy vey Ta - te - nyu. Far - vo - sze shlogt men uns

Ta - te - nyu, Far vo - sze plugt men unz

Ta - te - nyu. Ven vet zein a sŏf oy ven?

7. OY BRIDER ZOG*

Attributed to R. Levi-Yitzhak of Berditchev

Oi bri - der zog vie heist der tog vos mir
Sha - bes a - lein kimt tsu gehn

al - le sei - nen frei - lach, Der yi - de - le der klein-ner der
zeit sze frei - lach a - le, Tanzt kind - er

ko - sher - er der shei - ner is doch dan - a -
ye - der - er ba - zun - der l'ko - vod der hei - li - ger

me - lech, Der yi - de - le der klein - er der
Ka - leh. Tantzt kin - der

ko-sher - er der shein - er iz doch dan— a - me - lech.
ye-der - er ba-zun - der l' ko - vod der hei li-ger Ka - leh.

8. SHREIT SZE

Shreit sze yi - den shab - bes oi ge - valt sha - bes

Volt Ich ge - hat koi - ach Volt Ich ge - lof - fen

dorch die gas - sen un volt ge - shri - gen Sha - bes.

*Arr. for female voices and piano in Z. Kisselgof, *Lieder Sammelbuch*, Yowal, Berlin.

9. THE CANTOR

(A Chazzendel)

Moderately fast and freely; Recitative   Folk Song

Iz ge-kum-men a cha-zan tsu fuh-ren in a klein shte-tel

da - ve-nen a shab-bes—da - ve-nen a shab - bes. Ze-nen ihm ge-

ku-men he-ren die drei shen-ste ba-le - ba - tim-fun-dem shte-tel—

— die drei shen-ste ba - le - ba - tim fun dem shte - tel.

Ei - ner a shnei - der - el der ander - er a ko - val

tshi - kel und der dri - ter a ba - le - gol - tshi - kel.

A little faster

Ruft zich	up - et	dus	schnei - der - el	Ruft zich
Ruft zich	up - et	dus ko - val - tshi - kel	Ruft zich
Ruft zich	up - et	dus bal-a-gul - tshi - kel	Ruft zich

10. THE SABBATH BRIDE

ISAAC S. MOSES

JACOB BEIMEL
Based on a traditional Sabbath mode

1. O ho - ly Sab - bath - day, draw near, Thou
2. Re - joice ye now with all your might: The
3. Now come thou bless - ed Sab - bath - Bride, Our

art the source of bliss and cheer; The first in God's cre -
Sab-bath free - dom brings you light; Let songs of praise to
joy, our com - fort and our pride; All cares and sor - rows

a - tive thought, The fi - nal aim of all He wrought, Wel-come,
God as - cend, And voic - es sweet in cho - rus blend. Wel-come,
bid thou cease, And fill our wait - ing hearts with peace. Wel-come,

wel - come, day of rest, Day of joy the Lord hath bless'd.
wel - come, day of rest, Day of joy the Lord hath bless'd.
wel - come, day of rest, Day of joy the Lord hath bless'd.

11. KI V'SIMCHOH — כִּי בְשִׂמְחָה

כִּי בְשִׂמְחָה תֵצֵאוּ וּבְשָׁלוֹם תּוּבָלוּן,

הֶהָרִים וְהַגְּבָעוֹת יִפְצְחוּ רִנָּה.

וּשְׁאַבְתֶּם מַיִם בְּשָׂשׂוֹן מִמַּעַיְנֵי הַיְשׁוּעָה.

צַהֲלִי, צַהֲלִי, וָרֹנִּי, יוֹשֶׁבֶת צִיּוֹן, יוֹשֶׁבֶת צִיּוֹ

הַלְלוּיָהּ, הַלְלוּיָהּ.

Allegretto   Palestinian Melody

1 Ki v'-sim-chah tē - tsē - u   u - v'-sho-lōm tu - vo - lun

2 He - ho - rim v' - ha-g'vo - ōs, yif - ts' - chu ri - noh.

U - sh'-av-tem ma - yim b' - so - sōn—— mi - ma-ai - nē ha -

y'—shu - oh— Tsa - ha - lī, tsa - ha - lī vo - rō - nī yō -

she - ves Tsi - yōn, yō - she - ves Tsi - yōn.

Ha - l' - lu - - yoh! Ha - l' - lu - - yoh!

12. BORUCH ELOHENU — בָּרוּךְ אֱלֹהֵינוּ

בָּרוּךְ אֱלֹהֵינוּ שֶׁבְּרָאָנוּ לִכְבוֹדוֹ.
עוֹד הַפַּעַם, עוֹד הַפַּעַם, לִכְבוֹדוֹ.
וְהִבְדִּילָנוּ מִן הַתּוֹעִים.
עוֹד הַפַּעַם, עוֹד הַפַּעַם, מִן הַתּוֹעִים.

וְנָתַן לָנוּ תּוֹרַת אֱמֶת.
עוֹד הַפַּעַם, עוֹד הַפַּעַם, תּוֹרַת אֱמֶת.
וְחַיֵּי עוֹלָם נָטַע בְּתוֹכֵנוּ.
עוֹד הַפַּעַם, עוֹד הַפַּעַם, בְּתוֹכֵנוּ.

13. V'TAHER LIBENU — וְטַהֵר לִבֵּנוּ

וְטַהֵר לִבֵּנוּ לְעָבְדְּךָ בֶּאֱמֶת

V. CANTILLATION MODES ON THE SABBATH

1. THE USUAL TORAH CHANT

בְּרֵאשִׁית בָּרָא אֱלֹהִים אֵת הַשָּׁמַיִם וְאֵת הָאָרֶץ: וְהָאָרֶץ
הָיְתָה תֹהוּ וָבֹהוּ וְחֹשֶׁךְ עַל־פְּנֵי תְהוֹם וְרוּחַ אֱלֹהִים מְרַחֶפֶת עַל־
פְּנֵי הַמָּיִם:

2. THE USUAL *HAFTARAH* CHANT

כֹּה אָמַר יְהֹוָה הַשָּׁמַיִם כִּסְאִי וְהָאָרֶץ הֲדֹם רַגְלָי אֵי־זֶה בַּיִת

אֲשֶׁר תִּבְנוּ־לִי וְאֵי־זֶה מָקוֹם מְנוּחָתִי:

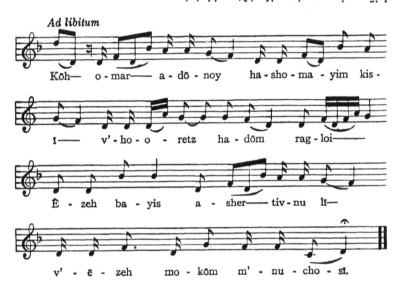

3. CANTILLATION OF "THE SONG OF THE SEA"

אָשִׁירָה לַיהֹוָה כִּי־גָאֹה גָּאָה סוּס וְרֹכְבוֹ רָמָה בַיָּם:

4. CANTILLATION OF THE BOOK OF LAMENTATIONS

אֵיכָה יָשְׁבָה בָדָד הָעִיר רַבָּתִי עָם הָיְתָה כְּאַלְמָנָה רַבָּתִי

בַגּוֹיִם שָׂרָתִי בַּמְּדִינוֹת הָיְתָה לָמַס׃

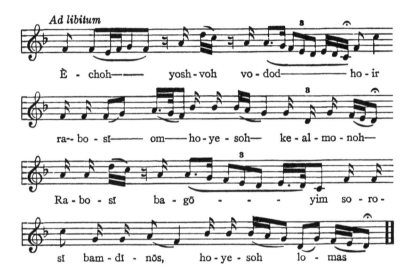

GLOSSARY

AUFRUFUNG — The calling to the Torah of a bridegroom on the Sabbath prior to his wedding.

BA'AL DARSHAN — Preacher; *Maggid*.

BARCHES — See *Ḥallah*.

BESAMIM — Spices used in the *Habdalah* service.

BESAMIM BOX — The box which contains the spices used in the *Habdalah* service.

CHOLENT — See *Schalet*.

'EREV SHABBOS — Friday.

'ERUB — A talmudic legal fiction which removes some of the restrictions dealing largely with the transportation of objects on the Sabbath.

'ERUBIN — Second treatise of the Mishnah, *Seder Mo'ed*, dealing with the types of *'Erub*.

ESHET ḤAYIL —"A woman of valor;" the biblical verses of Prov. 31.10–31, which the husband recites on Friday evening as a tribute to his wife.

GEFILTE FISH —"Stuffed fish," a favorite Sabbath dish.

GUT SHABBOS —"Good Sabbath," a Sabbath greeting.

HABDALAH —"Separation," the service at the conclusion of the Sabbath, which marks the separation of the Sabbath from the week days.

HABDALAH CANDLE — A candle of many wicks used in the *Habdalah* service.

HAFTARAH — Portion from the prophets, read on Sabbath morning immediately after the reading of the portion of the Torah.

ḤALLAH — Sabbath bread.

ḤIZZUK SHABBAT — Strengthening Sabbath observance.

474

KABBALAT SHABBAT —"Receiving the Sabbath," refers specifically to Ps. 95–99, 29, 92, 93 and the hymn *Lekah Dodi*, which are recited at the beginning of the Friday evening services in honor of the incoming Sabbath.

KIDDUSH —"Sanctification," the Friday evening home service in which the holiness of the Sabbath is declared over a cup of wine.

KIDDUSHA RABBA —"The great *Kiddush*," the *Kiddush* recited before the Saturday noon meal.

KUGEL — Sabbath pudding.

LEKAH DODI —"Come, my beloved," a hymn recited in the Friday evening services in honor of the incoming Sabbath.

LICHT BENCHEN —"Blessing the candles," the act of kindling the Sabbath lights and reciting the customary blessing.

MAFTIR — The concluding portion of the Sabbath Torah reading; also the person who reads the *Haftarah*.

MAGGID — See *Ba'al Darshan*.

MASSEKET SHABBAT — The talmudic treatise named *Shabbat*.

MEHALLEL SHABBAT — A desecrator of the Sabbath; a Sabbath-breaker.

MELAVVEH MALKAH —"Escorting the Queen," special meal eaten on Saturday night as a farewell party to the outgoing Queen Sabbath.

MOZA'E SHABBAT —"The evening when Sabbath departs," Saturday night.

MUKZEH —"Set aside," the prohibition to handle certain objects on the Sabbath because they are "set aside" for use in weekday work.

NESHAMAH YETERAH —"Extra soul," the additional soul which the observant Jew is said to possess on the Sabbath.

NIDHEH —"Postponed," a fast which falls on the Sabbath and is postponed to Sunday.

PARASHAH — The weekly portion of the Pentateuch which is read during the Saturday morning services.

PASTETTEN — Medieval German-Jewish Sabbath cakes.

PEREḴ — See *Pirḵe Abot.*

PIRḴE ABOT — "Chapters of the Fathers," a mishnaic treatise more commonly known as *Ethics of the Fathers.*

ROSH ḤODESH BENCHEN — "Blessing the new month," a special prayer recited on the Sabbath preceding the appearance of the new moon.

SABBATICAL YEAR — Every seventh year when the land in Palestine was left fallow.

SATURDAY — "Day of Saturn," so named in honor of the Roman god Saturn who was worshiped as the deity of seed sowing.

SCHALET — Sabbath food kept warm overnight in an oven and eaten on Saturday.

SEʻUDAH SHELISHIT — "Third meal," the third Sabbath meal eaten late Saturday afternoon.

SHABBAT BERESHIT — The Sabbath after the Feast of Tabernacles when the first portion of the Pentateuch is read in the synagogue. The first word of that biblical portion is *Bereshit,* "In the beginning."

SHABBAT HA-GADOL — "The great Sabbath," the Sabbath before Passover when the *Haftarah* mentions "the *great* day of the Lord."

SHABBAT HA-ḤODESH — "The Sabbath of the month," one of the Special Sabbaths when the *Haftarah* (Ezek. 45.16–46.18) extols *the month* of Nisan as the most important of all months because of the redemption of Israel that occurred in it.

SHABBAT ḤANUKKAH — "The Sabbath of Ḥanukkah," the Sabbath that occurs during the Feast of Lights.

SHABBAT ḤAZON — The Sabbath before the Black Fast (Ninth Day of Ab) when the *Haftarah* (Isa. 1.1–27) begins with the word *Ḥazon,* "The Vision" of Isaiah.

SHABBAT ḤOL HA-MOʻED — The Sabbath that occurs during the intermediate days of the Feasts of Passover and Tabernacles.

SHABBAT KALLAH — The Sabbath preceding the Feast of Weeks. It is called the "Sabbath of the Bride" because Shabuʻot celebrates the everlasting union of Israel with its "Bride," the Torah.

SHABBAT MEBAREKIM — The Sabbath preceding each new moon when the people "bless" the new month.

SHABBAT NAHAMU — The Sabbath after the Black Fast (Ninth Day of Ab) when the *Haftarah* (Isa. 40.1–26) begins with the word *Nahamu*, "Comfort ye."

SHABBAT PARAH — The Sabbath preceding *Shabbat ha-Hodesh*, when a special portion of the Torah is read. This portion (Num. 19) deals with the ancient custom of ritually purifying oneself for the Passover by means of the ashes of the *Parah Adumah*, the red heifer.

SHABBAT ROSH HODESH — Any Sabbath which coincides with the observance of the New Moon (*Rosh Hodesh*).

SHABBAT SHALOM —"A peaceful Sabbath," a Sabbath greeting.

SHABBAT SHALOM U-BERAKAH—"A peaceful and blessed Sabbath," the customary response to the greeting, *Shabbat Shalom*.

SHABBAT SHEKALIM — The Sabbath before the first of Adar when the portion of the Torah read deals with the half-*shekel* poll tax which used to be paid annually by every Jew for the support of the Temple. The tax was paid on the first of Adar, and the congregation was reminded of its obligation on the preceding Sabbath.

SHABBAT SHIRAH — "Sabbath of Song," the Sabbath before Hamishah 'Asar bi-Shebat when the Song of Moses (Ex. 15) is part of the Torah reading, and the song of Deborah (Judg. 5) is the *Haftarah* for the day.

SHABBAT SHUBAH —"Sabbath of Return," the Sabbath before the Day of Atonement, when the *Haftarah* begins with the word *Shubah*, "Return, O Israel, unto the Lord thy God" (Hosea 14.2).

SHABBAT ZAKOR —"The Sabbath of Remembrance," the Sabbath before Purim when the portion of the Torah read begins with the word *Zakor*, "Remember 'Amalek." Tradition regards 'Amalek as the ancestor of Haman.

SHABBOS GOY —"Sabbath Gentile," a Gentile who on Saturday performs chores forbidden to Jews, such as kindling lights and making a fire.

SHALOM 'ALEKEM—"Peace Be Unto You," a hymn recited on Friday evening, welcoming the Sabbath angels of peace.

SHALOSH SE'UDOT—"Three meals," usually designates the third Sabbath meal which is eaten late Saturday afternoon.

SHEBUT — An act forbidden on the Sabbath because it is contrary to the spirit of the Sabbath though not specifically prohibited by law.

SHOMER SHABBAT — A person who observes the Sabbath despite personal inconveniences and financial sacrifices.

SIDRAH — The weekly portion of the Pentateuch which is read in the synagogue during the Saturday morning services.

SUBOTNIKI — A Russian Sabbatarian sect that observes the seventh-day Sabbath and many other Jewish traditional practices.

TEḤUM — Sabbath walking distance (2,000 cubits beyond the city limit) beyond which a Jew may not walk on the Sabbath.

TSIMES — A Sabbath dessert usually made of cooked carrots.

ZEMIROT — Sabbath table hymns.

BIBLIOGRAPHY

I. GENERAL

SAMUEL, MAURICE, *The World of Sholom Aleichem*, New York, 1943, pp. 53–61.

SCHAUSS, HAYYIM, *The Jewish Festivals*, Cincinnati, 1938, pp. 13–37.

KAPLAN, MORDECAI M., *The Meaning of God in Modern Jewish Religion*, New York, 1937, pp. 40–103.

JOSEPH, MORRIS, *Judaism as Creed and Life*, London, 1925, pp. 200–11.

GREENSTONE, JULIUS H., *The Jewish Religion*, Philadelphia, 1929, pp. 12–23.

EDIDIN, BEN M., *Jewish Holidays and Festivals*, New York, 1940, pp. 17–34.

FRIEDLANDER, M., *The Jewish Religion*, London, 1922, pp. 336–360.

EISENSTEIN, IRA, *What We Mean by Religion*, New York, 1938, pp. 1–25.

MELAMED, DEBORAH M., *The Three Pillars*, New York, 1927, pp. 67–76.

GAMORAN, EMANUEL, *Changing Conceptions in Jewish Education*, New York, 1925, pp. 126–134.

COHON, BERYL D., *Introduction to Judaism*, Cincinnati, 1931, pp. 97–102.

HERTZ, J. H., *The Pentateuch and Haftorahs*, London, 1938, pp. 297–8, 355–6, 766–7.

IDELSOHN, ABRAHAM Z., *The Ceremonies of Judaism*, Cincinnati, 1930, pp. 3–11.

MONTEFIORE, C. G., *The Bible for Home Reading*, New York, 1905, Vol. I, pp. 86–91.

ABRAHAMS, I., "Sabbath (Jewish)" in *Encyclopedia of Religion and Ethics* (James Hastings), New York, Vol. X, pp. 891–3.

HASTINGS, JAMES, "Sabbath" in *Dictionary of the Bible*, New York, 1937, pp. 807–8.

SEGAL, SAMUEL M., *The Sabbath Book*, New York, 1938.

Sefer ha-Shabbat (in Hebrew), compiled by I. L. Baruch, Tel-Aviv, 1936.

Thieberger, Friedrich, "Der Sabbat" (in German), in *Jüdische Feste Jüdischer Brauch, Ein Sammelwerk*, Berlin, 1936, pp. 71–144.

ZOBEL, MORITZ, *Der Sabbat* (in German), Berlin, 1932.

II. THE SABBATH IN THE HOME

COHEN ISRAEL, *Jewish Life in Modern Times*, London, 1914, pp. 60–66.

ABRAHAMS, ISRAEL, *A Companion to the Authorized Prayer Book*, London, 1922.

"The Sabbath Lights," pp. 118–119.
"*Kiddush*," pp. 139–141; 169–170.
"The Parents Blessing," pp. 134–5.
"The Ideal Woman," pp. 135–9.
"The *Habdalah*," pp. 182–184.
"Table Hymns," pp. 260–272.

ROSENAU, WILLIAM, *Jewish Ceremonial Institutions and Customs*, New York, 1929 chap. VII.

GLICENSTEIN, ENRICO, and DUSHKIN, ALEXANDER, *The Tree of Life* ("Sketches from Jewish life of yesterday and today, poems and illustrations"), Chicago, 1933.

GREENBERG, BETTY D., and SILVERMAN, ALTHEA O., *The Jewish Home Beautiful,* New York, 1941. (Recipes for Sabbath foods, pp. 125–131).

FRIEDMANN, M., "The Sabbath Light," in *The Jewish Quarterly Review* (Old Series), London, Vol. III, pp. 707–721.

Jewish Encyclopedia, "Lamp, Sabbath," Vol. VII, pp. 600–601 (Julius H. Greenstone); "*Kiddush,*" Vol. VII, pp. 483–484 (Lewis N. Dembitz); "Barches," Vol. II, p. 529 (Kaufman Kohler); "*Habdalah,*" Vol. VI, pp. 118–121 (Bernard Drachman, Kaufman Kohler and Joseph Jacobs).

LEVINGER, ELMA E., *With the Jewish Child in Home and Synagogue*, New York, 1930, Chap. VI (For younger children).

GOLDIN, HYMAN E., *The Jewish Woman and Her Home*, New York, 1941.

III. HOME SERVICE FOR THE SABBATH

DEMBITZ, LEWIS, M., *Jewish Services in Synagogue and Home*, Philadelphia, 1898, pp. 348–355.

BERKOWITZ, HENRY, *Kiddush or Sabbath Sentiment in the Home*, Philadelphia, 1898.

IDELSOHN, A. Z., *Jewish Liturgy and Its Development*, New York, 1932, pp. 151–157.

Phonographic Records of Sabbath Melodies, Womens League of the United Synagogue of America, New York (consist of records of *Kiddush, Sholom Alekem, Sabbath Queen, Tsur Mishelo, Eliyahu ha-Navi*).

IV. SABBATH HOUR FOR CHILDREN

Any good Jewish story book will prove useful for a children's Sabbath hour. Lists of such books have been compiled by most of the Jewish book dealers and publishers, and are available on request. The following stories which have the Sabbath as their theme are especially appropriate:

WEILERSTEIN, SADIE R., "Come, O Queen" and "Farewell, O Queen," in *What the Moon Brought*, Philadelphia, 1942, pp. 47–54, 63–67; "Danny and His Red Express Wagon," "How Little-Bit-of-A-Boy Caught a Fish for Shabbos," "How Danny Watched Shabbos Go Away," "Judith Takes a Shabbos Walk," and "How Danny Helped for Shabbos," in *What Danny Did*, New York 1928, pp. 7–13, 14–24, 25–32, 61–67, and 100–103; and "K'tonton Plans a Palace for the Sabbath Queen," in *The Adventures of K'tonton*, New York, 1935, pp. 19–23.

BIALIK, ḤAYYIM NAḤMAN, "Which Was the Thief," in *And It Came to Pass*, New York, 1938, pp. 128–133.

ISH-KISHOR, SHULAMITH, "Sabbath in Heaven," in *Friday Night Stories*, New York, 1925, Series IV, pp. 31–39.

LEVINGER, ELMA EHRLICH, "The River of Dreams," in *In Many Lands*, New York, 1929, pp. 138–143; "Judith's Candlesticks," in *Jewish Holiday Stories*, New York, 1932, pp. 7–22.

GAMORAN, MAMIE G., "The Sabbath — A Holiday Every Week," in *Days and Ways*, Cincinnati, 1941, pp. 6–19.

V. THE SABBATH IN THE SYNAGOGUE

HARBURG, ISRAEL, "Observance of the Sabbath" in *Yearbook of the Central Conference of American Rabbis*, Cincinnati, Vol. XLVII (1937), pp. 324–50.

DEMBITZ, LEWIS N., *Jewish Services in Synagogue and Home*, Philadelphia, 1898.

ROSENAU, WILLIAM, *Jewish Ceremonial Institutions and Customs*, New York, 1929, Chap. III.

ABRAHAMS, ISRAEL, *A Companion to the Authorized Prayer Book*, London, 1922, pp. 120–180 (Notes on the origin and significance of the various Sabbath prayers and customs in the synagogue).

IDELSOHN, A. Z., *Jewish Liturgy and Its Development*, New York, 1932, pp. 128–150 (Description of the liturgy of the Sabbath).

LEVY, BERYL HAROLD, *Reform Judaism in America*, New York, 1933, pp. 14–37 (A comparison between the Traditional and Reform Sabbath morning service).

The A. Z. A. Monthly Program (for the month of March of any year), Aleph Zadik Aelph of the B'nai B'rith, Omaha, Nebraska. (Features a comprehensive program for a youth Sabbath service. The value of these programs lies in their attempt to teach the significance of the Sabbath to the members of youth organizations.)

EDIDIN, BEN M., "Conducting a Sabbath Service," in *Projects About Religious Ideas and Customs*, Cincinnati, 1938, pp. 26–33 (for youth groups).

LEVINGER, ELMA EHRLICH, *With the Jewish Child in Home and Synagogue*, New York, 1930, Chap. VII (for younger children).

DAVIS, MOSHE, "Towards a Modern Children's Service," in *Jewish Education*, Vol. IX, No. 1, Jan.-March, 1937 (A new approach to the problem of organizing and conducting a Children's Service).

BRILLIANT, NATHAN, "Children's Service," in *Jewish Teacher*, Vol. I, No. 3 (April, 1933), p. 12.

SILVERMAN, MORRIS, *The Junior Congregation*, Buffalo, N. Y. (A Guide for the Organization and Conduct of Services for Children).

ARZT, MAX, "The Junior Congregation," in *The Bulletin of the Rabbinical Assembly*, Vol. II, No. 3 (Mar. 1939), pp. 13–15 (A description of the techniques employed at Temple Israel, Scranton, Pa.).

VI. THE 'ONEG SHABBAT

Oneg Shabbat, Jewish National Workers Alliance, New York (selections dealing with the significance of the Sabbath, Sabbath talks, and Sabbath songs).

EPHRAIM, MIRIAM R., and LEIBEL, JEANETTE N., *Introductory Pamphlet on Oneg Shabbat Programs*, Hadassah, New York.

Papers and Dramatizations for *Oneg Shabbat* meetings, Hadassah, New York.

ROSMARIN, TRUDE WEISS, *The Oneg Shabbat Book*, New York, 1940.

Ongei Shabbat, Habonim, New York (for camp programs).

ELKIN, HARRY, "The Synagogue Service From a Pedagogic Viewpoint," in *The Reconstructionist*, Vol. IX, No. 10 (June 25, 1943). (Contains practical suggestions for *Oneg Shabbat* functions).

GREENBERG, BETTY D., and SILVERMAN, ALTHEA O., *The Jewish Home Beautiful*, New York, 1941 (A pageant of the Jewish festivals in a "Narrative Version" and in a "Dramatic Version." Portions on Sabbath are on pp. 35–37; 65–66).

Facts and Fictions Concerning the Jew (24 pamphlets for fire-side chats on some of the most pressing Jewish problems suitable for *'Oneg Shabbat* discussions), Anti-defamation League of B'nai B'rith, Chicago.

Popular Studies in Judaism, Tract Commission of the Union of American Hebrew Congregations, Cincinnati (30 pamphlets on problems of the Jewish religion and Jewish history).

Bibliographies for Twelve Discussion Topics, Department of Synagogue and School Extension, Cincinnati.

For music books for *'Oneg Shabbat* meetings see bibliography for Chapter XVI.

VII. THE LAW OF THE SABBATH

GOLDIN, HYMAN E., *Code of Jewish Law*, New York, 1928, Vol. II, pp. 63–148.

"Toward a Guide for Jewish Ritual Usage," in *The Reconstructionist*, Vol. VII, No. 16 (Dec. 12, 1941), pp. 10–15.

YISROEL, BEN, *Laws and Customs of Israel*, London, 1916, Part III, pp. 238–305 (compiled from the traditional codes).

MOORE, GEORGE FOOT, *Judaism in the First Centuries of Christianity*, Cambridge, 1927, Vol. II, pp. 21–39.

GREENSTONE, JULIUS H., "Sabbath," in *Jewish Encyclopedia*, Vol. X, pp. 598–602.

FRIEDLÄNDER, MICHAEL, "Erub," in *Jewish Encyclopedia*, Vol. V, pp. 203–204.

VIII. SABBATH SPICE

The Friday Night Book, London, 1933 (A Jewish Miscellany for Sabbath Home Entertainment).

RICHMAN, JACOB, *Laughs From Jewish Lore*, New York, 1926, pp. 282–289.

NECHES, S. M., *Humorous Tales of Latter Day Rabbis*, New York, 1938 (Humorous Sabbath stories will be found on pp. 24, 36, 54, 56, 64, 77, 80, 83, 94, 116 and 117).

IX-XV. THE SABBATH IN LITERATURE

HIRSCH, EMIL G., "Sabbath," in *Jewish Encyclopedia*, Vol. X, pp. 587–590.
SEGAL, SAMUEL M., *The Sabbath Book*, New York, 1942 ("Sabbath Legends," pp. 141–164).
Sefer ha-Shabbat, Tel-Aviv, Palestine, 1936.
ROTH, CECIL, "The Sabbath to Abraham Ibn Ezra," in *Anglo-Jewish Letters*, London, 1938, pp. 3–6.

Many good Sabbath stories were not selected for publication here either because they are too long, or because they duplicate the themes of other stories. The following short stories are recommended:

"The Short Friday," by Ḥayyim Naḥman Bialik, in *Aftergrowth and Other Stories*, Philadelphia, 1939, pp. 191–216.

"The Rav and the Rav's Son," by Hirsch David Naumberg, translated from the Yiddish by Helena Frank, in *Yiddish Tales*, Philadelphia, 1912, pp. 435–446.

"The Sabbath Question in Sudminster," by Israel Zangwill, in *Ghetto Comedies*, Philadelphia, 1938, pp. 139–196.

"A Union for Shabbos," by Sholem Asch, in *The National Jewish Monthly*, Nov. 1939.

"A Mystified Angel," by Louis Schnabel, in *Voegele's Marriage and Other Tales*, Philadelphia, 1892, pp. 30–33.

"The Land of Giants," by David L. Meckler, in *Miracle Men*, New York, 1936, pp. 152–164.

"Sabbathai," by S. J. Agnon, in *Yisroel*, by Joseph Leftwich, London, 1933, pp. 851–855.

"What the Tax-Collector Learned," by J. L. Perez, in *The Young Judaean*, Vol. XV, Oct. 1925, pp. 12–13, 22.

"The Disturbed Sabbath" (a Ḥasidic story), in *Jewish Mysticism and the Legends of the Baalshem*, by Martin Buber, London, 1931.

"God's Bread," by Sholom Asch, in *Children of Abraham*, New York.

XVI. THE SABBATH IN MUSIC

Synagogue Music for the Sabbath

BINDER, A. W., *Hibbath Shabbath* (Sabbath Eve Service)
Rinnath Shabbath (Sabbath Eve Service).
Kabbalath Shabbath (Sabbath Eve Service).

BLOCH, ERNEST, *Avodath Hakodesh*, Sabbath Morning Service.
FREED, ISADORE, *Sabbath Morning Service*.
GOLDFARB, I. and LEVINTHAL, I., *Songs and Praise for Sabbath Eve.*
KATCHKO, ADOLPH, *Avodath Aharon*, Sabbath Eve Service.
LEWANDOWSKI, LOUIS, *Kol Rinnah*, Sabbath Eve and Morning Services.
NAUMBOURG, SOLOMON, *Zemirot Yisroel*, Sabbath Eve and Morning Services.
SPICKER, MAX, *Emanu-El Service*, Books 1 & 2, Sabbath Eve and Morning Services.
STARK, EDWARD, *Sabbath Eve and Morning Services.*
SULZER, SOLOMON, *Shir Zion*, Vol. 1, Sabbath Eve and Morning Services; American Edition of *Shir Zion* (Sabbath Eve Service).
SCHALIT, HEINRICH, *Sabbath Eve Service.*
WEINBERG, JACOB, *Sabbath Eve and Morning Service.*
Union Hymnal, Cincinnati, Third Edition.

Zemirot and Folk Song Collections

Die schoensten Lieder der Ostjuden, Fritz Mordechai Kaufmann, Leipzig.
Die Hauslichen Sabbatgesange, Arno Nadel, Berlin, 1937.
Jewish Year in Song, A. W. Binder, G. Schirmer, New York.
Jewish Songster, S. and I. Goldfarb, New York.
Mediaeval Jewish Minstrelsy, Herbert Loewe, London, 1926.
Musikalisher Pinkas, A. M. Bernstein, Vilna.
Mizimrath Haaretz, S. Rosowsky, Jerusalem.
New Palestinian Songs, 4 volumes, A. W. Binder.
Shirenu, Texts and Music, M. Nathanson, Hebrew Publishing Company, New York.
Shire Eretz Yisrael, J. Schoenberg, Berlin.
Songs of My People, H. Coopersmith, Chicago, Ill.
Union Hymnal, Central Conference of American Rabbis (Third Edition).
Songs of Zion, H. Coopersmith, New York.

XVIII.   THE ORIGIN AND DEVELOPMENT OF THE SABBATH

JASTROW, MORRIS, "The Hebrew and Babylonian Sabbath," in *Hebrew and Babylonian Traditions*, New York, 1914, pp. 134–195.
JASTROW, MORRIS, "The Original Character of the Hebrew Sabbath," in *The American Journal of Theology*, Chicago, 1898, Vol. II, pp. 312–352.
WEBSTER, HUTTON, *Rest Days*, New York, 1916, pp. 242–271.
SCHAUSS, HAYYIM, *The Jewish Festivals*, Cincinnati, 1938, pp. 3–12.
EDIDIN, BEN M., *Jewish Holidays and Festivals*, New York, 1940, pp. 18–21.
GINZBERG, LOUIS, "The Sabbath in Ancient Times," in *United Synagogue Recorder*, New York, Vol. I, No. 1 (Jan. 1921).
KOHLER, K., "The Sabbath and Festivals in Pre-Exilic and Exilic Times," in *Studies, Addresses and Personal Papers*, New York, 1931, pp. 86–91.

BARTON, GEORGE A., *Archaeology and the Bible*, Philadelphia, 1927, Part II, pp. 281-282.

OESTERLEY, W. O. E., and ROBINSON, THEODORE H., *Hebrew Religion, Its Origin and Development*, New York, 1930, pp. 93-96.

COLSON, F. H., *The Week, an Essay on the Origin and Development of the Seven-Day Cycle*, London, 1926.

MANN, J., "The Observance of the Sabbath and the Festivals in the First Two Centuries of the Current Era According to Philo, Josephus, the New Testament, and the Rabbinic Sources," in *The Jewish Review*, London, Vol. IV (1914), pp. 433-456, 498-532.

RADIN, MAX, *The Life of the People in Biblical Times*, Philadelphia, 1929, pp. 206-7.

KOHLER, K., *Jewish Theology*, New York, 1918, pp. 455-8.

WEBSTER, HUTTON, "Sabbath (Primitive)," in *Encyclopedia of Religion and Ethics* (James Hastings), New York, 1928, Vol. X, pp. 885-9.

PINCHES, T. G., "Sabbath (Babylonian)," in *Encyclopedia of Religion and Ethics* (James Hastings), New York, 1928, Vol. X, pp. 889-91.

XIX. THE STRUGGLE FOR THE PRESERVATION OF THE SABBATH

"The Sabbath Question," and "Discussion," in *Yearbook of the Central Conference of American Rabbis*, Vols. XII (1902), XIII (1903), XIV (1904), and XV (1905).

LEVY, BERYL HAROLD, *Reform Judaism in America*, New York, 1933, pp. 92-108 (A detailed analysis of the problem of "Sabbath Observance and Sunday Sabbath").

PHILIPSON, DAVID, *The Reform Movement in Judaism*, New York, 1907, pp. 275-302; 447-449; 503-510.

KOHLER, K., *Jewish Theology*, New York, 1918, pp. 458-9.

HERTZ, J. H., "The Battle for the Sabbath at Geneva," in *Sermons, Addresses and Studies*, London, 1938, Vol. II, pp. 265-295.

HYAMSON, MOSES, "The Blank Day Device in Proposed Plans for Calendar Reform," a memorandum submitted to the League of Nations by the League for Safeguarding the Fixity of the Sabbath, New York, 1931.

HYAMSON, MOSES, "Reply to Marvin and Cosworth's Pamphlet, 'Moses the Greatest of Calendar Reformers,' " New York.

HYAMSON, MOSES, "The Proposed Reform of the Calendar," in *The Jewish Forum*, New York, Jan., 1929.

JUNG, MOSES, "The Opposition to the Thirteen Month Calendar," in *The Jewish Forum*, Nov., 1930.

ROSENGARTEN, ISAAC, "Religious Freedom and Calendar Reform," in *The Jewish Forum*, Jan., 1930.

BLOOM, SOL, "Calendar Reform," in *Congressional Record*, Seventy-First Congress, First Session, Jan. 11, 1929.

XX. THE JEWISH SABBATH AND THE CHRISTIAN SUNDAY

COTTON, PAUL, *From Sabbath to Sunday*, Bethlehem, Pa., 1933.

HIRSCH, EMIL G., "Sabbath and Sunday," in *Jewish Encyclopedia*, Vol. X, pp. 603–605.

FISHER, WILLIAM LOGAN, *The History of the Instituion of the Sabbath Day, Its Uses and Abuses*, Philadelphia, 1845.

GLAZENBROOK, M. G., "Sunday" in *Encyclopedia of Religion and Ethics*, New York, 1928, Vol. XII, pp. 103–111.

NOTES

NOTES TO CHAPTER I
THE TRADITIONAL SABBATH

[1] Ex. 20.8.
[2] See pp. 295–6.
[3] Finkelstein, Louis, "The Origin of the Synagogue," in *Proceedings of the American Academy for Jewish Research*, Vol. I., pp. 49–59.
[4] Moore, George Foot, *Judaism in the First Centuries of the Christian Era*, Cambridge, 1927, Vol. II, p. 24.
[5] Shab. 10b.
[6] Kaplan, Mordecai M., "Affiliation with the Synagogue," in *The Jewish Communal Register*, New York, 1917, pp. 118–119.
[7] Nissenbaum, I., in *Sefer Ha-Shabbat*, Tel-Aviv, 1936, p. 142.

NOTES TO CHAPTER II
THE SABBATH IN THE HOME

[1] The greetings *Shabbat Shalom* and *Shabbat Shalom u-Berakah* are used mainly by the *Sefardim* (Spanish-Portuguese Jews) while the greeting *Gut Shabbos* is used by the *Ashkenazim* (Central and East European Jews and their American descendants).
[2] Most of what follows in this chapter is based on lectures delivered by Prof. Louis Ginzberg of the Jewish Theological Seminary of America. For this instruction and for the clarification of many points in private conference the author expresses his profound gratitude.
[3] See below, Chap. XVIII, p. 337 ff.

NOTES TO CHAPTER III
HOME SERVICE FOR THE SABBATH

[1] For the music, complete with piano acc., see A. W. Binder, *Kabbalath Shabbath*, Bloch Pub. Co., N. Y.
[2] Ibid.
[3] For the music, complete with piano acc., see A. W. Binder, *The Jewish Year in Song*, G. Schirmer, N. Y.

NOTES TO CHAPTER IV
SABBATH HOUR FOR CHILDREN

[1] Weilerstein, Sadie Rose, *What Danny Did*, Bloch Publishing Co., New York, 1928, pp. 100–103.

[2] Weilerstein, Sadie Rose, *The Adventures of K'tonton*, The Women's League of the United Synagogue of America, New York, 1935, pp. 15–18.

[3] Weilerstein, Sadie R., *What the Moon Brought*, The Jewish Publication Society of America, Philadelphia, 1942, pp. 55–62.

[4] This story is based on a briefer account in Shab. 119a.

[5] *The Young Judaean*, Vol. XVII (1927), pp. 21–26.

[6] Gaer, Joseph, *The Unconquered*, The Sinai Press, Cincinnati, 1932, pp. 3–11.

[7] *The Young Judaean*, Vol. II (1912), pp. 23–24.

[8] Segal, Samuel M., *Elijah, A Study in Folklore*, Behrman's Jewish Book House, New York, 1935, pp. 119–122.

[9] From *The Jewish Child*, Vol. I (1912), p. 3.

[10] *"Oneg Shabbat,"* Jewish National Workers Alliance, New York, pp. 32–35.

[11] Learsi, Rufus, *Kasriel the Watchman*, The Jewish Publication Society of America, Philadelphia, 1925, pp. 267–275.

[12] Schnabel, Louis, *Voegele's Marriage and Other Tales*, The Jewish Publication Society of America, Philadelphia, 1892, pp. 66–71.

[13] Wolfenstein, Martha, *Idyls of the Gass*, The Jewish Publication Society of America, Philadelphia, 1901, pp. 167–180.

[14] *Poems for Young Judaeans*, New York, 1917, p. 59.

[15] *The Jewish Child*, Vol. VI, No. 30 (Aug. 23, 1918), p. 1.

[16] Raskin, Philip M., *Anthology of Modern Jewish Poetry*, Behrman's Jewish Book House, New York, 1927, pp. 104–105.

[17] Sampter, Jessie E., *Around the Year in Rhymes for the Jewish Child*, Bloch Publishing Co., New York, 1932, p. 12.

[18] Ibid., p. 13. Abridged.

[19] Fein, Harry H., *Gems of Hebrew Verse*, Bruce, Humphries, Boston, 1940, p. 17.

[20] Ibid., p. 15.

[21] Klein, A. M., *Hath Not the Jew*, Behrman's Jewish Book House, New York, 1940, p. 85.

[22] *The Jewish Child*, Vol. IV (1916), No. 11, p. 1.

[23] Schwarz, Leo W., *Sabbath Program*, Young Judaea, New York, 1928, p. 8.

[24] Sampter, Jessie E., *Around the Year in Rhymes for the Jewish Child*, Bloch. Publishing Co., New York, 1932, p. 12.

[25] Ibid., p. 45.

NOTES TO CHAPTER V

THE SABBATH IN THE SYNAGOGUE

[1] Stamm, Frederick K., "Millions of Backsliders," in *The Country Home Magazine*, Dec. 1939.

[2] Bell, Bernard I., "Stay-at-Home Christians," in *Atlantic Monthly*, Vol. CLXIII (Apr. 1939).

[3] Psalms 95–99, 29, 92, 93 and the hymn *Lekah Dodi*.

[4] See *Song and Praise for Sabbath Eve*, by Goldfarb and Levinthal, N. Y., 1922.

[5] *C.C.A.R. Yearbook*, Vol. XV (1905), p. 62.

[6] *C.C.A.R. Yearbook*, Vol. XII (1902), pp. 145–146.

NOTES TO CHAPTER VI
THE 'ONEG SHABBAT

[1] The Society for the Advancement of Judaism, New York.
[2] Euclid Avenue Temple, Cleveland, Ohio.
[3] Habonim Kevuzah.

NOTES TO CHAPTER VII
THE LAW OF THE SABBATH

[1] See Num. 35.5 for a definition of city limits.
[2] Kaplan, Mordecai M., *Judaism as a Civilization*, New York, 1934, p. 445.
[3] Selected from the *Code of Jewish Law* (*Kizur Shulḥan 'Aruk*) by Hyman E. Goldin, Hebrew Publishing Co., New York, 1928, Vol. II, pp. 63–148.
[4] "Who createst the fruit of the vine."
[5] The benediction over bread.

NOTES TO CHAPTER VIII
SABBATH SPICE

[1] For the original meaning of the phrase "Sabbath Spice" see Chapter XI, p. 224 f.
[2] Drujanoff, A., *Sefer ha-Bediḥah veha-Ḥidud*, Tel-Aviv, 3 vols., 1935.
[3] Josephus, Flavius, *Against Apion*, 2.2.
[4] *The Friday Night Book*, The Soncino Press, London, 1933, p. 38.
[5] Marcion was the founder of the Marcionite sect of anti-Judaic gnostics of the second century.
[6] Epiphanius, "Against Heresies" (42.3) quoted by Paul Cotton, in *From Sabbath to Sunday*, Bethlehem, Pa., 1933, p. 46.
[7] Neuman, Abraham A., *The Jews in Spain*, Jewish Publication Society of America, Philadelphia, 1942, Vol. I, p. 29.
[8] Henriques, H. S. Q., *The Jews in the English Law*, Oxford, 1908, p. 247.
[9] Mandelbaum, David G., "The Jewish Way of Life in Cochin," in *Jewish Social Studies*, Vol. I, No. 4 (Oct. 1939), p. 429.
[10] See "The Sabbatic River," Chapter X, pp. 216–7.
[11] Greenberg, Hayim, "Shambat — An Episode," in *Furrows*, New York, Volume I, No. 1 (November 1942), pp. 21–26.

NOTES TO CHAPTER IX
THE SABBATH IN THE BIBLE

[1] The biblical excerpts were culled from the version of *The Holy Scriptures* issued by The Jewish Publication Society of America.

NOTES TO CHAPTER X

THE SABBATH IN JUDAEO-HELLENISTIC LITERATURE

[1] Baron, Salo W., *A Social and Religious History of the Jews*, Columbia University Press, 1937, Vol. I, p. 149.
[2] The Authorized Version, Oxford University Press, London.
[3] King Antiochus IV and his officers.
[4] This and the following excerpt were taken from *The Works of Philo-Judaeus*, translated by C. D. Younge, London, 1890, Vol. I, p. 26 and Vol. III, pp. 158–9.
[5] The rest of the excerpts in this chapter are from *The Works of Josephus*, trans. by William Whiston, Virtue & Yorston, New York.

NOTES TO CHAPTER XI

THE SABBATH IN THE TALMUD AND THE MIDRASH

[1] Friedlander, Gerald, *Pirke de-Rabbi Eliezer*, London, 1916, pp. 137–8.
[2] "They" refers to God and to the worshipper.
[3] The phrase *shabat vayinafash* means "He ceased from work and rested," but one might translate *shabat* as "He finished the Sabbath," while the word *vayinafash* can be separated into two parts — *vayi* (woe) *nafash* (for the soul).

NOTES TO CHAPTER XII

THE SABBATH IN MEDIEVAL JEWISH LITERATURE

[1] Halevi, Judah, *Kitab Al Khazari* (translated from the Arabic by Hartwig Hirschfeld), Bloch Publishing Co., New York, pp. 113–114.
[2] *The Cusari* was written in the form of a dialogue between the king of the Khazars and his teacher, the rabbi.
[3] Ibid., pp. 142–3.
[4] Abraham Ibn Ezra visited Cyprus prior to his arrival in London. It was probably there that he met a Jewish sect which celebrated the Sabbath from Saturday morning to Sunday morning instead of from Friday sunset to Saturday eve. This experience, as well as the appearance of some books defending this heterodox practice, induced Ibn Ezra to write the *Sabbath Epistle*.
[5] There is truce in hell during the Sabbath.
[6] The book was probably the commentary of Rabbi Samuel ben Meir (*Rashbam*) on the Pentateuch. He could not kindle a light because of the Sabbath. We can tell that December 7, 1158, was full moon because it was the 14th day of the Hebrew lunar month (Joseph Jacobs).
[7] Jacobs, Joseph, *The Jews of Angevin England*, New York, 1893, pp. 35–38.
[8] Maimonides, Moses, *The Guide for the Perplexed* (translated from the Arabic by M. Friedländer), E. P. Dutton Co., New York, 1910, p. 219.
[9] Ibid., p. 352.
[10] The *Mishneh Torah*.

[11] *Sefer Hasidim.*

[12] Shebu. 20b. "Remember" and "Keep" are the initial words of the Fourth Commandment in Ex. 20.8 and Deut. 5.12, respectively. The variation is explained by the rabbinic statement that the two words were pronounced on Sinai simultaneously. Albo in the sequel explains the rabbinic statement differently.

[13] Albo, Joseph, *Book of Principles* (trans. from the Hebrew by Isaac Husik), The Jewish Publication Society of America, Philadelphia, 1930, Vol. III, pp. 246–8.

NOTES TO CHAPTER XIII

THE SABBATH IN MODERN JEWISH LITERATURE

[1] Schechter, Solomon, *Studies in Judaism*, First Series, The Jewish Publication Society of America, Philadelphia, 1896, pp. 244–248.

[2] Kohler, K., *Jewish Theology*, The Macmillan Company, New York, 1918, pp. 455–6.

[3] Kaplan, Mordecai M., *The Meaning of God in Modern Jewish Religion*, Behrman's Jewish Book House, New York, 1937, p. 59.

[4] Ibid., pp. 60–61.

[5] Hertz, J. H., *The Pentateuch and Haftorahs*, Soncino Co., London, 1938, p. 929.

[6] Fleg, Edmond, *The Jewish Anthology* (trans. by Maurice Samuel), Harcourt, Brace and Co., New York, 1925, pp. 331–2.

[7] Levine, Joseph Cooper, *Echoes of the Jewish Soul*, Bloch Publishing Co., New York, 1931, pp. 32–33.

[8] Zangwill, Israel, *Children of the Ghetto*, The Jewish Publication Society of America, Philadelphia, 1892, Vol. I, pp. 324–331.

[9] Ibid., pp. 340–341.

[10] Asch, Sholom, *Kiddush Ha-Shem* (trans. by Rufus Learsi), The Jewish Publication Society of America, Philadelphia, 1936, pp. 45–48.

[11] Aḥad Ha'Am, *'Al Parashat Derakim*, Vol. III, 30.

[12] From address delivered by Ḥayyim Naḥman Bialik at the laying of the cornerstone of *'Ohel Shem*, the home of the *'Oneg Shabbat* gatherings in Tel-Aviv, Palestine, 1929 (*Sefer ha-Shabbat*, Tel-Aviv, 1938, p. 519).

[13] Bialik, H. N., *Law and Legend* (trans. by Julius L. Siegel), Bloch Publishing Company, New York, 1923, pp. 7–9.

NOTES TO CHAPTER XIV

THE SABBATH IN THE SHORT STORY

[1] Perez, Isaac Loeb, *Stories and Pictures* (translated from the Yiddish by Helena Frank), The Jewish Publication Society of America, Philadelphia, 1906, pp. 21–25.

[2] A Bible commentator of the sixteenth century.

[3] Frank, Helena, *Yiddish Tales*, The Jewish Publication Society of America, Philadelphia, 1912, pp. 62–66.

[4] Levin, Meyer, *The Golden Mountain*, Jonathan Cape & Robert Ballou, New York, 1932, pp. 115–124.

⁵ Buber, Martin, *Jewish Mysticism and the Legends of Baalshem* (trans. from the German by Lucy Cohen), J. M. Dent & Sons, London, 1931, pp. 217–218.

⁶ Levner, B., in *The Young Judaean*, Vol. XIII (1925), pp. 175, 178. Adapted from the Hebrew.

⁷ Zangwill, Israel, *Ghetto Tragedies*, The Jewish Publication Society of America, Philadelphia, 1899, pp. 479–486.

NOTES TO CHAPTER XV

THE SABBATH IN JEWISH POETRY

¹ Lucas, Alice, *The Jewish Year*, Bloch Publishing Co., 1926, pp. 70–71. Abridged from a translation from the Hebrew by Alice Lucas.

² Solis-Cohen, Solomon, *When Love Passed By and Other Poems*, The Rosenbach Co., Philadelphia, 1929, pp. 98–99. Translated from the Hebrew, *Lekah Dodi*, by Solomon Alkabiz.

³ Messiah.

⁴ Messiah (Perez was an ancestor of King David).

⁵ Davis, Edith Ella, *Echoes from the Temple*, Bloch Publishing Co., New York, 1926, p. 8.

⁶ Friedlander, Joseph, *The Standard Book of Jewish Verse*, Dodd, Mead and Co., New York, 1917, p. 270.

⁷ Raskin, Philip M., *Songs of a Wanderer*, Jewish Publication Society of America, Philadelphia, 1917, pp. 91–92. Abridged.

⁸ Salaman, Nina, *Apples and Honey*, Doubleday, Page and Co., Garden City, New York, 1922, pp. 12–14. Abridged.

⁹ Grindell, E., in *The Reconstructionist*, Vol. VIII, No. 5 (April 17, 1942), New York.

¹⁰ *The Works of Heinrich Heine*, translated from the German by Charles Godfrey Leland, vol. XX, Croscup & Sterling Co., New York, 1906, pp. 3–9. Abridged.

¹¹ Sampter, Jessie E., *Around the Year in Rhymes for the Jewish Child*, Bloch Publishing Co., New York, 1920, pp. 74–5.

¹² Misch, Marion L., *Selections for Homes and Schools*, Jewish Publication Society of America, Philadelphia, 1911, p. 226.

¹³ Lucas, Alice, *The Jewish Year*, Bloch Publishing Co., New York, 1926, pp. 162–163.

¹⁴ Leftwich, Joseph, *The Golden Peacock*, Sci-Art Publishers, Cambridge, Mass., 1939, p. 901. Translated from the Yiddish.

NOTES TO CHAPTER XVI

THE SABBATH IN MUSIC

¹ Kurt Sachs, *The History of Musical Instruments*, New York, 1940.

² Moses Azulai, *Leḥem min ha-Shammayim;* cf. *Sefer ha-Shabbat*, Tel-Aviv, 1936.

³ Megillah 32a.

⁴ Mishna 'Erubin 10.13.

[5] S. Rosowsky, *The Music of the Pentateuch*, London, 1934.
[6] A. Z. Idelsohn, *The Ceremonies in Judaism*, Cincinnati, 1929.
[7] See *Zemirot* for Friday evening, p. 39 ff. and Music Supplement.
[8] Herbert Loewe, *Mediaeval Jewish Minstrelsy*, London, 1926.
[9] Aguilar-DeSola, *The Ancient Melodies of the Liturgy of the Spanish and Portuguese Jews*, London, 1857.
[10] See musical illustrations in Music Supplement, pp. 404–5.
[11] See *Zemirot* for Friday evening, pp. 37–8.
[12] *Zohar*, II, p. 93a.
[13] *Cant. Rab.* 8.15.
[14] Israel Abrahams, *Jewish Life in the Middle Ages*, N. Y., 1917; London, 1932.
[15] Ibid.
[16] See *Hymn of Welcome to the Sabbath Angels of Peace*, pp. 26–8.
[17] See no. 1 in Music Supplement, p. 437.
[18] See no. 2 in Music Supplement, p. 435.
[19] See No. 3 in Music Supplement, p. 434.
[20] See Hymns for the Conclusion of the Sabbath, pp. 92 ff.
[21] The cabalistic cantor and rabbi of Frankfurt-on-Main of the 16th century, Rabbi Herz Treves, bitterly complains against the new movement and the strange view which the *Ḥazzanim* took of their holy functions. "They have ceased to be writers of Torah, *Tefilin* and *Mezuzahs*, nor do they care for the correct grammatical reading, nor for the reading of the prayers, only for their songs, without regard for the real sense of the words. They neglect the traditional tunes of their ancestors." Idelsohn, A. Z., "Songs and Singers in the 18th Century," in *Hebrew Union College Jubilee Volume*, Cincinnati, 1925.
[22] In the Library of the Jewish Institute of Religion, New York City, may be found the manuscripts of Isaac Offenbach, cantor at Cologne during the early part of the 19th century. He was the father of Jacques Offenbach, famous composer. Among these manuscripts are found violin parts to the *Kabbalat Shabbat* which Isaac Offenbach played as a young man, most likely in his home town, which was Offenbach, Germany.
[23] "In Vienna we knew the famous tenor, Sulzer, who served in the capacity of precentor in the synagogue, and whose reputation is so outstanding. For moments we could enter into his real soul, and recognize the secret doctrines of the fathers.... We went to his synagogue in order to hear him. Seldom were we so deeply stirred by emotion as on that evening, so shaken, that our soul was entirely given to meditation and to participation in the service." (Liszt, F., *Die Zigeuner und Ihre Musik in Ungarn*, Leipzig, 1883, trans. by L. Raman.)
[24] See No. V, 3, in Music Supplement.
[25] See p. 405 in Music Supplement.
[26] Isaiah 1.
[27] See No. V, 4, in Music Supplement.
[28] See No. V, 2, in Music Supplement.
[29] A. S. Sachs, *Worlds That Passed*, Philadelphia, 1928.
[30] See p. 415.
[31] See No. 8, p. 463.
[32] See No. 7, p. 463.
[33] See p. 464 f.
[34] See pp. 50 and 426.

³⁵ See p. 459.
³⁶ A fuller discussion of the *'Oneg Shabbat* will be found in Chapter VI, pp. 166 ff.
³⁷ Simon, Ernest, "Der Entführung Des Oneg Shabbath in Tel-Aviv," in *Jüdisches Fest Buch*, Berlin, 1936.
³⁸ See p. 412.

NOTES TO CHAPTER XVIII

THE ORIGIN AND DEVELOPMENT OF THE SABBATH

¹ See Webster, Hutton, *Rest Days*, New York, 1916, pp. 188 ff.
² Jastrow, Marcus, "The Day After the Sabbath," *American Journal of Semitic Languages and Literature*, vol. XXX (1914), p. 104.
³ II Macc. 5.25–26.
⁴ See I Macc. 2; II Macc. 4; Josephus, Flavius, *Antiquities of the Jews*, XIV, 4.2; XXIII, 9.2.
⁵ *Kos Shel Berakah.*
⁶ Ginzberg, Louis, "The Sabbath in Ancient Times," in *United Synagogue Recorder*, vol. I, no. 1 (Jan. 1921).

NOTES TO CHAPTER XIX

THE STRUGGLE FOR THE PRESERVATION OF THE SABBATH

¹ Mekilta, *Ki Tisa.*
² See Chap. X, pp. 212 f.
³ *Yearbook of the C.C.A.R.*, Vol. XII (1902).
⁴ Ibid., Vol. XIII (1903), p. 166.
⁵ Ibid., p. 141.
⁶ Ibid., pp. 157–158.
⁷ Ibid., p. 166.
⁸ Ibid., p. 163.
⁹ Ibid., p. 170.
¹⁰ Ibid., p. 142.
¹¹ Ibid., Vol. XII (1902), pp. 104–5.
¹² Wolsey, Louis, "Discussion of the Sabbath Question," *Yearbook of the C.C.A.R.*, Vol. XII (1902), pp. 134–5.
¹³ Sonneschein, S. H., ibid., p. 147.
¹⁴ Raisin, Jacob S., ibid., p. 124.
¹⁵ *Yearbook of the C.C.A.R.*, Vol. XIII (1903), pp. 79–80.
¹⁶ Ibid., pp. 77–78.
¹⁷ Harburg, Israel, "Observance of the Sabbath," *Yearbook of the C.C.A.R.*, Vol. XLVII (1937), p. 349.

[18] Drachman, Bernard, "Upholding the Sabbath in America," *The American Hebrew*, July 9, 1937, p. 7.
[19] Anyone interested in obtaining literature on Sabbath observance should communicate with The Sabbath Alliance of America, 302 East Fourteenth Street, New York City.
[20] Hertz, J. H., *The Pentateuch and Haftorahs*, London, 1938, p. 298.

NOTES TO CHAPTER XX

THE JEWISH SABBATH AND THE CHRISTIAN SUNDAY

[1] Moore, George Foot, *Judaism in the First Centuries of the Christian Era*, Cambridge, 1927, Vol. I, p. 90.
[2] Matt. 5.19.
[3] Mark 2.27.
[4] Yoma 85b.
[5] I Cor. 9.22.
[6] Origen, *Contra Celsum*, 2.1; Irenaeus, *Adversus Haereses*, 1.262.
[7] Fisher, William Logan, *History of the Institution of the Sabbath Day*, Philadelphia, 1846, pp. 37-38.

NOTES TO CHAPTER XXI

SABBATH OBSERVANCE IN THE FAR-FLUNG
JEWISH COMMUNITIES

[1] Gaster, Moses, *The Samaritans*, Oxford University Press, London, 1925, p. 71.
[2] *Sefer ha-Shabbat*, Tel Aviv, 1938, p. 205.
[3] Zobel, Moritz, *Der Shabbat*, Schocken Verlag, Berlin, 1935, pp. 151-3.
[4] Dr. J. Faitlovitch has devoted his life to the dissemination of Jewish learning among the Falashas of Abyssinia.
[5] *Sefer ha-Shabbat*, Tel Aviv, 1928, p. 208.
[6] Stern, Henry A., *Wanderings Among the Falashas in Abyssinia*, London, 1862, pp. 189-90; 191-2.
[7] *Sefer ha-Shabbat*, Tel Aviv, 1938, p. 207.
[8] Ibid., p. 210.
[9] Lea, Henry Charles, *A History of the Inquisition of Spain*, The Macmillan Company, New York, 1907, Vol. III, pp. 300-302.
[10] Neubauer, N. Adolf, *Miscellany of Hebrew Literature*, N. Trübner and Co., London, 1872.
[11] Kobrin, Leon, *A Lithuanian Village*, Brentanos, New York, 1920, pp. 9-20.
[12] Ginzberg, Louis, *Students, Scholars and Saints*, The Jewish Publication Society of America, Philadelphia, 1928, p. 74.
[13] Horodezky, S. A., *Leaders of Hassidism*, Hasefer Agency for Literature, London, 1928, pp. 131-132.
[14] *Oneg Shabbat*, Jewish National Workers Alliance, New York, pp. 17-18.
[15] Sampter, Jessie E., *The Emek*, Bloch Publishing Co., New York, 1927, pp. 23-26.

In the JPS Holiday Anthologies series

The Rosh Hashanah Anthology
edited by Philip Goodman

The Yom Kippur Anthology
edited by Philip Goodman

The Sukkot and Simhat Torah Anthology
edited by Philip Goodman

The Hanukkah Anthology
edited by Philip Goodman

The Purim Anthology
edited by Philip Goodman

The Passover Anthology
edited by Philip Goodman

The Shavuot Anthology
edited by Philip Goodman

The Sabbath Anthology
edited by Abraham E. Millgram

To order or obtain more information on these
or other Jewish Publication Society titles, visit jps.org.

CPSIA information can be obtained
at www.ICGtesting.com
Printed in the USA
LVHW03s0337120618
580397LV00002B/12/P

9 780827 613140